**The Elusive Quest**

# Studies in International Relations

Charles W. Kegley, Jr., and Donald J. Puchala,
*Series Editors*

Marvin S. Soroos
*Beyond Sovereignty: The Challenge of Global Policy*

Manus I. Midlarsky
*The Disintegration of Political Systems:*
*War and Revolution in Comparative Perspective*

Lloyd Jensen
*Bargaining for National Security:*
*The Postwar Disarmament Negotiations*

Lloyd Jensen
*Negotiating Nuclear Arms Control*

Yale H. Ferguson and Richard W. Mansbach
*The Elusive Quest:*
*Theory and International Politics*

# The Elusive Quest:

## Theory and International Politics

## by Yale H. Ferguson and Richard W. Mansbach

UNIVERSITY OF SOUTH CAROLINA PRESS

**Library of Congress Cataloging-in-Publication Data**

Ferguson, Yale H.
    The elusive quest.

    (Studies in international relations)
    Bibliography: p.
    Includes index.
    I. International relations. I. Mansbach, Richard W.,
1943-      . II. Title.    III. Series: Studies in
international relations  (Columbia, S.C.)
JX1391.F39    1988      327      87-19238
ISBN  0-87249-539-6
ISBN  0-87249-570-1 (pbk.)

# Contents

# Preface

*The Elusive Quest* is a very personal book. In some respects, it contradicts our previous work and presents assumptions that are quite dramatically at odds with those previously held by us and by most scholars of international relations. We expect it to be a controversial volume for it raises basic epistemological questions that have lain dormant for two decades yet are fundamental to much of the research that was conducted during that time. We appreciate that our conclusions implicitly (and in some instances explicitly) question the utility of much of this research, yet we trust that colleagues will accept such criticism in the positive spirit in which it is offered.

We do not intend *The Elusive Quest* to signify the end of an intellectual trek. Instead, it represents an important first step in looking at international relations theory from a different and more modest perspective. It is the initial statement in what we hope will prove to be a comprehensive and thematic analysis of the history and evolution of ideas about international relations, and we expect it will provoke debate among our colleagues. Before proceeding further, however, it was necessary to ask two key questions: Why do we think what we do about the world around us, and how do these ideas change? *The Elusive Quest* is our effort to address these questions.

We have benefited greatly from the advice and criticism of Chuck Kegley and Don Puchala and wish to thank them for their assistance and support. Yale Ferguson wishes to express his appreciation for the support provided him by the Rutgers University Graduate School– Newark. He wishes also to acknowledge the assistance of the Centre of International Studies and Clare Hall at the University of Cambridge, during his sabbatical leave. Both authors wish to acknowledge the assistance of the Rutgers University Research Council.

The authors wish to thank Rhoda Mansbach and Kitty, Colin, Duff and Caitlin Ferguson who have contributed beyond measure with their sustaining love. Special gratitude goes to Phyllis Moditz. This is not the first manuscript she has typed for us with skill and patience, nor—we hope—will it be the last.

Grateful acknowlegment is made to the University of Chicago Press for permission to quote from Bertrand Badie and Pierre Birnbaum's *The Sociology of the State,* © 1983 by The University of Chicago.

Finally, we wish to dedicate this book to our parents: In loving memory of Florence Appel Mansbach and Milton Mansbach, and Marion Hicks Ferguson and Phil Moss Ferguson.

**The Elusive Quest**

# Introduction:
# Taking Stock

Many students of international relations, like the present authors, were once convinced that they were participants in a quest for theory which would, in time, unravel the arcane secrets of world politics. That quest would deepen our theoretical insights as we tested our ideas according to the canons of science. Knowledge and understanding would be gradual and cumulative, but, in the end, they might even enable us to overcome age-old scourges like war.

In subsequent decades, we have witnessed changes in discourse in our field, the development of intriguing and ingenious methodologies, the creation of new forms of data, and the diffusion of American social science techniques throughout the world. Yet, our understanding of key phenomena is expanding only very modestly, if at all; and scholarly attention shifts back and forth among these phenomena with almost faddish regularity. If insight is to be understood as "the capacity of the mind for making a path through time and complexity,"[1] then little is evident in our field. "New" theories, often dressed in novel jargon, turn out, upon close examination, to be restatements of old ideas, and they enjoy only fleeting moments of academic adulation because fashions change soon again.[2] Graduate students are repeatedly forced to return to "a kind of 'old theories' home"[3] in which the lineage of the theories they meet is rarely revealed to them; the wheel is regularly rediscovered. Perhaps it is just as well that practitioners find themselves unable to understand the scholarly literature in international relations and, therefore, make little use of it, because otherwise they might decide that the emperor is indeed naked. Its exponential growth and profusion has rendered the literature unmanageable; there is too much to consume.

**3**

One historian has observed that "a number of currents converged to create a type of social inquiry whose methodological distinctiveness was a commitment to quantitative research."

> Underlying the application of quantification was the assumption that such a methodology could illuminate and explain social phenomena. Consequently, . . . social commentators became preoccupied with the development of elaborate classification systems capable of ordering a seemingly infinite variety of statistical data.[4]

Although this could be a splendid description of trends in the study of political science in general and international relations in particular beginning in the 1960s, the quotation actually refers to research in psychiatric epidemiology after 1800. The analysis goes on to explain why these methodological innovations failed to advance psychiatric understanding to any appreciable extent:

> Epidemiology, of course, required in part clear classes or categories of disease in order to facilitate the collection of statistical data. Prevailing nineteenth century psychiatric nosologies, however, did not lend themselves to any kind of precision.[5]

In other words, the conceptual apparatus of this field was inadequate for major theoretical advances to occur. Muddy concepts also precluded operationalizations that would permit valid measurement. So it is in contemporary international relations where the absence of conceptual consensus or clarity, perhaps more than any other factor, accounts for the appearance of theoretical gridlock.

Unfortunately, we are not merely disappointed with the slow progress that has been made in transforming the field of international relations into a scientific discipline. More importantly, we are increasingly uncertain whether such a transformation is possible at all. Like the nineteenth-century epidemiologists who were dedicated to applying their understanding "to a series of pressing social problems that seemed to threaten the very fabric of American society,"[6] the research of international relations scholars is, apparently inevitably, conditioned by deep normative commitments. These commitments, which effectively determine the research agenda, vary by time and place and, consequently, so do the key concepts in the field. In effect, then, international relations scholarship grows out of the social milieu in which it occurs; and, since that milieu is constantly in flux, linear theoretical growth is impossible.

The degree to which the intellectual enterprise is dependent upon social reality is reflected in many ways. Research orientations and the normative predilections of scholars are constantly reshaped by the political needs and preferences of political practitioners and the funding practices of government institutions. The latter especially account for the "scientific" bent of American international relations scholarship. Like our epidemiologists who utilized statistical data "to establish the legitimacy of public mental hospitals and build broad support among state officials and the public,"[7] contemporary international relations scholars often focus on methodology at the expense of theory in order to legitimize their "discipline" and coax greater resources from government and university sources.

The quest on which we embarked at the outset of our careers, then, seems to have become increasingly elusive. The time has come for us to address these concerns directly and to ask ourselves whether the intellectual map we expected to follow offers any prospect for reaching our destination. In order to do this, we will assess the state of theory in international relations and the progress we have made in apprehending the essence of our subject. We will also seek to explain the reasons for the condition in which the field finds itself.

The following chapter summaries are offered as a map to our readers so that they may descry more easily the path we have taken on our journey.

Part I. The Sources of Theory: The first four chapters of the book elaborate the authors' analysis of how theory construction takes place in the field of international relations.

1. In Search of a Paradigm

This chapter reviews the Kuhnian and Popperian versions of scientific advancement and assesses their applicability to the social sciences in general and to the study of international relations in particular. It argues that, in view of the noncumulative nature of the social sciences, the Kuhnian paradigm proved irresistibly seductive. Efforts to apply that framework to international relations, however, have not, it is shown, been successful, nor is there any agreement as to what constitutes a paradigm in that field or in other social sciences.

2. Values and Paradigm Change in International Relations

This chapter observes that significant differences exist between theory in the natural sciences and in international relations, notably the role of values in formulating the latter. It contends that ideas in international relations are contextual and emerge from and are dependent upon social norms. They, therefore, evolve in a manner quite uncharacteristic of the Kuhnian model. Theoretical controversies in international relations are shown to be less debates over "truth" than over normative commitments and political preferences. The chapter proceeds to elaborate the sources of social norms and the means by which they develop and change.

3. Changing Norms and Theory: The Middle Ages to Machiavelli

The manner in which theory evolves in international relations is illustrated in this chapter, which reviews key ideas about global politics and changes in them from the early medieval period in Europe until the Renaissance. The relationship between changing conditions, norms, and theory is revealed in the ideas of such thinkers as St. Augustine, John of Salisbury, St. Thomas Aquinas, Dante Alighieri, Pierre Dubois, Marsilio of Padua, and Niccolo Machiavelli. Dramatic differences exist among the normative commitments of such scholars and publicists, and the chapter elaborates the unique concatenation of conditions that underlies each of them.

4. The Vicissitudes of Norms and Theory: Realism and Idealism

This chapter suggests that those schools of thought labeled "realism" and "idealism" are less coherent bodies of theory than they are competing bundles of norms. An historical analysis of this competition, it is argued, reveals that the relative influence of each set of norms and, therefore, of the theories that reflect those norms has fluctuated in reaction to changing sociopolitical conditions. The manner in which norms oscillated between the founding of the modern state in Europe through the nineteenth century is briefly reviewed. Closer attention is paid to changing norms and theory in the present century. The rise of idealism after World War I and its subsequent decline along with the ascent of realism after World War II are analyzed and explained. Finally, the waning of realism in the 1970s and its partial reemergence the following decade are reviewed.

Part II. Conceptual Anarchy: The second section of the book illustrates the inadequacy of concepts in international relations for constructing theory and assesses the present state of theory in the field as well as its future prospects.

## 5. The State as an Obstacle to International Theory

The central purpose of this chapter is to illustrate the degree to which confusion about the concept of state acts as a barrier to constructing theory in the field. The general problem of the subjectivity of concepts in international relations is introduced and illustrated by reference to the state concept. The dimensions of the problem are portrayed by efforts to understand the state concept as an historical phenomenon. Sharp disagreements about the origins and evolution of the phenomenon, it is argued, reflect incompatible normative perspectives. Efforts to identify a Platonic state confront the same difficulties. The resulting confusion about the concept and the explanation for that confusion are illustrated by a brief discussion of some ten distinct conceptualizations of the state along with the normative intent underlying each.

## 6. The Uncertain Bounds of Bounded Rationality

This chapter explains the central role played by the concept of rationality in the development of foreign policy theory and explores the consequences and implications of abandoning or weakening the concept. Realist approaches to the field, it is shown, virtually depend upon some assumption of rationality and, without it, are severely circumscribed. But, as the chapter argues, growing disillusionment surrounding American foreign policy in the 1960s and 1970s produced a lack of confidence in existing models of policy formulation and encouraged models that no longer assumed rational decisionmakers. A number of the efforts to develop theoretically attractive alternatives to assuming rationality are then reviewed. Most of these, it is argued, have severe conceptual and data problems. Insights derived from them cannot be generalized and are unlikely to produce coherent or consensual bodies of theory.

7. The Making of Foreign Policy, or Opening the "Black Box"

This chapter analyzes how the retreat from realism and its assumption of rationality encouraged scholars to scrutinize their traditional claim that unitary nation-states are the key explanatory units in foreign policy. A survey of a number of alternative models reveals that, as in the case of the retreat from rationality, abandoning the unitary state-as-actor perspective has not produced coherent and generalizable theory. Key perspectives that are reviewed are the elite, shared images, groupthink, cybernetics, and governmental (bureaucratic) politics approaches to foreign policy. Efforts to integrate some of the insights from them— especially in the comparative study of foreign policy—have been disappointing. The chapter concludes that the overall results of this proliferation of approaches has been to increase confusion rather than coherence in the field.

8. The Challenge of Anarchy and the Search for Order

This chapter reviews a final pair of concepts central to international relations—anarchy and interdependence. These two concepts, it is argued, really represent the realist-idealist antimony and, as a consequence, conflicting normative commitments. Anarchy, it is shown, has been traditionally regarded as the defining characteristic of the field, even as the existence of social bonds in global politics and linked fates among actors has always been recognized. The 1970s, however, marked a retreat from the anarchy concept and an effort to raise the standard of interdependence (a concept no less muddy than anarchy). The anarchy-interdependence debate is not of recent vintage. Efforts to modify the assumption of anarchy include the systems approach and integration and development theory. All proved effective competitors with realism for a time until their popularity waned. A recent successor to these approaches, the chapter argues, is regime theory, but it is largely old wine in new bottles and has been no more successful than they in producing explanatory theory. Ultimately, it is suggested, the concept of interdependence is nontheoretical and is unlikely to prove an effective foundation upon which to build theory.

9. The Elusive Quest

This chapter sums up and looks ahead. It suggests that the nature of theory in international relations and the manner in which it evolves, along with the subjectivity of concepts in the field, make progress in theory construction difficult, at best, and, at worst, improbable. It points out that the analysis leading to this pessimistic conclusion is reinforced by the historical record and that persuasive arguments (except those based on faith) have not been offered that might lead to rosier conclusions.

# I

# The Sources of Theory

# 1

# In Search of a Paradigm[1]

It is difficult these days to find a major work in international relations that does not either urge that the field synthesize a new paradigm or does not itself offer such a synthesis.[2] "The tasks of the normal scientist," declares James Rosenau, "can be undertaken only after her revolutionary counterpart has paved the way—to use Thomas Kuhn's distinction. . . ."[3] And change in research agendas "does not represent a haphazard sequence of theoretical or topical 'fads' but is rooted in a 'core concern' or a set of puzzles which give coherence and identity to this field of study."[4]

Implicit in such claims is an assumption that the "constellation of beliefs, values, techniques . . . shared by members"[5] of the international relations fraternity is evolving in a manner similar to that of the natural sciences as depicted by Thomas Kuhn. In other words, our understanding of the world around us putatively grows even as theoretical consensus breaks down. Indeed, the Kuhnian assumption is that the breakdown of consensus may even signal step-level progress in such understanding.

The field of international relations, however, has *not* developed by a process of incremental or continuous theoretical growth. Paradoxically, this partly explains the magnetic effect the Kuhnian model has exerted on international relations scholars. Until after World War II, the study of international relations was largely the domain of political philosophers, historians, lawyers, and diplomats. Although a variety of theoretical orientations was identifiable, each with its own classical referents, the field lacked the attributes of a discipline. It lacked any consensus regarding the proper questions to be confronted, what methods or concepts were appropriate to the subject matter, and even what

**13**

was that subject matter. As the field lacked identifiable boundaries, it was not even clear who was part of it and who was not.[6] Accumulated knowledge, then, consisted of a welter of legal commentaries, diplomatic reminiscences, historical case studies, and ethical and theological tracts.

After World War II a generation of scholars emerged who were determined to bring about more order. They were committed to forging a discipline of international relations and attracted to the methods of the natural sciences. Analyses of international phenomena were to be made systematic and to be built on empirical observation.[7] Sociopolitical phenomena, like the subject matter of the natural sciences, were assumed to be part of the natural world with natural causes whose discovery was impeded only by the absence of suitable data, methods, and tools. Nothing was, in principle, unknowable if the search for patterned behavior was undertaken in systematic fashion.

This so-called behavioral revolution in political science was a self-conscious effort to break with previous tradition and quite explicitly assumed an ahistorical posture. New ideas regarding international relations, for instance, could not be viewed—as were discoveries in the natural sciences before Kuhn—"as the developing achievement of the successive commentators on Aristotle," nor were they the outcome of "a continuous development of Western thought."[8] International relations lacked a consensual set of beliefs and theories that could be regarded as the culmination of the analyses of previous generations. Nor did the history of the field reveal a process of persistent theoretical refinement consonant with Karl Popper's view of falsification and refutation.[9]

## THE PARADIGM APPROACH AND THE SOCIAL SCIENCES

To social scientists, who were wrestling with the claims of critics pointing out the noncumulative nature of their enterprise, Thomas Kuhn's critique of the accepted view of progress in the natural sciences was a *jeu d'esprit*. Kuhn questioned whether "the cognitive development of science is a rational process governed by timeless rules of procedure" and argued, instead, that the growth in scientific knowledge is the product of "a succession of points of view—each point of view constituting a self-authenticating tradition of thought."[10] Kuhn's idea that knowledge systems evolve by a process that is at once dynamic and unpredictable, marked by discontinuities and dramatic shifts, seemed to contrast starkly with the perspective that science evolves in a gradual but linear manner. Kuhn's claim that new theories and methods are not merely incremental adaptations of older ones, modified to incorporate new facts and findings, was eagerly accepted as legitimizing the revolutionary nature of the behavioral enterprise in the social sciences.

The central concept in Kuhn's framework, the "paradigm," was inevitably a magnet for scholars seeking to abolish tradition rather than to build upon it. Kuhn perceived science as evolving by means of a succession of comprehensive and mutually exclusive metatheories or paradigms that embrace and redefine disciplines, set new research agendas and boundaries, guide scholarly enquiry, and provide new criteria for theoretical acceptance. Despite the ambiguity of this concept, it appeared to legitimize abrupt intellectual shifts and the abandonment of traditional ways of viewing things.[11] Genuine paradigms, according to Kuhn, do not provide answers to specific research questions. Rather, the assumptions they incorporate define those problems, inform the scholar as to how solution should be sought, and so generate theory. Commonly, the dominant paradigm is incorporated in a single work or "exemplar."

> Aristotle's *Physica,* Ptolemy's *Almagest,*, Newton's *Principia* and *Opticks,* Franklin's *Electricity,* Lavoisier's *Chemistry,* and Lyell's *Geology*—these and many other works served for a time implicitly to define the legitimate problems and methods of a research field for succeeding generations of practitioners. They were able to do so because they shared two essential characteristics. Their achievement was sufficiently unprecedented to attract an enduring group of adherents away from competing modes of scientific activity. Simultaneously, it was sufficiently open-ended to leave all sorts of problems for the redefined group of practitioners to resolve.[12]

In other words, paradigms "do not so much confront the facts as tell us what we should see in the facts."[13]

Scholarship that follows paradigm assumptions and carries out the research agenda set by a paradigm is what Kuhn calls "normal science." Such scholarship does not aspire to theoretical originality but seeks to realize the promise of the paradigm by extending understanding of the facts toward which the paradigm points, "by increasing the extent of the match between those facts and the paradigm's predictions, and by further articulation of the paradigm itself."[14] This largely involves efforts to solve the numerous puzzles toward which the paradigm directs attention.[15] In other words, normal science attempts to force nature to conform to the assumptions of the dominant paradigm;

scholars who do not share these assumptions and eschew puzzle-solving are regarded as pariahs by the dominant scientific community.

Paradigm shifts occur because normal science will, in time, reveal puzzles for which the dominant paradigm affords no solution, and "their assimilation requires the elaboration of another set" of rules.[16] Such puzzles, which entail observations that are inconsistent with the assumptions of the dominant paradigm, are termed "anomalies" by Kuhn. In these conditions, there is growing recognition "that nature has somehow violated the paradigm-induced expectations that govern normal science."[17] If such anomalies persist, it at least becomes possible that normal scientific activity will cease and the discipline will enter a period of crisis. Disciplines are, then, "intermittently shaken by collective nervous break-downs followed by restored mental health."[18] Such crises, argued Kuhn, must be resolved in one of three ways.

> Sometimes normal science ultimately proves able to handle the crisis-provoking problem. . . . On other occasions the problem resists even apparently radical new approaches. Then scientists may conclude that no solution may be forthcoming in the present state of their field. The problem is labelled and set aside for a future generation with more developed tools. Or, finally . . . a crisis may end with the emergence of a new candidate for paradigm and with the ensuing battle over its acceptance.[19]

An existing paradigm is only discarded when an alternative is available. The latter must predict novel experimental outcomes, explain the unrefuted content of its predecessor, and succeed in corroborating some of its new predictions.[20] These requirements are what, in Kuhn's eyes, ensures progress in a science rather than perpetual conflict.[21]

"Scientific revolution" is, for Kuhn, the transition from crisis to the acceptance of a new paradigm during which time a field is fundamentally reconstructed. While progressive, such a process is not cumulative in the conventional sense even though those who triumph may wish it to appear so. In fact, earlier paradigms are either banished or regarded as historical curiosities by subsequent generations of scholars. "Why," asks Kuhn, "should the student of physics . . . read the works of Newton, Faraday, Einstein, or Schrodinger, when everything he needs to know about these works is recapitulated in a far briefer, more precise, and more systematic form in a number of up-to-date textbooks?"[22] Such a perspective fits precisely the aspirations of postwar social scientists who saw little reason to study directly the likes of Freud, Smith, Machiavelli and so forth. As modern social scientists, they were the heirs but not the linear descendants of these great figures.

For communities of social scientists aspiring to disciplinary status, seeking to emulate their counterparts in the natural sciences, yet unable to point to an unbroken history of progressive knowledge accumulation, Kuhn's analysis appeared at the right time. Their critics seemed not to appreciate that "during a pre-paradigm period, when there is a multiplicity of competing schools, evidence of progress is very hard to find," and "during periods of revolution . . . doubts are repeatedly expressed about the very possibility of continued progress if one or another of the opposed paradigms is adopted."[23] Many social scientists believed their revolution was underway, and, in joining it, they had nothing to lose except the chains of tradition. Those who had crossed the revolutionary divide, like the behavioralists in political science, could not expect their critics to understand them. The nature of discourse had been altered, and opponents were bound to speak past one another. Old language was being used in new ways. As "the proponents of competing paradigms," they were practicing "their trades in different worlds" so dooming them to "see different things" and to see them "in different relations one to the other."[24]

The Kuhnian framework served the interests of social scientists who were in the midst of declaring the scientific status of their fields. No longer would they have to apologize for the patently noncumulative histories of their disciplines. The paradigm concept was a tonic for social scientists who were seeking to map out the future direction of their professions and demarcate the boundaries of their disciplines in a period of unprecedented institutional growth.[25] In order to sustain proliferating graduate programs and enhanced government funding, social scientists felt compelled to jettison the image that they constituted no more than loose congeries of relatively independent and isolated scholars interested in vaguely similar problems. Considerations of professional status encouraged them to depict themselves as marching in unison toward the solution of commonly held problems; they wished to constitute themselves into "disciplines," not merely "fields" or "subjects." In order to do so social scientists had to identify their paradigms, for, as Kuhn observed, it is "sometimes just its reception of a paradigm that transforms a group previously interested in the study of nature into a profession or, at least, a discipline."[26] Social scientists could achieve the prestige of their cousins in the natural sciences if they could but fit the Kuhnian mold. "In the sciences," Kuhn argued, ". . . the formation of specialized journals, the foundation of specialists' societies, and the claim for a special place in the curriculum have usually been associated with a group's first reception of a single paradigm."[27]

Social scientists also believed that acceptance of dominant paradigms would bring order into fields historically rent by quarrels over beliefs, values, and expectations. With paradigms, scholars would no longer have to start afresh from first principles, repeatedly defining and justifying concepts necessary for theory construction and elaboration. For these reasons, social scientists set out to identify comprehensive metatheories that, at first blush, could fulfill the criteria of Kuhnian paradigms.

To date, however, their success has been modest at best. For the most part, there has been little agreement in any of the social sciences as to what have been or currently are its dominant paradigms. There exists considerable uncertainty as to whether paradigms must dominate entire disciplines or merely subareas within disciplines. Finally, the social sciences simply do not resemble Kuhn's scientific communities. At best, some of the social sciences have identified research traditions, consisting of sets "of general assumptions about the entities and processes" in subareas.[28]

There may be different schools of thought within the social sciences, but these do not function as communities working within their own distinct traditions. Instead they tend to act like partisan bands, with followers feuding among themselves as well as with the partisans of other schools of thought over norms, concepts, methods, and so forth. Individual academic departments are, from time to time, seized by particular partisan bands which distinguish themselves from departments elsewhere and seek to recruit graduate students by promulgating the superiority of their school of thought. The student must decide whether, for example, he wishes an education in traditional, behavioral, or postbehavioral political science, as his counterpart in economics might have to decide to be a Keynesian or a disciple of Milton Friedman. Often, schools of thought are so narrow that they are identified with individual institutions or scholars—the "Michigan" or "Rochester" schools of political science, Straussian political philosophy, and the like. It would surely be generous to describe these as "islands of theory," to use Harold Guetzkow's felicitous metaphor, which "are seldom synthesized."[29]

Having once selected his institutional affiliation, the graduate student will have defined his future professional friends and adversaries, and he will select his professional journals, associations, and even association panels at annual meetings to ensure a minimum of communication with those outside his school of thought.[30] Thereafter, he will communicate largely with those with whom he already is in agreement, and he and his colleagues will minister to and reinforce each other.

Sociology typifies the effort of the social sciences to avail themselves of Kuhn. In order to identify paradigms, sociologists, like other social scientists, tend to loosen the fairly rigid criteria of a Kuhnian paradigm. Thus, "the term comes most often to mean no more than a general theoretical perspective, or even . . . a collection of elements from several more or less distinct perspectives," and paradigms become "nebulous, shifting entities, indicating whatever one wishes them to indicate . . . limited only by the theorist's imagination."[31] Douglas Lee Eckberg and Lester Hill, Jr., identify twelve different groups of authors "who view the organization of sociology in at least ten fundamentally different ways—each claiming to present 'Kuhnian paradigms.' "[32] Are "structural-functionalism," "operationalism," and "ecological-interactionalism" the discipline's three great paradigms,[33] or should it be divided among "social facts," "social behavior," and "social definitions"?[34] Does the discipline host many paradigms each with its own disciples and distinct constellations of values, axioms, concepts and methods.[35] or does it remain in an immature and pre-paradigmatic state?[36] Or, is the term "paradigm" used by sociologists to legitimize parochial perspectives and mask the situation described by Eckberg and Hill:

> What we often actually find is research modeled upon no other research at all, upon a short, soon-extinguished line of research or upon a single theorist's speculations. There is little extended puzzle solving. There are few instances in the literature where an important puzzle has been solved. Indeed there are few puzzles, mostly problems. If a problem is considered important, it is never solved at all, but serves as a point of contention among variant perspectives. We find constant arguing, bickering, and debate, but very little agreement. This lack of agreement affects operationalization and manipulation of concepts, such that different research requires different, often incommensurable data. The concepts themselves seem to change from study to study.[37]

Other "protosciences," too, sought to avail themselves of the Kuhnian framework, with similar results—or lack thereof. For instance, "appeal to paradigmatic reasoning quickly became a regular feature of controversies in economics and 'paradigm' is now the byword of every historian of economic thought."[38] As for historians: "Not since the publication of R. G. Collingwood's *Idea of History* has a work of 'theory' won from historians the amount of interest recently accorded Thomas S. Kuhn's *The Structure of Scientific Revolutions.'*[39] Like sociologists, neither economists nor historians have been able to agree on what their paradigms are or on how to "fit" the paradigm concept to the development of their fields.[40] Again, part of the problem lies in Kuhn's own ambiguity and the willingness of his readers to interpret him in ways that suit their own claims. As a consequence, one economist argues in exasperation "that the term 'paradigm' ought to be banished from economic literature, unless surrounded by inverted commas."[41]

Yet theorists persist in trying to apply Kuhn in truncated form in order to provide a non-Popperian version of progress for the field they represent. Declares David Hollinger:

> While not "a science," the discipline of history is at least an academically organized branch of inquiry; it resembles Kuhn's scientific communities more obviously than do many of the cultural units that are said to partake of the same pattern of historical development. Increasingly, historians offer new interpretations, or suggestions for new research, as "paradigm-proposals," and historians have begun to regard basic changes in common outlook as "paradigm-shifts."[42]

In an especially ingenuous effort, political philosopher Sheldon Wolin argues that, although political theory is not a science, "political theories can best be understood as paradigms."[43] He proposes that political society itself be conceived as an operative paradigm which is reflected in its institutions and practices. Crises in societies serve, for Wolin, as Kuhnian anomalies; and, if such crises cannot be accounted for by existing theory, they produce novel theories. Wolin is really employing "paradigm" as a metaphor, but, although his usage is basically un-Kuhnian, its emphasis on factors *outside* the community of scholars provides an excellent starting place for analyzing the evolution of political ideas.

> Many of the great theories of the past arose in response to a crisis in the world, not in the community of theorists. . . . In each case political crisis was not the product of the theorist's hyper-active imagination but of the actual state of affairs. . . . In the natural course of its history a society undergoes changes which impose strains upon the existing paradigm. A society may find the paradigm being challenged directly, or it may experience difficulty in coping with the results of change. New social classes may have emerged; new economic relationships may have devel-

oped; or new racial or religious patterns may have appeared. In much the same way that a scientific community will seek to adjust its paradigm to account for "novelty," a political society will seek to adapt its system to the new developments brought by change.[44]

As this brief discussion implies, there are a number of inherent difficulties in transplanting the Kuhnian framework from the natural sciences to less congenial areas. For such a framework to be usable, genuine communities of scholars must be identified. Gary Gutting is on the mark when he argues that

Kuhn's account of the natural sciences emphasizes the fact that their scientific status depends essentially on the emergence of a consensus among the community of practitioners as to the authority of a given paradigm. Since this consensus is remarkably absent in the social sciences, there should be no question of Kuhn's account supporting the scientific status of these disciplines. . . . The very existence of so many attempts by social scientists to use Kuhn's work to arrive at a basic understanding of what is going on in their disciplines shows that they have no consensus in Kuhn's sense.[45]

In addition, social scientists are hard put to identify dominant areas of research that engage in normal science by generating and resolving puzzles. Quite to the contrary, research areas in the social sciences typically bear little resemblance to one another; individual lines of research tend to be pursued in relative isolation; and idiosyncratic speculation remains the norm. Scholars remain embroiled in controversies over first principles; consensual operational concepts are rare; and data are often incommensurable. Little wonder that Kuhn denied that he had intended to guide social scientists in their quest for scientific status:

. . . I claim no therapy to assist the transformation of a proto-science to a science. . . . If . . . some social scientists take from me the view that they can improve the status of their field by first legislating agreement on fundamentals and then turning to puzzle solving, they are badly misconstruing my point.[46]

## INTERNATIONAL RELATIONS AND THE CUMULATION OF KNOWLEDGE

For scholars of international relations, as for other social scientists, Kuhn's work was highly seductive. The 1960s and early 1970s were decades of intellectual ferment in the field during which realist doctrine was under assault and halloos were raised in the name of science. Increasingly, international relations scholars subscribed to James Rosenau's claim that "the same methods that unraveled the mysteries of atomic structure can reveal the dynamics of societal behavior."[47] Thus, it was widely believed to be critical that "scholars, who seek to solve the same puzzles, build on their colleagues' findings."[48]

The claim that international relations is, or could become, a science entails more than methodological controversy. It is, at once, an article of faith and a matter of some desperation. Underlying it is a widespread belief that such acknowledgment is necessary in order to sustain professional and institutional well-being in the face of theoretical disarray and disciplinary adversity.

The Kuhnian framework constituted a device that allowed international relations scholars to see progress in their field while surrounded by theoretical incoherence.[49] It provided criteria for the establishment and maintenance of a discipline and a means to argue that, although international relations had not experienced linear development, the subject could still be equated with the natural sciences. It promised that international relations could become cumulative as scholars came to recognize a common set of puzzles needing solution and a set of rules that both defined the steps to achieve such solutions and provided criteria for their acceptability. For international relations scholars, the concept of paradigm came to be, in Richard Ashley's words, "a vaguely envisioned utopian destination which, like Hilton's Shangri-La, is not marked on any map."

> Of the little that is known of this destination, its most alluring feature is its orderliness . . . the Rousseauesque orderliness that comes when consensually shared beliefs, values, and expectations motivate a society's members to serve common ends by common means. It is widely believed that in a paradigmatic society each member's labor constitutes a cumulative contribution to the society's product, for each member is certain of the form that the product has taken and is taking. The member is not nagged by doubts about the sturdiness of the prior contributions upon which he builds; after all, these have been subjected to reliable quality controls that screen out those contributions in which he should not be confident. He even knows the general form that his contribution must take, if it is to "fit."[50]

International relations has not, however, agreed on a set of puzzles requiring solution, and it is at least as difficult as it is in economics or sociology to discern genuine paradigms.[51] Kuhn, as already noted, viewed such puzzles as determining acceptable research and as prerequisites for cumulation through normal science. In a word, they are necessary to draw the boundaries of a discipline and to impose an orthodoxy upon it. Consequently, "the primary obstacle to cumulation in international relations research," as P. Terence Hopmann observes, "seems to be that we have lacked any broadly shared conceptualizations of the important puzzles or problems to be solved and any adequate theory to guide us in the solution of those problems."[52]

Surely part of the problem is the nature of the beast itself. The study of politics—that "master-art" in Aristotle's view—is peculiarly unamenable to empiricism. Its concepts, as we shall emphasize later, lack objective referents and tend to be highly abstract. As such they defy consensual definition. To the degree it is genuinely architectonic the study of politics necessarily encompasses ideas, concepts, and perspectives from other disciplines—psychology, biology, economics, sociology, anthropology, to name a few.

But, whatever the reason, far from having institutionalized a consensual set of puzzles, international relations theorists continue to debate basic concepts and pursue idiosyncratic lines of research with scant reference to prior achievements or research being pursued by others. Idiosyncratic research is commonly justified by reference to the putative rewards of "middle range" theory in contrast to the impracticality of building "grand" theory. Paradoxically, normal science—ostensibly the clearest reflection of maturity in a discipline—is eschewed by international relations scholars and their students because "someone who tests or builds on someone else's theory receives less credit than someone who can claim to have developed his own."[53] After all, few of our colleagues see much of a future in being relegated to what Kuhn calls "mopping up operations."[54] Far from cumulation, then, the field is consistently in the grip of fads that, like novas, light up the scholarly heavens for a brief time and then disappear. Along with Richard Ashley,

> We are disturbed by the scarcity of firm theoretical propositions on which to build. We are concerned by the absence of cooperation: the disregard that others seem to have for our contributions, the vaporous qualities of others' contributions. . . . We are confused and perplexed by the number of competing blueprints and the fact that each is incomplete. We often conclude that, by the standards set by our vision, our progress has been dismal.[55]

Despite the absence of a well-defined set of puzzles, international relations theorists are largely unwilling to concede that theirs may be less a discipline than a limited convergence of scholarly interests—that is, a field. Many believe that there has been some accumulation of knowledge, although they disagree on the extent to which this has occurred. This disagreement reflects their varying usages of Kuhn's concept of paradigm, their competing versions of how cumulation should be defined, their confusion between methodological and theoretical progress, and the enormous difficulty in evaluating progress itself. G. R. Boynton is probably correct, then, in declaring that "cumulativeness in any discipline is, at least in part, a frame of mind of the practitioners of the field."[56]

The growing suspicion that cumulation was, at best, occurring in painfully slow fashion and, at worst, occurring not at all increased the attraction of the Kuhnian framework. Arguably, some cumulation has occurred in a few subareas, for example, the study of regional integration and the comparative study of foreign policy where replication does take place. However, the efforts have not been sustained. Instead, as the editors of a volume dedicated to the question of cumulation in international relations declare, "the absence of substantial cumulation is particularly disappointing,"[57] and the same theme was echoed by other contributors in describing their own subfields. Among those who study war, for example, "there is a pronounced tendency to conceptualize current research orientations without recognizing the way in which these relate to previous research."[58] Brian Job's assessment of the lack of progress in understanding alliances reveals the disappointment many of us share when he concludes that "international relations research is highly susceptible to fads and . . . the appeal of studying alliances was just another passing fancy in the late sixties and early seventies."[59] "In conclusion," declare the editors, "all these articles indicate that cumulative development of international conflict research still leaves much to be desired."[60] Yet, even in the absence of cumulation, the Kuhnian framework allowed scholars to believe in the possibility of progress.

Disagreement over the degree of cumulation in international relations results in part from confusion about the meaning of Kuhn's "scientific revolution." Richard Smith Beal suggests that

> Scientific revolutions are, by their very nature, noncumulative
> developments. They are radical breaks with past paradigms; they
> are possible only insofar as they destroy the very foundations
> upon which the previous paradigm was based.[61]

Sheldon Wolin offers a similar interpretation, arguing that, for Kuhn, cumulation takes place only through the process of normal science.[62]

Yet while Kuhn's model emphasizes the discontinuous and non-incremental nature of progress, it should be stressed that the successful confrontation of anomalies, the solution of previously unsolved puzzles, and the generation of new sets of puzzles demanding solution imply step-level, if uneven, knowledge accumulation. And the natural sciences, at least, have surely "progressed" in the sense of an ability to exercise greater control over nature. For Kuhn, progress in science, though not the product of "a rational process governed by timeless rules of procedure," is assured "by its social character—by the nature of science as a social system."[63] Hence, although there is a significant element of ideological, professional, and political contention in the confrontation between rival paradigms even in the natural sciences, as Wolin suggests, it is apparent that what takes place is more than "an adversary proceeding."[64] Indeed, since Kuhn argues that normal science does not even try "to produce major novelties, conceptual or phenomenal,"[65] there is arguably no place in his scheme for theoretical advance to take place except during periods of revolution and paradigm transition.

In light of the divergent meanings given to Kuhn's work, it is hardly surprising that there also exist several not entirely compatible views among international relations scholars as to what constitutes cumulation. Differing views are also encouraged because of the absence of cumulation in international relations in the conventional sense expressed by Boynton:

> The most obvious characteristic of cumulative thinking is that it
> is a temporal frame of reference which incorporates the past,
> present, and the future. From this perspective it is assumed that
> the present research could not have been done except for the
> work that preceded it. . . . [I]t also sees past and current re-
> search as leading to research in the future. . . . It is sometimes
> asserted that cumulativeness means that current research *builds*
> on previous research. But the more stark characterization, *that*
> *without which this work could not be done*, . . . may be a clearer
> way to present what is basic to the cumulative perspective.[66]

Richard Ashley, for example, suggests two forms of cumulation, "which can occur at confidence levels much below those demanded in our paradigm image," that he terms "expansive" and "selective" cumulation.[67] The former produces "an expanding, commonly perceived catalogue of models, concepts, variables, indices, relationships, data, and techniques"; the latter he describes "as a process of evolving shared *expectations* about models, relationships, variables, techniques, etc. such that a group of scientists' selections among these increasingly will be informed by prior experiences, including empirical research."[68] "Expansive cumulation," which Ashley sees as characterizing international relations, is closer to our notion of theoretical proliferation than cumulation in the standard sense and seems disturbingly antiparadigmatic in nature. This leads Ashley to conclude that "the field is not truly divisible into paradigms."[69]

Dina Zinnes dichotomizes cumulation rather differently than Ashley, distinguishing between an "additive" and "integrative" version. By the former she means that "one study adds some information to the existing literature on the subject" and by the latter "that a study ties together and *explains a set* of research findings."[70] It is difficult to see precisely where this dichotomy leads us. At first reading, it might appear that what Zinnes characterizes as "additive cumulation" is similar to Kuhn's normal science. Yet the mere accretion of facts is not equivalent to genuine puzzle solving and should not be considered cumulation in a theoretical sense. "Integrative cumulation," of which Zinnes sees little in international relations, appears to be equivalent to theory itself, at least as conceived by Kenneth Waltz: "A theory is not the occurrences seen and the associations recorded, but is instead the explanation of them."[71] Waltz argues that the "longest process of painful trial and error will not lead to the construction of a theory unless at some point a brilliant intuition flashes, a creative idea emerges."[72] He thus would presumably agree with Zinnes's criticism of what she calls "the additive mentality" as an impediment to cumulation in international relations:

> The principal characteristic of the additive mentality is its belief
> that integrative cumulation will occur of its own accord through
> the simple process of adding more and more facts and relations
> to a body of knowledge. It is assumed that integrative cumulation
> is the consequence of a sufficient quantity of additive cumulation;
> the bits and pieces will in effect arrange themselves into meaning-
> ful packages, if only enough parts of the puzzle are supplied. . . .
> The problem is, as many philosophers of science have noted and
> a careful scrutiny of the physical sciences shows, we cannot
> achieve explanation through induction. At some point someone
> must make the leap and *propose* an explanation.[73]

The Zinnes/Waltz conception of theory construction is precisely what was largely absent from the so-called behavioral revolution in international relations. With them, we suggest that theory consists of more than strategic simplification or the linking of tested hypotheses. Theory is explanation and must exhibit deductive power. Ironically, the behavioralists rose to prominence on the claim that traditional international relations had failed to produce cumulative knowledge because theorists had been contented with assertions that were in principle untestable and unfalsifiable.[74] "Until systematic observation, operationally derived evidence, and replicable analytical procedures were introduced," declared J. David Singer, "skillful rhetoric and academic gamesmanship often carried the day."[75] The absence of procedures for empirical verification and testable hypotheses had precluded the possibility of resolving conflicting claims or of establishing the reliable foundation of knowledge that behavioralists considered essential for cumulation to take place. Thus, charged behavioralists, traditional scholarship in international relations assured that no controversy could ever be resolved in final fashion. By contrast, systematic testing and replication of operationalized hypotheses utilizing quantitative data promised orderly, cumulative knowledge.

For these reasons, the ascendance of behavioralism in political science was itself perceived by some scholars as a paradigm revolution. Wolin declares:

> In striking ways, the behavioural movement satisfies most of
> Kuhn's specifications for a successful paradigm. It has come to
> dominate the curricula of many political science departments
> throughout the country; a new generation of students is being
> taught the new methods of survey analysis, data processing, and
> scaling; and there are even signs that the past is being reinter-
> preted in order to demonstrate that the revolution is merely the
> culmination of "trends" in political science over the past few
> decades.[76]

Arend Lijphart saw behavioralism as playing this role in international relations and as having succeeded a traditional paradigm whose core was the concepts of state sovereignty and international anarchy.[77]

What such enthusiasts did not understand is that the behavioralists in international relations lacked the sort of dominant theory that might have allowed them to deduce hypotheses that would have served as Kuhnian puzzles. The absence of an overarching theoretical framework necessarily reduced the relevance and impact of the ensuing richness of the empirical effort.[78] The "revolution" was largely methodological, not theoretical, and so encouraged practitioners to set off, without a common and coherent research agenda. Accordingly, they were to develop and use a variety of new tools to study problems that were not inherently linked. Induction was confused with theory construction, and probabilism—or, more accurately, possibilism or even "maybe-ism"—was confused with explanation. P. Terrence Hopmann, himself a persuasive proponent of increasing the scientific content of international relations theory, posed the issue rather well:

> [T]he development of cumulative international relations theory is not likely to come through purely inductive data gathering or through beginning with descriptions unencumbered by explanatory or predictive theory. Unless the standard of logical interrelatedness is upheld, the solution of one problem or puzzle will tell one nothing about where to turn next. The testing and subsequent confirmation or disconfirmation of an ad hoc proposition tells us nothing about what should be investigated next and *hence provides no basis for cumulative research.* On the other hand, the deductive interdependence upon which scientific theories depend should suggest the logical nature of the interrelationships among puzzles. This means that the solution of one puzzle may suggest new puzzles to be solved. . . . It is . . . through the logical interrelationships of these puzzles provided by a fundamental set of axioms that research is likely to become cumulative, since the answer which one researcher obtains to his or her particular puzzle will have important implications for himself or herself as well as for other researchers in solving other puzzles and in suggesting new puzzles which require solution.[79]

Although packaged as a paradigm, behavioral scholarship was preoccupied by questions of methodology rather than theory,[80] and its practitioners have had little impact on the ways in which international phenomena are conceived. Significantly, behavioral scholars tacitly accepted many of the assumptions of those "traditionalists" whom they vigorously criticized. As John Vasquez has persuasively argued, much of the behavioral research of the 1950s and 1960s employed the three key realist axioms—the centrality of nation-states as actors, the bifurcation of domestic and international politics, and the dominance of the struggle for power and peace.[81] "Political scientists," as Boynton notes, "have been busy testing hypotheses for more than 20 years, and . . . there has been little theoretical development in coordination with research findings."[82] Ultimately, we must "question the utility of hypothesis testing, in and of itself, as a road to theory."[83]

A number of seriously debilitating consequences flowed from the fetish with data and method. The most important of these was the propensity to confuse correlative findings with genuine theoretical explanation despite the repeated caution that correlation is not causation. Indeed, scholars even tried to construct hypotheses *after* obtaining the sort of statistical results they sought. As Zinnes contends

> The computer printout, with the addition of a few sentences
> indicating how the data were collected and a summary paragraph
> of interpretation, became a fast and easy publication in a world
> of publish or perish. We began to succumb more and more to the
> belief that explanations were found in amounts of variance ex-
> plained or in levels of significance. Even our hypotheses . . .
> now became products of statistical results—when bivariate corre-
> lations were significant we then formulated the relevant hypothe-
> ses.[84]

However robust their statistical associations, scholars could neither be certain that critical causal factors were absent nor sure that their operational procedures did not encourage tautology. More importantly, in the absence of prior theorizing, it is possible to subject even the relatively few hypotheses that have not been falsified to a variety of explanations depending upon the theoretical perspective employed.

Certain sophisticated statistical procedures actually encouraged theoretical anarchy. The "naming" of factors in the course of factor analysis, for example, permitted researchers to impose their own theoretical predispositions upon data without having to spell out the assumptions with which they were working. The same data could be manipulated endlessly in the search for different outcomes.[85] In a deeper sense, this reflected a propensity to view data and data collection as ends in themselves and to confuse data with truth itself. "We began to believe in our data sets," admits Zinnes, "as if they contained some kind of objective truth, forgetting that someone had to make decisions on what was to be measured and how."[86] Statistical analysis can reveal patterns in data, but such analysis cannot in itself point to patterns that have theoretical significance unless observations are conditioned by a sophisticated theoretical scheme.

And what of the data themselves? Here we come upon a paradox: the more ingenious that data-creation became, the further away international relations scholars moved from the behavior in which they were interested. Behaviorialism was intended as a focus upon people rather than institutions or abstractions.[87] Yet, neither what leaders say (content analysis) nor what the media report that actors do (events data) constitutes actual behavior. At best, they are the consequences or traces of decisions and behavior; at worst, they are pale reflections of behavior filtered through processes that homogenize the behavior itself. Events data, for example, *necessarily* incorporate the perceptions and prejudices of a journalistic profession characterized by a set of interests and preferences. When a researcher uses such data, he is surrendering much of the task of making theoretical choices to the media whose reports he studies. To the degree that events data collection is limited to the media of a single country or set of countries owing to resource constraints (including language skills), the impact of cultural and social diversity is lost. Indeed, the impact of sociocultural and psychological factors in a heterogeneous world is attenuated by the need of researchers to impose a single set of standards on a data set. Yet the meaning of language (e.g., "war," "peace," "truth," and so forth) varies by culture and is probably culturally determined, and superficially identical "acts" have different meanings in different cultures (e.g., the function of "lying" or "corruption" in Eastern versus Western societies).

There have been other, though perhaps more remediable, consequences of the behavioral fetish for data collection and analysis. One consequence is the propensity to study phenomena for which data are already available or can be constructed with relative ease. As the present authors have argued before, this problem contributes to an unwillingness to study actors other than sovereign nation-states and imposes an unwarranted conservatism and ethnocentricity on theoretical speculation.[88] Whatever the relative impact of actors other than states or governments on world politics, the objects of human loyalties appear to vary both in time and place. Thus, contemporary violence in the Middle East, Asia, and Africa often entails fierce tribal and ethnic collisions rather than conventional "inter-state" politics.

All too often the availability of data and a desire to use a particular methodology have determined the theoretical framework rather than the reverse. It is almost as though "data collectors have virtually attributed the characteristics of a paradigm to data collection and analysis techniques themselves."[89] Reversing the horse and cart in this manner not only runs the risk of trivial research but of trivializing the field as a whole.

## CONCLUSION

Efforts to impose a Kuhnian framework upon international relations, although no more successful than in other social sciences, did, for a time, boost the morale of a generation of scholars who thought they had been provided a guide to disciplinary maturity. Although it is increasingly apparent that behavioralism itself does not constitute a Kuhnian paradigm, the field has not surrendered its disciplinary vision, and the search continues for paradigm candidates. For some, that search entails efforts to fuse elements from diverse frameworks into a synthetic paradigm of "shreds and patches." Such efforts, however, entail a fundamental misunderstanding of the paradigm concept because, in Braillard's words, "although one can hope to integrate within a common model the various aspects of international relations channelled by the paradigms, that integration can be effected only by dissociating those aspects from the philosophical and ideological framework within which they appear."[90] Whether, as we suggest, international relations is inherently unamenable to a Kuhnian perspective or whether it is simply a matter of one day prescribing the right theoretical lenses, at the present time we do look, as J. David Singer declares, "painfully like our friends the historians or perhaps even the couturiers. We are almost as trendy, and seem willing to scrap and return to our paradigms with the same alacrity as historical revisionists or fashion designers."[91]

# 2

# Values and Paradigm Change in International Relations

In the preceding chapter, we suggested that one consequence of the behavioral revolution in international relations was to evoke unrealistic expectations of cumulative progress. Yet, even in the absence of cumulation, acceptance of Thomas Kuhn's epistemology permitted optimism. The repeated invocation of Kuhn especially encouraged the belief—often unarticulated—that our understanding of the world around us was advancing in almost dialectical fashion. If progress had previously been imperceptible, this was no longer the case because "science" itself constituted something of a "revolution" in the field which would, as a consequence, shortly enter a stage of "normal science."

Our intention is not to reopen the stale and unrewarding "science" versus "traditionalist" controversy[1] but rather to suggest that there may be sufficient differences between the evolution of theory in the social sciences, including international relations, and Kuhn's version of the natural sciences to render his analysis inapplicable to the former. If that is the case, perceptions of progress in international relations may be unwarranted and illusory. Indeed, it shall become apparent that ideas emerge and compete in international relations scholarship in a most un-Kuhnian manner.

## THE SOURCE AND ROLE OF VALUES

Kuhn himself highlights the most significant difference between the natural and social sciences when he notes "the unparalleled insulation

**32**

of mature scientific communities from the demands of the laity and of everyday life."[2]

> In this respect . . . the contrast between natural scientists and many social scientists proves instructive. The latter often tend, as the former almost never do, to defend their choice of a research problem . . . chiefly in terms of the social importance of achieving a solution.[3]

In other words, the work of the social scientist is generally infused by a commitment to serve the needs of the society of which he is a member. For international relations scholars, research is exciting because, in the words of Patrick McGowan and Howard Shapiro, they "find it dramatic, gratifying, or fearsome, as well as puzzling. . . ."[4] They summarize well the impossibility of freeing research from its normative roots, although they shy from the full consequences of this:

> If normative preferences are not explicitly stated, then they are always implicit in the research—for even the desire to do a "scientific" study is a normative decision. In addition, scholarship is a social process which in the end must justify its cost to society by the benefits it creates. Many social scientists feel today that social science is a tool in the struggle for a better world—for example, a world with a more equitable distribution of wealth and less violence. . . . For many, then, their systematic orientation to the study of foreign policy derives from their normative interests in policy evaluation and prescription.[5]

The importance of Kuhn's observation was appreciated two decades before by E. H. Carr when he wrote:

> The science of international politics has . . . come into being in response to a popular demand. It has been created to serve a purpose. . . . At first sight, this pattern may appear illogical. Our first business, it will be said, is to collect, classify and analyse our facts and draw out inferences; and we shall then be ready to investigate the purpose to which our facts and our deductions can be put. The processes of the human mind do not, however, appear to develop in this logical order. . . . Purpose, which should logically follow analysis, is required to give it both its initial impulse and its direction.[6]

The facts that the scholar amasses and the phenomena which preoccupy him are selections derived initially from a set of specific value-based concerns. In proceeding in this fashion, he inevitably decides to ignore other facts and phenomena. If he chooses to take cognizance of the latter at a future date, that choice reflects a shift in normative concerns rather than a paradigm change in the Kuhnian sense.[7] Carr sees this to some extent as a condition of the physical sciences, as well, but notes correctly how much more difficult it is to isolate facts from values in the social sciences:

> The purpose is not, as in the physical sciences, irrelevant to the investigation and separable from it: it is itself one of the facts. In theory, the distinction may no doubt be drawn between the role of the investigator who establishes the facts and the role of the practitioner who considers the right course of action. In practice, one role shades imperceptibly into the other. Purpose and analysis become part and parcel of a single process.[8]

For the most part, both natural and social scientists are aware of the intrusion of their values into the research process and make efforts to control their impact. But it is far more difficult for a social scientist to do so successfully because of the pervasive influence of society upon him and his perceptions. The relative absence of objective concepts confounds the task even more.

The synthesis of purpose and analysis is clearly in evidence in R. J. Rummel's autobiographical reflection, which could probably be echoed by many in our profession. "My lifelong superordinate goal," Rummel declares, "has been to eliminate war and social violence; only by understanding this goal's genesis and enveloping cognitive structure can DON's [Dimensionality of Nations project] research and my current re-orientation be grasped. For to me science or quantitative research are not the aims, but tools to be pragmatically applied to doing something about war. . . ."[9] How different than this was the normative commitment of the German historian Heinrich von Treitschke, who equated war with the "grandeur of history." And how well do these contrasting admissions reveal the starkly different normative climates of the societies in which they were written! Nor is it uncommon for pundits in impoverished or subjugated societies to devalue peace in the name of goals like prosperity and independence and to promulgate theories that would achieve these ends through violence. At root, these preferences can be debated, but no final proof can be offered as to the inherent superiority of one set of values over the other. Given such divergences in purpose and commitment, it is hardly surprising that cumulation has not occurred in international relations.

Jacob Bronowski's arguments against the "naturalistic fallacy" in the natural sciences are, if anything, even more germane to the social sciences. Bronowski suggests that normative consequences inhere in scientific discovery for at least three reasons.[10] The first is that discovery reveals that certain forms of conduct are "obviously ridiculous" and that one ought to tailor one's own actions so as not to be ridiculous. The second is that science informs us of our capabilities as human beings and "that it is right that we should practice those gifts." Finally, and most importantly for Bronowski, the scientist must behave in certain ways in order to learn what is true, which is the object of his calling:

> What is the good of talking about what is, when in fact you are told how to behave in order to discover what is true. "Ought" is dictated by "is" in the actual inquiry for knowledge. Knowledge cannot be gained unless you behave in certain ways.[11]

In large measure theoretical debates among political scientists reflect different normative commitments that are indirectly revealed in competing claims over which actors should be studied, which level of analysis is most appropriate, which variables are critical, and which issues are most pressing. What is striking about these debates and what distinguishes them from debates in the natural sciences is that essentially the same arguments and emphases tend to recur over and over again through time despite superficial changes in concepts and language. And, as we shall suggest, such debates recur because they revolve around enduring normative themes.[12] The key assertions of realism and idealism, for example, have been present in intellectual discourse about international relations at least since Thucydides.[13]

Thucydides' *Melian Dialogue* and Thrasymachus' argument with Socrates in Plato's *Republic* are enduring reflections of the antimony between power and justice. Sophocles' *Antigone* confronts this tension directly. Centuries of European political theorists served the roles of "realists" and "idealists." Machiavelli and those later known as Machiavellians consciously propounded their versions of realism in contrast to the so-called idealists of their time.[14] The old realist-idealist debate is currently manifested in debates among structural realists, neo-Marxists and unrepentent neofunctionalists.

Although the normative elements in these debates are, perhaps, less evident in contemporary international relations discourse than in the past owing to self-conscious efforts of many social scientists *to appear* to be "scientific" and "value-free," the debates are no less value-laden than their precursors. Dominant schools of thought in international relations are as much a part of the *Zeitgeist* of their age as are dominant theories of art and literature; all are part of the *ductus* of a culture.[15] Indeed, the contemporary devotion to science in international relations is a phenomenon that will always be associated with late twentieth-century America and the numerous symbols of its "modernity"—pragmatism, technology, nonrepresentational art, functional architecture, and so forth. All reflect a similar ethos, fully as much as did *The Trojan Women* of Euripides and Thucydides's *History*.

Changing fashions in art and literature, changing social values, and the wrenching nature of such shifts are commonly reflected in fierce, though often arcane, conflicts over aesthetics and purpose. The triumph of baroque forms, for instance, gave testimony to a growing belief in human perfectability and rationality, whereas the ascendance of nonrepresentational art was but one of many clues that society had come to sense the growing impact of the "unconscious" and the nonrational on human behavior. More obviously, we are repeatedly reminded of the unbreakable link between art and political ideology—both the reflections of more fundamental social values—in the legacies of great artists like Rudyard Kipling (imperialism), Maxim Gorky (socialist realism), and many others. The values reflected in their work reveal the social context in which they were formed and allow us to glimpse the collective values of their time and place. The intimate relationship between politics and art has been appreciated and commented upon by successive generations of scholars; Plato, Hegel, Kant, and Marx are but a few of those who have been preoccupied by this relationship. Ultimately, art, like political theory, reflects choices among competing value systems. Thus, Pierre Bourdieu's analysis of the consumers of culture might equally be applied to consumers of political ideas:

> The science of taste and cultural consumption begins with a transgression that is in no way aesthetic: it has to abolish the sacred frontier which makes legitimate culture a separate universe, in order to discover the intelligible relations which unite apparently incommensurable "choices," such as preference in music and food, painting and sport, literature and hairstyle.[17]

But what is the source and nature of the values to which we have been alluding?[18] Values are abstract aspirations for improving the human condition that may be pursued only indirectly by the acquisition of scarce tangible objects that serve as stakes in political contests. In this sense, then, politics may be regarded as an unending quest for value

satisfaction and as a process in which values are allocated and reallo-
cated. Abstract values are sought as consummatory ends with intrinsic
worth, while the stakes that represent them are merely instrumental in
terms of value satisfaction. The former are universal or nearly so,
while the latter are subject to significant sociocultural variation.[19]

Although values are largely universal, value hierarchies periodically
change in response to contextual and situational factors that heighten
perceptions of deprivation of some values and reduce anxieties about
others. Such shifts may be slow and imperceptible, resulting from evolutionary or secular environmental changes (e.g., technological development and ecological change), or they may be sharp and clear as a
consequence of cataclysmic events (e.g., wars, plagues, and famines).[20]
Although individual value hierarchies vary, they can largely be deduced
from socially specific collective norms. Thus, individual Americans,
however different may be their backgrounds and experiences, do, as a
rule, value material well-being more than do Burmese or Tibetans. The
collectivity determines the limits of what is culturally and socially acceptable and legitimizes certain values at the expense of others.

Value hierarchies represent *collective* perceptions of value deprivation (though there may be variation among individuals) and reflect
*collective* experiences and neuroses. Their collective nature is institutionalized and reinforced by mechanisms of socialization including
family, education, and role. Political leaders must share and articulate
key values and, in turn, seek to anchor them ever more firmly in order
to foster cohesion and consensus. The scope and domain of such hierarchies are determined by additional factors such as the extent to which
environmental changes or cataclysmic events are shared symmetrically
and the degree to which peoples are interdependent or isolated. Thus,
the Black Death, which afflicted all of Europe, had a profound impact
on the value hierarchy of all those who witnessed it. Ignorant of the
causes of the plague, Christian Europe regarded it as the wrath of God:

> The general acceptance of this view created an expanded sense of
> guilt, for if the plague were punishment there had to be terrible
> sin to have occasioned it. What sins were on the 14th century
> conscience? Primarily greed, the sin of avarice, followed by
> usury, worldliness, adultery, blasphemy, falsehood, luxury, irreli-
> gion. . . . The result was an underground lake of guilt in the
> soul that the plague now tapped.[21]

And the disappearance of the plague "did much perhaps to revive a
spirit of optimism in European affairs."[22]

Value hierarchies find expression in the normative temper of a society and an era, which in turn conditions intellectual direction and philosophic predisposition. Theories of human nature, for instance, which are commonly the bases of elaborate theoretical edifices, are among the most obvious manifestations of changing value hierarchies and consequent normative predispositions. The "timeless" commentaries on human nature by the early Christian scholars or by the likes of Rousseau, Locke, and Hobbes are not timeless at all; they are concrete articulations of the value hierarchies of particular eras and places.

Whatever the prospects, then, for applying scientific methods to studying political phenomena, political science will continue to develop more like one of the arts than one of the sciences unless or until political scientists can isolate themselves from the milieu whose problems they seek to address. This, we believe, is an impossible task and probably not one worth undertaking.

## THE NORMATIVE BASIS OF THEORY

Although a feedback loop of sorts is obviously involved, political dialogue is most accurately seen as a *reflection*, rather than a *cause*, of the normative temper of an era. And it is the shift in that temper, rather than the appearance of Kuhnian anomalies, that seems to stimulate what are characterized as paradigm shifts in international relations theory. Such shifts occur under conditions of rapid change and stressful events that generate an atmosphere of unpredictability and instability, a sense that somehow new and baleful forces are at work that will alter existing conditions in ways as yet not fully apprehended. In these circumstances, prior patterns of behavior and standard procedures no longer seem able to perform the tasks for which they were established or appear unsuited for new tasks that are identified. What James Rosenau has felicitously termed the "habit pool . . . that is fed and sustained by the diverse wellsprings of human experience"[23] is dramatically changed during such moments.

Although the causal sequence remains unclear, such periods seem to be associated with the genesis of sharply different religious, scientific, social, and ideological concepts; qualitative technological changes; and major unanticipated events, especially wars and environmental disasters. Often these occur together, though not necessarily so. Fifth-century Greece was one such period: this era witnessed the development of tragedy by the Athenian poets, the philosophic relativism of the Sophists, the introduction of empirical diagnosis by Hippocrates of Cos, the development of mining at Mount Laurion (which provided precious metals for a monied economy), the earthquake and helot revolt in Sparta (464 B.C.), the plague in Athens (430 B.C.), and the Peloponnesian War. These developments provided the framework for Thucydides's view of the world. The late fifteenth-through-the-early-seventeenth century in Europe was another tumultuous period: a renewal of the plague; the rise of Protestantism; the ideas of Brahe, Galileo, and Kepler regarding the physical universe; the spread of movable type; the rifling of guns and the boring of cannon; and, finally, the Thirty Years' War—all combined to constitute a sharp break with the past and to usher in fundamental revisions of the normative order. Changes of such magnitude pointed to new issues in need of resolution and/or new opportunities to be exploited.

Intervening between changing conditions and revision of the normative order are perceptions of linkages among stakes at issue in the global arena and the hierarchy of issues on the global agenda.[24] Fears of value deprivation and/or identification of new opportunities for value satisfaction occur as old stakes disappear and new ones emerge. Although these processes are continuous, they are especially intense during periods of potential or actual shifts in the global status hierarchy when the enfeeblement of high-status actors encourages challenges to an existing distribution of stakes and the energizing of low-status actors spurs their ambition.[25] For instance, the dramatic increase in German industrial and military strength and the significant advances in medical science during the second half of the nineteenth century, coupled with the relative decline of Great Britain and France, made available as stakes territories in Africa that previously had been seen as preempted or qualitatively inaccessible. Similarly, the decline of traditional trade unions in the West and the growing obsolescence of traditional industries at a time of recession and high unemployment in the 1980s have transformed into stakes many social and economic benefits and "entitlements" that until recently were regarded as sacrosanct.

As new stakes become available for contention and old ones are removed from contention, new issues emerge, old ones are redefined, and the salience of issues on the global agenda may be dramatically revised. Changes in issue salience redirect attention toward the values that underlie the newly important issues and away from values that are associated with declining issues. Accordingly, the value of prosperity, which in the United States had dominated the value hierarchy during the Great Depression, became a secondary concern with the outbreak of World War II and its aftermath, during which time physical security and freedom became principal preoccupations. As memories of the war receded in the 1960s and 1970s and the relative salience of key issues continued to change, values like peace, health, and human dignity assumed greater importance.

## KEY NORMATIVE DIMENSIONS

Changes in the global agenda of issues and in the value hierarchy invariably produce new normative emphases, which are reflected in what we have called the normative temper of an era. Normative shifts occur along several dimensions, often at the same time. Among the most important of these are mutability/immutability, optimism/pessimism, competitiveness/community, and elitism/nonelitism.

*Mutability/immutability* is the degree to which it is believed that human affairs and the conditions that shape them can or will be purposefully modified. In traditional cultures the status quo in human affairs is accepted as inevitable and unchanging, and the conditions in which men find themselves are viewed as not subject to manipulation. Arguments that attribute behavior to the supernatural or to human nature commonly assume immutability. By contrast, modern Western science assumes almost unlimited mutability.

The normative implication of a belief in immutability is that efforts to change the human condition are, at best, a waste of time and, at worst, dangerous and illusory. In any event, such efforts ought not to be made. Political realism in its several versions tends to view political conditions as relatively immutable, whether owing to "human nature" (Morgenthau), "original sin" (Niebuhr), or "system anarchy" (Waltz). Following Hegel, such theorists believe that the dilemmas of politics "cannot be rejuvenated, but only known."[26] Although realists accept that alterations in the distribution of power continuously occur, they see the struggle for power as a permanent feature of the international landscape. Nowhere is this emphasis on immutability more succinctly expressed than in Hans Morgenthau's observation that

> Human nature, in which the laws of politics have their roots, has not changed since the classical philosophies of China, India, and Greece endeavored to discover these laws. Hence novelty is not necessarily a virtue in political theory, nor is old age a defect.[27]

This emphasis leads political realists to criticize those who seek to reform prevailing conditions; such individuals are "divorced from the facts . . . and informed by prejudice and wishful thinking," and the laws of politics, rooted as they are in human nature, are "impervious to our preferences."[28] In the United States and Europe, at least, such an emphasis found ready acceptance after World War II with the apparent failure of bold experiments like the League of Nations. Those who sought to make fundamental changes were dismissed as "idealists." Even Marxism-Leninism, with its putative belief in the march of history and the uplifting of humanity, seemed to have lost its vigor in Stalin's conservative empire. Since experimentation entailed an element of peril, "prudence" became the prescriptive hallmark of political realism. The prudent leader understands the immutability of historical laws and eschews bold efforts to transform mankind or the global system.

In contrast, those whom realists dismiss as idealists blame "the failure of the social order to measure up to the rational standards on lack of knowledge and understanding, obsolescent social institutions or the depravity of certain isolated individuals or groups."[29] For them, social engineering is both possible and morally compelling.

*Optimism/pessimism* constitutes a second key normative dimension. Unlike mutability/immutability, which describes the degree to which it is believed that change can be engineered by human intervention, optimism/pessimism refers to the direction in which change is taking place, whether such change is the consequence of purposeful modification or not. More simply, it describes the answer given to the question: "Are conditions likely to improve or not?" Nevertheless, as the previous discussion of realism suggests, those who see conditions as relatively immutable are also likely to view change in a distinctly pessimistic light. After all, if the forces of change cannot be governed and directed, change itself is likely to be fickle, unpredictable and, ultimately, dangerous. There are, of course, significant exceptions to this intellectual propensity. Classical Marxists, for example, view history itself as an engine of progress governed by laws of economic development that will in time improve the human condition. And, as Kenneth Waltz points out, even those who start from an assumption that human nature is relatively immutable can be divided into "optimists" and "pessimists."[30] There are obviously degrees of immutability that allow for varying assessments of the potential for change.

Overall, however, optimism is at least partly a function of belief in mutability. Natural and behavioral scientists and social reformers share a common acceptance of the possibility that conditions and behavior can be improved by the accumulation of knowledge and the application of that knowledge. (How clearly this emerges from the passages cited earlier from Bronowski!) The normative implication of such optimism is that it is the obligation of those with knowledge and insight to apply these for the benefit of humanity.[31] And in the context of political life, liberalism tends to be associated with optimism and conservatism with pessimism.[32] Since degrees of optimism/pessimism would appear to be associated with discernible psychological profiles, it may be possible to predict the future political and scholarly orientations of individuals by suitable tests administered during their formative years.

The synthesis of optimism and mutability is typified by Jeremy Bentham, who sought to deduce a universal ethic by the application of reason. Buoyed by the apparently limitless prospects opened by the industrial revolution, Bentham decreed that, since man sought pleasure, "the greatest happiness of the greatest number" was the only possible guideline for collectivities. Such a guideline could only be followed by cooperation, and its content could only be determined by informed public opinion. Hence, Bentham and James Mill lauded the egalitarian effects which they saw as flowing from education, public knowledge, and, by inference, political democracy.[33] And it was this dedication to the cause of democracy which, perhaps more than any other factor, characterized nineteenth- and early twentieth-century idealism. Since individuals sought their own happiness and since peace was instrumental to achieving this, only democracies could assure international peace, as only this form of government could accurately reflect popular interests and sentiments.[34]

It is no coincidence that intellectual optimism and scientific advance are associated with eras and places in which the norms of a culture were also characterized by waves of optimism—Renaissance Italy, late eighteenth-century France, Edwardian England, and pre-Depression America. And while pessimism encourages political conservatism and inertia, waves of optimism inspire great efforts to give history a nudge. Political revolutions, for example, generally occur in the context of growing optimism, or at least a belief that the improvement of conditions is probable once the weight of existing institutions is swept away. As the historian George Soule observed:

> When the people are in their most desperate and miserable condition, they are often least inclined to revolt, for then they are hopeless. . . . Only after their position is somewhat improved and they have sensed the possibility of change, do they revolt effectively against oppression and injustice. What touches off insurrection is hope, not lack of it, rising confidence, not bleak suffering.[35]

Wordsworth's ecstatic description of his feelings at the time of the French Revolution captures perfectly the optimism of that era:

> Bliss was it in that dawn to be alive,
> But to be young was very heaven![36]

Not surprisingly, advances in natural science suggest to laymen that optimism is not misplaced.

In the context of international relations theory, the postwar ascendance of political realism in part reflected a rejection of the prevailing optimism of the 1920s and early 1930s. Yet realism is not a doctrine of unrelieved gloom. Realists do see it as possible to ameliorate the effects of international conflict by the judicious management of power. Indeed, some neorealists (or structural realists), like Kenneth Waltz, can be regarded as cautiously optimistic.[37] As a whole, advocates of a scientific approach to the discipline in the 1960s, while retaining many of realism's critical assumptions, reflected an increasing optimism about the prospects for overcoming the most dangerous problems of international relations insofar as the methods of the natural sciences were to be applied to an understanding of them. However, growing fears about environmental, political, and economic trends in the early 1970s produced a renewal of pessimism that was perhaps most vividly reflected in Robert Heilbroner's *An Inquiry into the Human Prospect*:

> At this final stage of our inquiry, with the full spectacle of the
> human prospect before us, the spirit quails and the will falters.
> We find ourselves pressed to the very limit of our personal capac-
> ities, not alone in summoning up the courage to look squarely at
> the dimensions of the impending predicament, but in finding
> words that can offer some plausible relief in a situation so bleak.
> There is now nowhere to turn other than to those private beliefs
> and disbeliefs that guide each of us through life . . . .[38]

And although perhaps not quite so extreme, the pessimism of the 1970s was a significant aspect of the revolt against realism, a new emphasis on "spaceship Earth," and the re-emergence of doubts regarding the ultimate prospects for a science of international relations.

A third normative variable that is central to international relations theory is that of *competitiveness/community,* that is, the degree to which welfare and/or deprivation is perceived in relative or absolute terms. Are evaluations of status and value satisfaction made in comparison to others, or are they made in terms of an absolute level that changes over time? The former emphasize competition for scarce re-

sources and the latter, linked fates and interdependence. When evaluation is made in relative terms, it implies that greater value satisfaction
can be achieved only at the expense of others; changes in the absolute
level of well-being matter less than the distribution of costs and benefits
among competitors. Outcomes are viewed in zero-sum, rather than
positive- or negative-sum terms.

It is commonly argued that the emphasis on competition intensifies
as perceptions of scarcity grow. This connection is vividly articulated
in Sheldon Wolin's description of Renaissance political life: "Minds
that knew no repose, ambitions that were boundless, an insatiable
pride, a restless species of political man which, when not bedeviled by
ambition, was stirred by sheer boredom—all of these considerations
conspired to shrink political space, to create a dense and overcrowded
world. A terrain with few areas open for unrestricted movement left
one course for the politically ambitious: to dislodge those already occu-
pying specific areas."[39] One need not, however, necessarily assume
such a convenient relationship between the two dimensions. Highly
competitive doctrines such as Adam Smith's version of capitalism or
late nineteenth-century social Darwinism became popular in exuber-
antly expansionist eras. By contrast, recent doctrines of interdependence and "limits to growth," which are at least in part based on
perceptions of scarcity, emphasize the shared condition of mankind and
the absolute nature of value enhancement and deprivation. Nor does
there seem to be any *necessary* connection between competitiveness/
community and optimism/pessimism, despite the common assertion
that pessimism encourages competitive evaluations.

Political realism, with its emphasis on "national interest," clearly
falls on the competitive end of the spectrum. Morgenthau's definition
of international politics "as a continuing effort to maintain and to increase the power of one's own nation and to keep in check or reduce the
power of other nations"[40] highlights the realist emphasis on the relative
nature of status and security in the global system. Although there is no
implication that a scarcity of political goods conditions the intensity of
competition, it is the assumption of an absence of central power and
trust that is fundamental to the analysis. Efforts to equate the national
interest with a global interest through international law and organization are dismissed as "legalistic-moralistic,"[41] "too wildly improbable,"[42] or, more generally, idealistic. Efforts to achieve justice must, in
the realist vision, give way to the more basic search for security that
can limit the prospect of relative loss with scant possibility for universal gain.[43] "International politics is," declared Kenneth Thompson,

"the study of rivalry among nations and the conditions and institutions which ameliorate or exacerbate these relationships."[44] However, the competitive world that political realists see is not anarchic, though it has the potential to become so. Classical realists, from Thucydides on, have seen their task as preventing such potential anarchy from becoming reality. The prevention of unrestrained violence in the international system and management of the sources of such violence are key values that loom behind realist claims of the inevitability of interstate conflict.

By contrast, those whom realists have labeled idealists have argued that informed reason reveals a harmony of interests that can be sustained only by cooperation. Peace, for instance, constitutes a public good that cannot survive intense competition and parochial rivalries. "I believe," declared John Stuart Mill, "that the good of no country can be obtained by any means but such as tend to that of all countries, nor ought to be sought otherwise, even if obtainable."[45] Since democracies share the same values, there is no reason for conflict among them, and it is these values—nurtured and disseminated by education and a free press—which, to many so-called idealists, provide the real bases for a world community even in the presence of sovereign states.

In practice, emphasizing competitive elements in global politics necessitates undervaluing prospects for international, supranational, or transnational organization, whether formal or informal. Actors that are more powerful, wealthier, or more skillful should, it is implied, see to their own well-being and security before concerning themselves with some "abstract" global good unless it can somehow be shown that the two are identical.[46] The global good may be secured but only in the manner of Smith's "invisible hand," if actors follow the dictates of national interest.

By contrast, idealists perceive individual and collective good as identical, and, in any event, believe that the former must give way to the latter if they are somehow incompatible. It is not the interests of states—fictitious corporations—which hold their attention, but rather the shared interests of the individuals who constitute them. "If it were not for extraneous interference, and a remediable measure of ignorance and misunderstanding," wrote Arnold Wolfers of this perspective, "there would be harmony, peace, and a complete absence of concern for national power."[47]

The devaluation of the norm of equality by those who emphasize competition tends as well to make them relatively *elitist* in their perceptions of global politics. This normative dimension entails perceptions of who ought to be involved in the making of decisions and the management of issues. Elitists emphasize that the possession of some attribute—for example, wealth, power, or skill—renders some individuals or groups legitimate leaders (and others, followers).

Among international relations theorists, elitism takes the form of an assertion that certain actors in the global system are and ought to be responsible for significant outcomes that affect the system as a whole. An elitist emphasis can be manifested at different levels of analysis. At the system level, for instance, it may assume the form of claims that the discipline should limit its focus to "sovereign" entities and exclude nongovernmental and transnational interactions. In more extreme form, it may implicitly or explicitly entail the assertion that only the governments of "great powers" or "superpowers" matter and that the interests and aspirations of minor states can (and by implication, ought to) be ignored except in unusual circumstances. This realist bias is, in part, a reflection of a belief that order and stability is best assured in a system governed by a few who share common norms and are relatively satisfied with their status.

Realist admiration for the virtues of the eighteenth-century European state system, which was characterized by a shared value consensus within the narrow stratum of rulers and professional diplomats, is elitist in this sense. Among contemporary scholars, Kenneth Waltz's unabashed preference for bipolarity is perhaps the clearest expression of the elitist norm.[48] Waltz believes that the world has remained fundamentally bipolar since 1945 and, more importantly, thinks this is a virtue. He argues persuasively that bipolarity assures greater stability than any alternative structure and appears to restrict himself to empirical and prescriptive analysis. However, there is a clear, if unstated, normative position underlying the analysis. For both Waltz and realists in general, the avoidance of catastrophic war is the most important of values. In order to secure this, they are prepared to assume as irrational the value hierarchies of those for whom the risks of war might be preferable to the perpetuation of unbearable political, economic, and social conditions. They assume that the great powers are somehow more responsible than lesser powers, presumably because the former have so much more to lose than the latter. The poor or the weak might be tempted to behave rashly and promote instability in order to improve their status. Whether this argument takes the form of opposition to nuclear proliferation or praise for the ability of the balance of power to preserve the independence of *major* states, it is profoundly conservative and elitist.[49] In effect, it is an international version of the argument that there should be a property or educational qualification as a prerequisite for enfranchisement.[50]

The Wilsonian critique of balance-of-power politics was dismissed by realists as utopian because it did not sufficiently take account of the role of power in international relations. Yet however "unscientific" was Woodrow Wilson's analysis of international politics, what probably incensed realists most was his denunciation of the prevailing elitist ethic. It is not simply that Wilson denounced aristocratic rule within states but also that he rejected a condominium of the great powers. His assertion of the rights of nationalities and ethnic minorities, along with his praise of democracy and the rights of small states, constituted a brief in favor of greater participation at all levels of global decisionmaking. There is an added irony in the fact that, although Wilson was accused of being naive for advocating such participation, he effectively predicted what has become an elemental process in the global politics of the late twentieth century.

At a different level of analysis, elitism may also take the form of assertions that foreign policy should be left in the hands of small coteries of professional diplomats.[51] Such arguments are often made in the context of expressions of concern about the allegedly injurious impact of public opinion or shifting electoral majorities on the possibility for formulating consistent and farsighted foreign policy. Walter Lippmann, for instance, saw the "devitalization of the governing power" as "the malady of democratic states,"[52] and Alexis de Tocqueville concluded that "a democracy can only with great difficulty regulate the details of an important undertaking, persevere in a fixed design, and work out its execution in spite of serious obstacles."[53] For their part, realists consistently lament the passing of the age of the professional diplomat and the onset of the era of mass politics. George Kennan believes that "a good deal of our trouble seems to have stemmed from the extent to which the executive has felt itself beholden to short-term trends of public opinion in the country and from . . . the erratic and subjective nature of public reaction to foreign-policy questions,"[54] and Morgenthau cites as one of his "four fundamental rules": "The government is the leader of public opinion, not its slave."[55] In sum, the elitist bias of political realists is characteristic of their perception of all levels of analysis just as Wilson's anti-elitist bent was present in his views of both internal and external political life.

## CONCLUSION

This brief analysis of the sources and nature of evolving theory in international relations is self-consciously gloomy both about the prospects for developing a cumulative science in the discipline and for paradigm advances of a Kuhnian sort. Notwithstanding significant advances in data-collection and method, the analysis views the discipline as mired in an unceasing set of theoretical debates in which competing empirical assertions grow out of competing normative emphases that have their roots in a broader sociocultural milieu. Dominant norms tend to vary through time along with shifts in perceptions of the sources of value deprivation and satisfaction; and such norms, therefore, reflect the hierarchy of issues on the global political agenda. In effect, social norms mediate between circumstances and events and the perceptions of analysts and practitioners.

This analysis suggests, furthermore, that the dominant theories of an age are more the products of ideology and fashion than of science in the Kuhnian sense. Their sources are relentlessly subjective. If the natural sciences somehow evolve in linear fashion regardless of their social and cultural contexts, "knowledge" generation in the social sciences— including international relations—may more closely resemble that of the humanities which are inevitably infused by the ethos of their era. International relations will, therefore, continue to be characterized by a welter of competing theories that reflect significant political, subjective and normative differences.[56] Only when the global system enters a period of rapid and stressful change will a dominant theory, *superficially* resembling a Kuhnian paradigm, possibly emerge for some period of time. In all likelihood that "new" theory will be old wine in a new bottle. It will reflect a changing normative environment and will yield pride of place once that environment again changes.

# 3

# Changing Norms and Theory: The Middle Ages to Machiavelli

We have suggested that prevailing theory in international relations—the way in which we explain the world around us—is an epiphenomenon of the normative temper of an era and that social norms evolve in response to perceptions of a changing "reality." In contrast to models of progressive paradigm shifts, this perspective assumes that international relations theory is closer to what is conventionally conceived of as ideology rather than an intersubjective body of knowledge. In this chapter, we shall examine this assumption in the context of the evolution of "reality," norms, and theory from medieval Europe to the Renaissance.[1]

Norms tend to evolve in leisurely fashion so that significant shifts—their sources and their impact—may only become visible after prolonged periods of time. For this reason, an historical approach of the sort we have selected to use in the following pages is very useful.

## MEDIEVAL INTERNATIONAL RELATIONS

Medieval ideas about international relations are, at first blush, almost unrecognizable to contemporary theorists. Prior to the emergence of what is usually termed a "modern" state system and characterized by complex overlapping jurisdictions, the international politics of that millenium has been virtually ignored by scholars. The apparent absence of the sorts of explanatory variables that are central to contemporary international thought—nation-states, bureaucracies, and so forth—seems to divorce the period even more from contemporary international problems than the earlier epochs of classical Greece and Rome. Yet all the elements of international relations as we understand them—autonomous actors, violence and war, system solidarity and culture, and supranational organization—were in fact present and were topics of great moment to scholars of the period. Moreover, there existed a corpus of ideas about these issues that, while not systematically articulated and presented in a manner peculiarly remote to contemporary empiricists, reflected the social and cultural realities of the period. For an empiricist, it is difficult to tease out many of these ideas because much of medieval theory is self-consciously normative, revealing the operation of the system only indirectly in expressing aspirations for order and universality quite at odds with the disorder and fragmentation that existed.

In part, the Middle Ages have been ignored by international relations theorists because of the absence of a clear differentiation between politics within communities and among them. This is ironic for two reasons: First, the absence of a clear "domestic" arena during much of the period entailed a "purer" and more complete *inter*state arena than was the case before or after; second, the erosion of the boundary between the domestic and international realms in contemporary politics has played a major role in undermining acceptance of traditional theories about international relations. Indeed, one of the most compelling characteristics of the medieval period was the gradual evolution of territorial entities and the rediscovery of the boundary between those two arenas. As realities changed, so too did ideas about international relations, and by the end of the period it was a relatively brief journey to the "modern" ideas of Machiavelli, Bodin, and Hobbes.

## CHRISTIAN UNIVERSALISM AND THE CHRISTIAN COMMONWEALTH

The dominant medieval myth—that Latinized Europe constituted a special community distinct from the pagan world—was partly an inheritance from pagan Rome, which had been reinforced by Jewish tradition, biblical scripture, and Roman persecution. Only Christian believers, argued St. Augustine, could guide the universal family of peoples to the inevitable City of God. The disappearance of the Roman Empire of the West and the schism between the Latin Church and Byzantium institutionalized this sense of exclusivity and isolation. With the waning of Byzantine authority, the Roman Church increasingly assumed temporal as well as spiritual authority.

In fact, the idea of a unified Christian commonweath, which made its appearance as the Roman Empire faded, coincided with the breakdown of central authority during which territorial rulership on any significant scale virtually disappeared. If, as we shall suggest later, the idea of international anarchy that came to characterize so much of international theory during the era of the sovereign territorial state entailed overstatement for purposes of drama, anarchy—in the sense of chaos—was a close approximation of Europe in the early Middle Ages. In this sense, the period was an archetypal international system.

Rome had been a centrally governed territorial unit characterized by relatively clear frontiers, a central army supported by taxation of the community, centralized civil and military bureaucracies. A clear delineation existed between international war and internal disturbances. "In principle," declares Philippe Contamine, "by using a continuous line of defence around Roman territory, it had been expected that peace would reign within the Empire and that there would be no reason for bearing arms, that violence would be illegal and recourse to justice would be the normal means of resolving litigious questions whatever they concerned."[2] By contrast, early medieval society witnessed the virtual disappearance of direct taxation, central bureaucracy, and regular armies.

> The resources of monarchies were largely absorbed by the imme-
> diate private expenses of kings and their entourages. The idea of
> a frontier (*limes*) was almost completely lost. At a stroke insecu-
> rity became general; no region was able to claim immunity from
> war. Each individual, every social or family group, had to look
> to their own security, to defend their rights and interest by
> arms. . . . The differences were obliterated between public war-
> fare and private violence, between the feud or vendetta and a
> conflict waged by the king in the name of his people.[3]

The inability of Byzantium to screen Italy from the eighth-century invasion of the Lombards confirmed western Europe's isolation and produced an alliance between the Latin Church and the Frankish empire of Charlemagne. The Carolingians, having united Gaul, western Germany, and other western territories, became the second pillar of Christian Europe and enabled the Roman Church to distance itself from Byzantium with relative impunity. The Franks, as the new protectors of the western Christian tradition, were induced to accept the idea of the Christian community. Frankish emperors viewed themselves as the heirs of the Roman emperors and founded the Holy Roman Empire. What evolved thereafter was an acceptance of unity and diversity—a society based on an amalgam of German tribal traditions and law, Roman law, and Church writings and law. Until the demise of the Frankish empire, the imperial-papal duopoly restored a measure of centralized rule to the West.

The myth of a unified Christian commonwealth was fostered by the continued expansion of Latin Christianity even after the Frankish empire waned. Poland, Hungary, Scandinavia, Spain, and Sicily were progressively added to this commonwealth, which achieved its greatest extent with the temporary establishment of Latinized enclaves in the Middle East. Paradoxically, however, this expansion was accompanied by the increasing dissolution of central authority within that commonwealth. This tendency was accelerated by the technology of warfare, most importantly the heavily armored horseman and the stone fortification. Philippe Contamine succinctly describes the extent of this fragmentation and the degree to which it contrasted with the myth of unity:

> It is true that between the tenth and twelfth centuries some relatively powerful, unified states survived or were created. . . . In France, however, as well as in the Empire, . . . duchies, marquisates, counties, baronies or simple lordships multiplied. All formed political units enjoying increased autonomy, even quasi-sovereignty. Even more than the relationships between one man and another, the rites of homage and vassalship, this is the outstanding feature of that complex phenomenon which historians call feudalism. In tens and hundreds, principalities of every size became centres of independent military systems, including, in addition to specific means of attack and defence, the right and power to declare, pursue and terminate war. From this sprang that multitude of skirmishes, sieges, raids, burnings, encounters and battles . . . whose recital constitutes the daily fare of contemporary annalists and chroniclers.[4]
>
> France in the tenth century, for example, witnessed first the proliferation of local principalities and then the growing autonomy of these from king and emperor. The extent of this phenomenon is extraordinary; from A.D. 900 to A.D. 975 the number of relatively independent counts and viscounts in southern France grew from about 12 to 150.[5]

## Public Versus Private Spheres

The idea of a homogeneous and unified Christian community masked the very real heterogeneity of those who lived within it and the existence of the innumerable autonomous units that constituted it and vied for power and prestige within it. Within an imperial framework, the demarcation of the public from the private realm was murky at best.

This obscurity was partly a consequence of the mixing of several legal traditions. Roman law, for instance, reinforced by canon law, promoted a sense of community and implied a single "domestic" arena, but it had to coexist alongside the traditions of the Germanic tribes that conquered Rome. For these tribes, law was largely an accretion of customary rights and duties that initially varied by tribal group and, as previously nomadic tribes settled down, became associated with territory. As described by one legal scholar: "Laws and systems of law became local. And the lines of division between them came to correspond roughly with the Roman provincial frontiers."[6] As customary law, such tribal customs were "personal" in the sense of applying to individuals by virtue of their membership in the tribal group. The stubborn persistence of such local law assured diversity within the empire and was the soil from which nationalism grew and could flourish.

It was not merely the diversity assured by customary law that worked against political centralization but also the idea that such law was not decreed from above but rather percolated up from below. In theory, legislation as understood today did not take place. Rather, law represented the codification of customary behavior that had been "discovered" and systematized. Law, therefore, though ultimately divine, derived from the people who, at least tacitly, had to give it their consent. And, in principle, rulers were subject to the same customary law. Overall, the effect was to enshrine tradition and impose a rigid conservatism upon society, a conservatism based on inherited inequalities. Thus, custom and, in consequence, the law served to perpetuate privileges and immunities determined by inherited status, and no authority, however august, dared tamper with these. In this manner, as well as for practical reasons of communication, limited coercive capability and geographic inaccessibility, the theoretical centralization of power implicit in the hierarchical organization of the system was extremely limited, at least on a day-to-day basis. As tacit consent was the basis of law, so too was it the basis of rulership. In time, the role of inheritance grew on the more "local" levels, but electorship remained the basis for selecting pope and Holy Roman Emperor.

In contrast to the rudimentary nationalism and localism fostered by customary law, the elaboration of canon law functioned to institutionalize the idea of a Christian commonwealth. Canon law, heir to Roman law, developed by the accretion of decrees of church leaders and the writings of religious scholars. The papal-Carolingian alliance encouraged the codification of canon law, a process that from the ninth through the twelfth centuries produced roughly forty systematic collections. All inhabitants, however noble or mean, were subject to canon law, with the threat of eternal damnation as its major sanction. The law was administered by ecclesiastical courts located in each diocese under papal authority.

For the most part, canon law was concerned with matters of faith and Christian ethics, and, while in principle this separated it from the secular law, its ethical content made it germane to otherwise secular issues like slavery, individual human rights, and contracts. It was only as the authority of the papacy waned and quarrels arose with increasing frequency between the pope, on the one hand, and the emperor and/or local kings and princes, on the other, that canon law began to lose its grip upon Europe. This development, of course, coincided with the waning of the Middle Ages and the emergence of territorial states. The Protestant Reformation which followed continued the process of secularization of the law. While canon law thrived, however, it bridged both the private and public spheres and provided an ideological basis for European unity. In Adda Bozeman's words:

> The international character of the canon law, which had been
> apparent in the law's double function as a general European
> system of public and private law applicable with equal force to
> each separate region and to each individual and as a set of norms
> guiding the relations between the separate Christian governments,
> derived, in the last analysis, from the recognition that the indi-
> vidual Christian, regardless of his residence or status, was the
> chief subject of the law's concern. As long, then, as the papacy
> could treat monarchs as individual Christians, the canon law
> could influence the relations between the kingdoms represented
> by the monarchs. But when the Christian kings became conscious
> of the unchristian sources of their own power, the papacy was
> left to fight its political battles without the aid and comfort of
> objective norms, and the canon law lost its character as a regula-
> tory force in the relations between governments.[7]

However complex and amorphous may appear the overlapping of public and private realms and the coexistence of several sources of law and authority, it accurately reflected the political, economic, and social circumstances of feudalism. Although that system (or more correctly systems) developed unequally in Western Europe, certain key features of it may be identified.[8] Fundamental was that feudalism was a system in which only the most local forms of direct rule were possible. The decline in systems of transportation and communication after the fall of

Rome and the limited coercive means available to those with pretensions to rule made local communities political foci. The economy was agricultural, and wealth was based on land and labor. Political power, therefore, was inextricably connected with landholding, and the complex hierarchical system of rights and obligations and indirect authority associated with feudalism reflected this. It was only with the emergence of trading cities after the twelfth century and the concentration of political power in the hands of temporal kings that direct political control was enlarged beyond the local community.

It is this extreme localism that makes feudalism appear so unlike the version of international relations to which we have become accustomed. Essential relationships were those among local communities and between local landholders and those who could provide them with some measure of security. It was in the latter that the overlap between public and private obligations was most pronounced. Although he might exercise a substantial degree of local control, the local landholder in effect turned over formal ownership of the land and rendered services to a lord in return for protection, and this was repeated to the apex of the feudal pyramid. Medieval kingdoms constituted states of a sort, but monarchs, like the barons who served them and the emperor and pope whom they all supposedly served, largely exercised authority indirectly and were rigidly constrained by their dependence upon others, as well as by customary and canon law. Military power was the lord's chief asset; he provided protection to those below him and reaped the profits of the land held in trust for his monarch, to whom, in turn, he was obligated to provide troops if the need arose. However great the formal authority of those on top, they depended upon those below them for economic and military wherewithal, and that authority could only be exercised in indirect fashion. A monarch, for example, had a personal contractual relationship with those who were entrusted with his lands at the same time as he represented the apogee of public authority, and the two roles implied different rights and obligations. The combination of private property relations and public obligations—reinforced by customary law that ensured the perpetuation of individual status—produced a system of international relations in Europe which gave unusual rein to the individual as actor.


## THE FOREIGN-DOMESTIC DICHOTOMY

The overriding ideal of a unified Christian community and the absence of a clear conception of the difference between the public and private

realms made it impossible for medieval thinkers to conceive of relations among automous princes as contemporary theorists do of relations between states. Nevertheless, such relations were characterized
by many of the same dilemmas that we associate with contemporary
international relations, including war.

In practice, the ideal of Christian unity starkly contrasted with the
genuine decentralization of feudalism. Owing to the absence of any
authority with the means to enforce peace, resort to military force by
local lords as a result of contested jurisdictions or other conflicts of
interest was not infrequent, especially after tribunals had failed to satisfy claims arising from incompatible rights and prerogatives. Such
wars were regarded by the papacy as "private" and, for the most part,
"unjust" (unless waged by the papacy itself). They were, nevertheless,
widely seen as necessary for adjudicating disputes and, by armed vassals, as welcome opportunities to exhibit military prowess. For the
latter, violence was a profession and a major source of income. If loot
or ransom could be obtained in the course of wars sanctioned by higher
authority, so much the better. In the absence of such wars, resort to
theft and pillage was common.

The nature of violence in the Middle Ages within Christian Europe
made it difficult to categorize as clearly public or private. On the one
hand, wars were waged among kings. Yet treaties were considered the
personal contracts of monarchs assumed under oath, rather than commitments by kingdoms; and were regulated in this fashion by canon
law. On the other hand, murder, personal vengeance, and brigandage,
especially after the decline of the Carolingian dynasty, were the most
common threats to order and peace and the major sources of universal
insecurity. Kings were expected to protect those who depended upon
them and to maintain peace in their realms, but their ability to do so
varied dramatically as their personal power and the loyalty they com-
manded waxed or waned.

It was in those areas of Europe where monarchical power had ebbed
and personal acts of violence had become most vexatious that movements arose to limit and regulate the nature of conflict.[9] Such efforts,
the most important consequences of which were the Peace of God and
the Truce of God, were initially associated with local bishops and,
temporarily at least, led to various forms of arms control. By the eleventh century, for instance, southern and central France had come to
lack any strong local power of the sort that was exercised by princes in
Flanders or Normandy. It was here that local agitation produced the
clearest articulation of limits on conflict. The Truce of God outlawed

fighting on selected days prior to the weekend and on holidays, and the Peace of God sought to protect various classes of people as well as religious and economic enterprises from the ravages of violence. To the degree that such efforts succeeded, they did so for reasons of common benefit, especially the maintenance of those sources of prosperity upon which entire regions depended. On occasion, princes sought to ally themselves with peace movements or associations, but, for the most part, such efforts enjoyed only limited success. Especially in cases where efforts to enforce limits on violence led to the organization of and/or arming of elements of the population, feudal nobles reacted harshly to what they feared were threats to their prerogatives and powers.

In contrast to wars within the Christian community of Europe, wars between that community and outsiders, or wars waged to repress heretics, were regarded as "public" and deemed to be "just." Such wars were "crusades" and were initiated for the most part with papal approbation between the end of the eleventh and thirteenth centuries to stem the tide of Islam and recover the Holy Land. If judged according to these objectives, the crusades were dismal failures, not only because they failed to secure and retain Jerusalem, but because they hastened the collapse of the Byzantine Empire. Jerusalem had fallen to Islam in 1187. It was not restored to Christian rule until 1229 when Emperor Frederick II, despite papal opposition, succeeded in negotiating its peaceful return. The restoration was only temporary, however, as disunion among Christian leaders assured its fall once more in 1244.

If, however, the crusades are viewed as a means of pacifying Europe itself by exporting violence, they may be judged more kindly. Medieval European nobility constituted a warrior caste that, as noted earlier, posed a constant threat to the "domestic" peace and prosperity of the Christian commonwealth. Improvements in armaments, especially after the tenth century, including the introduction of the stirrup, the heavy lance, and more effective armor, limited the number of individuals who could join the military profession, increased the need for wealth for those who practiced it, and made it difficult for societies to control the activities of its members. Boredom and the constant need for funds encouraged the nobility to seek profit either through war or brigandage, and neither the sorts of arms control described above nor the efforts to substitute symbolic equivalents for violence like tournaments was adequate to assure peace within western Europe. These warriors were attracted to wherever there arose an opportunity for excitement and profit.

These knights-errant. . . . helped the native Christians in Spain
to reconquer the northern part of the peninsula from Islam; they
set up the Norman states in southern Italy; even before the First
Crusade they enlisted as mercenaries in the service of Byzantium
and fought against its eastern foes; finally, they found in the
conquest and defence of the Tomb of Christ their chosen field of
action. Whether in Spain or in Syria, the holy war offered the
dual attraction of an adventure and a work of piety.[10].

Even more important, "fighting was also, and perhaps above all a
source of profit—in fact, the nobleman's chief industry," and "the fin-
est gift the chief could bestow was the right to a share of the plunder."[11]

Popes and monarchs repeatedly found it in their interest to purge
their own societies of the energy and destructiveness of these noble
warriors by declaring crusades that would export violence overseas.
Knights were summoned to fulfill their duty as Christians and vassals
and were afforded a legitimized opportunity for glory, booty, and salva-
tion. In this sense, the crusades were functional as it was realized that
"a common Christian cause against a declared enemy of all the Christians would defer fraternal bloodshed in Western Europe more effectively than any specially instituted Truce or Peace of God."[12]

[T]he bloodletting thus practised abroad by the most turbulent
groups in the West saved its civilization from being extinguished
by guerilla warfare. The chroniclers were well aware that at the
start of a crusade the people at home in the old countries always
breathed more freely, because now they could once more enjoy a
little peace.[13]

## THE SACERDOTAL AND THE TEMPORAL

The crusades were but one aspect of medieval society in which the
secular and the religious were merged. Indeed, an outstanding characteristic of the period was an omnipresent preoccupation with the hereafter. All aspects of medieval thought were infused with religion, and
the idealized unity of the European commonwealth grew out of the
belief that a Christian empire had succeeded the Roman.

During the early Middle Ages, reality tended to mirror this ideal in
political life despite the relative autonomy of local institutions. The
Frankish-papal condominium, the unifying effect of canon law, and the
combining of secular and religious authority in the persons of bishop-
nobles in large measure precluded friction between the temporal and
the sacerdotal. Early Christian thought, especially as articulated by St.

Augustine, was highly individualistic, distinguishing only between the spiritual and temporal aspects of men but not between two authorities. However, the division of Christianity into Eastern and Western churches and the flowering of the Frankish empire necessitated enquiry into the relationship between these two authorities.[14] From the end of the fifth until the ninth century, the answer was contained in the Gelasian doctrine or the "doctrine of the two swords," which admitted the existence of two authorities, each with its own exclusive jurisdiction. Although the emperor was expected to give way in matters of faith, it was declared, no one after Christ could exercise dominion in both realms, and both authorities were sanctioned directly by God. Potential friction, then, was diffused by the sense that, while each hierarchy was supreme in its own arena, each was simultaneously and inevitably dependent upon the other. What remained unresolved was the question of who was to determine whether a matter were spiritual or temporal.

In practice, however, during the period in which the Gelasian doctrine proved adequate, the empire tended to wield greater influence than the papacy; the latter, after all, remained dependent on the former for protection and resources, a condition that made it clear to Charlemagne, for instance, that he was responsible for both hierarchies. After the ninth century, the gradual growth in papal self-sufficiency and the weakening of the empire began to erode the equilibrium represented by the Gelasian doctrine. Increasingly, the church began to demand that its norms and laws govern the temporal, as well as the spiritual, realm and that its voice be determinant in the selection of secular leaders. This tendency was strengthened, in the first instance, by the publication of forgeries (the Pseudo-Isidorian Decretals) in the ninth century—intended to enhance the authority of bishops at the expense of archbishops, who were more beholden to secular authorities—and to expand the jurisdiction of the papal court. Their effect was to centralize the Roman Church and, therefore, to reduce its dependence on secular authorities. A century later a new source of energy and political influence was made available to the Roman Church in the reform movement associated with Cluny. The latter erected a semi-autonomous and tightly organized system of abbeys that sought to purify the Roman Church and strengthen papal control of the ecclesiastical hierarchy.

Imperial-papal friction almost inevitably intensified as the Roman Church acquired the trappings of a territorial principality. For centuries individual clergymen had been landowners and, as such, had exercised secular power in the feudal system. This fusion of temporal and religious functions had been encouraged, as well, by making bishops in several areas responsible for local defenses; and, especially in Italy, such bishops had themselves become lords. Fusion was further reflected in the orders of knighthood—the Templars, the Hospitallers of St. John of Jerusalem, the Teutonic Order—that grew up to conquer the infidels. By the eleventh century, however,

> the church had acquired the characteristics of an earthly empire: it claimed all Italy with Corsica and Sardinia as "states of the church," Spain because it supposedly belonged of old to St. Peter, Hungary as a gift from King Stephen, Saxony as a Carolingian bequest, and the entire Christian Roman Empire as a fief of Rome.[15]

And by this time the higher clergy had become so enmeshed in secular affairs as individual nobles that it had become virtually impossible to draw a clear distinction between Europe's religious and temporal hierarchies. The higher clergy had both temporal and spiritual responsibilities and, consequently, divided loyalties. In some respects, at least, the European system we have called the Christian commonwealth began to assume the characteristics of a bipolar system in which the first great clash between contenders erupted at the end of the eleventh century when Pope Gregory VII sought to prohibit the lay investiture of bishops. The subsequent quarrel pitted the pope against Emperor Henry IV.

The papal claim for the superiority of the Roman Church entailed arguing that both swords had been given to popes by Peter. More importantly, the church, it was argued, was responsible for regulating the ethical lives of all Christians and that, at least in spiritual matters, this included the emperor himself. In excommunicating Henry IV, then, Gregory was also asserting an authority to depose the emperor. What this implied was that, although the church conceded temporal jurisdiction to the emperor, it could act as the highest court to determine the legitimacy of imperial behavior.

Perhaps the strongest argument in favor of papal supremacy was voiced by John of Salisbury, a twelfth-century English clergyman and close friend of Pope Adrian IV and Thomas Becket. In *Policraticus* (The Statesman's Book) John declared that princes received their authority from the church. Elaborating an organic theory of society in which each person had a distinct function, John concluded that "since the soul is. . . . the prince of the body, and has ruleship over the whole thereof, so those whom our author calls the prefects of religion preside over the entire body."[16]

Supporters of the emperor, for their part, argued for retaining the Gelasian doctrine which, in practice, meant conceding to the emperor significant influence in the selection of the pope and other high clergy. The emperor's argument was that both he and the pope were granted authority directly by God so that the temporal and spiritual hierarchies had to be kept separate and independent of each other. This claim, however, was fast losing its conviction. However steeped in tradition was the Gelasian doctrine, the very real decline in imperial fortunes, especially the growing incapacity of the emperor to control and command lesser princes, undermined imperial pretensions. Even though the Holy Roman Empire had continued to expand after Charlemagne, no later emperor enjoyed as much authority as had that great leader. The legatees of the emperor's authority were, in a sense, local princes.

Conflict between a waxing papacy and a waning empire persisted for several hundred years, made more complex as the dispute came to involve the delineation of jurisdictions between other secular princes and the papacy. Indeed, this issue—with which most political thinkers were preoccupied—was not resolved until the emergence of autonomous territorial kingdoms and city-states. Arguments regarding the questions raised in the conflicts must be regarded as major elements of international relations theory of the period and were the harbingers of later theory associated with the birth of the system of sovereign states lacking an overarching authority.

The proliferation of theory intended to buttress papal claims to universal ruleship went hand in hand with changes in papal organization and policy in the Middle Ages. The Clunaic movement, which began in the tenth century, provided a model of internationalism which the papacy sought to emulate. Clunaic clergy established themselves throughout Europe and were unwilling to be supervised by any but papal authority. In time the movement "was recognized generally as the chief support of the public peace, the most effective agency for the rallying of public opinion against feudal violence, a well-equipped bureau of information for the dissemination of Christian ideas, and a smoothly operating political machine that was to be ultimately responsible for the establishment of papal supremacy."[17]

With the assistance of Cluny, papal power grew dramatically after the tenth century. Adda Bozeman describes the consequences of this as follows:

> Under Innocent III the church had become an international state. It had the power to set large armies in motion, to create and

destroy coalitions, to control the mighty and the meek, to raise funds by direct taxation, and to bring offenders to justice. It controlled education, propaganda, social welfare, and the courts, and it wielded the awesome power of external life and death.[18]

As part of its effort to achieve international supremacy, the papacy assembled intelligence agents, propagandists, lawyers, and diplomats; and it maintained a central archival system. And at its peak, papal power was not merely theoretical. For example, Innocent III "laid an interdict upon France and withheld all rites of the church from the lands that were subject to France, until King Philip Augustus agreed to take back a Danish wife whom, in the pope's opinion, he had repudiated unjustly."

> He gave the empire to Otto of Brunswick and forced him to renounce his chief imperial claims in Italy (1201). A few years later (1211) he deposed Otto for perjury and placed Frederick II of Hohenstauffen upon the imperial throne. And by sentence of interdict, excommunication, and deposition he forced King John of England to surrender his crown in order to receive it as a vassal of the pope.[19]

## MEDIEVAL THEORISTS

Some of the most gifted of the medieval theorists sought to dispute papal pretensions, even during the period in which that institution enjoyed its greatest predominance. The flowering of scholarship, especially in the twelfth and thirteenth centuries, was associated with the universities of Paris and Oxford and the Dominican and Franciscan orders and was able to take advantage of the rediscovery of Roman law and the work of Aristotle. It is their reliance on Aristotelian precepts and reason—revolutionary at the time—combined with their use of theological argument that make medieval discourse and method appear so distant to contemporary empiricists. The overshadowing of the Platonic preoccupation with the ideal society that was so compatible with Christian revelation by Aristotelian secularism and rationalism fueled growing doubts about the superiority of the spiritual to the temporal realm and challenged the tradition that had dominated Christian thought until the thirteenth century. It also began to undermine the belief that the temporal state was no more than the consequence of human sin.

St. Thomas Aquinas, for example, argued for reinstating the Gelasian doctrine from the premise that the universe constituted a hierarchy with God at its apex, in which every creature sought its own perfection. Within this hierarchy, the lower was obliged to serve the higher, and God himself had entrusted the emperor to govern the temporal realm. Applying Aristotelian reasoning, St. Thomas saw human law as articulating for mankind the principles of order inherent in natural and divine law. In tone and substance, his Aristotelian humanism represented a dramatic departure from earlier Christian thinkers like Tertullian and St. Augustine. Temporal authority flowed naturally from man's social nature rather than from sin. For St. Thomas, imperial prerogatives were of double practical significance because of the growing claims of lesser princes and the growing propensity of the papacy itself to behave in ways similar to those princes. In consequence, politics within the Christian commonwealth was becoming less stable and was beginning to take on the attributes of a multipolar system. Notwithstanding these developments, St. Thomas remained firmly attached to the ideal of a unified Christian community. Despite his effort to revive the Gelasian tradition, he continued to regard the Roman Church as the basis of human unity.

Like St. Thomas, the great Italian poet Dante Alighieri also retained the vision of a united Christian commonwealth since it was "the intention of God that all created things should represent the likeness of God, so far as their proper nature will admit."[20] Unlike St. Thomas, he declared that such unity must be based on the temporal empire rather than the church; mankind could not be united "except when it is subject to one prince."[21] Of course such an empire had never existed. The source of Dante's concern was the conflict in Italy between papal and imperial parties. That conflict was manifested both in the internal politics of the maturing Italian city-states and in the politics among those actors; the demarcation of interstate from intrastate politics had begun to emerge but was far from complete at the time Dante wrote. The bases of wealth had begun to change, and a bourgeoisie had emerged in Italy to challenge both the clergy and the feudal nobility.

The theoretical side of Dante's argument proceeded from the claim that Christ himself had declared that his kingdom was not a temporal one and that only a secular monarch could provide the peace necessary for subjects to realize their full potential. Such had been the case during the Roman Empire, and the Holy Roman Emperor, as the heir to the Roman imperium, was the only possible candidate to impose unity and peace. The practical source of Dante's position, however, arose from his partisanship as a member of the imperial faction in the city of

Florence and his exile from that city during a time in which his political foes had achieved political ascendancy.

In reality, Dante's advocacy of a unified temporal empire was something of an anachronism insofar as the Hohenstauffen heirs to the imperial throne had already become impotent servants of the territorial princes whom they in theory governed. In his effort to unite traditional Christian theology with Aristotelian assumptions and in his belief in the unity of a Christian community, Dante stood with St. Thomas even while taking the opposite side in the papal-imperial controversy. They agreed, declares George Sabine, "that the distinguishing mark of human nature is its combination of a spiritual and a physical principle, each requiring an appropriate kind of authority."

> The government of the world is therefore shared between a spiritual and a temporal power. . . . This single world-wide society may be called . . . either a commonwealth or a church. Whether in church or state, power is justified ultimately as a factor in the moral or religious government of the world, and yet as equally a factor in the life of a self-sufficing human community. . . . The controlling social conception is that of an organic community in which the various classes are functioning parts. . . .[22]

Dante's "De Monarchia" was written almost a decade after the climactic collision between Pope Boniface VIII and the French king, Philip IV; yet, in its analysis of papal and imperial claims, it belonged to an earlier world. The chief competitors were no longer pope and emperor but rather pope and the secular princes of the emerging territorial states of western Europe, most importantly the kings of France and England (especially after the Norman conquest of 1066). This collision began to intensify at that moment when it appeared that papal authority was at its acme; the empire was in a state of progressive decay, and territorial princes were only beginning to appreciate the strength they possessed. Between 1150 and 1300 the kings of France and England had pacified their realms to a degree not seen for hundreds of years and had achieved significant visibility by their service in the crusades. Papal efforts to enlist such princes in opposition to imperial pretensions had, ironically, heightened the sensitivity of monarchs to any abridgement of their own autonomy. Nascent nationalism was beginning to prove an ally of the princes, and theorists like Pierre Dubois and John of Paris reflected both the new nationalist ethos and the willingness to assert national independence from both the empire and the papacy.

Dubois, for instance, a French lawyer, was something of a harbinger of Jean Bodin. He argued that all those who believed in the possibility of a universal ruler were hopelessly looking to the past. If a semblance of peace were to be provided for Europe, papal authority in secular matters had to be eliminated, and the equivalent of a collective security system consisting of independent princes would have to be constructed:

> No sane man could really believe that at this period of the
> world's history one individual could rule the whole world as a
> temporal monarch, with all men obeying him as their superior. If
> a tendency in this direction did appear, there would be wars and
> revolutions without end. No man could put them down because
> of the huge populations involved, the distance and diversity of
> the countries, and the natural propensity of human beings to
> quarrel.[23]

The controversy between papacy and princes that erupted at the end of the thirteenth century was triggered by a conflict over control of taxation. Initiated by a papal claim that secular officials had no authority over the clergy and could not tax church property, the ensuing struggle dramatically reduced papal power and confirmed the central place of territorial states in the new order of things. Papal claims were anathema to the monarchs of France and England because of their dependence on revenue from church property; both refused to accede and could not be coerced into doing so. In 1302 Boniface issued a papal bull that declared his authority to be supreme in both the spiritual and temporal realms; princes could be judged by the pope who, in turn, could be judged only by God. Philip of France was excommunicated, and the king then summoned a royal council— which included the higher French clergy—that indicted Boniface for a series of alleged crimes. Philip subsequently undertook an abortive effort to kidnap the pope, who died shortly thereafter. Boniface's immediate successors, Benedict VI and Clement V, abandoned their predecessor's bold claims, and Clement, a French cleric, came to reside at Avignon rather than Rome. There followed a long period of papal decline. Between 1305 and 1378, successive popes resided at Avignon ("the Babylonian captivity"), and for almost forty years thereafter rival popes resided at Avignon and Rome ("the Great Schism"). The feeble attempts by popes between 1323 and 1347 to reverse this decline, especially their efforts to intervene in imperial elections, were singularly unsuccessful.

In sum, the papacy at the peak of its power had confronted incipient nationalism and had been humbled by it. By the end of the conflict, the medieval myth of universal monarchy and community was, for all intents and purposes, finally dispelled. This dramatic shift was most clearly reflected in the ideas of Marsilio of Padua. His *Defensor Pacis* (The Defender of Peace), which appeared in 1324, was conditioned by key trends such as the rise of a new commercial middle class and the growing autonomy of territorial states. One emergent property of these trends was a fundamental transformation in the nature of the European interstate system, which was becoming characterized by behavior and norms quite unlike those of the medieval imperium.

Like the period in which he lived, Marsilio's ideas represent something of a bridge between the medieval system to the Renaissance and Protestant Reformation. The transitional nature of his thought is reflected in the combining of what is an essentially medieval mode of discourse with self-conscious advocacy of emergent nationalism and the prerogatives of territorial states. Like St. Thomas and Dante, Marsilio retained Aristotelian forms but abandoned the myth of Christian unity. Of equal importance was his propensity to legitimize authority on the basis of consent from below. Authority, for Marsilio, was legitimized by the will of the community in whose name and for whose benefit it existed. In this, Marsilio at once echoed early medieval conceptions of the law and later conceptualizations of national sovereignty. What was strikingly absent in his ideas were those conceptions of divine and canon law that constituted the pillars upon which the myth of Christian unity had been erected.

Not only did Marsilio reject the universal pretensions of the papacy, but he declared that bishops and pope alike were responsible to and derived their authority from the community of believers. Any additional claims by them represented efforts to usurp the authority of secular rulers. Nor were they entitled to exercise coercive power, even over heretics; the authority to do so belonged entirely to secular officials in this world and to God in the hereafter. Indeed, religious officials, he argued, should constitute no more than one of many functional classes within civil society and should be governed by temporal authorities like all such classes in order to maximize the peace and well-being of the communities of which they were a part. Religion, like agriculture or commerce, had social consequences and, therefore, logically must be regulated by those responsible for maintaining public order. Papal usurpation of temporal authority was, for Marsilio, the single greatest obstacle to peace and order:

> This wrong opinion of certain Roman bishops, and also perhaps
> their perverted desire for rulership, which they assert is owed to

them because of the plenitude of power given to them, as they say, by Christ—this is that singular cause which we have said produces the intranquillity of discord of the city or state.[24]

## THE MACHIAVELLIAN REVOLUTION: INTERNATIONAL RELATIONS AND THE RENAISSANCE

In the evolution of international relations theory from the medieval imperium to the European state system of the seventeenth and eighteenth centuries, Niccolo Machiavelli, like the Renaissance itself, must be regarded as transitional. He at once echoed the ideas of Marsilio and forecast the ideas of later balance-of-power and power-oriented theorists. Not quite a realist in the contemporary sense, he was a progenitor of realist thought. Having decisively rejected the Aristotelian rationalism of the later Middle Ages, he was an empiricist who sought lessons from classical history.

Like his medieval predecessors, Machiavelli was the product of his time and place, and he was conscious of the transitional nature of the period in which he was living. He understood that the myth of political and religious universalism had been eclipsed by the emergence of princely territorial states, and he knew, too, that Italy and its system of city-states were in transition between two political ages. He was at once an Italian patriot in the tradition of Marsilio and a theorist who sought to construct an autonomous model of politics. Thus, he simultaneously sought to rid Italy of its fiercely competitive parochialisms while seeking to provide a highly secular and timeless theory of political power.

Machiavelli was a political practitioner as well as a theorist, and his writings were self-consciously directed to both audiences. He was politically active between 1498 and 1512, following the ouster of the Medicis from his native Florence, and was a partisan of Piero Soderini. His participation in the government of Florence, most especially its effort to reconquer the city of Pisa, and his preoccupation with the status of Italy following the French invasion of 1494 made him keenly aware of the rapidly changing international environment and conditioned his political ideas. Those ideas are, of course, staples in all courses in the history of political thought, and Machiavelli is perhaps most readily—though somewhat inaccurately—recalled as the archetypal political amoralist. Hence, Marlowe has him speak of himself in the prologue to *The Jew of Malta*:

To some perhaps my name is odious,
But such as love me guard me from their tongues;

And let them know that I am Machiavel,
And weigh not men, and therefore not men's words.
Admired I am of those that hate me most.
Though some speak openly against my books,
Yet they will read me, and thereby attain
To Peter's chair; and when they cast me off,
Are poisoned by my climbing followers.[25]

Machiavelli's ideas are commonly cited by postwar realists as evidence for their assumptions and method.[26] Kenneth Waltz virtually credits Machiavelli with having found *Realpolitik*:

Ever since Machiavelli, interest and necessity . . . have remained
the key concepts of *Realpolitik*. From Machiavelli through
Meinecke and Morgenthau the elements of the approach and the
reasoning remain constant.[27]

E. H. Carr views him as "the first important political realist."[28] And
from the other end of the intellectual spectrum, the British scholar of
international law, J. L. Brierly, declares that "Machiavelli's
*Prince* . . . had already given to the world a relentless analysis of the
art of government based on the conception of the state as an entity
entirely self-sufficing and non-moral."[29] How redolent of what later
theorists would term realism is Machiavelli's declaration of independence from his predecessors:

I fear that my writing . . . may be deemed presumptuous, differing as I do . . . from the opinions of others. But my intention
being to write something of use to those who understand, it appears to me more proper to go to the real truth of the matter than
to its imagination; and many have imagined republics and principalities which have never been seen or known to exist in reality;
for how we live is so far removed from how we ought to live,
that he who abandons what is done for what ought to be done,
will rather learn to bring about his own ruin than his preservation. A man who wishes to make a profession of goodness in
everything must necessarily come to grief among so many who
are not good.[30]

In other words, counsels Machiavelli, observe what *really* exists, not
what one would wish into existence.

## The International System of Renaissance Italy
Although it was clear to Machiavelli writing in the early sixteenth century that the independent city-states of Italy had become anomalies in

the face of the large territorial states of Western Europe, the relatively long period in which those entities had developed had produced fertile soil in which his ideas might germinate and flourish. Except in the south, feudalism had not taken hold as fully in Italy as elsewhere in Europe. "Sometime during and after the final decades of the Hohenstaufen empire," writes Winfried Franke, "the Italian regional states and city-states coalesced, so to speak, from a multitude of politically rather 'atomized' and disjointed entities into several sets of regional actors and finally into one system of interlocking, independent states."[31] By the fifteenth century, city-states such as Venice, Milan, Genoa, Florence, and the Papal States had already enjoyed several hundred years of political independence and commercial development and had accumulated significant experience in "balance-of-power" politics. Indeed, Venetian diplomatic method served as a model for the emerging territorial states of Europe.[32] International trade and commerce, bourgeois political influence, and urban habits of life developed earlier and faster in Italy than elsewhere in Europe. It was also in Italy, as reflected in the thought of Dante and Marsilio, that recognition of and resistance to the secular pretensions of the Roman Church took root most deeply.

By the time of Machiavelli, then, the city-states of Italy had considerable experience with a decentralized system in which independent actors were sufficiently powerful to retain their autonomy but over which no one of them could exercise hegemony. Adda Bozeman's description of that system bears considerable resemblance to descriptions of the so-called European balance-of-power system of large sovereign states of the eighteenth century:

> It was characterized by a plurality of city-states among which Milan, Florence, Naples, the Papacy, and Venice were the strongest. Each of these five claimed to be sovereign, yet none could muster the necessary strength to realize its particular aspirations independently.[33]

Yet despite their early assertion of autonomy, the growth of the Italian city-states—as Machiavelli realized—had fallen well behind that of the territorial monarchies of Western Europe by the end of the fifteenth century. The city-states remained sufficiently small so that no clear distinction could be drawn between the interstate and intrastate realms. As noted earlier, the Guelph (papal)-Ghibelline (imperial) quarrels of Dante's era raged both within and among the city-states, and the tight linkage of internal and interstate conflicts continued to characterize

Italian politics during the Renaissance. In Bozeman's words:

> The struggle for supremacy within the state was . . . seldom
> confined to the local scene. For since the Italian cities were
> closely related to each other both physically and culturally, aspi-
> rants to power were always tempted to seek the supplementary
> strength they needed by conspiring with governments or factions
> in neighboring communities. The area of diplomatic activities,
> already disturbed as a result of the uneasy distribution of power
> in the Italian region as a whole, was thus still further confused
> by the espionage, intrigues and betrayals in which conspiring
> partisans engaged incessantly across the boundaries of their native
> states.[34]

To this extent, Italian politics stood somewhere between what we think
of as gangster politics and the politics of sovereign states. The autonomy of the city-states had come early, but, by the end of the fifteenth
century, nationalism in Italy was rudimentary indeed in comparison to
England and France.

Had Machiavelli not appreciated the anomalous nature of Italian politics before, he certainly did so after a French army under Charles VIII,
with artillery and Swiss mercenaries, descended on Italy in 1494. In
the words of his contemporary, the historian Francesco Guicciardini:

> [H]is passage into Italy not only gave rise to changes in domin-
> ions, subversion of kingdoms, desolation of countries, destruction
> of cities and the cruelest massacres, but also new fashions, new
> customs, new and bloody ways of waging warfare, and diseases
> which had been unknown up to that time. Furthermore, his incur-
> sion introduced so much disorder into Italian ways of governing
> and maintaining harmony, that we have never since been able to
> re-establish order, thus opening the possibility to other foreign
> nations and barbarous armies to trample upon our institutions
> and miserably oppress us.[35]

The effect of the invasion of Italy by the French and Spanish, the
decline in the independence of city-states like Naples and Milan, the
overthrow of the Florentine republic, and the triumphs by those whom
Italians looked upon as cultural upstarts infused Machiavelli with pas-
sionate nationalism and brought him to demand his country's unification so that it might restore and maintain its independence. He saw his
country as "more enslaved than the Hebrews, more oppressed than the
Persians, and more scattered than the Athenians; without a head, without order, beaten, despoiled, lacerated, and overrun. . . ."[36]

The French invasion of Italy not only impressed upon Machiavelli the advantages of the large territorial state over competing political entities like the Italian city-states but brought him to recognize the absolutely central role of military power in international politics, a belief handed down to subsequent generations of realist theorists and practitioners. In *The Prince*, he declared that the "chief foundations of all states . . . are good laws and good arms," neither of which could exist without the other (XII) and that a prince should "have no other aim or thought . . . but war and its organisation and discipline, for that is the only art that is necessary to one who commands. . ." (XIV).[37] And Machiavelli's understanding of warfare, like politics, was conditioned by his recognition of the relationship among changes in technology, economics, and society.

In the technological sphere, the introduction of firearms, gunpowder, and artillery had undermined the military role of the medieval knight and, consequently, his political and social status. The feudal system itself was a victim of these changes as the knight could no longer perform his legal functions. But it was not merely technological changes that doomed the feudal system but the growth in commerce and the spread of money. This shift in the economic basis of society weakened the religious and legal bonds that had constituted the bases of political loyalty and increasingly depreciated the centrality of landholding as a political-economic power factor. "It was primarily in the military field," declares Felix Gilbert, "that those who were the protagonists of the new economic developments—the cities and the wealthy overlords—could make greatest use of the new opportunities: namely, to accept money payments instead of services, or to secure services by money rewards and salaries."[38] Urban elites, then, were able to assemble professional armies in which allegiance was based on pay rather than vassalage. This revolution in the nature of military organization started earliest and proceeded fastest in Italy, where economic changes were most advanced.

The effect of these changes in technology and organization was to create the potential for more destructive and longer wars. Where medieval armies were largely recruited from the narrow caste of noble knights who served only for short periods of time, mercenary armies had a larger pool of manpower from which to draw. Artillery especially was responsible for degrading the defensive capacity of isolated strongholds and castles, the bastions of medieval knights. Mercenaries were willing to serve as long as they were paid. That this potential was not realized until the end of the fifteenth century was largely due to the

reluctance of mercenary commanders to squander their military resources in fierce campaigns and their preference for more leisurely and
indecisive conflicts that would earn them greater profits. In addition,
such mercenaries—unmoved by a higher cause—were rarely inclined to
die for their employers. The French invasion of Italy seemed to change
all this with dramatic ferocity. In Guicciardini's words:

> The effects of the invasion spread over Italy like a wildfire or
> like a pestilence, overthrowing not only the ruling powers, but
> changing also the methods of government and the methods of
> war. Previously there had been five leading states in Italy . . . ;
> and the foremost interest of all these states had been to maintain
> the status quo. . . . When war broke out, the forces were equal,
> the military organization slow and the artillery cumbersome, so
> that usually the entire summer was spent on the siege of one
> castle; the wars lasted very long and the battles ended with small
> losses or no losses at all. Through the invasion of the French,
> everything was thrown upside down, as though by a sudden hurri-
> cane. . . . Now the wars became quick and violent, a kingdom
> was devastated and conquered more quickly than previously a
> small village; the sieges of cities were very short and were suc-
> cessfully completed in days and hours instead of in months; the
> battles became embittered and bloody. Not subtle negotiations
> and the cleverness of diplomats, but military campaigns and the
> fist of the soldier decided over the fate of the states.[39]

Almost overnight, the Italian city-states had been reduced to pawns in
the emerging European state system, as the citadels upon which they
had relied for protection against each other swiftly fell before the
French onslaught.

Military disaster had a decisive effect on Machiavelli's political outlook. Not only did he come to appreciate the coming hegemony of
large, centrally organized, and secular territorial states, but he came to
understand instinctively the political and military necessity of popular
support and legitimacy. It was no longer possible, he believed, for a
narrow elite unilaterally to make itself responsible for the mass; the
former could only survive if it enlisted the latter. Repeatedly he ridi-
culed the fighting prowess of paid mercenaries in contrast to citizen
armies.

> The mercenaries and auxiliaries are useless and dangerous, and
> if any one supports his state by the arms of mercenaries, he will
> never stand firm or sure, as they are disunited, ambitious, with-
> out discipline, faithless, bold amongst friends, cowardly amongst

enemies, they have no fear of God, and keep no faith with men. Ruin is only deferred as long as the assault is postponed; in peace you are despoiled by them, and in war by the enemy. *The cause of this is that they have no love or other motive to keep them in the field beyond a trifling wage, which is not enough to make them ready to die for you.* They are quite willing to be your soldiers so long as you do not make war.[40]

Only if the sort of nationalist spirit, dimly perceived earlier by Marsilio, could be harnessed to the defense of the state would it be possible for Italy to regain its former independence. Translated into military practice, this meant that Machiavelli advocated reliance upon citizen militias rather than paid mercenaries despite his own disappointment with such a militia during the defense of Florence against the return of the Medici. It was his belief in the efficacy of the citizen soldier motivated by love of country that led him to downplay the importance of money in war. Overall, Machiavelli predicted by almost three centuries the military consequences of revolution in France, that tremendous infusion of martial energy and spirit that so frightened Clausewitz.

It was, moreover, the French invasion and Machiavelli's analysis of the reasons for Italian weakness that led him to his key idea that there existed a morality of states different than and independent of the conventional morality of individuals. "Although deceit is detestable in all other things," he argued, "yet in the conduct of war it is laudable and honorable. . . ."[41] In effect, Machiavelli was articulating the primacy of states' interests and the compelling proposition that the ends justify the means.

## The Primacy and Autonomy of Politics and Power

If, during the Middle Ages, the temporal and spiritual represented two sides of the same coin and were inextricably woven together, Machiavelli reflected the new reality in which the two realms were clearly demarcated.[42] Increasingly, political leaders were no longer subject to spiritual authority and no longer sought to play dual roles. Even the popes had come to respect and participate in the ebb and flow of balance-of-power politics. Moreover, especially in Italy, political leadership was no longer based on ascription or law but on the ability of parvenus to seize and hold the reins of government. Finally, the universalist ideal of the Middle Ages had surrendered to the clash of state egoisms; the apparent permanency of the past had given way to a scene of apparently ceaseless and turbulent change. Machiavelli's prince was, in Sheldon Wolin's apt phrase, "the offspring of an age of restless ambition, of the rapid transformation of institutions and quick shifts in power among the elite groups."[43] His skills were those of manipulation of symbols and people; his "right" to rule was confirmed by his ability to do so. Ethics, like religion, were instrumental rather than ends-in-themselves. For Machiavelli, observes E. H. Carr, "politics are not . . . a function of ethics, but ethics of politics. . . . Morality is the product of power."[44] In Machiavelli's eyes medieval rulership, like medieval theory, was obsolete—an idealist illusion of no theoretical value for Renaissance practitioners.[45]

Like later realists, Machiavelli's ideas followed from a gloomy assessment of human nature, especially that of political man, and he argued that "human desires are insatiable (because their nature is to have and to do everything whilst fortune limits their possessions and capacity of enjoyment), this gives rise to a constant discontent in the human mind. . . ."[46] The ambition that inevitably flowed from such discontent implied a perpetual scarcity of power among individuals as well as among states. This in turn implied a constant clash of wills and interests. In contrast to his medieval predecessors, then, Machiavelli viewed conflict and preparations for conflict as the norm rather than as exceptions to the norm. History was the repetition of cause and effect in which conflict was the motor force; it was no more possible to will away the dilemmas inherent in scarcity than to will away history itself. As the product of cause and effect, rather than the whim of God, history, for Machiavelli, could be and had to be approached empirically, as a science. It was the politician's task to do so, always sensitive however, to those unpredictable elements that Machiavelli labeled "fortuna" and always aware that political outcomes were as dependent on the actions of others as on his own decisions.

If, for Machiavelli, there existed an autonomous science of politics based on an understanding of history, then it followed that states, as the products of history, must be guided by principles of behavior and morality unique to them. States had interests unique to them that were not merely the sum of the interests of their citizens. To pursue these interests effectively in conflict with others, it followed that they must be guided by reason of state. And although reason of state consisted of certain very general common principles, it must also incorporate specific instructions determined by context and situation, especially the distribution of power. Later theorists would refine these assumptions and deduce what they would call the national interest.

In the Middle Ages, the idea of reason of state could not evolve because the concept of the secular state itself was boxed in by competing concepts such as divine law and religious obligation; and Machiavelli's own later conception remained limited owing to the immaturity of the city-state and the European state system. Yet he tapped its essence by combining his three master concepts of "virtue," "fortune," and "necessity." The first was that quality of heroic commitment that distinguished successful rulers from common men and which was a prerequisite to the founding of a state. That act, which was to Machiavelli a supreme achievement, could not be accomplished by blind obedience to conventional norms and should not be judged by such norms. Machiavelli's treatment of the myth of Romulus, in contrast to that of St. Augustus, as Wolin observes, reflects the step-level shift in thinking between ages:

> For Augustine the vile acts committed by Romulus in laying the foundations of Roman power constituted a political version of the drama of original sin. . . . Machiavelli . . . argued that the ends of national greatness legitimized Romulus' deeds: crimes committed by political actors fell under the judgments of history not morality.[47]

For Machiavelli the great task of princes was to instill "virtue" in his subjects, imbuing them with a healthy patriotism that created and sustained institutions. A high level of social "virtue" was the prerequisite of republics, which Machiavelli deemed superior to principalities. Like Romulus, a prince with "virtue" was responsive to something greater than his personal interests and was, therefore, not to be constrained by ordinary morality. "And because it [virtue] was for him the higher world," declared Friedrich Meinecke, "so it could be permitted to trespass and encroach on the moral world in order to achieve its aims."[48]

The state and its rulers are, however, constantly assailed by "fortune" which, to Machiavelli, consists of factors and events beyond deliberate control and rational planning.[49] While "fortune" cannot be overcome, its effects can be modified and constrained by rulers and states which have "virtue." "Fortune" creates "necessity" which provides, in Meinecke's words, "the causal pressure, the means of bringing the sluggish masses into the form required by virtu."[50] "Necessity" encourages "virtue" and, like the invasion of Italy, demands heroic actions; "virtue has more sway where labor is the result of necessity rather than of choice."[51] The state and its rulers must be responsive to the dictates of "necessity" even if such response flagrantly violates conventional morality; "necessity," in other words, is the basis of rea-

son of state, and it is in this sense that, for Machiavelli, the end justi-
fies the means.

From this equation, Machiavelli deduced a relativist morality for
states and their rulers. Declaring that everyone would wish a prince to
possess good qualities, he quickly adds, "but as they cannot all be
possessed or observed, human conditions not permitting of it,"[52] it is
necessary for rulers to do what they must if the state is endangered.
"Necessity," then, may require force and fraud if the state is to survive
and prosper,[53] but the idea of reason of state is, for Machiavelli, a
prudential and "utilitarian middle way"[54] between good and evil; it is
realism as opposed to idealism. Politics consistently requires, for Machiavelli, the confrontation of dilemmas, and reason of state entails the
selection of the lesser of evils that will ensure state survival.[55] All this is
summed up in that most realist of Machiavelli's conclusions:

> For where the very safety of the country depends upon the reso-
> lution to be taken, no considerations of justice or injustice, hu-
> manity or cruelty, nor of glory or of shame, should be allowed to
> prevail. But putting all other considerations aside, the only ques-
> tion should be, What course will save the life and liberty of the
> country?[56]

## MEDIEVAL IDEALISM AND MACHIAVELLIAN REALISM

In this brief review of medieval and Machiavellian theory, it has become clear that both were responses to social conditions and social
norms. While it is, of course, difficult to generalize about the medieval
millenium, the thrust of much of its theory reflected a world characterized by an economically and socially stratified universe in which political and military power were local and limited and in which
differentiation between individual and collective interests and between
domestic and international politics was almost impossible. Theory
tended to reflect these realities in a number of ways, most importantly
the myth of individuals united in a universal imperium and the dichotomy between the relative immutability of temporal conditions and the
ultimate perfectability of humanity as a spiritual collectivity. The
strong religious component and the very real authority of the Roman
Church entailed an idealism among theorists, especially those influenced by Platonism.

The dominance of Christianity itself was a reality that tended to
overshadow pervasive conflict and economic and social stagnation.
Christian belief in spiritual perfectability bred an optimism about the

course of human affairs as part of a divine plan. It fostered, too, a belief in the community and equality of Christians in the face of a temporal reality that was at once disunited, competitive, and hierarchical.

As the Middle Ages drew to a close, the underlying conditions that had evoked medieval idealism had begun to shift. The early decline of the Holy Roman Empire and the subsequent decline of the church both as a spiritual and temporal force inevitably stimulated new, and radically different, ideas about the political universe. The rise of the large and centrally administered territorial state, shifts in the bases of economic and military power, the breakdown of feudal social constraints, and growing secularization through the recovery of the classics— especially Aristotle—and advances in science produced a new spirit that was evident in Marsilio and dominant in Machiavelli.

All of these great changes are reflected in Machiavelli's historical empiricism, as well as in the substance of his ideas. Large territorial states governed by secular prices in the absence of any higher authority whose independence was ensured by force of arms and nascent nationalism were the focus of his attention. Written in what Jacob Burckhardt described as an "age of bastards"—the era of the Borgias— Machiavelli's ideas reflected the insecurity, the rapid shifts in political power, and the demise of traditional bases of authority that he saw all around him. Machiavelli's political realism reflected a belief in the immutability of the security dilemma while allowing for the waxing and waning of individual states and leaders.

From this and from his assumptions about human nature flowed a fundamental pessimism about the human condition. Individual heroes were capable of creative political acts just as were individual artists and scientists, and individual states could, at least for a time, encourage sufficient "virtue" among its citizens for them to prosper; all could not do so at once. Machiavelli's world was one of intense competition and turbulence in which the power and prosperity of individual leaders and states could be measured only in relation to one another. Finally, Machiavelli's ideas reflected elitism in the sense that only a relatively few individuals possessed the "virtue" of a prince, yet this elitism was tempered by his belief in the importance of republican legitimacy, his skepticism toward ascriptive bases of authority, and his rejection of an hierarchical international system.

Our analysis suggests, furthermore, that what we have termed idealism and realism are not "theories" in the scientific meaning of that term but rather conceptual and normatively inspired prisms through which theorists and practioners view the political world around them. These prisms, in turn, provide the assumptions on which decisions are made and from which specific hypotheses are generated in particular eras. With this perspective, it becomes easier to appreciate why it is so difficult for theorists to progress toward some abstract "truth." For international relations scholars, history itself provides the raw data from which inspiration is born. Yet, in the fundamental sense we have outlined, their data and its interpretation remain prisoners of history.

# 4

# The Vicissitudes of Norms and Theory: Realism and Idealism

International relations scholars who have sought to depict the evolution of theory in their field in accordance with the Kuhnian model almost inevitably point to realist theory as the discipline's outstanding paradigm. They argue as though postwar realism were a "revolution," a reaction to anomalies associated with what they describe as interwar "idealism." Their argument is strengthened, they believe, by the subsequent decline of realism, especially in the 1970s, which they offer as evidence that the paradigm process in international relations remains healthy and continues to operate as they would have predicted. Postwar realists like Hans Morgenthau, Kenneth Thompson, Reinhold Neibuhr, and E. H. Carr themselves contributed to the illusion by emphasizing the novelty of their ideas and depicting them as the antitheses of idealism. Although they recognized their debt to earlier scholars like Thucydides, Machiavelli, and Kautilya, they were more concerned with fundamentally reorienting the foreign policies of their countries and so tended to claim more for themselves than was justly theirs.

Yet, as we have suggested earlier, realism is less a theory than it is a set of normative emphases which shape theory.[1] Boiled down, it is a self-contained syllogism whose premises are

A. As long as human beings are organized into sovereign states, their survival and security can only be assured by acting according to the dictates of power.

B. Sovereign states are permanent features of the political landscape.
C. *Ergo*, competitive power politics, realist-style, is the alpha and omega of international relations, and any alternative system of thought is incompatible with "reality."

This is a closed system of analysis. Relying implicitly or explicitly upon such a syllogism condemns theory to the same conclusion regardless of methodology and reduces analysis to the level of ideology. Balance of power, for example, is merely a logical corollary, not an empirical "fact." No allowance is made for the possibility that realist assumptions are themselves based in empirical claims and that underlying phenomena on which these assumptions are based (e.g., the territorial nation-state) are the products of historical evolution rather than timeless constructs. Little effort is, therefore, made to hypothesize the conditions for further evolution. And when the behavior of leaders or collectivities fails to reflect this iron law, realists explain such deviance as "utopian" or, worse, suicidal stupidity. Unfortunately, such condemnation reveals the iron law to be no law at all but merely prescription laced with a good deal of subjectivism. Under these circumstances, the prospects for genuine theoretical breakthroughs are remote, especially since even much of contemporary behavioral analysis remains in the grip of this ideology.[2]

Historically, most societies have been characterized by the presence of several normative strains simultaneously competing with one another. For this reason, theories of international relations which reflected one or another extreme have rarely monopolized scholarly discourse. For every self-professed Machiavellian, there has been an anti-Machiavellian; Jeremy Bentham and Richard Cobden flourished alongside of the nineteenth-century advocates of balance of power and imperialism. However, as illustrated in the preceding chapter, the normative temper of any era is likely to have distinctive emphases. Typically, if these are extreme in one period, a compensating shift will take place during an ensuing period. These shifts are reflected in changing fashions in the social sciences, including international relations.

Realists have often recognized their own role in this ancient drama, and they have themselves pointed to the shifting nature of ideas in their field. For John Herz, this takes the form of movement between extremes—"a utopian and often chiliastic Political Idealism, or—when disillusionment with the ideal's ability to mold the 'realist' facts frustrates expectations—it [the ideal] has taken refuge in an equally extreme power-political and power-glorifying Political Realism."[3] Realists have also been prepared to describe in clear and forceful terms the repeated collision between themselves and their putatively idealist adversaries and have provided histories of foreign policy that depict the cyclical domination of one or the other set of normative claims.[4]

Earlier we described the key normative continua along which conflicting theories of international relations are distributed and suggested the circumstances under which shifts tend to occur. Although it is not easy to predict which normative emphases will dominate at a particular moment, two observations are in order at this point: Self-styled realists and idealists are prone to identify different aspects of the same phenomena as evidence for their positions, and it is a profound error to accept the realist contention that their adversaries are merely misty-minded dreamers and utopians with no sense of the "real" conditions that shape and condition human behavior. The first of these observations helps to explain why realist and idealist theoretical strains coexist in time and place regardless of which is dominant, and the second is essentially a corollary of the first.

Scholars whose theories emphasize immutability, pessimism, competition, or elitism (e.g., realists) are fundamentally conservative. They are alert to the perils posed by the inherent unpredictability of change. For them, the great challenge is to control and manipulate the forces of change against human error, stupidity, and avarice. Theirs is a world of limited resources and unlimited ambition. Those conditions, at least, are immutable. In contrast, those whose theories reflect mutability, optimism, community, and nonelitism (e.g., idealists) see the forces of change as opportunities for reducing stupidity and avarice and for expanding spiritual and material resources. For the former, the calamities of major wars provide evidence of the failure to use violence scientifically, the risk of unleashing human passions, and the folly of reformist zeal. For the latter, such tragedies reflect the futility of prevailing rules of the game and afford opportunities to alter these rules. The former regard technological innovation as providing new, and often dangerous, capabilities with which struggles can be waged, whereas the latter view science and technology as means for enlarging the resource pie and overcoming the superstitions, ignorance, and parochialisms that they see as sources of conflict. To some extent, both are correct, just as repeated plays of the same nonzero sum games provide evidence for the virtues both of cooperative and noncooperative strategies. From time to time, one or the other normative strand will appear to have triumphed, because the values that preoccupy them most seem—temporarily—at greater risk; yet neither can triumph in any permanent way.

## OSCILLATING NORMS

Realism and idealism, as we have portrayed them to this point, appear as antitheses, and it might be inferred that we are proposing a simple theoretical dichotomy. Of course, this is not the case, as scholars rarely place themselves at one or the other extreme. Just as Morgenthau and Machiavelli were prepared to admit of the role of law and justice, so Wilsonians were not ignorant of the importance of national power and ambition.[5] For us, realism and idealism represent logical extremes or ideal types, much as Clausewitz, influenced by Kant, distinguished between "absolute" and "real" war. The insightful theorist sees the pitfalls and virtues of both and refuses to embrace either without reservation. So it is that the realist Thucydides gives voice to Pericles' Funeral Oration and depicts the tragedy of the *hubris* of Athens' undiluted policy of power in its dealings with Melos and its subsequent Sicilian expedition. In paying homage to Thucydides, Sir Alfred Zimmern also expressed more eloquently than could the present authors a key theme of the present book: "All great art is like a ghost seeking to express more than it can utter and beckoning to regions beyond. This is as true in history . . . as in poetry or any more personal art."[6] This was only partly understood by the great German historian Friedrich Meinecke when he described the "compromise" that seventeenth-century thinkers professed to find between Machiavelli's creed and natural law:

> The immense power of the old tradition of Natural law is shown
> by the fact that even the most emancipated thinkers of the century
> lay under its spell and made no attempt to grasp the handhold
> which the doctrine of raison d'etat offered towards a new empiri-
> cal doctrine of the state. But, being great and profound thinkers,
> besides imbibing the old tradition they also mentally digested the
> living reality of state life. . . .[7]

Yet there is oscillation among the norms that condition theory in international relations. We have seen this to be the case in the evolution of medieval theory and in its transition to the realism of Machiavelli. Such oscillation does not necessarily reflect major shifts in the subjects that preoccupy theorists and practitioners of international relations as much as in the salience of those subjects and in strategies for coping with them. Indeed, at a general level there is a remarkable consistency in the subjects that the international relations literature treats. As expressed by Arnold Wolfers and Laurence Martin:

> The problems of self-preservation in the light of external danger,
> of expansion into new territories or of contraction, of intervention

in the affairs of others, of alliances, peace-making, and the conduct of wars are as much matters of concern and controversy as they were when a More, Hume or Bentham put their minds to them.[8]

Hence, we are repeatedly confronted with theoretical "novelties" that, on close inspection, turn out to be rediscoveries of old ideas, themes, and hypotheses.

That historical and geopolitical circumstances at least partly determine theoretical outlook is borne out by the distinctive intellectual traditions of continental Europe and the Anglo-Saxon world. Historically, realist doctrines appear to have enjoyed greater prominence and to have become more firmly anchored in the former owing to geographic factors and the consequent presence of powerful countries on one another's frontiers, all posing potential threats to one another. By contrast, the long-time isolation and greater sense of security enjoyed by the United States and Great Britain produced more fertile ground for ideas of an idealist stripe.[9] Even today, the relatively greater realism, even cynicism, of Soviet than American leaders is partly the legacy of historical insecurity and seems strangely at odds with the optimism of classical Marxism. Anglo-Saxon theorists and practitioners, then, have typically viewed themselves as enjoying greater latitude in foreign affairs than their continental brethren who saw themselves under the spell of Machiavelli's "necessity." The traditional faith of Americans in the benefits of science and technology, their optimism about the future and the prospects of improving the human condition, and their general problem-solving ethos are products of America's unique historical experience.

There have, of course, been notable Anglo-Saxon realists as well as continental idealists. What is singular about them is that they seem to have emerged in "exceptional" historical periods. Thomas Hobbes, for example, can only be understood as the product of a period of civil war in England, and Alexander Hamilton was, at once, the product of the American Revolution and the relatively brief era of extreme American vulnerability to European power that followed the Revolution.

At root, mature realism and the theories and doctrines of international politics and foreign affairs that emerged from it entail an acceptance, even an endorsement, of the state system. The relationship between this acceptance and the norm of competitiveness is quite obvious. What is more important is the realist propensity to view the state as a phenomenon greater than the sum of its parts, as an organic entity endowed with personality and interests that are not to be understood as the mere sum of individual personalities and interests. It is this propensity that partly explains the elitist bias in realist theory. By contrast, political and intellectual challenges to state authority over individuals domestically or to the state system internationally are viewed by the realist with suspicion and even fear. This accounts, in part, for the realist's preference for system-level analyses and antipathy to "reductionist" theory.[10] Consequently, individualism is equated with utopianism; individual preferences, interests, and ethics are regarded as inconsistent and feckless and are, therefore, dangerous. In this manner, the realist tends to equate currents of thought or political movements that threaten revolution within states with transnationalist and supranationalist currents that threaten the state system itself. Commonly, such movements prove to be individualist in content and are associated with norms of harmony and equality.

Clashes between these competing norms have, historically, produced remarkable ironies. Some of the more interesting of these grew out of the great philosophical and political conflicts that enveloped Europe during the Protestant Reformation. In its most general sense, Protestantism was a doctrine of individual conscience and personal piety, yet the outcome of the Reformation was to strengthen temporal monarchies, affirm the doctrine of state sovereignty, and usher in the halcyon era of realpolitik. This generalization, however, masks specific consequences that were even more paradoxical. Martin Luther, for instance, espoused a highly personal and individual doctrine of faith; yet, upon discovering that the secular German princes could, for their own reasons, serve as the instruments of this faith, he denounced resistance to state authority and legitimized princely tyranny as God's vengeance for sin.[11] By contrast, John Calvin and his followers, especially John Knox, were more inclined to see the state as a secular instrument to impose and sustain religious purity, yet force of circumstance in France, Holland, and Scotland transformed Calvinism into a fundamentally revolutionary movement that legitimized individual resistance against those states and monarchs that failed to adopt Protestant reforms. In a word, where Protestantism found acceptance, it became allied to the state; and where it did not, it either reaffirmed feudal localism or individual conscience against the power of states.[12]

Given the association between the evolution of the state system and the emergence of realism, it is not surprising that the doctrine gained new adherents following the articulation of the doctrine of state sovereignty. It was in France, the country that served as Machiavelli's model of the emerging territorial state, that the latter doctrine was born. Between 1562 and 1598 the French state was rent by religious strife. Caught between extremist Catholics aided by Spain and Protestant Huguenots supported by coreligionists in England and Holland, the authority of the French monarchy was increasingly circumscribed. For their part, the Huguenots allied themselves with centrifugal forces that threatened the dismemberment of the state and became spokesmen for the feudal privileges of cities and provinces. It was to bring an end to civil disunion and restore the majesty of the monarchy that Jean Bodin, a member of the moderate Catholic "Politiques," published, in 1576, *Six Books on the State*. Bodin defined sovereignty as "the absolute and perpetual power of the state, that is, the greatest power to command." Sovereignty, as Bodin used the concept, was neither an attribute of government nor of individual monarchs but rather a permanent characteristic of the state itself as an entity apart from and greater than the inhabitants of the realm. The doctrine was equally directed against those subnational forces that threatened the state from within and those transnational and supranational forces of religion and empire that threatened it from without. Bodin's sovereign power could neither be divided nor delegated, and it was this doctrine that became the rallying cry of later realists.[13]

The defeat of the Huguenots and the triumph of the monarchy in France set in train a process that culminated in the centralized state of Louis XIV and the doctrine of divine right of kings. And it was the Peace of Westphalia of 1648, which ended the Thirty Years' War, that ratified the absolute power of the state over its subjects and the state system internationally. It also ushered in the period known as the "classical balance of power" to which realists point with such approbation. In a sense, the state system and the balance of power were indivisible.

> A balance of power apparatus could not function without the existence of a state system. . . .[14]

> Balance of power theorists assumed, first of all, the existence of a *state system*, that is, a group of independent "neighboring states more or less connected with one another." . . .[15]

Generations of international relations scholars, especially realists, have virtually defined their field in terms of sovereign states, thereby seeking to build an empirical discipline on the weak reed of a legal fiction. Even the "model" French state only briefly resembled the sovereign monolith described by Bodin. Neither of the key stipulations of the doctrine—absolute power of the state domestically and legal equality of states internationally—has been an accurate depiction of the global community. Their irrelevance at the present time accounts for the apparently unreal and "backwater" quality of much of contemporary scholarship in public international law. Historically, sovereignty was a potent psychological symbol, but it is hyperbole, indeed, to term the symbol, as does one scholar, "a source of vitality for the state."[16]

Yet the apparent congruence between the fictional world of sovereign states and the real world of eighteenth-century Europe enabled that period to become the "age of realism." It was an era of absolutist monarchy, intense interstate competition featuring transitory alliances and limited wars, as well as a period of cosmopolitan diplomacy and political stability. The entire edifice was reinforced by a rejection of the political and religious extremism that had characterized the bloody centuries that had preceded it. Statesmen of the era, like generations of realists that followed, could believe with Sir Harold Nicolson that "the worst kind of diplomatists are missionaries, fanatics and lawyers; the best kind are the reasonable and humane sceptics."[17] Yet it was the very conditions of this era—relative toleration, cosmopolitanism, economic growth, scientific advance, and relative peace—that were prerequisites for the belief in the possibilities of change and the spirit of optimism that pervaded late eighteenth-century thought.

The normative transition had already begun and would generate some very different ideas about politics. Cosmopolitan humanists, especially French *philosophes* like Voltaire, Montesquieu, and Diderot, gave voice to a new individualism, a belief in the brotherhood and harmony of mankind, and a dedication to applying enlightened rationalism to overcoming social and political woes. It was this resurgent emphasis on the possibilities of human mutability, cooperation, and equality that constitutes the "Age of Enlightenment," and it was sufficiently strong that it even persuaded monarchs like Catherine the Great and Frederick the Great to attempt novel experiments to foster the cultural and economic well-being of their subjects. It was also a prerequisite for the great surge of idealistic optimism that culminated in the American and French revolutions. Writing of the latter, Thomas Paine expressed the optimism of this mood and its consequences for the system in which it had been fostered.

> Monarchical sovereignty, the enemy of mankind and the source
> of misery, is abolished; and sovereignty itself is restored to its
> natural and original place, the nation. Were this the case through-
> out Europe, the cause of war would be taken way.[18]

And when Crane Brinton defined the enlightenment as "the belief that all human beings can attain here on this earth a state of perfection hitherto in the West thought to be possible only for Christians in a state of grace, and for them only after death,"[19] he, too, captured the optimism and belief in mutability that characterized the tremendous burst of energy that engulfed all of Europe at the time of the French Revolution and France's effort to export its new-found creed.[20]

The French Revolution and the Napoleonic Wars placed in great peril the European state system itself; yet, as though an additional irony were needed, the fusion of state and nation brought about by the revolution seemed to give further evidence of the durability, even permanence, of the state concept. The full potential of this fusion was not realized until the end of the nineteenth century with the flowering of political romanticism, especially in Germany. For the time being, the skill of statesmen like Metternich, Talleyrand, Castlereagh, and, later, Bismarck postponed this development as they sought to reestablish the beneficent system that had existed prior to the French Revolution, buttressed by the institutional framework of the Concert of Europe and reinforced by a conservative ideological harmony. That they appreciated the dangers of national fervor wedded to state power was revealed in their "condemnation of the revolutionary principle"[21] at the Congress of Vienna and in their strong endorsement of the "legitimacy principle" as the basis of the new order. Fearful of abrupt change either within or between states and advocates of a highly elitist international system run by professional diplomats in the service of conservative monarchs, the architects of the Concert were by instinct and training cautious realists. And, at least in the years immediately after the Napoleonic Wars, their conservative philosophy reflected the prevailing mood. As Richard Rosecrance observes:

> The Concert of Europe was created at a uniquely favorable time.
> The ravages of war and revolution demanded a new effort for
> peace and domestic stability. . . . Even the philosophic fashions
> of the age railed at the doctrinaire rationalism of the Enlighten-
> ment and fostered a new attention to traditionalism and romanti-
> cism. . . . Even the peoples themselves were ready for a period
> of stability and order.[22]

This mood was, however, transitory, and the implications of fusing the ideas of nation and state could not long be delayed. Within a few years of the Congress of Vienna, the national idea swept Europe and left in its wake the wreckage of those institutions established in 1818. In some cases, the effects were relatively benign as in the liberalization of British institutions, which had the effect of a withdrawal of British support for the Concert mechanism that Britain had helped to construct. In many cases, nationalist agitation was accompanied by violence and revolution—Spain (1820), Naples (1820), Moldavia and Wallachia (1821), Greece (1821), Sardinia (1821), France (1830), Belgium (1830), and France, Austria, Prussia and the German states (1848). Many of these outbursts were unsuccessful, but their overall effect was synergistic. Nationalism became a doctrine of both liberals (e.g., Mazzini) and reactionaries (e.g., Tsar Alexander I), but its overall impact was to strengthen greatly the vertical cleavages among states and to generate ideologies of national idolatry. The national idea was further institutionalized by the successive wars of German unification (1863, 1866, 1870), and by the unification of Italy (1861). And, notwithstanding Bismarck's efforts to impose a realist solution to Europe's instability after 1870, the sense of cosmopolitan solidarity and elite harmony of interests that underlay both the eighteenth-century balance of power and the later Concert was gradually but persistently eroded.

Perhaps the great irony of eighteenth- and nineteenth-century European realism was that, although a doctrine that assumed a world of fiercely competitive states, it prospered in an environment of cosmopolitan concern for the survival of the system as a whole and of the major state entities that constituted it. This was shortly to change. "As the classical theory had its limitations," observed John Bowle, "romanticism had its dangers, in the loss of political realism and of the old sense of European order."[23]

As the hold of classical realism weakened, societies were infected by a romanticism that glorified state and nation and, especially in Germany, realism deteriorated into a crude parody of itself. As leading victims of French expansionism, the peoples of the disunited German states were eager recipients of the national idea which Napoleon's armies brought with them.[24] It was there as well that the romantic image of the nation developed and took root. This process was intensified by the frustration of German liberalism in 1848.

Johann Gottfried Herder presaged this romantic obsession with the nation—the *Volk*—as an historical and cultural organism arising from a distant past and exhibiting a collective personality and a collective consciousness. Only the "people" constituted a natural entity, united in blood and a common history; all other interests, whether of individuals, groups, or mankind as a whole, were either artificial, parochial, transitory, or chimerical and so must give way to the interests of the historical nation. And the political imagery of nationalist romanticism was but a part of broader intellectual currents. "It was," in Bowle's words, "bound up with the new philology, with the study of ancient languages; embodied in Percy's *Reliques*, in Macpherson's *Ossian* and in weird Scandinavian mythology."[25] It was, in addition, influenced by Montesquieu's political geography and by the botany of Linnaeus with its predilection for taxonomy and classification.

The political imagery of this romantic movement was, in Herder's version, relatively benign. In contrast to some of those who followed him, he perceived the possibility of nations living in harmony. But nationalist imagery grew more dangerous when seized upon first by Fichte and then by Hegel. J. G. Fichte added to Herder's romantic historicism the belief in a strong state; individual freedom, in his view, could be secured only through such a state, not apart from it. Georg Wilhelm Friedrich Hegel went a step further. "He endowed the state with a dangerous glamour and lacked the salutary suspicion of power which has inspired more realist thinkers."[26] For Hegel, world history was the story of the awakening, growth, clash, and decay of states as the agents of the Dialectic. Widely read and highly influential, Hegel's ideas, especially in relation to the international sphere, seemed to endorse perpetual and unlimited conflict among nations, unrelieved by any vision of individual or collective well-being. As Bowle observes:

> Here . . . is a manifestation of romantic early nineteenth-century
> nationalism; the cult of the Volk; the cult, of course, of Germany.
> And Hegel gives the nation a charter which would have made
> Bodin shudder. "The Nation State,' he writes, 'is mind in its
> substantive rationality and immediate actuality, and is . . . abso-
> lute power on earth." This hideous remark is followed by a joyful
> acceptance of war.[27]

War, to Hegel, was the means by which the will of each nation could be asserted as it sought domination. Law and ethics, he believed, were mere artifacts, having no moderating role to play in the collision of national destinies; and neither society, nor government, nor individuals had any reality or interest apart from the collective destiny.

Hegel, and more importantly, his cruder imitators and popularizers, both reflected the broad upsurge of nationalism in Europe in the first half of the nineteenth century and provided intellectual legitimacy for its intensification in the second half. Theirs was a dark and fundamentally reactionary philosophy, in contrast to the liberal nationalism of Mazzini, Garibaldi, and Kossuth; and it was this darker strain that persisted, especially in Germany but elsewhere as well, after the failure of the 1848 revolutions. The more liberal nationalism which saw the realization of self-determination and democracy as ushering in an era of individual freedom and international peace was aborted by the events of that year. If the spirit of the earlier period found expression in the music of Beethoven and the art of Delacroix, the spirit of the latter was reflected in the older Wagner.[28]

Despite the ultimate failure of the revolutions of 1848, conservative leaders increasingly found it necessary to appeal to nationalist emotions in order to justify their continuance in office. The legitimacy principle no longer sufficed. Both public and elite opinion in Europe became captive to nationalist doctrine of one or another stripe. Consequently, however much traditional realist leaders may have remained convinced of the need to retain a cosmopolitan balance-of-power system, they found themselves increasingly compelled to violate its principles. Even Bismarck, who after the final unification of Germany sought to restore such a system, played the nationalist card in 1871 when he seized and retained the provinces of Alsace and Lorraine from France. From that point until his ouster in 1890, the realism of the German chancellor was bedevilled by nationalist resentments in France and Russia.[29]

The intellectual and practical consequences of the fusion of nation and state were increasingly felt as the nineteenth century waned, and the world began its descent toward World War I. A crude and violent nationalist philosophy—typified by the work of Heinrich von Treitschke—combined with Social Darwinism, imperialism, and outright racism to produce a climate in which war was regarded as a necessary engine of social change and a vehicle by which nations could prove their vitality and their superiority. This violently nationalist ideology retained something of the trappings of classical realism in its emphases on national sovereignty and international competition, but, at root, it was a perverse caricature of the genuine article. It represented an unbridled egoism and lacked any vestige of the cosmopolitan sense of responsibility and prudence that characterized the Machiavellian tradition.

Treitschke, for instance, cited Machiavelli to justify his claim that war is natural and inevitable and that international law is chimerical. But where Machiavelli and his followers appreciated the necessity of mechanisms like the balance of power to limit the effects of the anarchy they believed to exist, Treitschke glorified war. "The State," he argued, "is power"[30]; it may not "renounce the 'I' in its sovereignty."[31] "War," he continued, "is justified because the great national personalities can suffer no compelling force superior to themselves, and because history must always be in constant flux; war . . . must be taken as part of the divinely appointed order."[32] Neither peace nor international solidarity held any attraction for Treitschke.

> Brave peoples alone have an existence, an evolution or a future; the weak and cowardly perish, and perish justly. The grandeur of history lies in the perpetual conflict of nations, and it is simply foolish to desire the suppression of their rivalry.[33]

It was this ethos that influenced German foreign policy after Bismarck, a policy inimical to the ideas of the cautious realists who had created the Concert of Europe.

If there was a popular alternative to the unbridled and perverse realism that dominated European thinking in the final decades of the nineteenth century and first decade of the twentieth, it was Marxist socialism. Indeed, Marxism may be regarded as an idealist variant with its vision of a world in which states had "withered away," its belief in the limitless mutability of man, and its optimistic and egalitarian biases. Marxists saw classes, not nations, as the bases of historical analysis and not only rejected the static assumptions of realist theory but insisted upon the inevitability of change owing to the evolution of modes of production. From the standpoint of international relations, at least, a paradox is apparent here. Hegelians are regarded by political philosophers as Idealists owing to their metaphysical version of the Dialectic. Yet they were more firmly rooted in the realist tradition than the Marxist materialists. For their part, as Bowle observes, "Marx and Engels were at heart revolutionary romantics, in the tradition of 1789."[34]

Like the worshippers of the state, the Marxists reflected social and cultural currents of their time, most importantly the rapid industrialization of the later nineteenth century and its companions, the urbanization and proletarianization of societies. Ultimately, the currents of nationalism proved stronger, and the Marxist prediction of class solidarity against war proved baseless in 1914. Even in Russia, where Marxism triumphed in 1917, Lenin and, later, Stalin found nationalism a more congenial ally than internationalism and rapidly abandoned any notion of dismantling the state.

## THE 20TH CENTURY: IDEALISM ASCENDANT

The futile bloodletting of World War I produced an atmosphere very congenial to a resurgence of idealist theory. One effect was to intensify demands that the study and practice of international relations and foreign affairs be opened to greater popular participation. The bloody waste that had just come to an end suggested that issues of war and peace were too important to be left to professional diplomats and soldiers. Diplomats' virtual abdication of responsibility to the generals and their military plans in 1914 and overblown rhetoric that accompanied the intensification of the war contributed to this disillusionment. The consequences of inverting Clausewitz's formula of the relationship between politics and war proved to be very dangerous indeed. Agitation focused especially on secret treaties and on so-called merchants of death, and in general reflected a revulsion against "The Old Diplomacy."[35] It entailed a rejection of elitism in foreign affairs and the belief that the arcane issues of international politics could be left safely in the hands of a narrow stratum of professionals.[36] Professional diplomacy, especially in the United States, has never recovered the status it lost at that time.

Nineteenth-century developments such as mass education, yellow journalism and inexpensive books, and the broadening of electorates in the West had already begun the process of democratizing foreign affairs, but the war dramatically increased public mistrust in the capacity and wisdom of foreign-policy establishments. In addition, changing technology (e.g., machine guns, barbed wire), had debased the value of cavalry and had transformed the First World War into a struggle of attrition in which infantry played the principal role. This had a significant social leveling effect, as the cavalry had traditionally been the "gentlemen's service." At home, too, the increasing involvement of civilians in the war effort and their increasing vulnerability to enemy action (e.g., the use of zeppelins in the bombing of London) generated antielitist sentiment.

Under these conditions, scholars entered a new idealist phase characterized by optimism (at least until the Depression and the rise of Hitler), a belief in social and political mutability, an emphasis on global interests and cooperation through international law and organization, and a renewed faith in public opinion.[37] Science and reason were regarded as tools that could be applied to understanding the causes of war as the first step toward engineering international society in ways that would prevent its recurrence.

Dr. Lewis Richardson exemplified this new spirit as it was manifested in the social sciences. Richardson pioneered in the application of mathematical modeling to identify patterns and sequences of interstate behavior associated with the outbreak of war in order to "improve public debate by making it easier to discern the likely consequences for peace of various proposed policies and thus to create peace plans actually more likely to promote peace than to incite war."[38] Richardson's approach assumed that the human condition was malleable, and his faith in the efficacy of science was adopted by a generation of his followers, especially in the United States. Science and reason combined could uncover the conditions necessary to realize the harmony of interests to which idealist scholars aspired. "The scholar's purpose," declares John Vasquez, "was to reveal this fundamental truth and to delineate those conditions so that it would be possible to establish a set of institutions that by their very structure would force nations to act peacefully and thereby cause a revolution in the way international politics was conducted."[39]

History, then, was looked to by scholars as the great data source that would reveal errors of the past in order to avoid their recurrence. Thus, the first two occupants of the Chair of International Politics at the University College of Wales—the first of its kind—were diplomatic historians (Professors Alfred Zimmern and C. K. Webster). Describing the study of international relations at this time, Kenneth Thompson suggested that "what most distinguishes this period is the high level of historical accuracy and the faithful attention to the canons of historiography and historical method by which it was characterized."[40]

The widespread belief that international harmony would exist if the system of competitive nation-states could be modified and reformed provided an impetus to the study of international law and organization. Indeed, of the twenty-four scholars of international relations who had attained the rank of professor by 1930, eighteen were specialists in law and organization.[41] And the purposes of such analysis were "the stimulation and advancement of international cooperation and good will among the world's people."[42] As this description suggests, international relations scholarship in the years after World War I had a decidedly antinationalist bias. Peoples, not states, were viewed as the key units of analysis. States were impediments to the achievement of a natural harmony of interests and to an understanding of the degree to which the fates of individuals everywhere were linked. Public opinion, channeled by supranational organizations like the League of Nations and the Permanent Court of International Justice, would, it was believed, generate pacifist pressures sufficient to prevent the outbreak of war.

The ideas of President Woodrow Wilson significantly contributed to international relations scholarship in the years after 1918. As noted earlier, international relations scholars regularly seek cues from political practitioners, and the latter play a major role, intentionally and unintentionally, in structuring scholarly research agendas. This was as much the case in post-World War I America as it had been during the late nineteenth-century era of imperial expansion and as it would prove to be during the Cold War and the brief era of U.S.-Soviet détente. Wilson shared the optimism that inspired the industrialist Andrew Carnegie to instruct the trustees of the Carnegie Endowment for International Peace that

> When . . . war is discarded as disgraceful to civilized man, the trustees will please then consider what is the next most degrading evil or evils whose banishment . . . would most advance the progress, elevation, and happiness of man.[43]

War was merely one of many problems confronting civilized man which could be conquered if sufficient zeal and energy were applied. Wilson's optimism and belief in mutability are conveyed in Hedley Bull's description of the president's conviction that "the system of international relations that had given rise to the First World War was capable of being transformed into a fundamentally more peaceful and just world order; that under the impact of the awakening of democracy, the growth of the 'international mind,' the development of the League, the good works of men of peace or the enlightenment spread by their own teachings, it was in fact being transformed; and that the responsibility of students of international relations was to assist this march of progress to overcome the ignorance, the prejudices, the ill-will and the sinister interests that stood in its way."[44]

Wilson's belief in the culpability of narrow nationalism, authoritarianism, and selfish interest reveals an antipathy toward competitiveness and elitism. Thus, democracies shared an obligation "to turn wars from the object of the narrowly defined safety of the state into crusades to establish the conditions under which all states can coexist in perpetual peace."[45] Only democracies could prevent preemption of the common interest by wilful minorities which might benefit from war. This is clearly conveyed in Wilson's message to Congress asking that war be declared against Germany.

> A steadfast concern for peace can never be maintained except by a partnership of democratic states. . . . [O]nly free people can hold their purpose and their honor steady to a common end and prefer the interests of mankind to any narrow interest of their own.[46]

And if some miscreant state initiated war in defiance of the common will of mankind, the United States and the other democracies would take up the burden of that common will.

> All the peoples of the world are . . . partners in this interest,
> and for our part we see very clearly that unless justice be done
> to others it will not be done to us. The program of the world's
> peace, therefore, is our program. . . .[47]

Although Wilson did not share the Marxist vision of ultimately eliminating nation-states, his conception of states was vastly different than that of the nineteenth-century practitioners and theorists of realpolitik. States were not, in his view, anthropomorphic entities with interests greater than those of their citizens. Governments were established to represent those individual interests rather than to mobilize them in the name of parochial elites. It was this conception of the state that allowed idealists to draw upon domestic analogies in analyzing international relations.[48]

Public opinion was not something to be feared as an impediment to rational decisionmaking but was something to be revered as a source of rationality and good sense. Individuals, not corporate entities called states, were the key units of analysis. It was this last assumption, so different than that of realists, which allowed Wilson to predict that, once democracy were universally established, the peace of the world would rest on "the organized major force of mankind," which would constitute "a community of power" rather than a balance of power.[49] Public opinion was a more certain guarantor of peace than national armies. "What we seek," declared Wilson, "is the reign of law, based upon the consent of the governed and sustained by the organized opinion of mankind."[50]

So different a conception of the state *alone* would have made it difficult for Wilson and other so-called idealists to communicate with classical realists. Basic definitions reveal ideological predispositions, and differences among them reflect much more than the scientific "immaturity" that many international relations scholars expect to be shortly overcome.

Realists have repeatedly argued that idealist scholarship, unlike their own, consists of "normative and prescriptive analysis."[51] This claim was perhaps most eloquently articulated by E. H. Carr in his critique of idealism, *The Twenty Years' Crisis*. Carr argued that idealists had confounded aspiration with reality and that it was necessary to understand how things really are before a science of politics could be developed. In this, Carr echoed his great realist predecessor, Machiavelli.[52] In this way, realists set the agenda for the "debate" they proposed to have with their idealist adversaries, just as Machiavelli had done four centuries earlier.[53]

But in successfully setting the agenda, realists also succeeded in perpetuating a false dichotomy; that is, that they were hard-headed empiricists—in contrast to their quixotic adversaries—whose close reading of history enabled them to discern general laws of politics by means of induction. In fact, the general laws that realists propounded were value-laden assumptions buttressed by a ransacking of history. And those assumptions reflect normative commitments antithetical to the beliefs of idealists. It is not that idealist analyses were more "normative and prescriptive," but that were more *overtly* so.

Despite the realists' repeated invocation of idealist strawmen, twentieth-century realists, like those whom they criticized, were less concerned with imposing a new methodology on a discipline than with reorienting foreign policy. While realists rarely articulated clearly the norms that guided them, they were not at all shy about prescribing "correct" and "prudent" foreign policy behavior. Indeed, in providing advice to practitioners, realists implicitly recognized that idealism was not merely a mode of scholarship. Rather, especially in the United States, it represented a broad mood of optimism that came with the end of World War I and that was sustained by booming economic conditions. Within a relatively short time, Wilsonian internationalism was replaced by isolationism, tinged with pacifism, but the mood remained optimistic.

Post-World War I political, economic, and social conditions suggested to many Americans that their time had come to assume world leadership and that the examples and practices of Europe, believed to have been shown a failure, could be safely ignored. Americans, including many in the scholarly community, assumed that the practices of businessmen and lawyers—practices that had built the United States— could be applied internationally. What was termed isolationism was, in reality, a disavowal of the practices of power politics—political and military intervention in the name of a balance of power—accompanied by economic globalism. Underlying partial isolationism was a sense that global peace and prosperity required the conditions of a free market and that interventionism would, in effect, distort this market. This belief system constituted a unique blend of nationalism and internationalism, the former manifested as a belief in the superiority of the American system and the latter as a belief that America's interests and the world's interests were identical.

Realists have suggested that this mood was responsible for the failures of the 1930s. On one level, they are correct; America's political and military noninvolvement made it difficult to contain German and Japanese revisionism. But what realists call American idealism did not take root in Europe (except in some British circles). European pacifism and failure to confront Hitler in timely fashion had very different roots than American isolationism. In Europe, this behavior was largely the product of a mood of pessimism and cynicism and an absence of self-confidence produced by the fearful waste of World War I, the Bolshevik Revolution in Russia, and America's earlier refusal to incur the obligations of collective security. British and French leaders repeatedly sought to apply the principles of balance of power, but they at once lacked available alliance partners and did not grasp that Hitler would not play by the prudential rules of realism.

## THE REALIST "PARADIGM"

Western inability to cope effectively with German and Japanese revisionism and the catastrophe of World War II brought on an eclipse of idealism and set the stage for the reascension of realist perspectives. The international institutions that had been established after 1919 did not evolve as Wilsonians had anticipated and achieved neither the political nor functional ends for which they had been created. Following E. H. Carr, realists argued that self-abnegation in the face of growing German and Japanese power had culminated in the disasters of the 1930s. But Hitler, as we have observed, was no more in the tradition of classical realpolitik than the most ardent of idealists. Would the postwar experiments have succeeded if the German Army had seized power or if the world had not been gripped by economic depression? We shall never know.

In any event, the experience of World War II and the onset of the Cold War provided fertile soil for the reassertion of realist doctrine. As initial postwar optimism gave way to a growing pessimism that accompanied apparent Soviet victories in Eastern Europe and Asia, realist assumptions once more found public and intellectual acceptance. So dominant did realism become in academic and policy-making circles in the 1950s and 1960s that, to many international relations scholars, it assumed the status of a genuine Kuhnian paradigm. Postwar realism even seemed to have an "exemplar" in Hans J. Morgenthau's *Politics Among Nations* (1948), and, until the end of the 1960s, most textbooks tended to share realist assumptions.[54] Morgenthau, as John Vasquez declares, "expressed, promulgated and synthesized" postwar realism

and was the "single most important vehicle for establishing the dominance of the realist paradigm within the field."[55]

Realist theory, especially as articulated by Morgenthau, was at once
elegant and parsimonious, emphasizing national goals and objectives in
the context of a global distribution of power. But—and this cannot be
stressed strongly enough—the doctrine did *not* achieve ascendance because it was able to account for anomalies that its competitors had
failed to explain. In fact, idealist and Marxist theories can explain the
outbreak of Word War II quite as persuasively as can realism. The
ascendance of realism merely revealed once more that, although the
facts of history do not change, scholars are free to select from among
them in constructing plausible explanations. Consequently, dominant
explanations vary, as some facts are emphasized and others deempha-
sized and as phenomena are viewed through changing normative
lenses. And the inevitable disputes that arise in academic circles as
norms shift are anchored in genuine policy quarrels among practitioners preoccupied with life-and-death issues; they are *not* the stuff of
ivory towers alone.[56]

Realists accused Western statesmen of the interwar period of having
"deprecated" power in favor of legal and moral solutions (e.g., the
1928 Kellogg-Briand Treaty that "outlawed" war) to the problems of
their time. In doing so, according to realists, idealists confused theory
with practice and confounded scientific with normative analysis. Yet,
for the most part, the supposedly offending statesmen were quite as
aware of the balance of power concept as their realist critics but were,
in practice, as unable as are contemporary analysts to assess that balance in a manner that could provide clear policy guidelines.

At best, power is an elusive concept that has become increasingly
difficult to measure as the pace of technological change has accelerated. National power, as Morgenthau himself notes, includes such un-
measurable elements as "national character," "national morale," "the
quality of diplomacy," and "the quality of government."[57] The efforts of
interwar diplomats to formulate policy sought to account for these several factors, yet realist criticisms of them come perilously near to focusing only on military factors. Ultimately, Morgenthau admits that the
calculation of national power "is an ideal task and, hence, incapable of
achievement,"[58] and this admission forces us to ask why realists think
that they could have done better. Ironically, the factor that was least
understood by interwar politicians was one for which realists cannot
account either, the motives and personality of Hitler, who refused to
behave according to the dictates of balance of power. In short, realists

would have been unable to explain or predict the behavior of a leader who did not act according to the dictates of realist rationality. History revealed to the realists (and to many of the practitioners of that time as well) that the interwar statesmen *should* have acted differently. Unfortunately, theory that can only provide answers retrospectively is of limited value.

The manner in which realism triumphed after World War II reveals again that theory in international relations evolves in a significantly different fashion than the almost dialectical manner in which Kuhn views paradigm change in the natural sciences.[59] The revival of realism was not merely a product of, as Kuhn expresses it, "the recognition that nature has somehow violated the paradigm-induced expectations"[60] but also represented a condemnation of earlier norms brought about by the revolutionary effects of the war and the onset of the Cold War. For Kuhn, a paradigm shift occurs, *not* because the natural universe itself changes but because something about the universe becomes manifest for which the existing paradigm cannot account. Realism triumphed precisely because the political universe that had existed in the interwar period had been shattered and had been replaced by a dramatically different one in which the United States was pressed to play a leading role.

The outbreak of the Second World War served less to reveal anomalies in an existing paradigm than to provide legitimacy for the claims of power thinkers who had been competing with "idealist" rivals for centuries. In the same way, World War I had previously provided normative justification for Wilsonians to assert the bankruptcy of "narrow nationalism" and the superiority of moral universalism. Thus, the early interwar period seemed to represent a final victory of the Gladstone-Cobden school over the adherents of Disraeli. It was in each and every case, of course, only a Pyrrhic victory.

In fact, twentieth-century realists were not especially innovative theoretically. We have noted their debt to their predecessors, eighteenth-century European political practice, and the ideas of early American realists like Alexander Hamilton.[61] It was not, then, that they could account for anomalies in an existing body of thought but that they eloquently asserted the normative superiority of the "national interest" over "universalism" and "globalism." The key to their victory lay less in the power of their assumptions or logic than in the climate of the times, as well as the claim that their work was, in Morgenthau's words, "abstract but empirical and pragmatic"[62] and that they could discern a "science of international politics."[63] For a number of reasons, this claim exercised a powerful attraction in the years after World War II; the soil was indeed fertile for what Morgenthau declared to be "another great debate." Realism entailed a rejection of ideologies such as those that had legitimized the excesses of the previous years, as well as of those institutional and legal efforts to eliminate world conflict that had failed in the 1920s and 1930s. Moreover, realism meshed nicely with America's self-image at a time that the United States had so clearly emerged as *primus inter pares* in the global system.[64]

American science and economic productivity had won the war, and the atom bomb would secure the peace. Of course, pragmatism, positivism, faith in scientific advancement, and free enterprise themselves constituted an ideology, but one that appeared to be objective and rational. In this context, realism was especially attractive because it, too, appeared to offer an alternative to ideological and moralistic analysis. "Intellectually," declared Morgenthau, "the political realist maintains the autonomy of the political sphere, as the economist, the lawyer, the moralist maintain theirs."[65] This claim seemed to serve the paradigmatic purpose of providing disciplinary boundaries. Although, like Machiavelli, realists were accused of being amoral; like Machiavelli, they, in fact, provided a rather clear set of moral and prescriptive dicta that constituted the obligations of official decisionmakers seeking to serve the national interest. Indeed, one of the ironies of their triumph is that realists were able to make a powerful moral case against their intellectual adversaries by asserting the value-free character of their theories, while simultaneously providing moral and prescriptive guidelines for a generation of scholars and statesmen.

Surveys have shown that Morgenthau is the political theorist whose ideas have been most familiar to United States policy makers.[66] Among other reasons, his derogation of moral concerns has appealed to them. Thus, Bernard Brodie writes of a strong "professional tradition" among American practitioners that views the intrusion of moral considerations into policymaking to be "inherently mischievous, that is, . . . likely to cause the warping of what otherwise would be trimly correct thinking about foreign affairs."[67] Richard J. Barnet summarizes this position:

> Those who run nations cannot be unselfish, generous, or even honest in the jungle world of international relations because such impulses are not reciprocated. To recognize external limits on discretion is to compromise the interests of the American people and of future generations for whom the statesman is supposed to act as trustee.

To the realist, he continues, "What was expedient also became right. . . . Neither God, law, world opinion, right reason, or any other outside standard was recognized as a limit on their own discretion, for that discretion, they convinced themselves, would be exercised in pursuit of the highest moral values."[68]

In justifying expediency, realism neatly reinforced the ideological tenet of "pragmatism" that has been central to American culture and to policymakers who are the product of that culture. For instance, David Halberstam reports:

> In the early days of the [Kennedy] Administration [the word pragmatism] had been used so frequently that David Brinkley, writing the introduction of an early book of portraits of the Kennedy people, would dwell on that single word, and note that at an early Washington cocktail party a woman had gone around the room asking each of the hundred people there if he was a pragmatist.[69]

Pragmatism is an example of what might be termed "the attitude of ideology toward itself," advancing as it does the proposition that "practical" responses to the "real world" should take precedence over the dictates of ideology (other than pragmatism). In fact, pragmatism has regularly allowed decisionmakers to conceal from themselves the ideological premises behind their policies and, less often, to congratulate themselves on the "rightness" of their policies when the dictates of ideology and the demands of the "real world" have seemed to coincide. The concealing function of pragmatism has been enhanced by its links to the realist concept of the "national interest," purporting as that does to provide an "objective" standard for national policy. Of course, as numerous critics have pointed out, this supposed standard is so vague that its interpretation cannot but involve a highly subjective judgment. As Arnold Wolfers declares,

> When political formulas such as "national interest" or "national security" gain popularity they need to be scrutinized with particular care. They may not mean the same thing to different people. They may not have any precise meaning at all. Thus, while appearing to offer guidance and a basis for broad consensus, they may be permitting everyone to label whatever policy he favors with an attractive and possibly deceptive name.[70]

Realism thus provided the legerdemain through which the sow's ear of the pragmatist's expediency could be converted into the silk purse of the pursuit of the national interest.

The realist's association of the national interest concept with the "struggle for power," in turn, has reinforced yet another aspect of what Richard Barnet sees as part of the American tradition, a phenomenon that he terms "bureaucratic machismo." "One of the first lessons a national security manager learns after a day in the bureaucratic climate of the Pentagon, State Department, White House, or CIA is that toughness is the most highly prized virtue." United States officials have customarily adopted a self-consciously "tough," "hard-nosed" brand of decisionmaking and have evidenced a profound distrust of policies favored by "soft-headed," "liberal" "idealists" and "intellectuals".[71]

Many intellectuals, too, were influenced by realism. Realism's apparent rejection of institutional and legal mechanisms and its assertion of the value-free nature of theory were instrumental in encouraging the behavioral and scientific revolutions in international politics. Morgenthau's assertion that realism "requires . . . a sharp distinction between the desirable and the possible"[72] was, especially in the 1960s, repeated by a generation of scholars who believed that it was possible to isolate values from the analysis of political phenomena. For the most part, these scholars retained the assumptions of realism and, in retrospect, performed something approaching the task of "normal science" in the Kuhnian sense.[73] Their contributions were primarily methodological rather than theoretical and unwittingly served to institutionalize and legitimize many of realism's key assumptions.

## NEW NORMS AND OLD THEORY: THE DECLINE
## OF REALISM

The 1970s witnessed a concerted assault on the several realist assumptions—the centrality of the unitary state-as-actor, the autonomy of the international and domestic realms of politics, and the existence of the single issue of managing power—accompanied by an implicit "declaration of independence" from the doctrine.

Among the principal lines of attack were those that highlighted nonrational sources of decisionmakers' behavior,[74] the impact of changing situations on decisionmaking,[75] the importance of bureaucratic politics and organizational behavior,[76] the significance of transnationalism and interdependence,[77] the role of nonstate actors,[78] and the influence of issues on behavior.[79] In a word, realism was no longer a "disciplinary matrix."[80]

None of the above phenomena identified by these scholars as detracting from realism was new, and none was in any sense "discovered" in the 1970s. For example, even as realism was in the ascendant the ideas of Freud about nonrational sources of behavior were entering the discipline[81]; the evolution of the containment policy and the reorganization of the U.S. defense and foreign policy establishment were providing clear cases of the impact of situation and bureaucracies[82]; the integration of Western Europe was revealing some of the implications of interdependence and transnationalism[83]; the emergence of revolutionary and anticolonial movements and of multinational corporations reflected the potential roles of nonstate actors; while the appearance of a North-South axis, alongside an East-West axis, illustrated the role of issues.[84]

What had changed most dramatically were the frame of reference of scholars and the ethos of the society in which they were working. Many factors were involved in bringing about these changes. The decline in American hegemony symbolized by Vietnam, the growing salience of nonmilitary problems with an economic or environmental basis, and growing fears of nuclear war all encouraged scholarly criticisms that were grounded in an unarticulated dissatisfaction with realist norms.

The Vietnam debacle suggested that the elements of power were even more obscure than had been realized, that national power was contextual, and that military capabilities had limited utility. Recognition of the limits of American power—perceived by some as a process of decline and by others as the restoration of normalcy after a unique and "unnatural" era of postwar hegemony—was especially important in shifting the scholarly agenda in the United States from how American power could be utilized unilaterally to shape world events in U.S. interests to how relatively uncontrollable forces in an interdependent world could be channeled and tamed by multilateral cooperation.[85] Successive energy crises highlighted the existence of fragile economic interdependence and the finite nature of key resources. Apparently endemic stagflation in the West pointed to the central role of economics in national power, reinforced the growing sense of interdependence, and focused attention upon issues without any evident military dimension. In many ways, the process of détente and successive environmental traumas had the same effects. Finally, the eventual demise of détente and the achievement of technomilitary breakthroughs unleashed dormant fears in the United States and Europe regarding the adequacy of nuclear deterrence as a formula for managing conflict.[86]

These and other events promoted a shift in the nature of political vocabulary and dialogue. That altered vocabulary emphasized the linked fate of humanity as a whole, processes and interactions only partly controlled by national decisionmakers, and potential outcomes in which the differences between "winning" and "losing" were unclear. For the most part, these were precisely the concerns that had motivated political thinkers after 1919 and had shaped their vocabulary and dialogue. The cycle had come full turn, and no one seemed to notice.

Such a shift was well under way by the early 1970s. In its postwar heyday, realism emphasized immutability, pessimism, competitiveness, and elitism. These emphases were at least partly the product of a global preoccupation with the value of security in the wake of World War II, and this preoccupation was manifested in the overriding salience of a single critical issue, the Cold War.[87] Having emerged from a catastrophic conflict that had been inflicted by the aggressive behavior of a small group of dissatisfied and expansionist actors, publics and governments were ready to embrace policies and theories that focused upon the prevention of war through strength.

By the 1970s, the salience of the Cold War issue had begun to recede, permitting renewed attention to be paid to a host of other global issues that had been "hidden" in the previous years. These issues involved disputes and concerns that revolved around global resource allocation, the maintenance of postwar prosperity and environmental decay.[88] Many were, of course, not new issues but old issues that had been quietly managed after the war by international institutions and regimes that had been elaborated largely by American efforts. The growing prominence of these issues in the 1970s, however, coincided with a decline in the preoccupation with security in a military sense that accompanied the flowering of détente, along with an intensified sense of potential deprivation of other base values. In a more general sense, their prominence grew as the United States found itself increasingly less able to dominate unilaterally key international regimes like oil and money.

In this climate, realism and the norms it reflected seemed less relevant.[89] The decline in Cold War anxieties was largely responsible for reducing, at least in the West, the belief in human immutability and competitiveness; and the apparent emergence of power centers other than Washington and Moscow necessarily diluted the atmosphere of postwar elitism. There was, however, little change along the dimension of optimism/pessimism because, even as acute anxieties concerning some survival issues eased, new anxieties about other survival issues increased.

This change in the global agenda and shift in normative emphases was mirrored by the breakdown of consensus about international relations theory and the proliferation of new approaches, frameworks, and theories that rejected some or all of the realist assumptions. There was a retreat from grand theory and an impulse to the investigation of specific issues and cases in inductive fashion. The nonmilitary nature of many issues encouraged the introduction of concepts and ideas from allied disciplines, especially economics, psychology, biology, and sociology; and such migrations increased doubts about the disciplinary autonomy of political science. Although the heterogeneity and ecumenical nature of postrealist international relations scholarship makes it difficult to generalize about, some of the key concepts have been "linkage," "interdependence," "regimes," "political economy," and "transnationalism."[90] Greater attention is once more being paid to power factors, but the relative de-emphasis of the unitary state-as-actor is a reminder that nonrealist elements remain.

The shift in normative emphases that is reflected in postrealism is perhaps best seen in the work of Robert Keohane, who explicitly seeks to graft such concepts onto realist insights about power.[91] Among other reasons, Keohane is especially interesting because he has been a prolific writer during the 1970s and early 1980s, has been usually self-conscious regarding the evolution of his ideas, and has openly discussed the normative content of those ideas. Keohane regards international relations as more mutable than do realists, viewing a significant degree of cooperation among actors through international regimes as both possible and desirable. And, although cautious, he suggests that such cooperation could bring about fundamental changes in political behavior. He is relatively sanguine about postwar developments, while taking pains to preclude accusations of "idealism"; and he views global society through less elitist and competitive lenses than did his realist precursors.

Will these new concepts and ideas provide the bases for a paradigm for international relations in the Kuhnian sense? If our analysis of the sources of intellectual change is correct, the answer is probably no. Even as major syntheses of postrealist theory are emerging, such as Keohane's *After Hegemony*, it appears that the agenda of global issues is once more in transition, with military security concerns and East-West relations beginning to assume greater salience since the late 1970s. Concomitantly, an upturn in economic conditions in the West and a prolonged oil glut have reduced anxieties about these matters, even though the international economic system continues to face serious threats from trade imbalances, monetary instability, and debts. Barring major war or some other systemwide catastrophe, we would anticipate a partial return to realist norms, though realism is unlikely to achieve the dominance it once enjoyed. Its resurgence was in part forecast by the impact that Waltz's *Theory of World Politics* and its reassertion of the primacy of structural realism had on the discipline when it appeared in 1979.[92]

Keohane's own work offers considerable latitude for an increased emphasis on realist assumptions. While retaining some of the language and insights of scholars who had predicted decline in the autonomy of nation-states, the growing irrelevance of military security issues and the inevitable growth of regional and global cooperation on functional or neofunctional lines, he carefully asserts his debt to realism:

> My analysis has assumed that governments calculate their interests minutely on every issue facing them. It has not relied at all on assumptions about the "public interest" or the General Will; no idealism whatever is posited.[93]

The growing appeal of realist norms owes much to yet another apparent shift in the global agenda of critical issues. The shift is less the product of new scholarly insights than of political change in the United States and the preferences of political leaders. Jimmy Carter had sought to emphasize human rights and to focus attention both at home and abroad on global resource and economic issues. His successful negotiation of the Panama Canal Treaty, his initial attitude toward the Nicaraguan and Iranian revolutions, the apartheid issue, and the developing world in general were symbolic of his belief that American power was declining and that the United States must learn to function as but one of many in an interdependent world. And in large measure he succeeded in reorienting the agenda of the academic community. Then, he apparently "rediscovered" the Cold War following events in Afghanistan and, in the waning days of his administration, gave much more attention to the East-West and military side of the global equation. Nicaragua became more of a concern, with the Sandinistas' consolidation of power and the escalation of guerrilla violence in El Salvador.

Ronald Reagan was predisposed to emphasize these issues in any event. Open hostility to the Sandinistas and Angolan Marxists replaced the relatively flexible attitude of his predecessor. The symbols of Reagan's administration have been Euromissiles, the Strategic Defense Initiative, aid to the Nicaraguan contras, antiterrorism, and an upgrading of American military and intelligence capabilities. He was at once less prepared than Carter to see evidence of American decline, except as an argument for military spending, and more prepared to see America act unilaterally. As was the case before, the scholarly agenda reflected this official shift in perception. *International Security* replaced *International Organization* as a journal of preferred publication, and the Jeanne Kirkpatrick–Edward Luttwack school of academics replaced the intellectual courtiers of the Carter years.

Although specific events helped to trigger these policy and intellectual metamorphoses, the basic issues they reflected were relatively constant. East-West relations in which realists were most interested did not disappear in the Carter years; nor did North-South relations and nonmilitary concerns, of interest especially to theorists of interdependence and political economy, vanish after 1980. National and international moods, however, did change and were orchestrated by leaders. Intellectual fashion dutifully responded, as in the past, to these shifting social and political currents.

## CONCLUSIONS

Three conclusions emerge from the foregoing analysis: (1) There has been a tendency historically for dominant normative emphases to move back and forth along the dimensions described earlier, and, as a consequence, for so-called realist and idealist theories to alternate as the nearest thing to "paradigms" in international relations. (2) Shifting terminology notwithstanding, genuinely new theoretical visions regarding international relations have been few and far between. (3) Intellectuals and practitioners in any era tend to reinforce one another's theoretical preferences, and their relationship is generally more intimate than contemporary social scientists care to believe.

Perhaps the most important reason for the alternation between realist and idealist dominance in international relations thought and practice has been the key role played by unanticipated and disillusioning events in producing revisions in the dominant normative order of an era. Examples of such events include the Peloponnesian War and its impact on Thucydides, the fall of Rome, the French invasion of Italy of 1498 which so influenced Machiavelli, the destructive religious wars of the sixteenth and seventeenth centuries, the French Revolution and the Napoleonic Wars, the two world wars, the Vietnam War, and the seizure of American hostages in Iran. Following each, there has been a tendency to place the blame on existing values and modes of thought and to embrace "new" norms and theories.[94]

These dramatic shifts, however, have rarely produced genuinely new visions. Instead, they hastened a return to earlier values and the consequent rediscovery of earlier theories enhanced by new vocabularies. A survey of most grand theories of international relations reveals them to be built upon bundles of social and political preferences that grow out of shifting political and social contexts. The more fundamental the restructuring of existing institutions, the more likely it is dominant theories will be—at least temporarily—abandoned.

That this should occur is in no way surprising in light of the relationship between pundits and practitioners. With few exceptions, the former represent specific social and political interests and may even seek the patronage (or, at a minimum, the passive approval) of those in authority. Even Hegel, after the metaphysical debris has been cleared, is revealed to have concluded that imperial Prussia represented the ultimate stage in historical evolution. In return, intellectuals structure and articulate the perspectives of practitioners, and legitimize their behavior. On the other hand, as Charles Lindblom and David Cohen observe, contemporary practitioners, even when not directly utilizing the work of social scientists, "may take the whole organizing framework or perspective for their work from academic social science."[95] Additionally, practitioners crave theoretical justification for what they intend to do in any case, and they have the means today, as in the past, to encourage this.[96] Social science, even more than natural science, is, as Bernard Barber declares, "a social activity" that has "determinate connections . . . with the different parts of a society, for example, with political authority . . . and with cultural ideas and values. . . ."[97]

Behavioral research, while failing to produce the cumulative knowledge to which its pioneers aspired, has had the important consequence of disconfirming many of the assumed verities of the past and producing healthy scholarly scepticism about such verities. It has contributed to theoretical disarray by undermining existing general theories yet has failed to generate any of its own. Part of the problem is that the stable of concepts available to us cannot easily sustain theory construction. It is to some of these concepts that we now turn.

# II

# Conceptual Anarchy

# 5

# The State
# as an Obstacle
# to International Theory

Almost two decades ago, Martin Wight addressed the question: "Why Is There No International Theory?" His answer was that political theory had traditionally focused on "speculation about the state."[1] Humanity lived within states, not in the interstices between them, so that analyses of international relations could be no more than logical extensions of the study of the state. "If political theory," declared Wight, "is the tradition of speculation about the state, then international theory may be supposed to be a tradition of speculation about the society of states, or the family of nations, or the international community."[2] In other words, it became altogether too natural "to think of international politics as the untidy fringe of domestic politics."[3] Theorists like Hobbes and Marx, for example, directed their attention to international politics only briefly, extrapolating conclusions about the global community from observations about the relations of individuals *within* states. The absence of the sort of sovereign power that constrained human passions within states led Hobbes to posit international anarchy. For his part, Marx and his followers viewed states as extensions of class domination that must logically vanish with the establishment of classless societies.

Wight's analysis highlights one reason why international relations theorists, unlike other self-conscious communities of scholars, have been unable to establish an autonomous discipline. Even today, the most fundamental concepts in the field—its linguistic building blocks— are derivative. The very notion of "international," for instance, can be

**111**

understood only in respect of that which is *not* "national" or "domestic." The same, of course, is true of concepts like "transnational," "interstate," and "foreign policy." A field whose concepts can only be defined negatively can scarcely aspire to disciplinary status. Nor, as we shall show, does there exist any agreement about the meaning of the state concept or, for that matter, about most other core concepts in international relations.

Even postwar realism, which leans so heavily upon the state concept, exhibits confusion as regards the meaning of "state." Hans J. Morgenthau, for example, uses "state" interchangeably with "nation," and the waters are further muddied by the equating of "national interest" with the "struggle" for "national power."[4] And Inis Claude, having suggested that states are "those important political, legal, and administrative units into which the world is divided,"[5] proceeds to inform us in some detail of what the state is *not* while never informing us of what its attributes *are*.[6]

An autonomous discipline requires a stable of concepts unique to it and over which there is substantial agreement. In the absence of such concepts, international relations will remain a derivative field of study. Unique and consensual concepts are the bases of disciplinary boundaries and are prerequisites to identifying a common set of problems and puzzles that constitute the raisons d'être of its practitioners. In the absence of such boundaries, it is not even clear who is in the field and who is not. The moral theologian, the psychiatrist, the agricultural specialist, and many others may equally and plausibly claim to be involved in international relations research. Under these conditions, individual scholars or groups of scholars will continue to pursue idiosyncratic lines of research, often in isolation from one another. They will continue to contemplate different, even unrelated, problems or, what is even worse, may believe that they are addressing the same problem, only to discover that this is not the case. Put differently, international relations specialists commonly discover that they are giving the same "names" to quite different phenomena; if they fail to discover this, they will inevitably speak past each other. Quarrels over satisfactory operational definitions may mask deeper divisions over meaning, thereby aborting the voyage of scientific discovery even before it is launched. Competing methodological claims will continue to obscure more fundamental questions of meaning and language.

International relations, then, remains in a condition of conceptual anarchy; and, owing to the normative core of theory, it is unlikely that the field will transcend this condition in the foreseeable future. In Justice Benjamin Cardozo's words: "We may try to see things as objectively as we please. None the less, we can never see them with any eyes except our own."[7]

Normatively infused theory is the product of normatively infused concepts, and the meaning of concepts is bound to change along with the changing normative temper of society. Thus, the meaning of the state concept (like so many other political concepts) cannot live apart from the conditions in which it is used. In this, it is like the concept of human dignity as described by Justice William Brennan: "The precise rules by which we have protected fundamental human dignity have been transformed over time in response to both transformations of social conditions and evolution of our concepts of human dignity."[8] In other words, the value of human dignity has remained prominent in American thinking for two hundred years, but its content and meaning have changed dramatically. The reference to jurisprudence is instructive. For the most part, concepts in international relations evolve in a manner similar to that of law as described by Justice Holmes:

> The life of the law has not been logic: it has been experience.
> The felt necessities of the time, the prevalent moral and political
> theories, intuitions of public policy, avowed or unconscious, even
> the prejudices which judges share with their fellowmen, have had
> a good deal more to do than the syllogism in determining the
> rules by which men should be governed.[9]

Concepts like "state" are forged and reforged in accordance with shifting life habits and critical global issues, and the process of interaction between them. As social mores evolve in response to perceptions of necessity and social utility, the fundamental meaning associated with the sorts of abstract and artificial concepts inherent in political science is bound to change as well. Justice Cardozo's analysis of the changing meaning of "liberty" could easily be applied to the state concept:

> Does liberty mean the same thing for successive generations?
> May restraints that were arbitrary yesterday be useful and rational
> and therefore lawful today? May restraints that are arbitrary today
> become useful and rational and therefore lawful tomorrow? I
> have no doubt that the answer to these questions must be
> yes. . . . The same fluid and dynamic conception which under-
> lies the modern notion of liberty . . . must also underlie the
> cognate notion of equality. . . . From all this it results that the
> content of constitutional immunities is not constant, but varies
> from age to age.[10]

The general problems of the field are epitomized by the state concept. That concept is so central to international relations that there is virtually no possibility of developing unified and cumulative theory in the absence of universal agreement as to what the concept connotes.[11] Historically, however, that concept has had widely different connotations for scholars. Mainly for this reason, no doubt, they have not been in agreement as to when the "state" or the "modern state" emerged or even as to whether all contemporary "sovereign" entities are "true" states. To the extent that the state remains a variable, so too does a key part of the subject matter of the discipline that most of us keep hoping will someday, somehow evolve.

Historically, efforts to define the state have inevitably combined views of what it is with what it ought to be, views conditioned by context-bound issues of practical significance. For Aristotle, the notion of the state was inseparable from that of the Greek polis. For Romans, the state evolved from the polis of Rome itself into a vast empire with an emperor who in later stages was seen by many as being both "above the law" and divine. In the medieval era, for St. Thomas Aquinas and his contemporaries, there were, in a sense, many overlapping states or none—a diffuse and fragmented hierarchy of power, ranging from pope and emperor (or perhaps God alone) at the pinnacle through local monarchs down to the humblest manor, town, or cloister. Machiavelli's idea of the state and its prince was, of course, derived from the Medici Italian city-state universe in which he lived and, more immediately, from his desire for a job at court; although the French occupation of Italy subsequently convinced him of the need for republican-limited government. As for Bodin, who is usually credited with having articulated the first full-blown notion of state "sovereignty," F. H. Hinsley puts it: "Bodin's book was a direct outcome of the confusion brought about by civil and religious wars in a France which had known no peace between the conflicts arising from the dissolution of its feudalized segmentary structure and the onset of the Reformation in the form of a new kind of rebellion against the state."[12] Likewise, Hobbes's *Leviathan* was the product of his preoccupation with civil strife in England.

A colleague in English tells us that the first time the term "the state" actually came into general use in England was during the Cromwellian era when the Crown's properties were seized and the Cromwellians scratched their round heads trying to decide who or what the properties now belonged to. John Locke, Adam Smith, and others adopted the perspective of a liberal state in which the people reigned, which perspective neatly coincided with the political and economic interests of a rising middle class—and of upper class revolutionaries and capitalists in America. (Contract became the watchword in more ways than one!) Karl Marx, on the other hand, saw the state as the instrument (until it withered away) of the urban proletariat that he saw growing and restive all around him in the western Europe of his day.

The same process took place outside of Europe. Confucian thought held that China and, indeed, all the earth was united under an emperor who was the Son of Heaven; and the ideal of Chinese unity persisted, even, as so often was the case, when China was politically fragmented. The early Indian conception of the state (articulated circa 300 B.C. by Chanakya Kautilya, sometimes likened to Machiavelli) saw the ruler as essentially an executive for Brahmin law (dharma) and envisaged realist-style power relations prevailing among local rulers. This conception gave way some years later under the influence of Buddhism to an idea of a peaceful empire under one emperor who was the defender and chief missionary of a universalist faith. In the Moslem world, from the outset to the present day, there has been a tension between the secular state in its local manifestations and the state seen as a servant of the universalist religion of Islam.

In Europe, Rousseau's vague notion of popular sovereignty as the "general will" formed part of the background of the French Revolution, and Napoleon gave a major thrust to the identification of the state with the nation. Hegel's concept of the state as a moral idea, the realization of self, meshed nicely with later Social Darwinism and found a particularly nasty echo in German extreme glorifiers of the state like Treitschke—and finally, of course, Hitler. By contrast, the limited democratic state and national self-determination were the hallmarks of Wilsonian thought.

Contemporary analyses of the state have been no less infused by normative commitment. "The mark of the modern world," writes Immanuel Wallerstein, "is the imagination of its profiteers and the counter-assertiveness of the oppressed. Exploitation and the refusal to accept exploitation as either inevitable or just constitute the continuing antinomy of the modern era. . . ."[13] Nor are such analyses less context-bound, as reflected in Nicos Poulantzas's initial comments on his "theory of the state":

The urgency behind this book derives above all from the political situation in Europe, since although the question of democratic socialism is far from being everywhere on the agenda, it is being posed in a number of European countries. The urgency also stems from the emergence of the new phenomenon of State authoritarianism, which affects virtually all the so-called developed countries. Finally, it refers to the discussion on the State and power that is developing in France and elsewhere.[14]

For a time, except for die-hard realists, the concept of the state actually fell out of intellectual fashion, only to return in recent years. The same year (1968) that Wight's essay complaining about the concept's negative impact on international theory appeared, J. P. Nettl was writing: "The concept of the state is not much in vogue in the social sciences right now. Yet it retains a skeletal, ghostly existence largely because, for all the changes in emphasis and interest in research, the thing exists and no amount of conceptual restructuring can dissolve it."[15] Stephen D. Krasner confirmed the trend away from the state concept when he wrote: "From the late 1950s until the mid-1970s, the term state virtually disappeared from the professional academic lexicon. Political scientists wrote about governments, political development, interest groups, voting, legislative behavior, leadership, and bureaucratic politics, almost everything but 'the state'."[16] Why this trend? For one thing, there was increasing recognition that the realists' world of objective national interests and nonideological behavior is as much a normative conception as the League of Nations. Analysts began asking realists hard questions like "whose national interest?" and "power for what?" and "isn't ideology part of power?"

As Krasner's list suggests, many scholars started to peer within the "black box" or "billiard ball" of the state, explicitly or implicitly questioning its autonomy and stressing the degree to which policy outcomes are shaped by domestic political actors and processes. Alternatively some of the same scholars and others emphasized the constraints on state autonomy emanating from the international environment—from the basic structure of the international system, international law, a great variety of international governmental and nongovernmental actors (IGOs and INGOs), "regimes," and so on. In the sense that theirs was an "international" emphasis, it was reminiscent of the Wilsonian "idealism" against which the realists had harangued. However, that is where the similarity ended. The proponents of what might be called the new internationalism were a disparate group, including Marxist, neo-Marxist, and/or *dependencia* theorists, as well as theorists who were responsive to the fact that the receding of Cold War issues in the late 1960s allowed other previously "hidden" global issues to come to the fore. The latter category of scholars were preoccupied with issues of international political economy such as resource allocation, recession, monetary instability, trade, transnational corporations, and environmental decay. Temporarily, the state as traditionally conceived was no longer the principal focus of analysis, and the familiar issues of "power and peace" were no longer seen as necessarily delimiting the boundaries of the discipline. By 1976 Krasner concluded: "In recent years, students of international relations have multinationalized, transnationalized, bureaucratized, and transgovernmentalized the state until it has virtually ceased to exist as an analytic construct."[17]

If this was the situation in the mid-1970s, Krasner and others have subsequently succeeded in resurrecting the notion of state autonomy. In their view, the state has significant resources of its own that often allow it to overcome constraints deriving from both domestic and international environments. Krasner's 1984 assessment was that "the agenda is already changing." Reviewing several important works relevant to this subject, he predicted: " 'The state' will once again become a major concern of scholarly discourse."[18] So it has. The current fashion is "neorealism," which seems to be attempting to find a middle ground between the divisions of the past. The so-called crisis of the state has moved beyond discussion among political economists to become a principal concern of behavioral scholars as well.

Yet the essential ambiguity of the concept of the state remains. For that matter, there is not even full agreement on the meaning of "autonomy." Furthermore, while state (however defined) and autonomy (however defined) may have been underrated in the rush to give adequate weight to domestic and systemic constraints, important constraints do continue to derive from other actors/levels. The state's surrogates may well be the primary actors in international affairs, but they are not the only significant actors. Recognizing the essential validity of this familiar statement, however, is far from being able to generalize with precision about the relationships involved. Although neorealists are attempting a synthesis, we have little reason to expect that a satisfactory one will be achieved. Kenneth Waltz and Robert Keohane, for instance, both acknowledge a debt to realism but are otherwise light years apart in their main concerns and approaches.

## THE HISTORICAL STATE

Since the absence of a consensual state concept inhibits the development of international relations theory, it might seem that an analysis of the historical roots of the phenomenon might provide a basis for identifying its essential qualities. In fact, such an analysis offers little solace to the investigator. He will discover that, while there have existed since prehistoric times self-conscious subgroupings able to distinguish themselves from other groupings and conduct relations with them, there is no agreement that such entities have always been states. On the other hand, those who view the state as the relatively recent outcome of a period of Western political development run the risk of assuming the nonexistence of international relations prior to that time. "If this is the actual history of the state," declares Sabino Cassese acerbically, "there is no need to disturb Plato and Aristotle in a search for the origin of the concept of the state unless we want to attribute to them, and to other thinkers who followed them, extraordinary abilities to foresee the future."[19]

By contrast, if the observer concludes that the state is an historically omnipresent phenomenon, he is confronted with a bewildering array of entities with so little in common that he is forced to adopt highly abstract and effectively nonoperational definitions of the phenomenon he is seeking. Thus, the state tends to become, in J. W. Burton's conception, "linked systems and their administrative controls"[20] or some "structural-functional" entity with no clear objective referent.

Identifying the origins of the state poses less of an historical than a conceptual problem. In other words, whether one conceives the state as having always existed or having been born in a particular era depends largely on one's definition of the state. And, as Donald J. Puchala suggests, "the first questions we must ask about the modern state are: What is it? and What are its origins? These questions answer each other."[21] Unfortunately, that is exactly what they do *not* do, since questions are not answers, and neither question *has* a satisfactory answer (as we shall attempt to explain).

Puchala's questions do, however, help to reveal the circularity of the problem we face. One cannot pinpoint the origins of the state unless one can identify and operationalize the phenomenon one is seeking, and history does not afford an example that one would feel confident of offering as a "state for all seasons." This problem is discernible in the argument of two eminent French scholars, Bertrand Badie and Pierre Birnbaum:

> [T]he writer who wishes to treat the concept of the state faces a dilemma: either he must settle for a broad and therefore useless definition of the state or he must concede that "the state" is not

a universal concept but rather the product of a specific historical crisis to which different premodern societies are vulnerable in different degrees. . . . On the other hand, we do not wish to argue that the state is peculiar to a single country or even to a small number of countries. Our point is simply this: in each society, particular historical processes foster state building to a greater or lesser degree. . . .

The sociology of the state should . . . be careful to avoid . . . the conclusion that once the state is established, its nature and form are determined and will never change. In particular, we think it would be useful to study the conditions under which one type of state is transformed into another.[22]

However, if the state is not a "universal concept" but "the product of a specific historical crisis," how are we to assess the "greater or lesser degree" of "state building" in each society, much less meaningfully typologize "states" and study the dynamics of their transformation?

Anthropologist Ronald Cohen runs into similar difficulties in the course of maintaining that "the state" had its origins in both social conflict (competition over scarce resources) and integration (benefits flowing from centralized authority):

It is now becoming clear that there are multiple roads to state-hood, that whatever sets off the process tends as well to set off other changes which, no matter how different they are to begin with, all tend to produce similar results. It is this similarity of result, I believe, that has clouded the issue of causality. Similar results—the state—imply common antecedents. Unfortunately, as the data are compared, as more cases appear in the literature, historical sequences support the notion of multiple and varied causes producing similar effects.[23]

The reader who has been following the reasoning thus far may be somewhat disconcerted to learn that Cohen's principal focus is on the "early state." He says: "Early states as far removed as Incan Peru, ancient China, Egypt, early Europe, and precolonial West Africa exhibit striking similarities. Thus the state as a form of organization is an emergent selective force that has sent humankind along a converging path."[24] Cohen acknowledges that "*Homo sapiens* has evolved a number of quite different and distinct political systems; one of these is the state." Moreover, "[f]rom this baseline of agreement, our notions about what to emphasize in a definition of 'state' begin to diverge sharply." He himself lists three classes of definitions.[25] How, then, can we be confident that the "similar results" of "multiple and varied causes" that he has identified are, in fact, "the state"?

Jonathan Haas's analysis of the "prehistoric state" is worth citing at length because it illustrates just how uncoordinated have been efforts to achieve understanding of the phenomenon's origins.

> [T]he first problem that needs to be confronted concerns the concept of the "state" itself. The myriad definitions presented in the literature tend to be either idiosyncratic or tied to a particular theoretical perspective. . . .
>
> First, "State" is seen as representing the discrete complex of social institutions that operate together to govern a particular, highly evolved society. Under this conceptualization, *the* state operates as a concrete entity within the social whole. Lenin, for example, argues that "the state is an organ of class *domination,*". . .
>
> The second notion of "state" sees it as referring to a particular kind of society characterized by specific attributes. In an evolutionary sense, this conception uses "state" as a label to classify societies that have reached a particular level of cultural development. . . .
>
> Finally, "state" is used in a way that is somewhat complementary to the second usage. Specifically, it is used to simply identify individual bounded societies that are characterized by a "state" level of organization. In this sense, a "state" is analogous to a "tribe" or a "chiefdom." For example, one might refer to the Aztec *state* or the Zulu *state*, just as one might refer to the Zuni *tribe* or the Kwakuitl *chiefdom.* In contrast to the idea of the state being a part of a society, the third conception sees the state as the entire society.
>
> *These three notions of "state" do refer to different things, and lack of awareness of the distinctions between them has introduced a degree of confusion in the literature. What is one person's "state" is another person's "government" and vice versa.*[26]

By inference, we must conclude that a state is *any* form of political organization, and we are left in the dark about the level of organization necessary for an entity to qualify for statehood.

Let us examine how the authors of two other works treat the state as an historical and even prehistorical phenomenon, even while failing to denote that which they are seeking to describe. In the view of Ernest Gellner:

> Mankind has passed through three fundamental stages in its history: the pre-agrarian, the agrarian, and the industrial. Hunting and gathering bands were and are too small to allow the kind of

political division of labour which constitutes the state; and so, for them, the question of the state, of a stable specialized order-enforcing institution, does not really arise. By contrast, most, but by no means all, agrarian societies have been state-endowed. . . . They differ a great deal in their form. The agrarian phase of human history is the period during which, so to speak, the very existence of the state is an option. . . . During the hunting-gathering stage, the option was not available.

By contrast, in the post-agrarian, industrial age there is, again, no option; but now the *presence*, not the absence of the state is inescapable. Paraphrasing Hegel, once none had the state, then some had it, and finally all have it. The form it takes still remains variable. There are some traditions of social thought—anarchism, Marxism—which hold that even, or especially, in an industrial order the state is dispensable, at least under favourable conditions or under conditions due to be realized in the fullness of time. There are obvious and powerful reasons for doubting this. . . .[27]

Gellner thus admits the appearance of "the state" at a relatively early, "agrarian" stage of human history. Since the form of the "state" is said to be "variable" at any stage, the only apparent requirement is that the entity involved must have been a "stable specialized order-enforcing institution." Yet that is a characteristic of a polity *sui generis*!

For their part, Badie and Birnbaum assert:

To be sure, centralized political systems have been a feature not only of modern but also of many ancient or classical societies. The novelty of modern times is that exceptions to the law of centralization are no longer tolerated, the division of labor in modern society being such that none can escape the need for coordination through a centralized political structure or structures. But this is the only common feature of modern political systems, and as soon as the political sociologist begins to concern himself with history or simply with the empirical data he is forced to admit that political centralization may take many forms and that the particular form that emerges in any given case is largely related to cultural and conjunctural factors: state-building is only one form of political centralization among others, and the models followed in building states vary widely from one society to the next.[28]

According to Badie and Birnbaum, the state is not omnipresent:

Even in the West, however, civil society has at times been able to make do without a state. It has often been able to organize itself and by doing so to prevent the development of a state with some claim to the right to wield absolute power. Wherever a state exists, the entire social system is affected. Civil society invariably organizes around the state once a state has come into existence. . . . Class relations vary widely depending on whether there is a highly institutionalized state or a mere political center whose main function is to coordinate the activities of civil society.[29]

What, then, do Badie and Birnbaum regard as a "true state" as distinct from a "mere political center"? The closest they come to a definition is the following:

[T]he true state (as distinguished from what is merely the center of a centralized political system) is one that has achieved a certain level of differentiation, autonomy, universality, and institutionalization. These features remain characteristic, even if . . . all of the features named may coexist with dedifferentiation and epigenesis.[30]

So a "true state" has "certain" "characteristic features"—or does it? If only selected entities are "true states," what does that imply for other entities that behave in statish ways? In the end, Badie and Birnbaum settle on France as "the ideal type of the state" or "the state model," arguing that the political center of that country carried out the "process of differentiation and institutionalization"[31] further than others in Europe because it needed to do so to overcome greater resistance from feudal vestiges in French society.[32] As for the contemporary West:

It is still possible even today to distinguish between political systems in which there is both a center and a state (France), a state but no center (Italy), a center but no true state (Great Britain and the United States), and neither a center nor a true state (Switzerland). In the first two cases the state dominates civil society and is responsible for its organization albeit in different degrees. In the last two cases civil society organizes itself. It is therefore possible to distinguish between societies in which the state attempts to run the social system through a powerful bureaucracy (of which France is the ideal type, with Prussia, Spain, and Italy exhibiting similar trajectories) and societies in which there is no need for a strong state and governing bureaucracy because civil society is capable of organizing itself (of which Great Britain is the ideal type, with the United States and "consociational democracies" . . . such as Switzerland exhibiting similar trajectories).[33]

Note that, in Badie and Birnbaum's analysis, less emphasis is laid on the state's autonomy from societal influences than on society's lack of autonomy from organizational influences emanating from the state's "center" (where one exists).

Although it is apparently true, as Morton H. Fried observes, that "the ancients left no self-conscious history of the evolution of their earliest states,"[34] there have clearly been territorial-political entities—some of substantial size and/or authority—in the global system for many thousands of years. As Oran Young maintains: "Over the bulk of recorded history, man has organized himself for political purposes on bases other than those now subsumed under the concepts 'state' and 'nation-state'."[35] Whether one chooses to term them "chiefdoms," "empires," "city-states," "principalities," "states," or something else seems to us to rest exclusively on the nature of the entity in question and on one's choice of definitions.

This statement is a truism of sorts, but it highlights, first, the important fact that early entities evinced several or many of the characteristics customarily associated with the "modern state": for example, territory, executives, legislatures, judges, bureaucrats, taxes, an army, interest groups, social classes; as well as problems of succession, center-periphery relations, alliances, wars, trade, ecology. The list could go on and on.[36]

Second, institutional artifacts from every stage of human political evolution may still be found in the present "industrial" or "post-industrial" era, even as the "progress" of industrialization has varied tremendously from place to place. Just as there are a few remaining pockets of Stone Age culture and many predominately agrarian societies, so, too, do there continue to be tribes, city-states, surprisingly autonomous cities, and other political subdivisions (like "states" in the U.S. federal system), monarchs (albeit mostly enfeebled), myriad ethnicities, latent and more substantial "nations," complex bureaucracies, classes and masses, a host of interest groups, political parties, transnational corporations, transgovernmental organizations, alliances, ideological empires, and other putative neo-imperialisms. To borrow a felicitous phrase that Charles Anderson coined for Latin America, the world is indeed a "living museum."

Third and finally, many "modern states" are sadly lacking in many of the same "state-like" qualities that characterized the "sovereign" European states that evolved in the seventeenth and eighteenth centuries. Some old and other not-so-old states in the immediate spheres of influence of the superpowers face grave political constraints, enforced when necessary by military occupation. Moreover, it is no secret that many of the states spawned by decolonialization in the twentieth century are shaky enterprises indeed. The explosion in the number of states in the world has been striking. There were about fifteen such entities in 1871, twenty-five by the outbreak of World War I, and over thirty by the 1930s.[37] The vast expansion in numbers, of course, took place in the years following World War II. Fifty-one states were charter members of the United Nations, and the number of legally independent units looks to round out at well over three times that many within the foreseeable future. By almost any standard—size of territory, size of population, ethnic homogeneity, GNP, degree of industrialization, military forces, forms of government, ideologies, and so on—these units present a wide range of differences. As David Vital observes:

> There is surely at least a *prima facie* case for asserting that one of the notable characteristics of the modern international scene is the growing disparity in human and material resources to be found where important categories of states are compared—with the result that the only genuine common denominator left is the purely *legal* equality of states that carries with it only such tenuous advantages as membership in the United Nations.[38]

And Oran Young is surely correct when he implicitly contrasts contemporary with "classical" states as follows:

> If the basic attributes of statehood are taken to be such things as a clearly demarcated territorial base, a relatively stable population, more or less viable central institutions of government and external sovereignty, the contemporary situation immediately begins to appear unclear and confusing.[39]

The world is further complicated by the presence of an unspecified number (because there is no precise definition here either) of "microstates." This issue has long troubled international organizations. For example, the League of Nations denied Liechtenstein membership on the grounds that "by reason of her limited area, small population, and her geographical position, she has chosen to depute to others some of the attributes of sovereignty" and "has no army" and, therefore, "could not discharge all the international obligations which would be imposed on her by the Covenant." Along with Liechtenstein, the League and the United Nations also refused to admit other microstates like Andorra, Monaco, and San Marino. However, like the Vatican, they have held membership in various technical international organizations. In addition, Liechtenstein and San Marino have participated in the activities of the international Court of Justice, and Liechtenstein was even a party to the 1955 Nottebohm case on dual nationality (Liechtenstein vs. Guatemala).[40] Bruce Russett and Harvey Starr report that when Liechtenstein entered the Council of Europe in 1978, "a British representative warned, 'If we let Liechtenstein join, we may face similar demands from other microstates like Monaco, the Faroe Islands, Guernsey, San Marino and all sorts of others.' More importantly, some members warned that if such microunits were to apply, the Council might have to raise the whole question of what a state *is*!"[41] For theorists, then, these mice continue to roar.

## THE SEARCH FOR AN IDEAL TYPE

The absence of a consensus regarding the attributes of a "true" state and the absence of agreement about the historical origins of the phenomenon suggest that we are dealing with a condition of *relative* political institutionalization, power, and vulnerability across the millenia. Yet lacking such agreement may entail regarding virtually all relatively autonomous global subdivisions as variants of the state; the state then indeed becomes a "conceptual variable" and can no longer be used by scholars of international relations solely as an independent variable.

Under these conditions the problem of constructing generalizable propositions of either a synchronic or diachronic sort becomes exceedingly difficult.[42] Contemporary comparison of state behavior is encumbered by the quite dramatic disparities in the units of analysis. Historical analysis of the sort attempted by projects like the Correlates of War is at least partly undermined also by gross difference—both across time and space—among the units defined as states.[43]

Is there an ideal type of state which can be used as a baseline for comparison with other variants of the state phenomenon—an entity that, on the one hand, is largely free from external control and, on the other, is distinct from its own society? Such an entity would not be a political subdivision of a larger entity, and it would be based on a different organizational principle from its own society as a whole. It would not be a "colony" or a "local government," or a tribal "chiefdom." Its institutions would symbolize the political community within its boundaries. Leaders and bureaucratic agents of "the state" would be readily recognizable as such, however "strong" or "weak" their capacity to mobilize human and material resources.[44]

The basic difficulty with such an approach is really twofold: First, even in hunter-gatherer and more complex tribal groups, political decisions are made—the "authoritative allocation of values" (in David Easton's terminology) as a process takes place. There are distinct political decisionmaking roles within the group, even though the same individuals simultaneously occupy other social roles. There is usually little doubt about how (in the sense of a process and the individuals involved) it will be decided, for example, whether or not to move the tents to a different pasture, or whether to fight or run from a neighboring group. Moreover, most groups have a defined territory or at least a "home range," and few of them are unclear about who is "we" and who is "they" in relationships with other groups. Second, political entities have never been and, one can safely say, never will be, fundamentally distinct or separate from their societies, because political decisionmakers simultaneously do occupy social roles and must be responsive both to their own societies and to external influences. Indeed, as John Hall and other have stressed, the societies in which political entities are enmeshed with regard to matters like defense or trade typically extend far beyond their own "borders."[45]

Political leaders interact differentially with *parts* of their own societies and the external world. Decisions of significance and considerable authority with regard to the allocation of values are regularly made at many different levels. Thus, if we we interested in explaining behavior rather than abstractions alone, we have to look both within and without the political entity in question. As we shall argue later, establishing that an entity is widely seen as "a state" may tell the analyst something relevant to the explanation of behavior, but it is normally far from all that is relevant and may even be the least illuminating explanation or even misleading.

Consider the "modern state," that "ideal type" that many scholars conveniently date from the Treaty of Westphalia in 1648. (Some scholars would suggest an earlier date, which is symptomatic of the problem). This "state" is credited, to some extent correctly, with having overcome the universalist pretensions of the Church and the Holy Roman Empire, as well as the internal challenge of segmentary feudalism. Monarchs became "Divine right" "absolute" "sovereigns," viewed as such from both inside and outside their domains, and the "state" itself took on the attribute—the key one for John H. Herz—of "territoriality" (a "hard shell" of "impenetrability").[46]

How simple it was in the age of *"l'État, c'est moi."* Perhaps, after all, it was not so very simple. The "absolute" monarchs of Europe—those few whose realms were sufficiently integrated for them to claim the title—might beg to disagree. Shakespeare expressed it well when he said, "Uneasy lies the head that wears the crown." There always seemed to be a "pretender" raising an army, or dissident nobles to curb, or rebellious towns and peasants from whom adequate taxes had to be extracted to pay for a mercenary army to defend the "hard shell."

Nor were things all that much more secure in the "model state" of France.[47] Part of the "Sun King's" genius was his capacity to make life at the royal court of Versailles more attractive for his nobles than subversive activities back at the chateau. Had Louis XIV been a little less shrewd in adopting flamboyant architecture, dress, and furniture, his sun might soon have set. Moreover, he had to rule, in part, through his *intendants* and continue to be alert to clientele relations developing between them and various private interests.[48] Badie and Birnbaum comment that "not until the eighteenth century do we find Frenchmen beginning to think of France's borders as 'natural,' as later became commonplace."[49] Also, France was considerably less than a unified cultural community. Peter Worsley quotes Eugen Weber on the point that: "As late as 1863, 'French was a foreign language for a substantial number of Frenchmen, including about half the children who would reach adulthood in the last quarter of the century'.[50] Louis XIV ran headlong into the later-celebrated "balance of power" when he embarked on a campaign of conquest; his eventual defeat, in turn, may be regarded as both a ratification of the "hard shells" of some of his neighbors and as testimony to the rise of a new "external" systemic constraint that had replaced the much less formidable Holy Roman Empire. Most significantly, a scant seventy-seven years after Louis XIV's death, the model state dissolved (or was fundamentally transformed) in Revolution, and the "sovereign" head of the "absolute" monarchy landed in the basket at the foot of the guillotine.[51]

The American and French Revolutions had an impact on the basic units in the international system at least as significant as the emergence of the "modern state" in Europe. The liberal doctrine of the era held that "sovereignty" belonged not so much in a personal sense to a divinely appointed monarch but, variously, to "the people," "the general will," "the law," and/or "the nation." The doctrine could justify authoritarianism or even rule by a monarch or self-styled emperor (e.g., Napoleon I), as well as republican experiments, but it forever banished the notion that "sovereignty" necessarily implies the acceptance of a flesh-and-blood sovereign. It was, of course, the concept of "nation," mutating into "nationalism" and "national self-determination"—the idea that each "nation" should have its own "state"—which subsequently had the greatest effect on global political boundaries.[52] This ethnocentric European idea was transmitted to the world, Worsley notes, via the very European imperialisms that had the most to lose were it to be taken seriously. With the assistance of Napoleon's campaigns, two world wars in the twentieth century, the League of Nations and the United Nations, and the Cold War rivalry between the United States and the Soviet Union, a multitude of new "nation-states" have emerged.

Perhaps, as Gellner insists, one should not "conclude, erroneously, that nationalism is a contingent, artificial, ideological invention, which might not have happened, if only those damned busy-body interfering European thinkers, not content to leave well enough alone, had not concocted it and fatefully injected it into the bloodstream of otherwise viable political communities."[53] Nationalism did provide an ideological justification for those who wanted to throw off the yoke of colonial repression and also later provided an ideological justification for the leaders of the new "nation-state" to rule. One can be charitable, with Gellner, and point out that the achievement of greater political centralization, the maintenance of political order, and the imposition of a "high culture" were essential if "Third World" countries were ever to "develop" in a world that was moving inexorably from agrarianism to industrialization. For Gellner, in fact, the imposition of a high culture was the most critical need: "At the base of the modern social order stands not the executioner but the professor. Not the guillotine, but the (aptly named) *doctorat d'état* is the main tool and symbol of state power. The monopoly of legitimate education is now more important, more central than is the monopoly of legitimate violence."[54] Or, one can stress, with Worsley, the persecution of dissident groups, ethnic and otherwise; the fact that nationalism has frequently degenerated into "chauvinism, from a pride in Self to a contempt for the Other," resulting, in the extreme in "genocidal brutality."[55]

Most analysts agree, however, that the basic concept of "nation" itself is little more than a fiction, which perhaps had some initial substance, especially in a few European contexts[56] (albeit incomplete, e.g., Welsh, Basques, Alsatians) but is truly a "mystification" (Worsley's term) applied to most of the "Third World." Gellner observes:

> It is nationalism which engenders nations, and not the other way round. Admittedly, nationalism uses the pre-existing, historically inherited proliferation of cultures or cultural wealth, though it uses them very selectively, and it most often transforms them radically. Dead languages can be revived, traditions invented, quite fictitious pristine purities restored. . . . The cultural shreds

and patches used by nationalism are often arbitrary inventions.
Any old shred or patch would have served as well.[57]

As Worsley expresses it:

> [I]t is more heuristically useful to restrict the term "nation" to
> that mode of ethnicity which only emerges with the modern
> centralized State, and which therefore entails not so much conti-
> nuity with older ethnic identities as their supersession, if neces-
> sary, their repression. Nation-building . . . goes hand-in-hand
> with the formation of the State.[58]

In any event, nationalism is an ideology with proven power to inspire
millions to acts of heroism and brutality. The "nation" may be a legal
fiction that defies easy operationalization, but it continues to exercise a
powerful grip on the human imagination. An observer's understanding
of the concept of "nation-state," which has dominated international
relations discourse for two centuries, is basically ideological. This is
typical of the concepts that we utilize in international relations. At best,
it will be difficult to lend *objectivity* to concepts that are inherently
*subjective*; at worst, it may be impossible.

## THE MANY MEANINGS OF THE STATE

Against this background, then, and with some degree of skepticism, let
us briefly summarize and categorize some of the more prominent conceptions of "the state." As we shall see, these conceptions repeatedly
grow out of normative preferences and ideological predilections. They
are fashioned less in an effort to achieve the conceptual consensus
necessary for examining the phenomenon scientifically than in order to
advance these preferences and predelictions.

Although scholars have generally maintained a distinction between
"state" and "nation," the past century has witnessed an increasing
identification of the two concepts at the popular level. Groups with
sufficient ethnic and cultural homogeneity demand the legal autonomy
associated with the idea of the sovereign state. In this context, the state
is defined as an *ethno-cultural unit*. Commonly, they justify this demand by pointing to a common history or, if necessary, inventing one.
By contrast, ethnic heterogeneity has been frequently cited as a source
of state weakness and dissension (e.g., Austria-Hungary). Whether one
refers to the unifications of Germany and Italy, the spread of the new
imperialism, Hitler's campaign for *Lebensraum,* the founding of Israel,

the partition of India, or the Nigerian civil war, the potency of this variant of the state is undeniable.

Indeed, it can be argued that it is this definition of the state—widely invoked by political leaders—that is largely responsible for the proliferation of ungovernable and unviable units in Asia and Africa.[59] As we have noted, young states, especially, often reach for "shreds and patches" of past cultures in attempting to build a nation, and some states, through design or historical happenstance, are roughly conterminous with ethnic boundaries. But, as Worsley explains: "The nightmare of the unifiers is . . . the realization that there is no logical limit on the size or number of groups which can legitimately claim to possess a common culture or subculture. The possibility of infinite regress opens up, for any sizable group can always be further decomposed into regional subcultures, each with its own distinctive territory, dialect, history, and so forth, and into further subdivisions within the region."[60] Some "extinct" "nations" have actually been reborn. Worsley points out: "One of the most horrific cases of genocide known to history is the extermination of the Tasmanian aborigines. Everyone knows they were wiped out. . . . But what 'everybody knows' is wrong, for today there is a militant movement among the thousands who proudly trace their mixed, but nevertheless partly Tasmanian descent to their slaughtered forebears."[61] Some ethnicities, moreover, are much larger than many existing "nation-states"; Worsley's example is the 15 million Kurds stretching across Iran, Iraq, Turkey, and Syria—compared to small states like Dominica (pop. 80,000) or Nauru (pop. 8,000).[62]

Nor are the older and more established states immune to the "absent nation" phenomenon. For instance, W. Raymond Duncan emphasizes that in Latin America, where most state boundaries have been in place since the early nineteenth century: "[Indians] differentiate between highland and lowland Indians in Bolivia or village identities in Guatemala or Peru. Linguistic differentiation between Quechua, Aymara, and Guarani throughout the Andean countries also fragments the Indian community. . . . At least 73 languages are spoken [by Indian groupings in Latin America] and more than 355 separate tribes have been identified."[63] The United States has at least partially "melted" numerous ethnicities, but Black, Brown, and Red "underclass" tensions remain; ethnic divisions continue to threaten the Soviet conglomerates; Canada has to contend with its Québecois; Britain has the Scots and Irish as well as the Welsh; France, its Bretons and Corsicans; Spain its Basques; and so on.

A second definition is that of the *state as a normative order*. The state in this conception is a symbol (or cluster of symbols) for a particular society and the laws, norms, and beliefs that bind its people ("the nation") together. From the vantagepoint of national *and* international society, a state has a juridical "sovereign" identity. Typical of this perspective is the observation of Alessandro Passerin d'Entreves: "The modern state is a legal system. The power it exercises is not mere force, but force applied in the name of, and in accordance with, a body of rules, from which in fact we infer that a state 'exists' . . . the birth of the modern state is no other than . . . the rise and final acceptance of the concept of sovereignty."[64] Clifford Geertz has written persuasively about the symbolic role of the "theater state" in Bali, which he sees as highlighting a "pomp and ceremony" dimension common even to more complex states.[65] One is also reminded of the glorification of the state under National Socialism or under other regimes, like Getulio Vargas's *O Estado Novo* in Brazil (1937–45). Virtually all states have their national flag. their national anthem, their leaders' frequent appeals to the mystical "national interest," their ideological banners, usually an Unknown Soldier or other martyrs, and so on.

The definition, however, fails to deal with the fact that many countries, including multicultural ones, are often deeply divided over norms. The civil strife that today rends societies like Lebanon, South Africa, the Sudan, Peru, the Phillipines, and El Salvador is merely the most graphic manifestation of these normative schisms. As the example of the United States in the 1960s illustrates, severe political turmoil lies closer to the surface almost everywhere than one might think. Aggravating internal divisions are normative conflicts sweeping across boundaries: ethnic ties, communism vs. capitalism or vs. catholicism (in Poland), Sunni vs. Shiite Islam, and so forth.

Of "sovereignty," J. P. Nettl wrote in the late 1960s:

> . . . nowadays the problem of sovereignty is, for social scientists, a dead duck. More than thirty years ago, Frederick Watkins pushed sovereignty to the margin of political science concerns by insisting that it be regarded as a "limiting concept"—an idealtypical situation that had to be qualified in all sorts of ways. He qualified it with the notion of autonomy, another limiting concept that applied both to the state itself and to all the associations within or below it, and as such eroded the value of sovereignty as a unique political factor. Since then we hear little of sovereignty except in the context of historical and philosophical (and, of course, legal) discussions.[66]

Nettl failed to foresee the situation today. For a "dead duck," "sovereignty" continues to generate a surprising amount of quackery!

What do we mean by "sovereignty"? Theorists have been working on *that* question for hundreds of years. One can easily see the linkage to the state as a normative order in Hinsley's definition—"the idea that there is a final and absolute authority in the political community,"[67] which legitimizes the decrees of the state. However central this conception may have been to political struggles centuries ago, it seems doubtful that many citizens the world over today ever think about the "sovereignty" of the state as somehow being the reason they pay taxes, serve in the military, get a marriage license, or whatever. Partly for this reason, the most useful definition for contemporary times, in our view, is a narrower and legal one advanced by Alan James that looks primarily outward from the state—just constitutional independence.[68]

Let us not underestimate the importance of a state's possessing constitutional independence. As James points out, it is usually a necessary (although not always sufficient) condition for a state's participation in international organizations and many other formal aspects of international life. Legally independent states can lay claim to various widely recognized rights under international law, including the right to send and receive ambassadors; and with rights come such duties as not allowing the state's territory to be used as a staging base for attack on another state's homeland by its dissident groups.[69]

Also, in a very practical sense, legal sovereignty offers a modestly extra dimension of stability to states and freedom from external interference that they would not otherwise possess. As James notes, for example, there was much more of a controversy over the Soviet Union's invasion of Hungary, Czechoslovakia, or Afghanistan than there would have been had these areas been formal parts of the USSR. It is not insignificant that the Soviets went to great pains to avoid the embarrassment of sending massive numbers of their own troops into Poland during the Solidarity crisis. For its part, the United States ran into much more criticism of its role in the 1954 overthrow of the Arbenz government in Guatemala, its marine intervention in the Dominican Republic in 1965, and the 1983 Grenada episode than ever would have occurred had any of the target countries been a state in the U.S. federal system.[70]

Robert Jackson has written eloquently[71] about the fact that so many states in Africa possess "juridical statehood" derived from a right of "self-determination"—what he calls "negative sovereignty"— "without yet possessing much in the way of empirical statehood disclosed by a capacity for effective and civil government"—what he calls "positive sovereignty." He remarks: "[A]part from a few qualified exceptions such as Morocco, Zanzibar, Swaziland, Lesotho, Botswana,

Rwanda, and Burundi—sovereignty in Africa has never reverted to anything remotely resembling traditional states."[72] Most were "novel European creations" and are today what James Mayall terms "anachronistic" states or what others term "nascent," "quasi," or "pseudo" states.[73] Why, asks Jackson, are such flimsy states still in existence years after independence? He offers a number of explanations: "Once juridical statehood is acquired . . . diplomatic civilities are set in motion which support it, exaggerate it, and conceal its lack of real substance and value. A new international momentum is inaugurated."[74] Many African states have themselves been too insecure to wish to see boundaries adjusted; the ideology of Pan-Africanism has frowned on regional states sitting in judgment on their neighbors, and what Jackson terms "racial sovereignty" forbids the rest of the world from criticizing the affairs of black African countries. Fledgling African states have gained status from participation in regional and world international organizations; and, apart from rivalry over Angola and Ethiopia/Somalia, powerful external states have been reluctant to intervene extensively in African affairs. Most of all, Jackson argues, African ruling elites are doing very well, thank you—their countries are a mansion of great privilege for them, while the masses often starve. Jackson thus takes partial exception to J.D.B. Miller's assertion that sovereignty confers "vitality" on states; often "in Africa," Jackson observes, "it debilitates them and confers luxury on statesmen."[75]

So the legal concept of sovereignty tells us something about the "real" world, but it nevertheless speaks not at all to a great deal that is important about states and international politics. Start with the legal problem of how constitutional independence is, in fact, established, although that is not the most important issue. In fact, there is no mechanism except the consensus—or lack thereof—in the international community. Let us leave aside technical problems regarding associated states and microstates. Consider the Turkish Republic of North Cyprus. Or the state of Israel. Or the fall-out from apartheid: the "black homeland" entities like the Transkei that no state but South Africa recognizes. In contrast, "the former British territory of Lesotho, which is also an enclave within South Africa, but was never ruled by Pretoria and has gained independence from Britain, is a recognized state and enjoys full rights. . . ."[76] As these examples confirm, the status question is a highly variable one; an entity's "sovereignty" is highly dependent on external recognition (a contradiction in terms?), and some entities are "states" for some purposes but not for others.

Neorealists tend to skip over the issue of how sovereignty is conferred and prefer to concentrate on its subsequent effects. Nevertheless, how to describe those effects has caused neorealists no end of trouble. All tend to denigrate empirical tests of state autonomy. John Gerard Ruggie, for example, complains: "The concept of sovereignty is critical. Unfortunately, it has become utterly trivialized by recent usage . . . as a descriptive category expressing unit attributes, roughly synonymous with material autonomy."[77] Turning to what he calls "liberal writings on interdependence," he takes the present authors to task for having spoken some years ago of "the relative irrelevance of sovereignty" and a world wherein all "states are subject to diverse internal and external conditioning factors that induce and constrain their behavior" and some states are apparently "more 'sovereign' than others."[78]

Kenneth Waltz, another neorealist, is also troubled by limiting the meaning of sovereignty:

> The error lies in identifying the sovereignty of states with their ability to do as they wish. To say that states are sovereign is not to say that they can do as they want. Sovereign states may be hardpressed all around, constrained to act in ways they would like to avoid, and able to do hardly anything just as they would like to. The sovereignty of states has never entailed their insulation from the effects of other states' actions. To be sovereign and to be dependent are not contradictory conditions. Sovereign states have seldom led free and easy lives. What then is sovereignty? To say that a state is sovereign means that it decides for itself how it will cope with its internal and external problems.[79]

Ruggie is equally disturbed by Waltz's definition: "If sovereignty meant no more than this, then I would agree with Ernst Haas, who once declared categorically: 'I do not use the concept at all and see no need to.' "[80] For Ruggie, in contrast, sovereignty "signifies a form of *legitimation* that pertains to a *system* of relations. . . ."[81] It sets up a world of "possessive individualist" states which interact largely on the basis of what Waltz calls an "exchange of considerations." According to Ruggie, domestic private property rights and state sovereignty are analogous. Consequently:

> [T]hose who would dispense with the concept of sovereignty . . . must first show why the idea of private property rights should not have been dispensed with long ago in the capitalist societies, where they are continuously invaded and interfered with by actions of the state. Yet we know that, at a minimum, the structure of private property rights will influence *when* the

state intervenes; usually it will also affect *how* the state intervenes. If this concept still has utility domestically . . . then its international analogue ought, if anything, to be even more relevant. The reason for the continued significance of the concepts is that they are not simply descriptive categories. Rather, they are components of generative structures: they shape, condition, and constrain social behavior.[82]

But, the reader might argue, how effective is that shaping, conditioning, and constraining? In some states like the United States, the concept of private property has greater currency than the concept of "sovereignty," and there is a traditional distrust of "government"; yet government at all levels continues to impose a substantial tax burden, seize property through eminent domain, and the like. The fact is that the concepts of private property and sovereignty both pretend to a degree of "autonomy" that is often fictitious, and this, indeed, makes the concepts "relatively irrelevant."

The fundamental objection to focusing on the state as a sovereign entity is that it tells us much too little about a state's autonomy from its society and from external influences. Theoretical or legal sovereignty is often small solace to a unit facing severe constraints from within and without; it is by no means the same as having a viable government or economy or society or a unit that is significantly independent from others. All things considered, some actors *do* seem a great deal more sovereign than others, and sovereignty itself appears relatively irrelevant as a guide to understanding actual behavior. Perhaps the concept's principal utility, which has endeared it to neorealists, is that it speaks to the legal framework of state participation in the international system and especially international organizations and "regimes." Politicians can use it in speeches opposing more involvement in transnational schemes. However, even they know at heart that participation in interdependence is not nearly as "voluntary" as the notion of sovereignty suggests, and we must look elsewhere for an explanation of why "states" do what they do in this regard. It is not enough to wave the tattered banner of "the national interest"; one must be able to specify the source of that "interest," why it is—or is perceived—as it is.

The subject of internal constraints brings to mind the very lengthy debate after Bodin and Hobbes about where exactly in the system of government "sovereignty" resided. In England, was it in the Crown, Parliament, or where? In the United States, was it in "the people," the Constitution, "the law" generally, Congress, the president, or where?

Theorists debated the question, but what was really happening were struggles over authority. The contest is still going on within countries, in the United States, for example: among the president, various bureaucracies, Congress, interest groups, political parties and voters.

In light of the current popularity of neorealism, it is worth reiterating something that many of us working in the field used to take almost for granted: Thinking about a world of sovereign states confuses more than it clarifies and certainly does not get us very far in theory-building. *In explaining behavior in international politics, there are almost always any number of more interesting and important things to say about almost any state than that it is sovereign*! States find other states, international regimes, nonstate actors like consortia of banks or multinational corporations limiting their options—even as they (states) have an impact on all of them (other state and nonstate actors) in turn. For example, the international debt negotiations or international monetary matters generally involve a wide range of intrastate governmental actors, the IMF (International Monetary Fund) and various international lending institutions, and any number of nonstate private and semi-private actors. Again, it is a contest both within and across state boundaries.

A third definition of the state, associated with Max Weber, is that the state is that *entity which has a monopoly of legitimate violence within a society.* A curiously atavistic definition, Weber's definition is usually associated with his writings on the rise of a "rational" state bureaucracy, of that presumably evolutionary process whereby a society eventually rises above the awarding of offices on the basis of patrimony and as sources of profit for the individuals involved.[83] Echoes of Weber may be found in many quarters, including Eric A. Nordlinger's brief for the relative autonomy of those groups of individuals who occupy decision-making roles in the modern democratic state.[84] Weber himself apparently recognized some of the deficiencies in his own generalizations about bureaucracy, acknowledging that not all major "states" in history had evolved extensive bureaucracies and that even in Germany the bureaucracy had not achieved independence from the landed aristocracy.[85]

As for violence, one might well insist that what matters most is not whether a state possesses a monopoly of legitimate violence emanating from within *and* without. Weber's definition speaks not at all to the challenge of military intervention from outside state boundaries. The challenge within is often even more serious. Many a Third World leader has found his arguments as to the illegitimacy of military coups singularly unpersuasive. It is also difficult to picture a Latin American or Asian president broadcasting Weber to guerrillas in the hills, convincing them to lay down their arms on the grounds that their violence is "illegitimate." In a sense, of course, that is what the government of El Salvador does when it insists that it alone acts for all El Salvadoreans—for El Salvador as a state. However, if there is no normative order, if there are no accepted ideological ground rules in a society, how can the exercise of violence by the government ever be truly legitimate? If there is no consensus as to whose violence is legitimate in El Salvador, does that mean El Salvador is not a state?

Insofar as Weber's definition is evolutionary in character, it does provide a bridge to a fourth conception of the state as *a functional unit*. Emile Durkheim, for example, reasoned: ". . . the greater the development of society, the greater the development of the state. The state takes on more and more functions and becomes increasingly involved in all other social functions, thereby centralizing and unifying them. Advances in centralization parallel advances in civilization."[86] In particular, according to Durkheim, the growth of the state goes hand in hand with a pattern of an increasing division of labor in a society. Talcott Parsons's "cybernetic model" of this process stresses the differentiation of the political system from other social systems, which he sees as influenced by economic factors like the development of a market economy and cultural events like the Protestant Reformation.[87] Badie and Birnbaum characterize this model of the state as follows: "[T]he state is one aspect of the rationalizing process that takes place in all societies undergoing modernization. State building therefore plays a part in what functionalists regard as the four central processes of modernization: differentiation, autonomization, universalization, and institutionalization."[88]

Badie and Birnbaum object, initially, to what they see as a neofunctionalist view of the nation-state as a "perfect functional substitute for vanished community solidarities," an aspect of the theory that shades off into the conception of the state as a normative order. They observe that ". . . once the state becomes an autonomous power center, with access to previously unavailable sources of power, it becomes a target of political action, an objective to be seized by every organized group that wishes to impose its own ends on society as a whole. The state thus tends not to quell conflict but to exacerbate it."[89] In addition, the neofunctionalist model appears to confuse the idea of state with that of a centralized political system.[90] Finally, neofunctionalists seem to imply that "the state" is a "universally valid political form suitable for all societies."[91] In Badie and Birnbaum's view, the crises experienced by political systems in Latin America, Africa, and Asia stem primarily from an attempt to transfer historical Western models to "radically different cultural traditions."[92]

> [T]he economic, social and political problems faced by third-world countries are utterly unlike the problems faced by European countries when states first emerged in Europe. Europe had to deal with a crisis of feudalism involving the private ownership of land by feudal lords. Most third-world societies, particularly in Africa, are currently faced by a quite different sort of crisis, involving the persistence of tribal structures, the crucial importance of kinship, and the limited individualization of property rights in land. Whereas European societies had to find ways to integrate already existing economic elites, the developing countries today need to create a market economy, to say nothing of a full-blown industrial society, from the ground up. Finally, whereas Renaissance Europe had only to contend with a gradual increase in the demand for popular participation, an increase more or less kept in check by organized civil society, today's newly independent societies have to face a much more dramatic rise in the desire for participation, which traditional allegiances by themselves cannot hold back.[93]

We should also recall two of our earlier observations. Contrary to Parsons's view, we have argued that political systems are never fundamentally differentiated from their own societies. Moreover, the societies in which political entities are enmeshed typically extend far beyond "domestic" borders. Jobs in the United States today may be as much or more a function of the global economic system and the politics of international economic relations as they are of government policy in Washington, not to mention the domestic private sector. The international dimension is even more critical and visible in Europe and certainly throughout the Third World. Neorealists like to picture governments acting jointly as functional managers of these larger societies, but it is far from clear who or what is managing whom, at what level(s) which values are being allocated, and with what degree of authority.

We may discern at least six additional conceptions of "the state." However, there is no need to do more than mention them here, because they point directly to the issue of the extent to which the state is autonomous from society. One conception (our fifth) is the Marxist model of the state as *a ruling class*. Marxist analysts differ as to the precise nature of the relationship involved: whether a capitalist economic elite actually occupies governmental roles or only influences decisionmakers (or a little of both) and whether government always acts as the ruling class desires or may occasionally act contrary to the immediate demands of the ruling class so as to uphold the best long-range interests of the capitalist system as a whole. (Stephen Krasner distinguishes in this regard between "instrumental" and "structural" Marxists.[94]) Of course, in classical Marxism, once the capitalist class is replaced (as it must inevitably be) by a "dictatorship of the proletariat," the state itself will eventually "wither away." Paradoxically, the ultimate ruling class is thus not expected to be interested in "ruling"!

Liberal "pluralists," on the other hand, have advanced a sixth conception applied at least to democratic political systems—the state as *an arena of interest-group competition,* where governmental policies are little more than a reflection of prevailing interest group pressures. As Krasner emphasizes, pluralist analysts and instrumental Marxists both "view formal governmental institutions as relatively passive recipients of societal pressure." The difference is that for "Marxists, power is basically in the hands of a capitalist class; for pluralists, it may be exercised by individuals motivated by any interest that is salient enough to affect behavior."[95]

A seventh definition, which Krasner sees as "the dominant conceptualization in the non-Marxist literature" is the state as *"a bureaucratic apparatus and institutionalized legal order in its totality."* As he explains, the "final phrase is critical, for it distinguishes statist orientations from the bureaucratic politics approaches which have parceled the state into little pieces, pieces that can be individually analyzed (where you stand depends on where you sit) and that float in a permissive environment (policies are a product of bargaining and compromise among bureaus)." An eighth definition is, thus, the state as *competing bureaucracies* or *governmental politics* in a somewhat broader sense.[96] Among other things, says Krasner, "statist" analysts view "politics more as a problem of rule and control than . . . of allocation"; it is "not just about 'who gets what, when, how': it is a struggle of us against them." The state, in this interpretation, is "an actor in its own right as either an exogenous or an intervening variable" and "cannot be understood as a reflection of societal characteristics or preferences."[97]

Eric Nordlinger, whom Krasner classifies as a fellow "statist," nonetheless cautions that any "definition of the state must refer to individuals rather than to some other kinds of phenomena, such as 'institutional arrangements' or the legal-normative order." In his eyes, "a conception of the state that does not have individuals at its core could lead directly into the anthropomorphic and reification fallacies." Therefore, we have Nordlinger's ninth conception of the state, which he characterizes as being somewhat "Weberian":

> . . . all those individuals who occupy offices that authorize them, and them alone, to make and apply decisions that are binding upon any and all segments of society. Quite simply, the state is made up of and limited to *those individuals who are endowed with society-wide decisionmaking authority.*[98]

*He adds:*

> [T]he state should include more than the government and/or the bureaucratic agencies that derive their authority from it. Although the executive and/or the bureaucracy have been said to constitute the "core" of the state, this in itself does not warrant a definition limited to them alone. Since we are concerned with all authoritative actions and all parts of the state as they relate to one another and to societal actors, the definition should include all public officials—elected and appointed, at high and low levels, at the center and the peripheries—who are involved in the making of public policy.[99]

Such a conception of the state invariably poses the problem of defining "autonomy." If the state is a conceptual variable, then it is impossible to say for certain what entity's autonomy we must attempt to weigh. On the other hand, if we cannot define autonomy, how then can we separate the state from other entities and influences that are not states but are said to constrain states? Can autonomy be merely symbolic, or must it mean a real capacity for independent decision and action? If a real capacity, must it be absolute or can it be relative? If relative, relative to what?

Nordlinger asserts: "The autonomy of any social entity refers to the correspondence between its preferences and actions."[100] The social entity of particular interest to him is the "democratic state," which, we have seen, he defines essentially as all individuals (at all levels) who are public officials with the authority to make binding decisions, as distinct both from public employees without that authority and private officials.

Utilizing this definition, he advances a "state-centered model," arguing that the autonomy of the democratic state has tended to be underestimated. Part of the reason, he believes, is that too much emphasis has been given to cases where state and societal preferences have diverged.

Equally significant, in his view, is the frequent convergence of state and societal preferences; and he stresses that, in such situations, state "preferences have at least as much explanatory importance as societal preferences."[101] (Query: Does it follow, then, that societal preferences have at least as much explanatory importance as state preferences?) Moreover, when state and societal preferences diverge, public officials have significant resources at their command to realign societal preferences with their own or even to act despite social preferences. Finally, according to Nordlinger: "Explanations based on societal groups dissuading American officials from making decisions they themselves prefer are undoubtedly valid in some instances, but not necessarily in most. More than likely, there are other important explanations having to do with the officials themselves being unable to agree upon what, if any, actions to take, what the most desirable and effective policies are thought to be." In fact, in the United States

> [T]he sharing of dispersed power turns public officials into competitors for power, while their distinctive responsibilities help generate incompatible policy preferences. There is also reason to suppose that American officials subscribe to values and beliefs which do *not* place much store upon promptly adopted, coherent, positive, decisive authoritative actions to begin with. On either interpretation the state's preferences are fulfilled; it is acting autonomously.[102]

Nordlinger thus attempts to sidestep a major problem—the extent to which a state finds itself "constrained" by divisions of authority and policy disputes among its own decisionmakers—by a neat definitional trick: The decisionmakers are inherently unified regardless of their differences because they collectively *are* "the state."[103]

A tenth and (for our purposes) final conception of the state is as *an executive.* Absolute monarchs of the old school would fit most neatly into this definition. Some traditional dictatorships would also appear to do so. The neon sign that loomed over the Santo Domingo harbor for many years read "Dios y Trujillo," accurately symbolizing (if not that the country was under God) that it was definitely indistinguishable from Trujillo. This definition shades off into the "great man" perspective on history, that is, the impact of particular individuals on state policies. For example, Manfred Wilhelmy describes the foreign policy roles of both Eduardo Frei (democratic president) and August Pinochet (military dictator) in Chile as that of an *animateur* rather than a "referee between contradictory positions."[104]

## CONCLUSION

Every discipline is defined in terms of a shared set of assumptions and concepts. Those assumptions and concepts at once provide both boundaries that distinguish that field of endeavor from others and a research agenda for the future. Few such assumptions and concepts have evolved in what is variously called "international," "interstate," "global," or "world" politics.

Our account of the multiple connotations accorded the concept of "state"—surely among the most central ideas in the field—and related concepts like "autonomy" casts doubt on the present existence of and prospects for a discipline of international relations. It is not simply that there have been multiple meanings from an historical perspective but that there is no greater consensus today than in the past. This is especially startling in light of the professed dedication of two generations of scholars to transform international relations into a science. Yet, perhaps it should not have been startling at all because, as we have seen, individual scholars have good (sometimes clear) *subjective* reasons for their definition.

Our concern is not merely that the field is characterized by intellectual disturbance or that, as Dina Zinnes notes, "the literature has not been very helpful in identifying the unit of analysis."[105] More importantly, we increasingly suspect that the concepts which bedevil us are inseparable from the norms, ideologies, and political aspirations that animate the practitioners and scholars in our field. If this is so, then concepts like "state" can never assume the objective and operational qualities that are prerequisites to scientific observation and analysis. To conclude that the phenomena we study change at a more rapid rate than, shall we say, the atoms of a physicist would only mean that social scientists face especially vexatious obstacles that need not dim their faith in the enterprise on which they have embarked. To conclude, as have the present authors, that those phenomena are inherently nonobjective must sorely try that faith.

# 6

# The Uncertain Bounds
# of Bounded Rationality

The sorts of conceptual problems that exist at the level of macroanalysis also are manifest at lower levels as well. The relationship of rationality and foreign policy illustrates the point. The capacity for rational behavior, whether of collectivities or of individual decision-makers, is perhaps the most important single assumption that can be made by scholars of international relations. It is only by making this assumption that an observer can remain confident that objective factors will, in time, be identified that can explain and predict international behavior. The assumption is thus essential for the construction of general theory and its application across time and space. Denial of rationality or disagreement about its meaning, by contrast, must inevitably force us to construct theory out of subjective factors and to reduce dramatically the prospects for fruitful comparison.

Foreign policy analysis is especially dependent upon the assumption of rationality for, without it, the concept of "interest" (national and other) must be distorted beyond recognition.[1] And without that sturdy signpost, scholars must embark on new and highly speculative paths of research. We require skills and insights from fields such as philosophy and psychology, which, in turn, further reduces the already limited autonomy of the "discipline" of international relations.

All of this notwithstanding, it is evident that recent decades have witnessed growing uneasiness about the utility of retaining the rationality assumption. And, in the end, probably no other trend is more likely to confound the already elusive quest.

## REALISM AND RATIONALITY

A leading critic of "power politics" models, John Vasquez, summarizes succinctly the major tenets of realism as follows:

> The first major assumption of the realist paradigm is that nation-states or their official decision-makers are the most important actors in international politics. At the core of the realist paradigm, the power politics explanation makes the additional assumption that nation-state behavior can be explained and predicted on the basis of a *rational-actor model.*[2]

This stress on the rational-actor assumption is surely central to realism, as well as other interest-based approaches to understanding politics. In one of his most dramatic passages, Hans Morgenthau declares:

> [W]e put ourselves in the position of a statesman who must meet a certain problem of foreign policy under certain circumstances, and we ask ourselves what the *rational alternatives* are . . . (presuming that he acts in a rational manner), and which of these rational alternatives this particular statesman, acting under those circumstances, is likely to choose. It is the testing of this *rational hypothesis* against the actual facts and their consequences that gives meaning to the facts of international politics and makes a theory of politics possible.[3]

Morgenthau, however, is definitely not talking about rationality exercised by the statesman in an open-ended sense. He condemns the search for a statesman's "motives" or ideological preferences as not only difficult but also entirely a waste of time. The theorist already knows what basic factors will shape the final policy choices; "his [Morgenthau's] *a priori* conception of human nature . . . and . . . his belief in the structural determinance of the international system."[4] Human nature, Morgenthau believes, is essentially imperfect and intensely selfish; and the international system, partly as a consequence, is anarchic and amoral, a struggle for power. The statesman's rational choices are "bounded" or constrained from within himself (human nature) and also by external factors, especially the Hobbesian international arena (itself, in a sense, a collective expression of human nature).

As we stressed earlier, despite Morgenthau's insistence that realism "is governed by objective laws that have their roots in human nature,"[5] the theoretical framework he advances is fundamentally normative. For Morgenthau and other realists, what is rational is also moral; that which detracts from rationality is fundamentally bad. The contradiction between Morgenthau's putative search for "objective laws" and his own subjective preferences creeps in even as he is waxing eloquent about the explanatory and predictive capacity of his assumption "that statesmen think and act in terms of [national] interest defined as power":

> That assumption allows us to retrace and anticipate, as it were, the steps a statesman—past, present, or future—has taken or will take on the political scene. We look over his shoulder when he writes his dispatches; we listen in on his conversation with other statesmen; we read and anticipate his very thoughts. Thinking in terms of interest defined as power, we think as he does, and as disinterested observers *we understand his thoughts and actions perhaps better than he, the actor on the political scene does himself.* [The concept of interest defined as power, on] the side of the actor . . . provides for rational discipline in action and creates that astounding continuity in foreign policy which makes American, British, or Russian foreign policy appear as an intelligible, rational continuum, by and large consistent within itself, regardless of the different motives, preferences, and intellectual and moral qualities of successive statesmen.[6]

One might be tempted to ask how "rational" a statesman is who thinks he is doing or wants to do X but ends up doing Y! In fact, Morgenthau acknowledges that policies are not always completely rational or predictable:

> The contingent demands of personality, prejudice, and subjective preference, and of all the weaknesses of intellect and will which flesh is heir to, are bound to deflect foreign policies from their rational course. Yet a theory of foreign policy which aims at rationality must for the time being, as it were, abstract from these irrational elements and seek to paint a picture of foreign policy which presents the rational essence to be found in experience, without the contingent deviations from rationality which are also found in experience.[7]

Finally, he admits what should already have become evident to his readers:

> Political realism contains not only a theoretical but also a normative element. It knows that political reality is replete with contingencies and systemic irrationalities and points to the typical influences they exert upon foreign policy. . . . Political realism wants the photographic picture of the political world to resemble as much as possible its painted portrait. Aware of the inevitable

gap between good—that is, rational—foreign policy and foreign
policy as it actually is, political realism maintains not only that
theory must focus upon the rational elements of political reality,
but also that foreign policy ought to be rational in view of its
own moral and practical purposes. Hence, it is no argument
against the theory presented here that actual foreign policy does
not or cannot live up to it.[8]

Accordingly, Morgenthau would probably not be too unhappy with
John Vasquez's intended criticism of the realist approach: "As an image of the world employed by policy makers, power politics promotes
certain kinds of behavior and often leads to self-fulfilling prophecies."[9]

Nevertheless, the normative dimension of realism does decidedly
limit its explanatory power. Vasquez again: "Power politics is not so
much an explanation as a description of one kind of behavior found in
the global political system. If this is correct, then power politics behavior itself must be explained; it does not explain."[10]

Part of the explanation, as Vasquez suggests, is the fact that Morgenthau's approach actually gained such wide acceptance, especially
among the post-World War II generation of U.S. policymakers.[11] There
was and is something ego-gratifying, *macho*, and even a little romantic
about picturing oneself as advancing the "national interest" in a
"struggle for power." Moreover, Morgenthau's stress on the amoral
nature of international affairs allows policymakers to indulge their
penchant for "pragmatism," thereby hiding from themselves any trou-
bling questions about the values that are actually being advanced by
their policies.

## THE RETREAT FROM RATIONALITY

The "rational" model, as usually conceived, maintains that an individual decisionmaker reaches a decision by a clearly defined intellectual
process: He or she clarifies and ranks values and goals; then weighs all
alternative courses of action (policies) and the likely consequences
(costs/benefits) of each; and ultimately chooses the optimal course(s)
of action with regard to the ends pursued. As Sidney Verba phrases it:
"Rational models of individual decision-making are those in which the
individual responding to an international event bases his response upon
a cool and clear-headed means-ends calculation. He uses the best information available and chooses from the universe of possible responses
that alternative most likely to maximize his goals."[12]

The rational model of decisionmaking was embedded not only in the dominant realist approach but also in the movement for a "scientific revolution" in the study of international politics that reached its zenith in the 1960s. Richard W. Cottam captures the spirit of this "golden age of American academia":

This was the "end of ideology" era. A new and heady positivism had triumphed, and a fierce competition was engaged in to discover what Stanley Hoffmann referred to as the "magic key"—a scientific method which would disclose the essence of man's sociopolitical behavior. . . . Leading figures in each discipline of the social sciences found ready acceptance in Washington. Indeed, formal or informal consultation with leading bureaucrats was as much a mark of achievement in a discipline as membership on boards of the relevant national foundations. Some theorists, especially those focusing on game theory and simulation, had the ultimate satisfaction of seeing their jargon incorporated into the bureaucratic lexicon.[13]

Reading Thomas Schelling[14] on bargaining, bureaucrats played zero-sum and nonzero-sum games, crafted "minimax" strategies, searched for "tacit" agreements, and on dull days perhaps contemplated an exciting round of "chicken." Dulles's earlier "brinkmanship" evolved into a full-blown policy of "deterrence," supported by a veritable torrent of scholarly literature that argued for a broad range of weaponry and adequate men at arms to allow for a "flexible response" to enemy challenges anywhere in the world. Herman Kahn thought about various levels of "unthinkable" nuclear war[15] and developed an escalation ladder with precise steps,[16] so that policymakers might apply just the appropriate degree of "compellence" to their adversaries at any stage of a conflict. All of this reached its apogee during the Kennedy years with Robert McNamara and the "whiz kids" brandishing new strategic theories and utilizing new technologies.

Theorizing rested upon the stated or unstated premise that policymakers are rational, that they pursue the national interest through Verba's cool and clear-headed means-ends calculations based on adequate information. John D. Steinbruner speaks of a "heavy investment of the culture in the concept of rationality":

The theory of deterrence, a direct embodiment of rational assumptions, has become a central element of United States foreign policy, and upon its principles are staked each year billions of dollars in expenditures and the risk of millions of lives. The common-sense mind has been substantially captured, and intuitive observers who would understand the processes of government have learned to impose rational assumptions on what they see and to work out explanations and expectations along lines required by these assumptions. These developments have all been laborious, consuming many decades and a great many intellectual careers.[17]

Richard J. Barnet observes that assumptions of rationality were implicit in the task of social scientists:

[A social scientist's] job was to tell officials how to do what they wanted to do in the most efficient way and then to help them measure what they had done. Criticizing policy goals or challenging the implicit values behind a policy were considered "counter-productive" by the managers of university contract teams and by ambitious professors themselves. . . . Built into the contract relationship were profound unspoken assumptions such as: Government is an instrument of problem-solving, not a problem itself. . . .[18]

And then, as Cottam reminds us, came the Vietnam experience, which (together with the continuing civil rights movement and the Watergate scandal) brought the United States to the edge of social upheaval and left a legacy of popular distrust of entanglement in foreign "dirty little wars" that is reflected in public opinion polls even to the present day. Government obviously *could be*—and indeed *was—itself* a problem! How could a vast foreign-policy "establishment," the "best and the brightest," have been so tragically misguided—so seemingly downright *irrational*?! Cottam remarks on shifting perceptions and the consequent dramatic change in the normative climate at the time:

When the United States took its first steps in Vietnam in 1954, governmental officials, academics, and the interested public overwhelmingly regarded them as necessary to contain [Soviet aggressiveness and ideological appeal]. By 1965 the picture for many . . . had changed drastically. . . . Communism was no longer a great international monolith. . . . The United States was . . . seen fighting North Vietnam, a fourth-class power that was receiving barely enough support to maintain the conflict. . . . For those who persisted in holding the aggressive international communism image, the policy was defensible and as moral as defensive wars ever are. For those who no longer saw the international communist menace, the policy was immoral and possibly racist.[19]

Moreover, the North Vietnamese appeared singularly unmoved by the "compelling" logic of the strategist's escalation ladder. The Johnson administration's "bomb 'em into the Stone Age" campaign was as out of touch with the "real world" as seen from Hanoi as it was with the shifting climate of opinion in the United States.

Against this background, then, it was not coincidental that theorizing about foreign-policy decisionmaking in the late sixties and the seventies moved increasingly away from reliance upon the rational model. The spotlight turned to decisionmakers' perceptions and the ways these are shaped by such factors as idiosyncratic variables and the organization/ bureaucratic context in which so many decisions are made. There was a new recognition both that policy is made by often fallible human beings and that a veritable "bureaucratic revolution"[20] had taken place since World War II in foreign policy decisionmaking processes, certainly in the United States, but also to varying degrees in many governments throughout the world.

As Steinbruner observes: "In common discourse the word 'rational' is drenched with normative connotations."[21] Indeed, the rational model always involved something of a tautology; "rational" decisions were presumed to result from "rational" decisionmaking even when they were as blatantly out of touch with the "real world" as Lyndon Johnson's bombing campaign of North Vietnam. Accordingly, Steinbruner prefers to substitute the label "analytic" for "rational" as a characterization of this kind of decisionmaking, that is, one "in which the decision problem is broken down into major components, and then a deliberate procedure for aggregation is evoked to achieve a decision."[22]

However the rational model is labeled and purged of normative connotations, as pioneering theorists Richard C. Snyder/H. W. Bruck/ Burton Sapin[23] and Harold and Margaret Sprout[24] emphasized, it is still undermined by a fundamental problem: the *dual* objective-subjective nature of reality or, as the Sprouts put it, the need to distinguish between the decisionmaker's "psychological milieu" (the world as he/she perceives it) and the "operational milieu" (the real world in which policies have to be implemented). According to Joseph de Rivera: "It is difficult even to intellectually grasp the fact that *we construct* the reality in which we operate. We take our perception of the world for granted. . . . It is precisely in this feeling of certainty that the danger lies."[25]

Unless one adopts the philosophical stance that everything "real" is inherently illusion, and even while recalling Plato's "simile of the cave," one must grant at least some validity to the concept of objective reality. Exactly how much validity is the hard question. In the words of a familiar maxim: "The Real World is Only a Special Case, Albeit an Important One."[26] Not all perceptions are equally legitimate, for, as de Rivera observes: "The stimulus has an *objective structure* that limits the number of possible legitimate interpretations."[27] Yet our awkward task as decisionmakers or analysts is how to perceive that "objective structure" from the vantage point of our own individual subjectivities. Policies that fail miserably surely often *seem* to be running up against a very substantial reality that turned out to be far different from that envisaged by the authors of the policy. Our own statement above, that the Johnson administration's strategy in Vietnam was blatantly out of touch with the real world, underscores the fact that things did not work out in Southeast Asia or back home in the United States as those who made the policy expected; it also betrays our own prejudices.

But was it the "wrong" policy for some "objective reality" in Southeast Asia? Right-wing ideologues in the United States still insist that the Johnson administration's "punish the enemy" approach was basically correct, that the Vietnam War would have been "winnable" if only treasonous left-wing intellectuals in the United States had not created so much domestic dissent that administration decisionmakers lost their nerve. Was it, then, only domestic "objective reality" that the Johnson team failed to read properly? Hans J. Morgenthau and other critics of the Vietnam War, who could hardly be classed as left-wingers, would heartily disagree with that interpretation. In their view, Vietnam was a quagmire into which the United States could continue to flounder deeper and deeper, but definitely not a contest of great strategic import nor one that could ever be "won" at acceptable cost.

On the other hand, "realist" critics like Morgenthau did not share the additional perspective of perhaps the majority of dissenters that, strategic and pragmatic assessments aside, the Johnson administration's policy was plainly "immoral." "Objective reality," as they saw it, had to include certain bedrock moral principles that the United States should not be violating. Also, they insisted, if the argument had to turn on strategic and pragmatic grounds, it was in the "national interest" of the United States to make a clear distinction between its own policies and the "aggressive" policies of the Soviet camp. Even the cynics should be able to see that morality, in this sense, could be an ideological weapon in the arsenal of democracy.

The dual objective-subjective nature of reality, of course, is far from the sole problem confronting the rational model. Sidney Verba summarized some of the others in his early pathbreaking article.[28] "One set of reasons why the rationality model is not an adequate description of decisionmaking," he stated, "lies in human frailty."[29] "There may be too many significant variables, inadequate information, variables that are not easily quantifiable, or decisional methods are not advanced enough."[30] Yet, according to Verba, human frailty is the "least important reason" why the rational model is insufficient. More important is the fact that a decisionmaker rarely is aware of his/her own values or has them neatly ordered in terms of personal significance. Values often conflict and even "depend in part upon the situation one is facing and what is attainable in that situation."[31] Personal preferences may change as the decisionmaking process advances, and means and ends are inextricably interwoven. Another problem is that most decisions relating to foreign policy are collective decisions, made by an ad hoc group of individuals or by a bureaucracy or other organizational unit. Ends-means calculations become much more difficult when various members of the group or different units have conflicting goals. Yet another objection to the rationality model is that "individuals do not consider all policy alternatives and, what is more important, make no attempt to do so."[32] They look for simple alternatives that are similar to those they have adopted in the past. In fact, fewer decisions are considered at the beginning of the process than toward the end, when other actors have raised their objections to the proposed policy. Finally, the rationality model "treats each decision as if it were a separate entity,"[33] while a decisionmaker cannot. The practitioner is operating not only in a personal context of limited time and energy but also "within a structure in which there has been previous commitment to policy and organizational vested interest in policy."

Verba approvingly cites early work by Herbert Simon and his associates to the effect that even optimal decisionmaking reflects merely "bounded rationality" and that decisionmakers are almost always "satisficing" rather than maximizing;[34] and also Charles Lindblom's characterization that most decisionmaking is essentially "incremental" and disjointed, just "muddling through."[35] Verba does concede that decisionmaking in international relations, for several reasons, may be somewhat more rational than that in other policy areas: First, foreign-policy actors presumably all have a shared loyalty to country that is inherent in citizenship. Second, there do exist groups within government whose primary purpose is to "coordinate and control the bargaining process among the various members of the foreign policy coalition," and "the greater the emergency, the more likely is decisionmaking to be concentrated among high officials whose commitments are to the overall system." Hence "it may be, paradoxically, that the model of means-ends rationality will be more closely approximated in an emergency when the time for careful deliberation is limited." Third, "unattached intellectuals" may be in a much better position to be rational in searching out policy alternatives than bureaucrats. Nevertheless, cautions Verba, "it may be just because this research approaches the rationality model that it is not often translatable into actual policy." In sum, Verba holds that the rationality model is useful "only if its limitations are appreciated," and he suggests that one of its principal utilities "may be that it facilitates the systematic consideration of deviations from rationality."

What is perhaps most striking about the literature on foreign policy decisionmaking since the mid-1960s is that systematic considerations of deviations from rationality have become the rule rather than the exception. Once enthusiasm for the notion of "bounded" rationality became unbounded, the theoretical challenge shifted from the task of attacking the rational model to that of establishing precisely what the "bounds" of bounded rationality were to be. Now that decisions no longer could be presumed to emanate from purely rational processes, what influences were, in fact, at work and what weights should be assigned to each of them as explanatory variables? Unfortunately, decisionmaking that was now seen as somewhat less than "rational" found its reflection in a substantial measure of theoretical chaos.

## ALTERNATIVES TO TRADITIONAL ASSUMPTIONS ABOUT RATIONALITY

Some theorists, looking for alternatives to rational theory, focused on the most basic level of analysis, that of the individual decisionmaker.[36] Following the pioneering psychobiographical work of Arnold A. Rogow on James Forrestal,[37] as well as Alexander and Juliette George on Woodrow Wilson,[38] the search was on for *idiosyncratic* (although not necessarily aberrant) *behavior* and its origins in such factors as a decisionmaker's personality, family background, education, and life experiences. Alexander George[39] and Ole Holsti[40] advanced and sought to refine the "operational code"/"belief system" concept; Ole Holsti attempted to reconstruct the "operational code" of John Foster Dulles.[41] Robert A. Isaak probed the personality of Henry Kissinger;[42] Joseph de Rivera,[43] as well as others,[44] explored the "psychological" dimension of leadership; and Lloyd Etheridge investigated the "private sources" of policy.[45] Some of these analysts and others have tried to go beyond case studies to develop general propositions about the relevance of the personality of individual decisionmakers to foreign policy[46]—for example, that personality is most likely to have a significant impact when the political system involved and/or particular circumstances (e.g., perceived crisis) concentrate(s) considerable authority in the hands of an individual decisionmaker; when that individual has the interest, ego, and/or charisma to impose his personal will; and so forth.

Nevertheless, this approach continues to confront several serious obstacles. Not the least of these is the sheer difficulty of gathering reliable data. Decisionmakers are understandably reluctant to recline on the foreign-policy analyst's couch, and thus most of the evidence has to be gleaned from such questionable sources as speeches, unclassified official documents, letters and diaries, and interviews with friends and associates. And since analysis of individual leaders is for the most part, possible only after their careers have reached an end, it is difficult to move beyond postdictive insights.

Even more vexatious is the absence of an acceptable conceptualization of the central variable of "personality." Attempts to develop a classification of personality "types" have not been particularly convincing, partly because the nagging question, "types of what?" remains always in the background. Joseph de Rivera asks: "How can we best conceptualize personality; what variables would be most efficient to use?"[47] And he concedes that there is no clear answer to these questions "because of our basic ignorance about many of the dynamics of personality."[48] He observes: "There are so many preferences, abilities, rules, and styles that it is difficult to know how to describe the behavior of a decisionmaker with some economy. Furthermore, it is not clear how to relate these individual differences in behavior to the deeper facets of personality they may reflect."[49] Nor does there appear to be an entirely satisfactory definition of an "operational code"/"belief system."[50]

In addition, as has often been pointed out, the individual-as-actor approach is likely to have limited explanatory potential because individual leaders are rarely in a position to give their individuality full rein. Their potentially idiosyncratic behavior is usually constrained by the decisionmaking role(s) they occupy, and, for that matter, it is often exceedingly hard to distinguish idiosyncratic behavior from that emanating from role or other influences. For example, did Margaret Thatcher's reaction to the Argentine military's seizure of the Falklands/ Malvinas represent yet another manifestation of her "Iron Lady" personality, what any British Prime Minister would likely have done faced with a blatant challenge of that nature and/or a response to the Conservative party's declining standing in public opinion polls? Or, why did such different personalities as John F. Kennedy, Lyndon Johnson, and Richard Nixon continue to wage war in Vietnam? Gunnar Sjoblom writes: "An interesting problem in the study of an individual's OC [operational code] is evidently to what degree it is influenced by personality factors and to what degree it is influenced by role factors."[51] Part of the issue here, as yet unresolved, is how to establish where the operating code of individuals shades off into the "standard operating procedures" (SOPs) of organizations and/or into bureaucratic parochialism (see below).[52] Finally, whether behavior is idiosyncratic or not, few individuals are regularly in a position to have a significant impact on the vast institutional network that is involved in making the bulk of foreign policy decisions in many countries.

Moving beyond the individual level of analysis, other theoretical approaches—somewhat distinct, albeit interrelated and overlapping—have moved to the forefront in recent years. These have explored the sources of perceptions and misperceptions which tend to be common to decisionmakers regardless of their place in the institutional network ("cognitive," elites, and shared images), the psychological dynamics of groups and organizations ("groupthink" and "cybernetic") , and the particular features of "governmental (bureaucratic) politics."

A quarter of a century ago Snyder/Bruck/Sapin observed: "It is difficult to see how we can account for specific actions and for continuities of policies without trying to discover how their operating environment is perceived by those responsible for choices, how particular situations are structured, what values and norms are applied to certain kinds of problems, what matters are selected for their attention, and how their past experience conditions present responses." They also commented: "[T]he foreign policy machinery mediates among internal and external demands and needs *and* among decisionmakers themselves. Three overlapping environments are implied. Any framework of analysis ought to accommodate the potential effects of these three groups of factors. . . ."[53] Without providing answers to by any means all of the questions raised by Snyder/Bruck/Sapin, subsequent theorists nevertheless have addressed them with considerable enthusiasm. While enriching the foreign-policy literature, these analyses have *not* yet provided anything approaching a coherent general theory. They cast doubt on prior theory and tempt us with tantalizing insights but, to date, have accomplished little more.

Robert Jervis, a leading advocate of the *cognitive* approach, maintains that "it is often impossible to explain crucial decisions and policies without reference to the decisionmakers' beliefs about the world and their images of others. That is to say, these cognitions are part of the proximate cause of the relevant behavior." He is especially interested in "how, when, and why highly intelligent and conscientious statesmen misperceive their environments" and engage in behavior that is "self-defeating . . . or generally lacking in a high degree of rationality."[54] Jervis, de Rivera,[55] Alexander George,[56] Steinbruner,[57] and others have identified a host of psychological mechanisms which commonly come into play when decisionmakers are forced to confront complex problems involving value conflicts and a great deal of uncertainty (Steinbruner's term is "structured uncertainty"). For example, decisionmakers tend to avoid recognizing conflicting values and the consequent inevitability of value trade-offs; they abhor cognitive dissonance and thus force the square peg of contrary information into the round hole of pre-existing beliefs; they see events in terms of the issues which concern them most (their own "evoked set") and not necessarily additional issues that are relevant and of primary concern to other decisionmakers; they misuse historical analogies;[58] they engage in wishful thinking; and so on.

The evidence is overwhelming that decisionmakers "differ in their perceptions of the world in general and of other actors in particular"[59] and that this is a matter of major importance. Jervis, for instance, is persuasive in his rebuttal of Arnold Wolfers's classic argument that external threats (a burning house in Wolfers's analogy) tend to unite decisionmakers regardless of their predispositions (they all head for the exits). Notes Jervis:

> For Churchill, the house was burning soon after Hitler took power in Germany; for Chamberlain, this was the case only after March 1939; and for others there was never a fire at all. To some decisionmakers, the Soviet Union is a threat to which the United States is compelled to respond. To others the threat passed years ago. Again, to a growing number of scholars it never existed. Similarly, American statesmen see a much greater threat from communism in both Europe and Southeast Asia than do the leaders of our allies. Decisionmakers may even agree that their state's existence is threatened but disagree about the source of the threat. This was true, for example, in the United States around the turn of the nineteenth century, when the Federalists believed

France so much a menace that they favored war with her. At the same time, the Republicans believed England an equal menace.[60]

Indeed, a growing body of writings has emerged of late specifically on the subject of "threat perception." Raymond Cohen, for his part, describes threat perception as a dynamic psychological process:

> Within any structure of relations which it is desired to preserve, certain "rules of the Game" will be developed to regulate permissible behavior between the actors. In a dangerously uncertain world they allow a minimal degree of certainty. But they are like a seamless web. Damaged at one point, the whole fabric begins to disintegrate. Threat, then, is like a tug on this web of rules, its perception an anticipation of a descent into disorder and uncertainty.[61]

Although Cohen believes that even tacit rules of the international game are well-understood by the players,[62] he does acknowledge that an expectation of occasional "cheating" is built-in. Moreover, it does seem obvious that occasional misperceptions of opponents' intentions are unavoidable.

This last observation is central to the "spiral model" that cognitive theorists are wont to substitute for the theory of deterrence. In this perspective, an opponent's acquisition of a new weapons system is more likely to be perceived as an attempt to "get ahead" rather than to "catch up" in the arms race, which, of course, leads to spiraling competition. Jervis comments that in the "Hobbesian state of nature" "anarchic setting of international relations," "we find that decisionmakers, and especially military leaders, worry about the most implausible threats."[63]

All of this to some extent undermines Charles F. Hermann's older conception of "crisis" as a "situational variable" independent of the minds of decisionmakers. According to Hermann, a "crisis" exists when a situation threatens high-priority goals of the decisionmaking unit, there is limited time for response, and decisionmakers are surprised.[64] Surely, however, decisionmakers have tremendous latitude in perceiving (or not perceiving) varying degrees of "threat" (if any) to "high-priority goals" ("core values") and the urgency of a response. Thus, another administration than President Johnson's might have regarded the 1965 revolt in the Dominican Republic as the "pro-Bosch" coup that its supporters declared it to be (and many still believe that it was, in fact), welcomed the pending restoration of the legitimate president and political democracy, and simply let the violence run its course. Richard Ned Lebow declares: "As is true with most important concepts in the social sciences, there is no generally accepted definition of international crisis." Yet it is interesting and significant that Lebow, writing over a decade after Hermann, includes policymakers' perceptions as a key factor in his own definition.[65]

Structural factors, as well as other objective explanations of the Cold War, are virtually dismissed by Richard Cottam when he declares that "historians will record the Soviet-American Cold War as one that rested predominantly on motivational attribution rather than on conflicting objectives."[66] In addition, he provides some excellent illustrations of perceptions at work in the categorization of "friends" and "enemies." Yugoslavia's Marshall Tito, for instance, appeared in descriptions by Americans "to be two utterly different men," a "simple satellite leader" when he was allied with the Soviets and "an almost liberal democratic leader" when he broke away from the Soviets.[67] According to Cottam (drawing on William Gilmore), the case of Spain's Francisco Franco "suggests both the limits of ideology as a determinant of foreign policy perceptions and the patterns ideology generates when it is a determinant of perceptions." Prior to World War II, before a threat to the United States was apparent, American Catholics (perceiving a threat to the Church in Spain) and American non-Catholic conservatives (responding to their political ideology) viewed Franco favorably, while American non-Catholic liberals did not. During World War II, when the United States was clearly threatened, Franco was seen by nearly all Americans negatively as a fascist who was a virtual ally of Hitler. Immediately after World War II, Franco regained his positive image among American Catholics and non-Catholic conservatives, but it was not until the Soviet threat loomed large with the intensification of the Cold War that American liberals came to view him as an ally.[68] Cottam cites the further cases of Patrice Lumumba and Moise Tshombe in the Belgian Congo as ones that evoked extremely different perceptions among decisionmakers around the world:

> In the United States the right saw Tshombe as one of them, and the far left equally identified with Lumumba. To the right, Lumumba was an instrument of international communism. To the left, Tshombe was an instrument of Western capitalist imperialism. For Egyptians, Lumumba was Nasser and Tshombe was the corrupt ex-King Farouk. For Indonesians, Lumumba was Sukarno; for Indians he was Jawaharlal Nehru or Mahatma Gandhi.[69]

Few cognitive theorists (except Cottam) have themselves perceived, or at least have explicitly acknowledged, the impetus that the shift in the normative climate over the Vietnam issue gave to their approach. On the other hand, they have been candid in admitting their own desire for improved decisionmaking and diligent in teasing out the normative implications of their work toward this end. Unfortunately, in no small part because of the problems of cognitive theory that we will be analyzing, the suggestions they have been able to make have been rather modest in nature. These actually reduce to little more than urging policymakers to make themselves alert to perceptual pitfalls and to try to avoid them, by building a measure of "multiple advocacy" into the decisionmaking process, consulting independent academics, and the like.[70] Perhaps cognitive theory's main contribution is, as Steinbruner assesses it, primarily a "negative one" of "challenging the conventional paths to reform." Certainly the theory offers little assurance that "merely" securing better quality leaders and/or persuading policymakers to pursue the "right" values will greatly improve the performance of government.[71]

Although the cognitive approach holds obvious interest and importance for students of foreign policy and practitioners alike, it, too, has grave weaknesses when considered as a potential basis for general theory. Snyder/Bruck/Sapin articulated a central issue early on:

> The fundamental question is whether we can do better than achieve the familiar *verstehen*—that is, whether we can obtain reliable data concerning the state of mind of actors whose behavior we wish to describe and explain. We are a long way from a hard methodology, but those who take an objectivist position have faith that such a methodology is possible. Can assumptions be replaced by evidence as a basis for inference? If not, we seem destined to remain puzzled about the combinations of determinacy and indeterminacy in the wellsprings of behavior.[72]

Part of the difficulty in obtaining reliable data is similar to that encountered by the individual-as-actor approach: the decisionmakers themselves are not normally available for analysis. Consequently, as Jonsson observes, "much of the relevant psychological literature rests on experimental research using subjects who are not—and are likely to differ significantly from—foreign policy decisionmakers."[73] Not only are the subjects of experimental research not the genuine article, they are usually observed in a laboratory setting that could hardly contrast more with the Oval Office or a ministry of foreign affairs.[74]

Yet the essential difficulty lies deeper still, in the fact that cognitive behavior varies not only by classes of persons and decisionmaking institutional setting but also *decision-by-decision*. Steinbruner, for instance, after outlining three "cognitive syndromes" ("grooved thinking," "uncommitted thinking," and "theoretical thinking"), readily acknowledges that "the three cognitive syndromes identified cannot be assumed to refer to personality types."

It is reasonably clear that every person at different times and, most critically, *in different decision problems,* is likely to operate according to different syndromes. Many decisionmakers doubtless could be observed fitting all three patterns at one time or another. Second, in any organizational situation the various positions of power are likely to be held by people operating in different modes of thinking. Awareness of this fact is likely to aid analysis when details of the specific context can be supplied, but it is difficult at the moment to provide general propositions of any power.[75]

So one suspects that even if more and better data could be secured, they would far outstrip the capacity of present cognitive theory to explain. Steinbruner himself is aware of the limitations of cognitive theory. He concludes:

Because the business of establishing the connection between theoretical assumptions and an actual decision is a process of particularization (inevitably a matter of setting up *ad hoc* assumptions), there are few generally applicable rules to follow. The standard rules of scientific method apply, of course, but they, too, need interpretation for any given situation, especially in that the pertinent data are largely non-quantitative. One relies ultimately on the judgment and care of the analysts.[76]

Jervis is no more optimistic about the prospects for coherent general theory using psychological insights:

[P]ropositions about both the causes and effects of images can only be probabilistic. There are too many variables to claim more. In the cases in which we are interested, decisionmakers are faced with a large number of competing values, highly complex situations, and very ambiguous information. The possibilities and reasons for misperceptions and disagreements are legion. For these reasons, generalizations in this area are difficult to develop, exceptions are common, and in many instances, the outcomes will be influenced by factors that, from the standpoint of most theories, must be considered accidental. Important perceptual predispositions can be discovered, but they will not be controlling.[77]

In other words, if we turn to cognitive theory to explain foreign-policy behavior, we shall be forced to abandon what Hedley Bull called the "scientific approach" in favor of the "classical approach" "that is characterized above all by explicit reliance upon the exercise of judgment. . . ."[78] As with so much of psychology, many conditioning factors will no longer be visible; only their consequences will be open to observation. And, like Freudians, we may have to subscribe to theories that are stubbornly nonempirical. When we are forced to consider outcomes "in many instances" to be "accidental," we are almost at the opposite pole from general theory. Indeed, one might wonder whether Jervis's description of cognitive-approach propositions as "probabilistic" might not be overstating the case.

### CONCLUSION: THE DECLINE OF THE NATIONAL INTEREST

Robert Jervis concludes his analysis of the cognitive approach to the study of foreign policy with what he calls a "simple plea": "let us, as best we can, stop fooling ourselves; let us understand better what we are really about."[79]

Most of us who labor in the vineyards of international relations theory have stopped fooling ourselves, at least as far as the usefulness of the rationality assumption is concerned. Few today would accord it more than very limited utility, at best, even while mourning its disappearance. Without it, however, little remains that might aid us to reconstruct consensual foreign-policy theory from the numerous hypotheses about decisionmaking that have been presented in recent years. If anarchy exists, it is less in the international system than in our theories.

# 7

# The Making of Foreign Policy, or Opening the "Black Box"

The traditional post-Westphalian picture of international politics is that of a universe of sovereign nation-states, each of which pursues an autonomous foreign policy. According to realist teachings, the foreign policy each state follows flows from a rational calculation of its "national interest" defined in terms of power. However, the inadequacy of the state concept and the wholesale retreat from the rationality assumption gravely undermine this traditional model and, more importantly, are devastating to the prospects for general theory. Nowhere has the disarray been more painfully evident than in the search for explanations of foreign-policy behavior.

Especially in the last several decades, the parsimonious realist view has been to some extent challenged by "new" approaches to the analysis of foreign policy that have emphasized a host of other factors. Some analysts focus upon variables external to the state like the essential "structure(s)" of the international system, although in some cases the arguments resemble realism clad in new raiment. Others have chosen to emphasize basic attributes of states like size, level of economic development, and the degree to which a political system is open or closed. Here, too, the essential "billiard ball" or "black box" model of the realists is retained, and there remains a tendency to anthropomorphize state entities in order to compare them.

Other scholars, however, have chosen to open up the black box in order to master subtleties and nuances that had eluded realists. In seeking more potent explanations and in combining clusters of different variables into single explanations, such scholars have, of course, introduced unprecedented complexity into the study of foreign policy. Some have studied the supposed linkages (posited by Marxists) between capitalist economies with attendant elite-mass social structures and foreign policy. Others have argued the primacy of "ruling elites" in determining foreign policy and, in so doing, have rejected "pluralist" assumptions about American politics. There has also been renewed interest in national cultural factors like ideology, "public opinion" at large, interest coalitions like the "military-industrial complex," and/or specific interest groups. Internal interactive processes have also attracted interest—cybernetics or information/communication factors like the "standard operating procedures" that characterize organizational process, bargaining among bureaucracies, role formation, and "situational variables." Finally, an increasing number of scholars (including many who were not trained as political scientists) are, as we have seen, investigating particular psychological perspectives on decisionmaking like personality, cognition, and motivation.

Owing to the long-time dominance of state-centric analyses of foreign policy, there is a tendency to think of these approaches as more novel than they really are. In fact, virtually all of them have had previous adherents. Arguments regarding the economic bases of foreign policy have been standard fare in Marxist analyses for more than a century, even though many universities have only recently rediscovered "political economy." Ideology was regarded by many nineteenth-century theorists as a critical factor, and "national character" arguments seem almost always to have permeated commentaries on foreign affairs. Observers as varied as Alexis de Tocqueville and Walter Lippmann grumbled about what they believed to be the pernicious effects of public opinion, and post-World War I accusations about the culpability of the so-called merchants of death were precursors to claims about the "military-industrial complex." And long before the current flurry of research into psychological factors, Sigmund Freud presented a "theory of the instincts which, after much tentative groping and many fluctuations of opinion, has been reached by workers in the field of psychoanalysis" to explain war.[1]

The reawakening of interest in these and other approaches has, nevertheless, vastly expanded the checklist of variables with which graduate students interested in foreign policy must become acquainted if they wish to pass their qualifying exams. However, these approaches have, if anything, vastly complicated the search for general theory. One is reminded of "Moore's Law," to wit: "The degree to which a topic is understood is inversely proportional to the amount of literature available on it. *Corollary:* That which seems vague is frequently meaningless."[2] With such a smorgasbord of factors from which to choose, the analyst is hard pressed to decide the relevance of and weight to be attached to each; many factors are so interrelated that they are virtually indistinguishable from one another; several factors bear the hallmark of ethnocentrism; and many are utilized as both independent and dependent variables. The parsimony of realist theory has disappeared; no theoretical alternative is available to reimpose discipline on the study of foreign policy; and coteries of scholars have ceased communicating with each other.

Moreover, no approach has as yet resolved the central ambiguities inherent in the study of "foreign policy": What exactly *is* "foreign" policy, when so much of "domestic" policy (e.g., interest rates, environmental protection regulations, tax rules, minimum wage legislation) has profound "international" consequences—and vice versa? Does the foreign-domestic dichotomy make sense at all? What, indeed, is "policy"? Who or what has the authority to "make" it? Who actually "makes" it? What, in fact, do we mean by "make"? Is "policy" a statement of goals or the presumed means to those ends? Is it what "policymakers" say they intend to do or what they actually do? Or, is it merely the behavior (intentional and unintentional) that flows outward from a state? What is a "decision," when most so-called decisions are almost always subject to modification either by their originators or by others, in the process of policy "implementation" (or nonimplementation)? Unfortunately, fundamental questions such as these are rarely addressed; and, when they are, are issues in methodological, rather than conceptual, disputes.[3]

All of this is so murky that we might be tempted to restate the central issue of foreign-policy analysis, only partially tongue-in-cheek, as follows: Can we make meaningful *generalizations* about the relative significance of many ill-defined variables in explaining decisions, often of dubious relevance and impact, made in various national contexts by a great number of potentially influential individuals and/or groups?! The outlook for doing so is, to say the least, hardly bright.

## REALISM, BLACK BOXES, AND FOREIGN POLICY

It is because realists take seriously the state as actor, perceive states as greater than the sum of their parts, and believe them to be endowed with unique interests that flow from their power position in the global arena that they find it unnecessary to peer within states for explanations of behavior. Strictly speaking, Morgenthau, as well as earlier realists, did distinguish between "nation-states" and "their decisionmakers," but this distinction carried little meaning because decisionmakers were conceived to be rational, basically fungible, and guided by a system-determined national interest. Morgenthau does indicate fairly clearly *who acts* on behalf of the nation-state and who inhabits the nation-state box, which is therefore not an entirely "black" box. In recognizing that supposedly rational "statesmen" act as surrogates for the nation-state, he avoids the worst excesses of reification. Nevertheless, realists tend to conceive of foreign-policy planning and execution as processes that are coherent and unitary; and, as Steve Smith observes, "one searches in vain through *Politics Among Nations* for any linkage between the domestic polity and the international system."[4] For Morgenthau, then, the "most important actor" in *causal* terms is not the decisionmaker either as an "individual" or as a representative of the nation-state. Rather, the "actor" with the most influence is two key attributes of the international arena—the selfish human nature of those who inhabit it and its jungle-like character.

Black box and billiard ball explanations, however, rely heavily on acceptance of the rationality assumption. For them to be plausible, it is absolutely crucial to assume that decisionmakers are capable of distinguishing between personal preferences and the dictates of official duty and that they are prepared to sacrifice the former for the latter.[5] And such decisionmakers must be able to calculate the national interest of the states for which they are responsible. With this assumption intact, it is perfectly reasonable to identify "nation-states" with "their decision-makers." Without it, black box explanations begin to fall apart. Sidney Verba understood some of these implications of rejecting the rationality assumption over a quarter of a century ago when raising questions about that assumption: "Different members [of the foreign-policy organization] will prefer different goals, and policy will often be formulated by bargaining among the members of a foreign-policy coalition. . . . Any policy alternative . . . will be considered in relation to a variety of goal systems that may not be consistent."[6] As we shall see, the governmental (bureaucratic) politics perspective, as well as studies of the influence of domestic interest groups and attentive publics, reinforce Verba's contention that nation-states cannot be conceived of as unitary actors.[7]

Realism has also been criticized from still other perspectives.[8] For example, its state-centric outlook seems to ignore the impact of non-state actors. Also, as we have seen, work on cognitive behavior and cybernetics has highlighted the extent to which the actions of individuals and groups vary according to their perceptions. Steve Smith comments:

> [Morgenthau's] key concepts—power, balance of power and national interest—are incapable of objective definition. To accept that these are subjective negates Morgenthau's claim to objectivity which is central to his argument. Once subjectivity enters into the definitions his epistemology collapses, for this is *not* an account of what decisionmakers *think* they are doing, it is an account of what we think we know they are doing.[9]

Finally, realism, as we have argued, tends to seesaw back and forth between empirical and normative analysis, never resolving the contradictions that this poses.

Yet the influence of realism goes on, not least today in the writings of so-called neorealists like Kenneth Waltz[10] and Robert Keohane,[11] and to a much lesser extent in the work of "neo-Marxists" like Immanuel Wallerstein.[12] What ties these two "schools" together with realism is primarily their emphasis on systemic determinants of state behavior, although neorealists also echo realism in stressing the role of states as the constituent units in world politics. On the other hand, there is nothing approaching a broad consensus as to the most significant attributes of the international system, the nature of the relationships within that system (or subsystems), or the dynamics of change. Everyone agrees that the international system is essentially "anarchical," in the very limited sense that no central government exists with a range of authority comparable to that found in many contemporary states. Also, nearly everyone admits the existence of at least an element of "order" arising from the "common interests" of states.

At this point, the consensus breaks down. For Waltz, it is the distribution of power, particularly the number of major powers, that is all important; and the only genuine cooperation possible in the system is a relatively minor "exchange of considerations."[13] As John Ruggie expresses Waltz's argument in this regard: "[T]he management of global problems is governed by 'the tyranny of small decisions'. . . . [T]he international system is not an entity that is capable of acting on its own behalf, for the greater social good. Thus, while a growing number of problems may be found at the global level, solutions continue to depend on national policies. . . ."[14] Keohane, in contrast, maintains:

> From a theoretical standpoint, regimes can be viewed as intermediate factors, or "intervening variables," between fundamental characteristics of world politics such as the international distribu-

tion of power on the one hand and the behavior of states and
nonstate actors such as the multinational corporations on the
other. . . . [T]he norms and rules of regimes can exert an influence on behavior even if they do not embody common ideals but
are used by self-interested states and corporations engaging in a
process of mutual adjustment.[15]

In Wallerstein's view, the international system is virtually synonymous with the "world-economy" and a present "world-system" of
capitalist "hegemony," which is slowly but inexorably being transformed by "antisystemic" forces that will one distant day ensure the
triumph of socialism. The system is divided by unequal development
patterns into core, periphery, and semiperiphery; in which framework,
the Soviet Union occupies a somewhat ambivalent position. A charter
antisystemic, the USSR evolved into a rather "establishment" figure,
itself challenged after the 1950s by such new phenomena as national
liberation movements in the Third World and Eurocommunism. What
is disappearing, according to Wallerstein, is not only the classical liberal economic consensus but also "schlerotic" official Marxism."[16]

All of this brings to mind *dependencia* theory, which in the 1960s
and 1970s was a prominent feature of writings about the North-South
relationship, but which today seems curiously dated. Paradoxically, the
calculatedly "independent" foreign policies pursued in recent years by
the likes of Argentina, Brazil, and Mexico derive much of their support
from nationalist resentments created by historical and continued United
States influence. The *dependencia* perspective also neglects the fact
that a sizable percentage of developed-country markets, investments,
and sources of supply are in the Third World.

There are obviously many forms of interdependence/dependency:
economic, political, military, social, cultural, psychological, and so
on. The extent of interdependence/dependency thus varies with the
issue-areas involved and the linkages among them. Ultimately, however, as we shall see in chapter 8, interdependence/dependency—like
power or national interest—are perceptions of the actors themselves.

While elements of realism, then, are alive and well, it is also the case
that fewer and fewer international relations scholars are any longer
prepared to accept the black box model of world politics. Our mental
maps of the world are probably growing closer to reality but at the cost
of parsimony, generalizability, and objectivity. A host of other approaches have emerged as competitors of realism in explaining foreign
policy. Unfortunately, none of these appears to have a potential to
achieve the same level of universal applicability as did realism. Such a

conclusion will emerge more clearly from a brief review of some of these approaches.

## ELITES AND SHARED IMAGES

Two closely related approaches—elites and shared images—share with cognitive theory a search for the sources of perceptions and misperceptions that are common to decisionmakers across institutional settings. On the other hand, these approaches are less daunted by what we have seen are the decision-specific ultimate implications of cognitive theory.

*Elites* theory seeks an explanation for foreign-policy behavior in "society," a different level of analysis from that stressed by students of decisionmaking who focus on "government." The concern is not only with the social origins of elites but also with their continued ties to powerful institutions and interests in society at large (e.g., the "military-industrial complex"). The elites approach, with an emphasis on the effects of various economic modes of production, is often—and quite correctly—associated with Marxist theory; however, one definitely need not be a Marxist analyst to recognize at least the existence of a foreign-policy "establishment" of sorts in most countries. Charles Kegley and Eugene Wittkopf, for example, write of the United States: "In terms of background and experience, the people making up the foreign policy-making elite are strikingly homogeneous. . . . [T]op-level decisionmakers are generally from the upper class and of WASP family origins, have been educated at the country's best schools and trained in law, and have extensive nongovernmental experience in major corporations and financial institutions." In addition: "Participation in politics and political aspiration may be functions of personality, with the consequence that those who seek positions of power share psychological traits that make them more like one another and less like 'average' Americans."[17] Of course, even if this description is accurate, it does not necessarily imply or allow the reader to infer any special impact on policy outcomes.

The work of Richard J. Barnet merits special attention because it is characteristic of elites analysis and also because its normative impulse is unusually explicit. Barnet states in *Roots of War:* "This analysis has grown out of a conviction that the United States had committed monumental crimes in Indochina and that these crimes are likely to be repeated unless we gain a much deeper understanding of what we have done as a nation and why we have done it."[18] His "thesis is that war is a social institution, that America's permanent war can be explained primarily by looking at American society, and that America's wars will cease only if that society is changed."[19] Barnet attempts to define "the elusive word 'we' so often invoked in state papers during the past generation."[20] He finds his explanations in a "governing class" with similar backgrounds that controls a vast bureaucracy; maintains a "partnership" with business interests; and rules over a public that tolerates and, even to some extent supports, the kind of international adventurism Barnet deplores. From this perspective, he argues: "The Vietnam War was certainly a mistake. But it was not an accident. The Vietnam policy arose from the same analysis of the national interest, from the same theories of statecraft and human behavior, from the same technological impetus, and from the same economic pressures that have been the driving forces behind America's successful wars."[21] And, once again, Barnet makes his normative agenda plain:

> If we are to recover our sanity as a nation and to earn again the decent opinion of those with whom we share the planet, including our own children, Americans must engage in serious self-examination of those drives within our society that impel us toward destruction. The chapters that follow offer a framework for such a social self-analysis, which, it is hoped, may lead to concrete acts of political and social reconstruction.[22]

While elites analysis seeks the wellsprings of foreign policy in society at large, what we have called (for want of a better term) the *shared images* approach looks variously for a national ideology, common national values, or at least shared assumptions among decisionmakers as to the nature of the world and desirability of certain policies (a "foreign policy consensus"). This approach, it is perhaps fair to say, cares less about the exact sources of shared images than the fact that some such images exist and that there appears to be a need to define them more clearly.

Even as one does not have to be a Marxist to have an interest in elites, one need not adopt the shared images approach exclusively to recognize that it has some validity and utility. Robert Jervis, a cognitive theorist, who, as we have seen, takes strong exception to Wolfers's fire-in-the-building analogy, nonetheless observes: "When we look at the major decisions of American foreign policy—those that set the terms for future debates and established the general framework within which policy was then conducted . . . what is most striking is the degree of unanimity."[23] Morton H. Halperin, drawing heavily on the work of Graham T. Allison—both of them primarily identified with the "governmental (bureaucratic) politics" approach (of which more later)—

lists some sixteen "shared images" of "American officials." In Halperin's formulation, these include items like the following: "The surest simple guide to U.S. interests in foreign policy is opposition to Communism"; "The United States has an obligation to aid any Free People resisting Communism at home or abroad"; "Nuclear war would be a great disaster and must be avoided."[24] According to Halperin, there are important reasons why such shared images tend to persist:

> [I]t is rare for the images shared within the government to diverge radically from those in society as a whole, and the appointment of individuals who cannot accept the broader images shared within the bureaucracy is probably equally rare. Moreover, the socialization process within the government is such that individuals who come in with doubts about, or in ignorance of, particular aspects of the set of shared images prevalent in the bureaucracy frequently find themselves quickly coming to support them.[25]

Similarly, Robert A. Packenham (following Louis Hartz) places his emphasis on four basic tenets of what he believes to be a "Liberal Tradition" in American political culture ("American exceptionalism"): Change and development are easy; all good things go together; radicalism and revolution are bad; and distributing political power is more important than accumulating it.[26]

The elites and shared images approaches perhaps help explain some of the unity and continuity in foreign-policy decisions in particular countries, but they fail miserably to account for what is often more interesting and significant—diversity and change. One of the perennial problems confronting the elites approach is how "elites" should be identified and the closely related question of to what extent they should be seen as unified or fragmented. Thomas R. Dye complains of "ideological disputation," "endless, unproductive debate," and a lack of "operational definitions, testable hypotheses, and reliable data" that have long confined this field of study to "the level of speculation, anecdote, or polemics."[27] He concludes his own in-depth study of elites in the United States with the summary statement: "Our findings do not all fit neatly into either an hierarchical, elitist model of power, or a polyarchical, pluralist model of power. We find evidence of both hierarchy and polyarchy in the nation's elite structure."[28] He illustrates this in the following manner:

> Approximately 6,000 individuals in 7,000 positions exercise formal authority over institutions that control roughly half of the nation's resources in industry, finance, utilities, insurance, mass

media, foundations, education, law, and civic and cultural affairs. This definition of the elite is fairly large numerically, yet these individuals constitute an extremely small percentage of the nation's total population—less than three-thousandths of 1 percent. . . . Perhaps the question of hierarchy or polyarchy depends upon whether one wants to emphasize numbers or percentages. To emphasize hierarchy, one can comment on the tiny *percentage* of the population that possesses such great authority. To emphasize polyarchy, one can comment on the fairly large *number* of individuals at the top of the nation's institutional structure; certainly there is room for competition within so large a group.[29]

Competition there has certainly been. Traditional pluralist theory posited overlapping contests between political parties, conservatives and liberals, business and labor, and so on. Elites theory, as Dye sees it, "emphasizes underlying cohesion among elite groups, but still admits of some factionalism." A widely recognized "source of factionalism is the emergence of new sources of wealth and new 'self-made' individuals who do not fully share the prevailing values of established elites." Dye labels these dissenters "the Sunbelt cowboys," and they have been major contributors to the Reagan "conservative" (some would say "radical reactionary") tide in recent years.[30] According to Dye:

The federal law-making process involves bargaining, competition, persuasion, and compromise, as generally set forth in "pluralist" political theory. But this interaction occurs *after* the agenda for policy-making has been established and the major directions of policy changes have already been determined. The decisions of proximate policy-makers are not unimportant, but they tend to center about the *means* rather than the *ends* of national policy.[31]

However, terming "decisions of proximate policy-makers" as "not unimportant" may be a serious understatement, not least because (as we have mentioned) in actual policymaking means and ends often become so intertwined as to be virtually indistinguishable.

An initial problem facing the shared image approach is the usual—and usually fatal—one of definition. It is no accident that, beyond a few obvious things like anticommunism, lists of such images/values almost invariably differ greatly, as do Packenham's and Halperin's. One cannot resist the temptation to ask questions like: If most United States officials have held it as an article of faith that "the United States has an obligation to aid any Free People resisting communism at home or abroad," why was there no more meaningful response to the Hungarian uprising in 1956 or the 1968 Russian intervention in Czechoslavakia? Was the shared image that only rhetorical "aid" need be given, or didn't the Hungarians or Czechs qualify as "Free People," or was the obligation to be waived in the event that a superpower confrontation loomed?

Nor is this approach capable of explaining (let alone predicting) changes in shared images,[32] like the apparent rise and fall of a U.S. commitment to the international advancement of human rights (except in communist countries) that took place between the Carter and Reagan administrations. Halperin speaks of the effect of changes in government personnel especially on regional policies, of the fact that "events in the outside world may bring about fundamental changes in the way American society looks at the world" (the sixties and Vietnam is his example), and of the phenomenon that "changes in national mood lead to changes in the images of the world held by the population at large" and "these changes come to be reflected in the bureaucracy."[33] Richard Cottam posits a "presidential decision-making level," with a "worldview" that becomes increasingly relevant in times of crisis and is more capable of change than the bureaucratic level.[34] However, claims such as these are remarkably vague and unsatisfying for the purposes of theory-building.

A final criticism of the shared images approach is perhaps the most significant and gets back to the matter of ends versus means that has already been raised: Even if we could agree on what the relevant shared images/values are, decisionmakers still must wrestle with value trade-offs and translate objectives into specific policies. For instance, a shared-images defender might insist, possibly quite correctly in the most general sense, that *both* the Carter and Reagan administrations recognized a United States obligation to support human rights abroad. Nevertheless, how does one then explain the relative priority attached to this goal in the two administrations, the different weights they assigned to Soviet violations versus violations in countries friendly to the United States, the contrast between Carter's pressure on South Africa and Reagan's "constructive engagement," and so on? Leading up to his own personal interest in bureaucratic politics, Halperin comments: "A proposed course of action that can be shown to be unambiguously necessary to preserve a shared objective will be agreed to by all. However, this is a very rare event."[35] In his view, shared images are more useful in predicting what decisionmakers will *not* do than what they will do: "Widely shared images often do lead to agreement on basic objectives and therefore to the exclusion of certain conceivable courses of action."[36] To be sure, Washington officials will be exceedingly unlikely to pop champagne corks and raise a glass in celebration of a victory for communism anywhere in the world. The shared values approach allows us an "insight" like that, but not much more.

## GROUP DYNAMICS

We turn next to two additional approaches, *groupthink* and *cybernetics,* that focus on the psychological dynamics of particular decisionmaking groups. "Groupthink" is identified primarily with the work of Irving Janis,[37] which found its inspiration in the Vietnam experience and then was extended to other case studies. The thrust of the groupthink perspective is the argument that decisionmaking groups, especially but not exclusively small groups, develop similar mind sets (attitudinal conformity). The cybernetic approach, according to John Steinbruner,[38] involves a search for the "routine behavior of men in organizational settings."[39] Steinbruner sees an organization as essentially a "servomechanism," that is, "a very simple decision mechanism but one with considerable logical power."[40] Organizations develop their own views of the world and standard operating procedures, which are designed to minimize uncertainty and to ensure institutional survival; hence, organizations respond to their environment in a remarkably stable, predictable, and unimaginative fashion. Joseph H. de Rivera discusses several related "constraints" affecting "organizational perception": There are always competing interests in an organization; officials are usually pressed for time; "the conflict of interests often prevents any action that is not absolutely necessary"; and "there are often legitimate differences of opinion as to what a situation is really like." Therefore, "the organization will 'view' as reality whatever will help to establish a consensus" and allow it to act; and the path of least resistance is normally "the policy they currently believe in."[41]

The cybernetic approach is distinguishable from other approaches, though just barely so in several instances. Insofar as it highlights attitudinal conformity—at least as expressed in an organization's traditional worldview, procedures, and policies (albeit masking internal divisions)—cybernetic theory might be regarded as groupthink writ large. Steinbruner, as we have seen, speaks of studying "the routine behavior of men in organizational settings," but his emphasis is mainly on organizations as actors because they develop their own identity into which decisionmakers *to a significant extent* submerge theirs. The separate identities of organizations quickly lead one into the realm of the "governmental (bureaucratic) politics" approach. Lastly, to the extent that decisionmakers *do not* submerge their own identities into the organizational whole, we must either refer to the individual as actor or return to the cognitive approaches.

As theory, both groupthink and the cybernetic approach are significantly limited. Despite what we have said, it is difficult to extend the concept of groupthink much beyond cases where a relatively small group of persons is involved in making important decisions and then only when a clear consensus emerges that appears to be based on shared misperceptions. On the other hand, as Steinbruner is the first to acknowledge, the cybernetic approach "still resides largely in the laboratories of basic research." In his opinion, it is not only insufficiently developed, but also "there are two critical problems with cybernetic logic":

> First . . . it is unclear how cybernetic decision processes might
> work for the complex environments of public policy, which are
> highly interactive and not rigidly or simply structured. Second,
> the cybernetic paradigm projects a view of the human mind
> (clearly the ultimate locus of decisionmaking), which does not
> account for one of its most critical faculties—the ability to make
> inductive inferences on its own initiative. Both problems indicate
> the need to supplement simple cybernetic theories in building a
> paradigm of the decision process competitive with that operating
> in rational decision theory.[42]

Steinbruner finds the required supplement in cognitive theory: "In essence," he says, "it is cognitive operations of the human mind working in interaction with the organizational structure of the government which set workable limits on highly diffuse decision problems, and it is cybernetic theory, thus supplemented, which offers a base paradigm for political analysis competitive with the rational position."[43]

Yet it is precisely what is meant by the "working in interaction" with the cognitive approach—not to mention groupthink and governmental (bureaucratic) politics—that is not adequately spelled out in cybernetic theory. De Rivera states the key problem succinctly: "Our current language and thinking is not precise enough to indicate exactly what an organization is and how it behaves; we are forced to rely on terms . . . which really apply to the behavior of individuals or machines."[44] He argues the need to exercise great care in the use of such terminology:

> It does not seem to me that we should speak of an organization
> as though it were either an individual or a machine. Its behavior
> is not motivated in the sense that a person feels himself to be

motivated, nor is it determined by the constraints that govern the behavior of even the most complicated machine. An organization does not really perceive events or make decisions; that is done by individuals in the organization. On the other hand, an organization does exist in its own right—it is not simply the sum total of the individuals in it—and it does act.[45]

### "PLAYERS IN POSITIONS"

A last approach we will consider, *governmental (bureaucratic) politics*, conceives of policymaking as an elaborate bargaining game among decisionmakers who are "players in positions." According to Graham T. Allison: "The governmental actor is neither a unitary agent nor a conglomerate of organizations, but rather is a number of individual players. . . . Players are men in jobs."[46] In this game, "where you sit influences what you see as well as where you stand (on any issue)"[47]; and the policy outcome is the result of competition and compromise, "pulling and hauling"—often an outcome that none of the individual players exactly wanted or anticipated. Assessing the normative implications of this perspective, Stephen D. Krasner complains that it appears to relieve decisionmakers of any ultimate responsibility for their actions:

> The failure of the American government to take decisive action in a number of critical areas reflects not so much the inertia of a large bureaucratic machine as a confusion over values which afflicts the society in general and its leaders in particular. It is, in such circumstances, too comforting to attribute failure to organizational inertia, although nothing could be more convenient for political leaders who have either not formulated any policy or advocated bad policies [than to] blame their failures on the governmental structure.[48]

The governmental (bureaucratic) politics approach suffered at its inception from some confusion regarding its label. As Kim Richard Nossel correctly explains:

> Because Allison chose to term it a "governmental (bureaucratic) politics" paradigm (and subsequently used, with Halperin, the term "bureaucratic politics"), the model is invariably interpreted as focusing on bureaucracies and bureaucrats alone. However, Allison makes it clear in *Essence of Decision* that the proper focus of the model should be on "players in positions," which includes players in bureaucracies, in the legislative branch, or in

the political executive. Similarly, there is no distinction between "Indians and Chiefs" (to use his term): a "player in position" can be a desk officer in the foreign ministry or the head of government.[49]

A careful reading of Allison does clarify his intentions as to the relevant players, but this, if anything, only compounds the problems inherent in the governmental (bureaucratic) approach.

A first major problem with the approach is that it appears to rest on the dubious assumption that "bureaucratic" actors behave in a "rational" fashion (though not according to some abstract criterion of national interest). To allow some of the insights of cognitive theory to creep in would completely change the nature of the "game." As Steinbruner points out, cognitive actors "will by-pass bargains which under analytic assumptions would appear to be obvious."[50] Yet the precise nature of this rationality is unclear. It is not the ideal rationality described by Verba, and it grows from more parochial roots than the rationality that realists derive from the national interest.

Second, to the extent that the actions of individual players in the game reflect their institutional role and loyalty—that is, insofar as their primary goal in the competition is to preserve their organization's health and mission—would it not be better to conceive of them as just extensions of the "organizational process"? This, of course, is the province of the cybernetic approach.

Third, it is decidedly unclear where the boundary exists (if it does at all) between institutional role performance and idiosyncratic behavior. Robert J. Art observes: "Organizational role (or institutional responsibility) is a component of a participant's outlook, but often only a component and often not even the overriding one."[51] Leading theorists of the governmental (bureaucratic) politics school only muddy the waters on this score. Halperin, for example, states: "The way an individual copes with . . . uncertainty is affected by his background—the personal experiences, intellectual baggage, and psychological needs he brings with him—as well as by his position in the bureaucracy."[52] And Allison throws everything into his kitchen but the veritable sink:

> The hard core of the bureaucratic politics mix is personality. How each man manages to stand the heat in *his* kitchen, each player's operating style, and the complementarity or contradiction among personalities and styles in the inner circle are irreducible pieces of the policy blend. Then, too, each person comes to his position with baggage in tow. His bags include sensitivities to

certain issues, commitments to various projects, and personal
standing with and debts to groups in the society.[53]

Yet the relative weight of the several variables identified by Halperin
and Allison and the relationship among them are not clarified.

A fourth criticism is that it is extremely hard to determine the degree
to which institutions like Congress or particular executive departments
are actors in their own right or are merely conduits for the demands of
their clientele. If the latter is the case, the analytical emphasis should
be on interest groups or "pluralism" rather than on governmental (bureaucratic) entities. Stephen Krasner, for example, classifies the United
States as basically "a weak political system":

> [C]entral decisionmakers may find it difficult to overcome the
> resistance of specific societal interest groups, because political
> power in the United States is fragmented and decentralized. There
> are many points of entry to the political system, especially in
> Congress and some executive bureaus. Once an issue falls into
> these decisionmaking arenas state preferences can be blocked.
> The American polity resembles a black ball system. Any major
> actor, public or private, can often prevent the adoption of a pol-
> icy.[54]

A fifth problem is how to establish the precise identity of the
governmental/bureaucratic "players" involved in the decisionmaking
process. Policy is often made by a shifting set of ad hoc committees.
Moreover, in most countries, numerous bureaucratic roles tend to overlap. In the United States, for example, the president's political appointments to top-level posts in the bureaucracy assure at least a modicum of
presidential control, even as the individuals concerned find themselves
immediately counterpressured to represent their agency's interests to
the president and to cultivate a close working relationship with key
committees and committee chairmen in Congress.

Bureaucratic divisions are further blurred by the fact that policy differences exist not only *among* various agencies but also *within* them
(and within clientele interest groups like "business" or "farmers," as
well), setting up the possibility (indeed, probability) of interagency and
interclientele factional alliances. Congress, in particular, is so fragmented that it has no true spokesperson and rarely expresses through
its votes anything approaching a genuine consensus. "There is no single theory of behavior," argues Stephen D. Cohen, "that can explain

all of the attitudes and actions of the two houses of the U.S. Congress."
He is probably correct when he argues:

> The concepts that the vast majority of its members wish to be
> reelected and that congressional members are responsive to out-
> side stimuli, mainly the constituents, the executive branch, and
> special interest groups, are too broad to predict or rationalize the
> nature and history of congressional performance. The U.S. Con-
> gress, while frequently adhering to general theories of organiza-
> tional behavior and specific behavioral models, is often a
> mystifying institution with a number of important idiosyncracies.
> It has been suggested that no one who has not served or worked
> in the legislative branch for many years can fully comprehend
> the techniques and vicissitudes of the Congress's pattern of opera-
> tion.[55]

The United States, following Krasner, may have its *black ball* dimension, but that is not to say that its governmental/bureaucratic entities
(any more than the state itself) should be treated as *black boxes*.

Putting aside the difficulty of identifying the players, yet a sixth
problem is the task of establishing their relative influence in the policy-
making process. Allison's answer is hopelessly tautological: "Power
(i.e., effective influence on government decisions and actions) is an
elusive blend of at least three elements: bargaining advantages [Allison
"explains" that these are such things as formal authority and control
over information], skill and will in using bargaining advantages, and
other players' perceptions of the first two ingredients."[56] "Elusive
blend" it certainly is! Krasner insists that Allison gives inadequate
attention to the role of the president as a "king" standing above all the
bureaucratic "chiefs."[57] Or, is it the perception that a "crisis" exists
that brings the president to the fore?

Is a more important variable the nature of the issues involved and
their attributes? James N. Rosenau, for example, points to what he
calls "interdependence issues" (food, seabed mining, pollution, and
the like) that are highly technical in nature, encompass many nongovernmental actors, and appear to require additional multilateral cooperation. Such issues, he argues, tend to "fragment the governmental
decision-making process" and therefore to give additional "authority
and clout" to bureaucratic agencies with appropriate technical expertise and links to specialized clientele.[58] Rosenau writes:

> Whereas the traditional issues of foreign and military policy are
> founded on nation-wide constituencies and can be managed by

heads of state and prime ministers through their foreign offices
and military establishments, interdependence issues render the
politically responsible leadership much more subject to the advice, direction, contradictions and compromises that emanate
from a fragmented bureaucratic structure. They normally do not
have the time or expertise to master the knowledge necessary to
grasp fully such issues and ordinarily they lack the political forti-
tude to resist, much less reject, the pressures from the special
clienteles that seek to be served. . . ."[59]

A seventh and final major problem with the governmental (bureaucratic) politics approach[60] is that its relevance depends upon the nature
of the particular political systems/societies in which players are enmeshed. This leads us to the subject of comparative foreign policy.

## THE COMPARATIVE STUDY OF FOREIGN POLICY: APPLES, ORANGES, BUT VERY LITTLE FRUIT

At the height of the "scientific" wave in the study of international
politics during the 1960s, significant empirical breakthroughs were
thought to be only just around the corner in the field of comparative
foreign policy. With great enthusiasm, James Rosenau declared that:
"All the signs are pointing in the same direction: as a television commercial might describe it, 'Comparative Foreign Policy is coming on
strong for the 1970s!' "[61]

Rosenau's seminal essay published in 1966 on "Pre-Theories and
Theories of Foreign Policy" speaks volumes in its very title about the
expectations that characterized that period, even as the number of categories (five variables, eight types of "societies") he advanced and the
difficulty of operationalizing such concepts as "small" versus "large"
country and "developed" versus "underdeveloped" society offered
more than a hint of grave problems lurking over the horizon.[62] As it
transpired, the theories to which his categories were to be "pre" never
materialized, and lacking theoretical guidelines, the veritable field day
of quantification that ensued contributed little to the task of comparison
and generalization. Christer Jonsson observes:

Whereas the early calls for nomothetic rather than idiographic
orientation, scientific rigour and statistical treatment of data met
with considerable enthusiasm, the subdiscipline is now accused
of using deterministic logic for indeterminate phenomena, of
confusing correlation with causation, of selecting variables in

terms of their quantifiability, and of using simple indicators of multidimensional concepts.[63]

Patrick J. McGowan and Howard B. Shapiro, two leading proponents of the "scientific" approach to comparative foreign policy, surveyed some 200 research studies in 1973 and candidly admitted: "Recognizably empirical theory is so scarce that our ability to explain and predict that it is uninteresting except to a few specialists." Unfortunately, there has been little improvement in this regard, for, as late as 1982, Linda Brady was suggesting, the most commonly and explicitly conceptualized properties [of] doing foreign policy [are] scattered throughout the literature [and] need to be developed into ...

McGowan and Shapiro's principal explanation for the lack of existing empirical theory was what they saw as a regrettable division of labor between "theorists" and "empiricists." In the empiricists' view: "Much of the systematically sophisticated work in comparative foreign policy studies has been theoretical ex post facto"; that is, "quantitatively oriented scholars have tended to collect data prior to theorizing and then they have proceeded to analyze these data in a bivariate fashion."[66] On the other hand, "theorists" had erred by concentrating on individual case studies rather than comparisons and by paying inadequate "attention to formal theory as embodied in mathematical models and computer simulations." Despite these problems and still other shortcomings that they identified, McGowan and Shapiro were confident that good empirical theory could yet be developed, which would, in turn, even serve as the basis for policy evaluation and prescription.[67]

Expressions of faith along these lines now seem as dated as the assumptions about the capacity to engineer "development" that undergirded the "foreign aid" programs of the 1960s. Much more common today are expressions of despair, like that of Bahgot Korany, the editor of a recent collection of essays on foreign policy in the Third World: "If the study of the foreign policies of underdeveloped countries is underdeveloped, the systematic analysis of their foreign policy decisions is not. It is simply nonexistent." Korany acknowledges that there are difficulties in securing (and creating) data, but he believes that the fundamental issue is "the relevance of foreign policy theory": "Not only is this 'theory's' applicability to the Third World situation still to be demonstrated, but the field is still dominated by debates over the best approach and even over basics such as the definition of foreign policy itself."[68] Indeed, it is improbable that the comparative study of foreign policy will make much headway until this and other basic questions that we articulated earlier in this chapter are satisfactorily answered.

The fragmentation of the field after the collapse of the rational model has greatly complicated not only the task of "explaining" the foreign policy of particular countries but also the search for valid bases for comparison. Idiosyncratic behavior as an approach might seem to have special relevance to the few countries dominated by old-style dictators, charismatic leaders, unusually strong elected chief executives, or powerful foreign ministers. However, the approach is, by definition, so tied to the idiosyncracies of particular individuals that it is obviously limited as a tool for comparison.

Nor do we know the extent to which the patterns of perceptions/ misperceptions highlighted by cognitive theory, groupthink, and cybernetics are applicable to decisionmakers in all countries or are significantly modified by different cultures or types of government. In any event, it is hard to imagine how "perceptions" or "motivations" can really be compared across national boundaries unless "decisionmakers" are treated—contrary to the most interesting insights of cognitive theory—as unified, rational actors. For this reason, Kal J. Holsti, for example, investigated what he called "national roles" through content analysis of the speeches of high-level policymakers of seventy-one countries.[69] In addition to the rational-actor issue, questions come to mind regarding the reliability of the data (speeches as indicators of perceived roles) and the extent to which "role" is defined by "self" or others.[70] Moreover, the results of Holsti's study, although thought-provoking, are at such a high level of generalization that it is difficult to link them to specific policies.

This last problem we have noted is also characteristic of the elites and shared values approaches. Consider, for instance, Henry Kissinger's classification of "leadership" into three types—"bureaucratic-pragmatic," "ideological," and "charismatic-revolutionary."[71] The scheme appears to allow little room, say, for the pursuit of pragmatic initiatives by Soviet leaders or by Fidel Castro, or for such ideological policies on the part of American leaders as Jimmy Carter's campaign for human rights and Ronald Reagan's crusade against the "evil empire."

However, the dangers of ethnocentrism are especially evident with regard to the governmental (bureaucratic) politics approach. This approach appears to be unusually applicable to the United States because of the sheer size and diversity of the U.S. bureaucracy, as well as for three other important reasons. First, the constitutional separation of powers gives the president and the executive branch, at once, major responsibility in the field of foreign policy, while allowing competition in the exercise thereof from an independent legislature (power over budget, treaties, appointments, and so on) and an independent judiciary. Power is thus, paradoxically, concentrated in the president and yet is still remarkably fragmented. Second, bureaucracies within the executive branch are expected to build close working relationships with both clientele interest groups and relevant congressional committees, which greatly increases bureaucratic autonomy from the White House. Third, the "rules of the game" of American politics allow for spirited and often public competition among bureaucratic agencies in the shaping of public policy.[72]

The foreign-policy role of the U.S. president is hardly identical with, for example, that of the British prime minister, a charismatic leader like Castro, a military junta, or a Soviet premier/general secretary. Moreover, the U.S. Congress has far more direct and indirect influence over foreign policy than any other national legislature, and, since Vietnam, there has been a greater propensity to exercise that influence. In contrast, with regard to external affairs, other national legislatures are little more than a cheering section or a rubber stamp for an executive or, at best, a debating society that gives air to a few key issues. With a more active contest between the president and Congress underway since the late 1960s, as well as the growing importance of international economic issues, the courts in the United States have also become more visible in affecting foreign policy; this, too, is a development unparalleled elsewhere in the world.[73]

When it comes to bureaucracies per se, the distinction between the United States pattern and that of other countries is somewhat more subtle, but substantial nevertheless. In the sense that the governments of even many Third World countries have become increasingly bureaucratized, rivalry among agencies is much more of a global phenomenon than it used to be. For instance, in Brazil the traditional dominance of the foreign ministry (Itamaraty) has recently been severely challenged by a host of entities—ministries of planning, finance, industry, commerce, mines and energy, along with the Bank of Brazil and the Central Bank—brought to the fore by international economic issues.[74]

However, the character of bureaucratic competition varies tremendously in different political systems, and the model may lack general applicability. Nossal concludes a Canadian case study with the observation that:

> [I]n parliamentary systems the concentration of political authority
> in the cabinet allows the political executive to impose constraints
> on legitimate conflict between policy-makers at lower levels in
> the decision process. This is not to suggest that there will not be
> divergences of interest between players in the foreign policy
> game in parliamentary systems, but rather that their propensities
> to engage in conflict to ensure that their preferences will be trans-
> formed into policy may be sharply reduced by the imposition of
> central authority.[75]

And Stephen Cohen's careful analysis of policymaking for international economic relations in a number of Western countries tends to
bear out Nossal's generalization: The style in Britain's Whitehall is to
mute policy differences so as to give every possible appearance of a
common front to the public. In Germany, the ministries seem almost to
coordinate themselves, insofar as top-level decisions rarely have to be
made to resolve which bureaucracies will prevail over particular issues.
Japanese decisionmaking proceeds in glacial fashion while bureaucrats
engage in polite negotiations leading to mutual accommodation. And so
on.[76]

Differences country to country are also pronounced with regard to
bureaucratic relations with their interest-group clienteles. A striking
and unique example is the relationship between the powerful Ministry
of International Trade and Industry (MITI) and big business in Japan.
Unlike Japan, in so-called corporatist systems, many groups are initially organized by government; only a few are officially recognized as
legitimate; and those that are recognized tend to exist in a symbiotic
relationship with government bureaucracies that is considerably more
dependent in nature than the MITI example or any notion of a "clientele" in the United States. Comparative politics specialists originally
developed the corporatist model, from Iberian and Italian precedents,
mainly in an attempt to characterize the "new" military regimes that
emerged in Latin America in the 1960s and 1970s.[77] Corporatist may
also be about as good a label as any for the Getulio Vargas and Juan
Perón regimes, as well as for the Mexican one-party system. On the
other hand, the current trend toward re-democratization suggests that
what transpires today in most Latin American countries is an uneasy
balance between corporatism and liberal democracy, both of which
have roots in the past. Meanwhile, a so-called neocorporatist approach

has been applied by some scholars to the analysis of collaboration between government and interest groups in the making and implementing of public policies in Western Europe, especially in Scandinavia.[78]

There are other relationships of potential significance to policymakers, as well, including those with political parties and "public opinion" at large. In one-party systems, of course, the line between "government" and "party" is at best poorly defined. Where more than one political party exists and there is any semblance of election campaigns (even when one party is clearly dominant and the system is thus not "competitive" in the fullest sense), parties can help to articulate foreign policy and other issues. Occasionally, however, party competition can be downright paralyzing, as it has often been, for example, in Italy, the Netherlands, or Bolivia.

Presumably, even leaders in authoritarian regimes have some concern about maintaining at least a minimum level of popular support for their policies. The Argentine military, for instance, found that initiating and then bungling the Falklands/Malvinas war made it impossible for them to go on ruling. In reasonably democratic systems, on the other hand, it is usually said that the public "mood" sets the broad constraints on policies, if only because many policymakers must face the voters at election time. To be sure, voters rarely have clear views on foreign-policy issues, nor are they often offered a clear "choice" as to policies in elections. However, Bernard C. Cohen writes of the United States that, "while officials routinely deny any *obligation* to pay attention to public opinion, in practice they admit—sometimes readily, sometimes reluctantly—to *responsive* behavior;"[79] and they often devote considerable time and effort to trying to manipulate public opinion. Cohen remarks:

> [W]e have to ask whether those efforts do not themselves constitute a significant *direct* opinion input into the policy process. The mechanism involved is a feedback loop, in the sense that foreign policy officials dominate the public discussion of a policy, which they (and Congressmen also) then monitor and on the basis of which they draw conclusions about their freedom to take next steps. The loop may not even go any further or deeper than the media of communication. . . .[80]

Cohen's observation points up yet another influence, the role of the media, whose impact, too, obviously varies greatly from country to country. It is noteworthy in this connection that Richard L. Merritt ends his examination of public opinion and foreign policy in West Germany with the caution:

> The striking differences between the structures of the West German and American political systems suggest that findings generated for one may not be directly applicable to the other.
> Moreover, neither set of findings may apply to France, Belgium, or any of the other industrialized countries of Western Europe, not to speak of the rest of the world.[81]

Finally, no meaningful comparison can fail to consider either the effect of the relative autonomy on certain issues granted to territorial components of various federal and decentralized unitary systems[82] or the impact of those "outlaw" groups that refuse to play by the political system's rules of the game. The Belgian government, for example, must pay careful attention to the relative impact that *any* policy decision (foreign or domestic) will have on the Flemish and French-speaking regions of the country. As for "outlaws," particularly in Latin America and Africa, to what extent should the military be regarded as "just another" bureaucratic actor? The military is certainly not like other bureaucracies in that it has a special capacity, regularly exercised, to wield force to impose its policy preferences and to protect its institutional interests. And what of large restive ethnic groups (as in South Africa, these may not be "minorities"),[83] multinational corporations, terrorist groups, or guerrilla movements—and their external allies?[84] Another example that springs to mind are organized criminals like drug dealers. Military involvement in drugs led to the 1980 "cocaine coup" of General Garcia Meza in Bolivia. Local drug peddlers have declared open warfare upon Colombian and United States enforcement officials, and Mexican cooperation in antidrug campaigns has been severely undercut by government corruption.


## CONCLUSION: A CONTINUING SEARCH FOR THE SOURCE(S) OF FOREIGN POLICY

Proponents of the comparative method looked to it for an answer to the persistent problem of ethnocentricity. In fact, it has proven more of a nostrum than a genuine cure. In part, this is because certain phenomena are genuinely unique to individual societies and are sufficiently important that masking them in an effort to highlight similarities effectively hides key conditioning factors. In addition, the effort to compare has necessitated casting other phenomena at such a level of abstraction and/or vagueness that resulting research has virtually no conceivable applicability to the real world. While it effectively focused attention on the need for precision in the study of foreign policy, many of the early hopes that accompanied the birth of the comparative foreign policy approach have been dashed.

The depreciation of the traditional "black box" model has left us with an acute case of theoretical overload, and, in this respect, to paraphrase Robert Jervis, we decidedly *do not* understand better what we are really about. Opening the "black box" may have been like opening Pandora's box.

To be fair, scholars like Allison, Jervis, Steinbruner, and Rosenau have never suggested that their particular approaches should be relied on to the exclusion of others. Quite the contrary, they have stressed that their contributions merely illuminate one or another of the significant dimensions of the complex reality that is the foreign-policymaking process, rather like a cubist painting depicts an object from various points of view. However, adding to the complexity does not, in itself, improve our understanding; in fact, in this instance the effect has been to leave us even more profoundly confused.

The essential difficulty is not the definitional and other weaknesses of each individual theoretical approach although, as we have seen, these are serious enough. Rather, the main problem is that we have too many choices of approaches, a host of "new" variables and less discrete levels of analysis that we have no effective means of ordering and integrating. We have an expanded checklist of factors that *may* influence foreign policy but no sure way of assessing their importance in particular cases, let alone comparing or generalizing. As a consequence, genuine empirical theory as convincing and useful, say, as that which students of American politics have in the field of voting behavior seems entirely beyond our grasp.

Our vase or bowl of fruit has now been left to each individual artist to paint as he/she wills. Theoretical cubism has been carried to such an extreme that the object under scrutiny has almost disappeared from view. In sum, despite our increasing theoretical sophistication and the accumulation of much more data since the heyday of realism, we still are far from *knowing* who or what makes foreign policy—or even how to go about finding out.

# 8

# The Challenge of Anarchy and the Search for Order

The development of theory regarding any phenomenon presupposes predictability, yet for many observers the defining characteristic of international relations remains anarchy. The effort to reconcile these apparently paradoxical assumptions has been a recurrent challenge to theorists for generations.[1] There were, for example, significant differences among classical scholars in the emphasis placed upon anarchy. Rousseau and Hobbes, for example, stressed the absence of bonds among international actors and the consequent propensity for conflict among them. In contrast, Hugo Grotius pointed to the presence of common interests and solidarity that constrain the autonomy of actors and limit conflict.[2]

## ANARCHY: THE DEFINING CHARACTERISTIC OF THE FIELD

Unpredictability is, of course, an extreme version of anarchy, and few scholars or statesmen have perceived international relations as equivalent to chaos. Minimally, scholars are forced to assume that behavior is patterned that prediction is possible and that the phenomena they are studying, while constantly changing, do so sufficiently slowly that descriptions and explanations provided one day will be valid the next.

The weaker definition of anarchy is simply the absence of central authority, allegedly in contrast to the well-ordered domesticity of inter-

**186**

nal politics. In other words, international politics consists of the interactions of sovereign nation-states, each of which enjoys a monopoly of
the means of coercion within its frontiers but above which there is no
higher authority. This simple dichotomy between the international and
domestic spheres—for centuries the basis for assuming that international politics was distinctive—appears an increasingly dubious proposition. "Linkages" among issues in both arenas are apparent, and it
has become virtually impossible to assess either sphere in isolation
from the other. Additionally, the distinction between the two spheres
based on the assumption of centralized authority in the one and its
absence in the other (the correlative of which is the assumption of
relative peace and order in the former and disorder and violence in the
other) is patently inaccurate.[3] If, however, there is nothing distinctive
about behavior in the international sphere, then it is necessary to ask
whether the traditional disciplinary boundaries serve any purpose and,
going further, to ask why so little effort has been made toward developing an integrated theory of politics *sui generis*.

In practice, the conventional definition of international politics as an
anarchical arena, although utilized by countless textbooks as a defining
characteristic of the field, serves more of a metaphorical than an analytic purpose. It signifies little more than the obvious absence of central authority in world politics, the corollary of which is that actors are
free to and, indeed, have no choice but to rely on their own devices
("self-help"). Despite its limited analytic value, we cannot dismiss the
"anarchy" concept lightly because, as a metaphor, it has exercised and
continues to exercise a powerful hold on the imagination of observers
and participants. Most importantly, it is used to explain and legitimize
the resort to coercion and the repeated occurrence of discord and conflict in international politics. It is widely accepted that the absence of
authority, as Kenneth Waltz declares, "is a permissive or underlying
cause of war" in the sense that "wars occur because there is nothing to
prevent them."[4]

There are both strong and weak variants of this claim, but, whatever
form it takes, it serves as the premise for most analyses of international
relations. In international law, it is the basis of permitting self-help and
self-defense; in game theory, it is the logic of "prisoner's dilemmas"
and, by extension, the nonmathematical application of "maximin"
strategies; and it is a lynchpin of foreign and defense policy even in the

nuclear age. One of its consequences is to focus scholarly and policy analyses on conflict—how to prevent it, minimize it, or engage in it effectively.

Unfortunately, this central metaphor of anarchy turns attention away from describing and explaining the *dominant* patterns of peace and cooperation in international relations, as well as from the fact that the threat of violence is probably greater within many societies than among them. While in no way denying the critical importance of conflict and the threat of war in international relations, such preoccupation has precluded concerted efforts to understand the causes of peace and order. The equivalent in microeconomics would be to study corporate failures rather than corporate successes when starting up a business enterprise and trying to comprehend what conditions are likely to bring prosperity to the organization.

## INTERDEPENDENCE: THE HIDDEN CONSTRAINT

Although the assumption of anarchy pervades analyses of conflict, there is also widespread recognition that actors are not free to do as they please, that conflict is minimized by the interests of actors in sustaining global patterns of cooperation, and that anarchy is severely attenuated by interdependence. Thus, maximin strategies are viable only in zero-sum games of which there are virtually none in international relations.

Increasingly disillusioned by the bankruptcy of seeking a military solution to the Vietnam conflict and attracted by the possibly revolutionary implications of East-West détente, scholars in the 1960s and 1970s began to turn their attention to those aspects of world politics that seemed to contradict the assumption of anarchy. These factors, generally lumped under the heading of interdependence, were viewed as providing the intellectual wherewithal for opening up new theoretical vistas in international politics and for escaping the sterility of analyses based on power politics.

The apparent futility of force revealed by Vietnam reinforced existing frustrations regarding the East-West arms race and the nuclear stalemate. In addition, there emerged a new generation of scholars who were persuaded that the critical issues of the future were fundamentally economic and environmental in nature. Moreover, they believed that the emphasis on power politics had involved their predecessors too closely with government, thereby limiting the independence of the academic community and precluding its addressing and starting to overcome these serious problems. In addition to Vietnam and détente, other events and factors that had influenced these scholars included the oil embargo of 1973 and predictions of energy and other resource shortfalls, the plight of the Palestinians and the growth in ethnic discontent globally, the increasing frequency of incidents of international terrorism, the report of the Club of Rome, the growing demands of developing societies for a greater share of the international economic pie, and high rates of inflation in the West.

Influenced by the growth in the flow of transactions across national boundaries, many theorists in the 1970s and 1980s concluded that interdependence was intensifying.[5] But they disagreed about what the concept means. For example, Richard Rosecrance et al. observed that: "In a very loose and general sense, one can say that interdependence is a state of affairs where what one nation does impinges directly upon other nations. In this most general sense, higher foreign trade, the ability to threaten atomic war, the development of worldwide inflation or recession all mean higher interdependence among states." However, this broad but vague conceptualization "is quite unsatisfactory for analytic purposes," embracing as it does everything from "fully cooperative" to "fully conflictful" relations among states—with the highest level of interdependence perhaps existing between "opponents in war," where "any improvement in one state's position would directly and adversely affect the other."[6] Instead, for Rosecrance et al.:

> "[I]nterdependence" [should be seen as] the direct and positive linkage of the interests of states such that when one state changes, the position of others is affected, *and in the same direction.* Interdependence, then, suggests a system in which states tend to go up or down the ladder of international position (economic strength, power, welfare, access to information and/or technology) together. . . . Wherever interdependence is high, there should be high cooperation.[7]

By contrast, Robert Keohane and Joseph Nye, Jr. insisted that the concept of interdependence should not be limited to situations of "mutual benefit":

> Where there are reciprocal (although not necessarily symmetrical) costly effects of transactions, there is interdependence. . . . [I]nterdependent relationships will always involve costs, since interdependence restricts autonomy; but it is impossible to specify *a priori* whether the benefits of a relationship will exceed the costs.

This will depend on the values of the actors as well as on the nature of the relationship.[8]

They go on to describe two dimensions of interdependence: "sensitivity" or the responsiveness of one actor to events occurring in another, and "vulnerability" or the ability of an actor to insulate itself from events occurring elsewhere.[9] Sadly, then, discussions of interdependence are, as Waltz puts it, "confused by the use of dissimilar definitions."[10]

Not surprisingly, considering divergences as to definitions, theorists differ even as to the degree of economic interdependence in contemporary global politics. Rosecrance and his colleagues argue that in the contemporary world industrialized societies no longer stand to profit—as they did prior to 1914—from the operation of free market forces; U.S. hegemony has been declining; the response of one economy to another has become less predictable; and the advantages that might be derived from greater multilateral cooperation have not been fully explored.[11] Stephen Cohen views the situation as one of "mutual dependency" arising from "the growing obsolescence of the nation-state as an entity capable of serving its people's economic needs."[12] Keohane argues that international cooperation among advanced industrial countries "has probably been more extensive than international cooperation among major states during any period of comparable length in history," yet "cooperation remains scarce relative to discord because the rapid growth of international economic interdependence since 1945, and the increasing involvement of governments in the operation of modern capitalist economies, have created more points of potential friction."[13] By contrast, Waltz—preoccupied as always by great power politics and striving to maintain a "pure" system-level perspective—concludes that contemporary interdependence is less than in the past.

> When I say that interdependence is tighter or looser I am saying something about the international system, with system-level characteristics defined by the situation of the great powers. In any international-political system, some of the major and minor states are closely interdependent; others are heavily dependent. The system, however, is tightly or loosely interdependent according to the relatively high or low dependence of the great powers. Interdependence is therefore looser now than it was before and between the two world wars of this century.[14]

As long as there are disagreements over the level of interdependence in global society, there will also be disagreements over asymmetrical interdependence or dependency relationships.[15] There is, for example, little consensus as to the actual degree of "dependency" inherent in North-South relations.[16] Alberto van Klaveren, for instance, argues that

> Latin American countries are now adopting foreign policies that are increasingly autonomous from the hegemonic power in the region. Those societies continue to be characterized by a general situation of structural dependency, but the new realities of the international system and the relative autonomy of the state and its bureaucracy vis-a-vis the dominant classes allow for considerable independence in the field of foreign policy.[17]

As we noted in the preceding chapter, it is rather paradoxical, but "independent" foreign policies pursued in recent years by the likes of Argentina, Brazil, Peru, and Mexico derive much of their support from nationalist resentments created by historical and continued United States influence. The *dependencia* perspective also fails to explore all the implications of the fact that the Third World accounts for a sizable percentage of developed-country markets, investments, and sources of supply. For example, former U.S. Trade Representative William E. Brock estimated that the Mexican debt crisis alone resulted in the loss of roughly 240,000 jobs for the U.S. economy.[18] The Alfonsín government in Argentina has been a hard bargainer in international debt negotiations, well aware that "if a country owes one billion, it's in trouble; if it owes 50 billion, the banks are in trouble."[19] Furthermore, the "pendulum" has swung and "the initial incursions of multinational enterprise have been responded to with a reassertion of state prerogatives."[20] Multinational corporations have themselves occasionally been "at bay" in host countries and nearly everywhere must contend with a web of restrictions on their investment strategies and day-to-day operations.

## CONTINUITY IN THE DEBATE

The idea of interdependence in the basic sense that the behavior of actors affects others or that changes in one part of the world usher in changes elsewhere is, of course, not new. What was different about the 1970s was that scholars began to emphasize the constraints that interdependence putatively placed on self-help. Not only did they deemphasize the effects of anarchy, but they tended to perceive interdependence as a force for cooperation—a claim the truth of which is by no means certain. *More than anything else this shift signified a*

*change in normative commitment among scholars and some statesmen.*
The apparent loss of American dominance and autonomy and the limits
of military power signaled by Vietnam, as well as the rise of OPEC,
produced echoes in the literature of Norman Angell's contention made
shortly before World War I that economic interdependence made war a
losing proposition for victors and vanquished alike.[21] Heirs also to integration theorists of the 1950s, especially communication, functionalist
and neofunctionalist theorists, who believed that the growth of a dense
web of transnational transactions reduced the probability of conflict,
interdependence theorists as a whole paid little attention to Rousseau's
contention that such transactions might actually provoke conflict.[22] It is
important to appreciate that these scholars, like Angell and the integration theorists, strongly favored the processes they were describing and
explaining.

Similar differences in the relative emphasis placed on anarchy versus
interdependence also existed among classical scholars, though such differences were masked by realists who emphasized anarchy and national
interest at the expense of interdependence and community interest, and
who polemically labeled those who optimistically believed in the pacific consequences of interdependence "idealists." For example, classical scholars who sought to institutionalize and legitimize the
independence and autonomy of city-states and territorial states stressed
the sovereign independence and equality of the new units and wrote at
length on "reason of state." In contrast, recognition of something
called the "balance of power" entailed a recognition of the limits of
anarchy even in a system that lacked central authority.

Balance-of-power theorists could not but recognize the constraints
imposed on independence by interstate ties. Yet among such theorists
were both optimists and pessimists who drew dramatically different
conclusions about the consequences of such ties. Representative of the
pessimists was Rousseau, who viewed the ties among states as making
war inevitable. They "touch each other at so many points that no one of
them can move without giving a jar to all the rest; their variances are
all the more deadly, as their ties are more closely woven."[23] For Rousseau, interdependence among states generated quarrels, and the absence of a central authority above them produced an environment
conducive to mistrust and obedience to short-term calculations of self-
interest:

All the Powers of Europe have rights, or claims, as against each
other. These rights are from the nature of the case, incapable of

ever being finally adjusted, because there is no common and unvarying standard for judging of their merits. . . .[24]

It was this version of a permissive environment, metaphorically depicted in Rousseau's stag-hare parable, that was largely adopted by the postwar generation of realists writing in the United States and Great Britain.[25]

Going beyond Rousseau, Edmund Burke saw the very interdependencies that flowed from the balance of power as enlarging and spreading conflict. Rousseau had, of course, shared this concern and had viewed the creation of relatively small and isolated communities as one means of establishing and institutionalizing peace. In Burke's view, the balance "has been the original of innumerable and fruitless wars. . . . The foreign ambassadors constantly residing in all courts, the negotiations incessantly carrying on, spread both confederacies and quarrels so wide, that whenever hostilities commence, the theater of war is always of a prodigious extent."[26] The pessimism of Rousseau and Burke concerning the balance of power, especially their belief that it fostered parochial perceptions of interest, was echoed in George Washington's admonition against "entangling alliances" and in Woodrow Wilson's reformist zeal.[27]

In contrast to Rousseau, thinkers such as Tomassio Campanella, Emeric Cruce, and William Penn believed that the balance of power contained the seeds of a greater European unity that would largely eliminate the opportunities for conflict that grew out of anarchy.[28] Still others, notably Hugo Grotius and Emmerich de Vattel, saw in the balance an interplay between the forces of anarchy and interdependence. De Vattel, for instance, believed that the balance was sufficiently institutionalized to be considered part of the law of Europe.

Europe forms a political system in which the Nations inhabiting this part of the world are bound together by their relations and various interests into a single body. It is no longer, as in former times, a confused heap of detached parts, each of which had but little concern for the lot of the others. . . . The constant attention of sovereigns to all that goes on, the custom of resident ministers, the continual negotiations that take place, make of modern Europe a sort of Republic, whose members—each independent, but all bound together by a common interest—unite for the maintenance of order and the preservation of liberty. This is what has given rise to the well-known principle of the balance of power. . . .[29]

Debates over the relationship between the balance of power and international order have as contemporary corollaries efforts to discern the relationship (if any) between polarity and conflict. Does concentration of power or its diffusion lead to peace?[30] Or, is the *change* in such concentration, rather than either condition, the key factor?[31] Overall, such analyses adopted what came to be termed the systems approach.

## THE SYSTEMS APPROACH

Scholars have a remarkable capacity for rediscovering the wheel, and so it was that in the 1950s students of political science in general and international relations in particular were smitten with the concept of "system." Although they had used different terminology, classical scholars like Rousseau and Grotius had, of course, viewed the relations of actors from a "systemic" perspective, appreciating keenly such implications as that of variables interacting with each other to produce patterned relationships among actors. As we have seen, they understood that because actors "touch each other at so many points" their behavior could be understood as a complex pattern of action/reaction in which individual acts served as "feedback" for targets. The balance-of-power metaphor was an expression of the consequence of patterned relationships out of which various forms and levels of dependency emerged.[32]

That metaphor, which continued to play a central role in realist theory, was rediscovered by scholars who sought to transform the metaphor into a scientific concept as part of their quest for grand theory based on macroanalysis.[33] In their eagerness to construct deductive models based on structural variables, they failed to heed those who argued that balance of power was either a value-laden/prescriptive concept[34] or a vanished historical reality.[35] It was not surprising, therefore, that efforts to extend the balance-of-power model beyond its original milieu were unsuccessful.[36]

In its most general sense—interdependence of variables and patterned interaction among parts—the idea of a system has an heuristic and descriptive value for international relations, de-emphasizing randomness as a consequence of anarchy. But its actual theoretical contribution, in the sense of explanation or prediction, is minimal. The systems approach, Robert Lieber argues, "is really a set of techniques for systematic analysis that facilitates the organizing of data, but which possesses no ideal theoretical goals."[37] For the most part, a whole new vocabulary was introduced into the analysis of international relations by scholars who seemed oblivious to the fact that they were still talking about the same old things. Thus, the "international system" was, for a majority of scholars, merely the old post-Westphalian state system; and "subsystems," "parts," and "units of analysis" were still largely understood to be sovereign nation-states or regions. Morton Kaplan, for instance, was simply reiterating that there is an absence of central authority in world politics when he characterized the contemporary system as "subsystem-dominant" in which "essential rules" are not treated as "givens" by the subsystems (i.e., nation-states).[38] One is compelled to ask with Harold and Margaret Sprout "whether one derives clearer and richer insight into the operations of political organizations by endowing them even metaphorically with pseudo-biological structures and pseudo-psychological functions."[39]

If the systems approach entailed little more than a restatement of classical observations about the relations among European states, why did the discipline so eagerly adopt the new jargon and regard the approach as so promising? Perhaps the most important reason was the currency of the system concept in the natural sciences, especially biology and cybernetics, at a time of growing enthusiasm among political scientists for adopting the techniques of the natural sciences into their own disciplines.[40] General Systems Theory, in particular, was attractive because it sought to cut across existing disciplinary boundaries; it seemed a "useful tool *providing,* on the one hand, models that can be used in, and transferred to, different fields, and *safeguarding,* on the other hand, from vague analogies which have often marred progress in these fields."[41] Even before the systems idea was taken up by political scientists, it had attracted scholars in other social sciences like economics (e.g., Kenneth Boulding) and sociology (e.g., Talcott Parsons), who were also committed to breaking down the walls separating disciplines.

A second reason for the acceptance of the idea, especially in international relations, was a realization that the scope and domain of international politics had become global. To some degree, international politics had always been global; but, for American scholars in particular, this fact was made more salient by a series of events and processes—the end of American isolationism, the relative decline of Western Europe in the scheme of things, the global nature of the 1939–45 war, the globalization of the Cold War as it spread outward from Europe after 1950, and the process of de-colonization and emergence of a multitude of newly independent societies in the developing world. Previously, American scholars, heirs to the classical European approach, had viewed the world through a largely European lens. Historical examples and cases were almost entirely drawn from European history between 1648 and 1914, and theoretical approaches like realism were largely based on assumptions inherited from Europe's classical tradition.

Typically, textbooks began to emphasize something called an "international system," which was said to encompass all independent actors and their interactions. Such a system was said to contrast with earlier systems of limited scope and domain that were relatively isolated from one another.[42] While it is true that in some sense the behavior of every actor affects all others either directly or indirectly, it is not at all clear that the conventional wisdom was correct in asserting a relatively abrupt evolution from historically local systems to an all-encompassing global one. Imperial powers had for centuries enjoyed global interests, and transnational activities like trade, immigration, and tourism had periodically waxed and waned as they continue to do. Indeed, there was an implicit recognition of the lack of explanatory power in positing a single global system in the proliferation of ideas about regional subsystems[43] and issue-based systems,[44] and the propensity of many scholars to invoke the international system metaphor but then routinely analyze the behavior of only a very few states other than the "superpowers." In sum, most actors matter little for key problems and issues that preoccupy observers of international relations, and there are variations in level of activity and in role by issue.

Almost inevitably the aspirations of systems enthusiasts were largely disappointed because, in the words of Jerome Stephens:

> In international relations, as well as in political science, no isomorphisms have been established, and the changes that have been made in GST (General Systems Theory) since its inception have not been any more beneficial in helping us find isomorphic relations than the original formulation was.[45]

This disappointment notwithstanding, international relations theory has remained littered with the debris of systems. We are left with formulations such as the following:

> The term "system" is used for two reasons. First, it encompasses all the sovereign states and therefore possesses the virtue of being comprehensive. . . . Second, it helps us to focus on the relations or interactions among the component units.[46]

The formulation is fundamentally atheoretical, but, so we are told, it at least reminds us that we are dealing with the entire world and that the behavior of nation-states affects other nation-states!

Ultimately, the concept of an "international system" is revealed to be as muddy as so many of our other key concepts. There is nothing approaching a consensus among students of international relations as to what constitutes the fundamental "structure" of that system or its sub-systems, or what lies behind change within it.

For general systems theorists what transpires in the international system is little more than a reflection of the nature of the whole, although there is hardly agreement as to what is the "essential" nature of that whole. For neo-Marxists like Immanuel Wallerstein, the key is the dominance of international capitalism within the system.[47] In striking contrast, structural realists like Kenneth Waltz, view the global distribution of power, especially the number of major powers, as the all-important system attribute. "Market structure," he writes, "is defined by counting firms; international political structure by counting states. In the counting, distinctions are made only according to capabilities."[48] In contrast to Waltz, whose model of the international system he believes lacks a "determinant of change," John Gerard Ruggie argues that anarchy is not a constant but varies according to "the quantity, velocity, and diversity of transactions that go on within society."[49] In fact, what *really* underlies the gap between Waltz and Wallerstein in conceptualizing the international system is a profound difference in normative commitment: Waltz sees a fundamental need for order; Wallerstein believes in the necessity of redistribution and change to bring about equity. Waltz wishes to tame anarchy; Wallerstein is prepared to encourage it if it would help to realize his preferred world.

Although systems have not enriched our theoretical understanding of global politics to any great extent, the language has remained because of its association with natural science, especially its apparent divorce from normative claims.[50] In fact, scholars who have employed the language of systems have had normative predispositions that are every bit as strong, though not as clearly drawn, as their classical predecessors, the balance-of-power theorists. Above all else, most of the latter valued the independence of those sovereignties that emerged from the Peace of Westphalia and the political and social status quo within the states of Europe. "[P]eace," declared Edward Vose Gulick, "was no more essential to equilibrist theory than the barnacle to the boat."[51] War was of concern only if it threatened the independence of states, the "liberties of Europe." "In war," wrote Edward Gibbon, "the European forces are exercised by temperate and undecisive contests," but such wars were only "partial events" that "cannot injure our general state of happiness."[52]

The degree to which balance-of-power theorists were committed to domestic stability or the "legitimacy principle," as well as international stability, became apparent after the collapse of the balance of power under the weight of the Napoleonic expansion. Meeting in Vienna after the defeat of Napoleon, European statesmen quarreled about many matters but agreed fully on "the condemnation of the revolutionary principle."[53] And the Concert of Europe structure was explicitly intended to enforce a domestic stability that the eighteenth-century balance had been unable to ensure.[54] Even among recent balance-of-power theorists, notably Henry Kissinger, domestic and international stability has been regarded as a cardinal virtue. Thus, Kissinger's "grand design" (a recent variant of the balance of power) and his interpretation of the meaning of détente were infused by the aim of achieving great global stability.

A similar propensity toward stability is evident in the work of systems theorists who do not invoke the balance. Although there is considerable variation among systems theorists regarding the degree to which the structural elements of global systems determine actor behavior, such theorists generally ascribe considerable importance to the impact of structure upon behavior.[55] In other words, global distributions of resources (especially power) and attitudes are generally perceived to govern what is possible and probable in the international realm, a view that follows logically from the original premise concerning the relative anarchy of global politics. For this reason, these theorists tend to agree that it is difficult to change substantially basic patterns of relations except at the margin. What is more, however, many of these theorists are openly pleased at the relative stability that they believe is the consequence of structural dominance and caution against efforts to alter things except at the margin.[56]

## INTEGRATION AND DEVELOPMENT THEORY

Although it highlighted the limiting conditions on anarchy in global politics, the systems approach has been largely sterile and undynamic. Heretics who sought to develop theory that might explain change were correctly seen as overt or closet advocates of such change and were commonly dismissed as utopians or moralists. However, two popular schools of thought in the 1950s and 1960s—political development and regional integration theory—were able to employ the system approach, address themselves to change, and still be regarded as mainstream.

Interestingly, the former, while concerned with the process of change toward "modernization," shared the bias toward stability already discussed. In the first place, political development theorists were profoundly ethnocentric; that is, "modernization" was seen to entail change of the sort that Western Europe and the United States had passed through and involved becoming more like "us." " 'Modern' means being Western,"[57] and modernization is "all those social and political changes that accompanied industrialization in . . . Western civilization."[58] In the second place, such theorists valued order highly. The study of politics itself was seen, in Leonard Binder's felicitous phrase, as "the study of the legitimation of social power."[59]

Regional integration theorists also sought to use variants of the systems approach to explain and predict change in global politics. Their normative agenda was, however, significantly different than that of modernization theorists. Unlike the latter, many of whom believed that the nation-state as it had evolved in the West represented the highest level of political, economic, and social organization, the former concluded, for the most part, that the nation-state was *and* ought to be but a way-station on the road to higher and more encompassing forms of organization.

Heirs to the "utopian" tradition of Kant and the Abbé St. Pierre, early integration theorists like David Mitrany were functionalists who argued that supplies of valued human goods like food, shelter, and security *must* keep pace with the growing demand for such goods.[60] Functionalists believed that growing exchanges of goods and people had increased the problem of satisfying demands which in turn increased the probability of war. Viewing history in teleological terms, they saw a progressive growth in the size and scope of political institutions in order to handle the ever greater problems confronting mankind. Like more recent WOMP (World Order Models' Project) theorists,[61] functionalists saw a close connection between security and non-security issues and were openly committed to encouraging trends which they believed would assure peace. In Sewell's words:

Is peace the aim? Its foundations must be laid by piecemeal international efforts in commonly recognized transnational problem areas which are readily acceptable to the procedures shaped and accepted by modern man.[62]

Functionalists pinned their hopes on the specialized organs of the United Nations which they saw as gradually assuming specialized burdens previously assumed by nation-states, and they believed that, as these agencies showed they could perform "nonpolitical" tasks, politicians would be willing to surrender greater authority to them in more overtly political areas. In this manner peace would ensue through the gradual erosion of the nation-state.

Functionalists recognized the importance of the anarchic qualities in global politics, especially the sovereign nation-state, which they sought to transcend by taking advantage of countervailing tendencies toward interdependence. Unfortunately, it became clear that there was no inevitability to the process they had identified; it became clear that there is no "necessity" that human wants be satisfied.[63] Nor was it easily possible to differentiate between "political" and "nonpolitical" issues in global politics. International agencies and even their parent organizations have proved quite expendable, and governments have generally been loath to surrender authority (a point to which we will return shortly). Nevertheless, functionalists did share with later integration theorists the idea that the nation-state was increasingly unequal to the burdens placed upon it and that its existence, as the main element of anarchy in global politics, was closely connected to war. Thus, Karl Deutsch has written:

> All the nation-state can do now is to risk or spend the lives of its soldiers and its cities as gambling stakes on the gaming tables of power, strategy or ideology, in games which none of the players control or fully understand. The nation-state is thus in danger of becoming for its people a cognitive trap in times of peace and a death trap in the event of war.[64]

Although elaborating the several strands of integration theory is beyond the scope of the present work, what is important is that such theorists tended to highlight processes and factors that were revived by interdependence theorists in the 1970s. One important group, deriving insights from cybernetic systems, theorized that high levels of communication and transactions among groups were linked to the formation of integrated societies. Whether these variables were causally connected to integration or whether they were merely indicators of the process remained an unanswered question. Restated, the question can be asked whether high levels of communication and transactions generate interdependence or are the result of it. Do they predict greater interdependence, or do they result from interdependence? The answer is unclear in part because of different definitions of the concept.[65] In any event, this group saw a relationship between the level of information exchange[66] and other transactions, especially trade, that heighten common perceptions and create material interdependencies.[67] Such exchanges were believed to increase mutual sensitivity and responsiveness to the needs and problems of the actors involved.[68] Richard Meier explained the logic of this claim as follows:

> A large continuous flow of information makes it possible to mobilize the requisite experience and data . . . to bring the anticipated crisis to the attention of decisionmakers sooner than would otherwise occur. Large flows of information . . . make it possible to reduce the chances of blundering into international conflicts.[69]

Rising communications and transactions, then, were seen to encourage learning; learning, in turn, supposedly generates the knowledge necessary for mutual responsiveness.

Interestingly, later international regime theorists continued to emphasize the central role of information exchange long after interest in regional integration had begun to wane. Robert Keohane, for instance, views information and institutional memory as key assets of international regimes. According to Keohane, these assets allow regimes to flourish even after the decline in American hegemony that, according to Keohane, was instrumental in their creation.

> Once an international regime has been established . . . it begins to benefit from the relatively high and asymmetrical level of information that it generates. . . . Viewing international regimes as information-providing and transaction cost-reducing entities rather than as quasi-governmental rule-makers helps us to understand such persistence.[70]

Insights from functionalist and communications theory were combined by a second important group into what became known as neofunctionalist theory.[71] Basically, neofunctionalism postulated that interstate agencies produced by agreements among nation-states, though initially based on common interests, could generate pressures for broadening or intensifying their own authority, as learning and socialization took place among participants. Elements of neofunctionalist theory, too, were later to reappear in regime theory.

Much of the initial enthusiasm for integration theory was, however, based on the limited experience of postwar Western Europe, and the several theories of regional integration suffered from the same kind of parochialism as had modernization theory. Efforts to apply insights derived from a European context proved largely disappointing, suggesting that the European experience was historically unique.[72] In addition, it became evident that even in Western Europe the movement toward political integration began to wane after achieving its acme with the Treaty of Rome (1957), which had created the European Common Market. Instead of greater supranational integration, the 1970s and 1980s witnessed significant subnational movements revolving around ethnicity, language, and culture. Research into regional integration then began to flag. Like so many of their predecessors, integration theorists knew what they wanted to happen, but the world failed to oblige. Not surprisingly, integration research flourished, especially in the United States, at a time American leaders were enthusiastic about the prospect of a united Europe as a buttress against the Soviet Union and as a reliable and prosperous trading partner. Its decline occurred as frictions grew between the United States and Western Europe and interest in U.S.-Soviet détente increased.[73] In the same way, modernization theory was partly a response to official American interest in the developing world during the era of decolonization and was associated with efforts to identify policies that could assure stability in the Third World and thus noncommunist solutions to socioeconomic problems.[74]

## REGIME THEORY

Theorizing about the relative impact of anarchy and interdependence on global politics did not, of course, cease with declining interest in regional integration. As we have observed, the 1970s witnessed an upsurge in concern over environmental and economic issues, especially after the several oil "shocks" and major changes in international monetary and trade practices. These concerns were shared by governments, publics, and scholars alike, though in different ways and to different degrees. "Interdependence" became the symbol for those who argued the existence of a "spaceship earth" in which narrow nationalism and egoistic behavior threatened the ecological and economic well-being of all. Intensified interest in the implications of interdependence was also encouraged by the political agenda of the Carter administration, quite different than that of its predecessor in its emphasis upon energy, human rights, environmentalism, and problems of developing societies. Consciousness was further raised by the growing global legitimacy accorded to the varied demands associated with the New International Economic Order (NIEO).

The interdependence concept was at the heart of a revised interest in international organization among theorists who were less concerned with formal institutional mechanisms like the United Nations than with more amorphous practices and institutions labeled variously "transnational actors and behavior" and "international regimes." The growing interest in transnationalism was reflected in the publication of a special issue of the journal *International Organization* (25:3) in 1971 entitled "Transnational Relations and World Politics."[75] The editors of this volume, Robert Keohane and Joseph Nye, Jr., argued that the traditional model of global politics—the "state-centric" model—ignored a vast web of interactions occurring directly between and among societies while attending exclusively to relations among governments or between governments and international organizations. "We can distinguish," they declared, "four major types of global interaction: (1) communication, the movement of information, including the transmission of beliefs, ideas, and doctrines; (2) transportation, the movement of physical objects . . . ; (3) finance, the movement of money and instruments of credit; (4) travel, the movement of persons."[76] Echoing proponents of regional integration, Keohane and Nye argued that one key effect of transnational interactions and organization was "increases in constraints on states through dependence and interdependence."[77]

Keohane and Nye admitted that the phenomena upon which they were focusing were not of recent origin.[78] Why then was the publication of their volume followed by an upsurge in research and theory on transnationalism, and why was there such renewed interest in the interdependent, as opposed to the anarchic, elements of global politics? As already noted, the key reasons were to be found in the realm of politics rather than scholarship. Thus, a large number of contributions to the volume dealing with transnational economic processes and institutions focused on matters like the collapse of the Bretton Woods arrangements, the prominence of multinational corporations in the world of international trade and finance, and the impact of subnational revolutionary groups on interstate politics highlighted by the behavior of the Viet Cong and Palestine Liberation Organization. Perhaps most important, as an influence on this trend in scholarship, however, was the declining preoccupation with East-West security issues that accompanied the rise of détente.

As the implications of these developments became clearer and additional events seemed to confirm their importance,[79] the initial insights about transnationalism were elaborated into theoretically tantalizing ideas about "complex interdependence" and "international regimes."

The idea of complex interdependence as elaborated by Keohane and Nye[80] included but went beyond the earlier transnational model to capture the features of a world dominated by interdependence rather than anarchy. In such a world, societies supposedly enjoy interstate, transgovernmental, and transnational ties across a wide variety of distinct, though often linked, issues.[81] This model Keohane and Nye explicitly contrasted with the realist model of world politics and its greater emphasis on the threat and use of military force. They believed that their model was applicable to certain issues, notably those of an economic nature, but that realist explanations still suited traditional security issues. Nevertheless, they argued that the world was becoming increasingly characterized by complex interdependence,[82] and that this was a good thing because it implied less frequent resort to military force. While applauding the growing constraints on state autonomy, they carefully hedged their bets, cautioning readers that

> So long as complex interdependence does not encompass all
> issue areas and relationships among all major states, the remain-
> ing role of military force will require sovereign states to maintain
> military capabilities. Moreover, so long as the world is character-
> ized by enormous inequality of incomes among states . . . citi-
> zens are likely to resist the dismantling of national sovereignty.[83]

In sidestepping the teleology of their functionalist predecessors and in developing a model of world politics that encompassed state bureaucracies as well as nonstate groups and international organizations, they avoided being branded utopians, which certainly would have happened twenty years earlier during the era of realist dominance.

Nor did Keohane and Nye envision a major change in the decentralized character of world politics. Indeed, they appreciated that among the key trends in world politics in the 1970s were a decline in control that could be exercised by the superpowers, a dispersion of resources, and growing difficulty in effectively using the conventional levers of power, especially coercion. How then did things get done in a world of complex interdependence lacking central authority? The answer, they contended, lay in the existence of "networks of rules, norms, and procedures that regularize behavior and control its effects."[84] These, they termed, "international regimes." Although such regimes may involve explicit rules for behavior, they are viewed as being less formal and more elastic than, for instance, international law. A strong or effective regime, then, does not require that the rules be explicit, but it does require that rules and norms be understood consensually so that "predictable, orderly behavior takes place."[85]

Regime theory was perhaps the most explicit challenge to the dominance of the classical emphasis on anarchy in international relations since "idealists" had been forced into hiding by the rhetorical wounds inflicted upon them by Hans Morgenthau and his followers. For the most part, regime theorists have been able to avoid this fate by accepting, in Krasner's words, "the basic analytic assumptions of structural realist approaches, which posit an international system of functionally symmetrical, power-maximizing states in an anarchic environment."[86] In other words, most regime theorists followed Keohane's view that international regimes could function effectively only under select conditions. Nevertheless, it is clear that all such theorists were grappling, as Arthur Stein puts it, "with the problem of trying to describe and explain patterns of order in the anarchic world of international politics" starting from an assumption of "the existence of interdependence."[87] Some like Donald Puchala and Raymond Hopkins, however, were prepared to go further, challenging frontally the classical assumption of anarchy by arguing the existence of regimes in virtually all aspects of global politics such that order exists even in the absence of centralized authority:

> [A] regime exists in *every* substantive issue-area in international relations where there is discernibly patterned behavior. Wherever there is regularity in behavior some kinds of principles, norms or rules must exist to account for it.[88]

Although there are significant differences in emphasis among regime theorists, they are all part of that strand of thinking in international relations that places great weight on the constraints imposed on actors by the existence of interdependence. Interestingly, those among them who accept the broadest conceptualization of regimes have been characterized by their own colleagues as heirs to the "Groatian tradition"[89]; yet in a very real sense all regime theorists owe something to this tradition that posits, in Hedley Bull's words, "the solidarity, or potential solidarity, of the states comprising international society, with respect to the enforcement of the law."[90]

Indeed, one repeatedly hears echoes of international law in descriptions of regime theory. Stephen Krasner, for instance, notes that since "regimes encompass principles and norms, the utility function that is being maximized must embody some sense of general obligation."[91] And Keohane argues that "the norms and rules of regimes can exert an effect on behavior even if they do not embody common ideals but are used by self-interested states and corporations engaging in a process of mutual adjustment."[92] No better reason could be proferred for claiming the existence of law or for explaining its origin! Certainly, regimes, like international law, have, as Bull argues, "helped to maintain, in a period of inevitably contracting consensus, some elements of a common framework."[93] Could not "international law" be substituted for "regime" when Krasner observes that: "The use of diplomatic cover by spies, the bugging of embassies, the assassination of diplomats by terrorists, and the failure to provide adequate local police are all indications that the classic regime protecting foreign envoys has weakened"?[94] Finally, the sense that regime is a rehabilitated version of law is heightened by Krasner's assertion that a major source of regimes is "usage and custom."[95] These are, of course, offered as key sources of positivist law. Ultimately, much of the disagreement among regime theorists regarding definition and applicability replicates in new guise the debate over definition and sources of international law between positivists and Grotians.

Indeed, the divergence in definition of international regime reflects not only the absence of sharp and consensual concepts in the discipline but also the lack of novelty in the idea itself. Arthur Stein, for instance, points out that broad definitions of regimes signify no more than "a disaggregated issue-area approach to the study of international relations" whereas narrower definitions that equate regimes with international institutions merely entail "an attempt to redress a tired and moribund field."[96] The broader definitions which identify regimes with enduring patterns of behavior in specific issue-areas reveal a clear debt to the original systems/subsystems approach described earlier. The narrower definitions not only recall earlier studies of international organization, as Stein suggests, but also functionalist and neofunctionalist formulations. And like functionalists and neofunctionalists, regime theorists do not distinguish what they analyze empirically from what they ardently desire. Regime theory, as Susan Strange observes, "takes for granted that what everyone wants is more and better regimes, that greater order and managed interdependence should be the collective goal."[97] Again, order is the implicit or explicit preferred value. Again, we confront a body of theory generated in response to policy preferences; that is, the maintenance of stability in an era of declining American control, a preference which Susan Strange contrasts to the earlier interest in integration theory that "started with the perceived U.S. need for a reliable junior partner in Europe."[98] Again, the theory is parochial, derived largely from the experience of the developed West and ignoring anomalies revealed by analysis of the developing world.

Ultimately, regime theory of whatever coloration reflects another occasion in the durable debate between those who see interdependence as severely limiting the impact of a decentralized world and those who think it only marginally lessens anarchy. Thus, as Susan Strange suggests, regime theory "tends to exaggerate the static quality of arrangements for managing the international system and introducing some confidence in the future of anarchy, some order out of uncertainty," and "gives the false impression (always argued by the neofunctionalists) that international regimes are indeed advancing against the forces of disorder and anarchy."[99]

## INTERDEPENDENCE: A NONTHEORETICAL CONCEPT?
Global politics has never been anarchic in the sense of chaos. Nor have actors ever enjoyed unbridled autonomy. Policymakers have always sought to reduce the prospect of surprise and to routinize their tasks to the greatest extent, even while resisting constraints on their autonomy. As a result, global politics is characterized today, as in the past, both by decentralization of power and purpose and a variety of allocation mechanisms and more or less institutionalized (though often tacit) rules that provide interaction with coherence.[100] Theorists who have argued the dominance of either anarchic or integrative features are largely driven by their own normative and policy predilections (e.g., for order or change), failing to appreciate the variability in such dominance by place, issue, and time.

International theory in the 1950s and 1960s tended to emphasize the role of anarchy in political life even while the United States and Soviet Union were tightly linked in a potentially deadly interdependent relationship. International theory in the 1970s and 1980s has accorded interdependence a more central role, even while international politics remained fundamentally decentralized, subject to the parochial decisions of independent (and occasionally maladjusted) leaders.

Contemporary theorists of interdependence and regimes do, for the most part, recognize this duality. Perhaps that is why neither they nor their predecessors have been able to give theoretical meaning to the impact of interdependence beyond pointing to a world of greater complexity. Similarly, realists and others who stressed anarchy could do little more than advise "prudence." Were we to admit that growing webs of transnational economic, informational, and technological flows are linking the fates of actors ever more tightly—a proposition that could be disputed by pointing to the explosion of independent sovereignties and nonstate actors and the decline in American hegemony[101]—

what would this tell us? Despite the best efforts of generations of theorists, we really do not know whether interdependence is related in any way to cooperation or conflict.[102] Those like Norman Angell who believed the former have been repeatedly disappointed, even while the ideas of Rousseau and other pessimists have not been confirmed. Whose "iron logic" are we to accept?

Minimally, the great costs potentially involved in escaping interdependence (or dependence) should endow selected actors with new forms of influence and should allow us to predict that those which are at once sensitive and vulnerable to commodity, financial and other pressures will succumb to influence attempts. The fact that this is not the case would not surprise anyone acquainted with the "puzzle of power." If the British retreat from Suez in 1956 under the threat of a U.S. veto of an IMF loan to London tends to confirm the thesis, the OPEC oil boycott of 1973 tends to disconfirm it. "On balance," observes Roy Licklider, "the short-term impact of the oil weapon on the foreign policies of the target countries toward the Arab-Israeli issue was small or negligible. . . . In the long run not much changed. . . ."[103]

A number of reasons account for the nonpredictive nature of analyses of interdependence. In the first place, the proliferation of transnational economic, political, military, social, cultural, and psychological ties on which much of the discussion of interdependence is based entails both potential benefits and costs. This is true even under conditions of asymmetrical interdependence; the relatively dependent actor will inevitably contain groups that could reap benefits from efforts to change the status quo even while leaders may judge the overall impact of such an effort as harmful to the "national interest." In the case of soaring energy prices that followed the oil boycott, for instance, Western banks stood to gain from the investment of recycled petrodollars; export industries acquired new markets for their products; and firms engaged in developing petroleum substitutes were suddenly provided with new economic incentives. At the same time, consumers and groups vulnerable to the inflationary effects of oil price rises were harmed. Thus, Licklider suggests that "the contribution of the oil weapon to Middle East policy change was at best indirect"; whatever change took place in policy he ascribes to "the increase in wealth rather than the fear of future oil supplies which the supply theory of economic sanctions would predict."[104] Ultimately, judgments regarding relative costs and benefits will be based on incomplete or very murky information, and the final balance sheet will be at best crude, heavily influenced by subjective factors.

That balance sheet is, moreover, importantly affected by countervailing currents in global politics. Rising international interdependence produces external pressures on governments in the form of potential costs and opportunities, while rising rates of participation at home create additional, often contradictory, pressures on leaders from within. The increasingly participant nature of political cultures in both democratic and nondemocratic societies places severe constraints on formal decisionmakers' ability to act autonomously. The stability and even the survival of governments increasingly depend on their ability to satisfy a diversity of economic, ethnic, linguistic, ideological and other interests; and many of these groups perceive their interests as contrary to the external pressures imposed by the logic of interdependence.

In the developing world, the growth in political consciousness and localist militancy has created powerful countercurrents to external pressures, making it extremely difficult and dangerous for elites to capitulate (or be seen to capitulate) to these pressures. Popular antipathy toward the IMF and the "banks," for instance, in a number of major debtors countries like Argentina, Brazil, Mexico, and Peru threaten the international monetary system. The intensification of local and sublocal "nationalisms" produces resistance to rising interdependence, repeatedly forcing local elites to act contrary to the logic of "national" or "global" interests produced by that interdependence. And it is less possible than ever to coerce apparently "dependent" societies to obey the norms of international regimes. Military intervention will produce massive local resistance; other forms of coercion will likely topple governments.

Developed societies have not escaped the consequences of this participation explosion. Its tremors were felt in the United States during the Vietnam War and are again being felt as intense pressures build in favor of protectionist policies that would erode international trading norms and strategic policies that would threaten the fragile arms control regime. In South Africa, Boer nationalism makes modification of the system of apartheid difficult for any government and creates resistance to external pressures for change. Similarly, in Israel, religious nationalism impedes resolution of Arab-Israeli differences and that nationalism is only exacerbated by foreign pressures.[105]

In Western Europe, too, the formerly protected character of policymaking in foreign and defense affairs is being challenged by social forces which threaten an Atlantic relationship that "serves the interests of so many states. . . ."[106] Until the late 1960s, the mutually profitable web of economic, political, and military arrangements was largely protected from attack by an elite consensus regarding the necessity of maintaining cooperative relations. Thereafter, the relative passivity of publics toward foreign and defense issues began to disappear, as greater accessibility to higher education and the increasing impact of the mass media familiarized and sensitized people, especially youth, to controversial issues such as Vietnam, nuclear power, environmental degradation, and nuclear arms.[107] Thus, during the debate over Intermediate Nuclear Forces (INF) European leaders came to appreciate the difficulty of steering a safe course between the Scylla of American pressure and the Charybdis of domestic protest.

In developed societies, too, the ability to respond effectively to the logic of interdependence has been complicated by the proliferation of giant bureaucracies with close ties to specific constituencies. In the ebb and flow of bureaucratic conflict and competition that often accompanies political decisions in developed societies, individual bureaucrats and organizations are apt to represent the interests of their constituencies as well as their own organizational interests. To the extent this takes place, decisions are further conditioned by internal pressures as opposed to external exigencies.[108]

Internal pressures, including bureaucracies, that push decisionmakers in several directions must be factored into any cost-benefit equation. As we have suggested, they may well outweigh pressures imposed by the apparent consequences of international interdependence. In the case of the 1973 oil embargo, for instance, the Arab effort to force developed societies to change their policies toward Israel enjoyed only modest success. A principal reason that such pressure did not succeed, according to Licklider, was the existence of "unwritten but real limits on the kinds of concessions which were 'politically possible.' "[109] When internal pressures make it impossible for governments to respond "rationally" to the costs liable to be imposed by violating the norms of an international regime or by severing ties, it may almost seem as though behavior is autistic.

Levels of interdependence, then, tell us little of a predictive nature, nor is interdependence adequate to explain behavior. Indeed, the fact of growing interdependence tells us little more than that life is increasingly complex for decisional elites. Ultimately, those elites must determine the relative balance of potential costs and benefits they are confronting on the basis of very incomplete information. Additionally, their evaluations of the impact of interdependence will likely vary by issue-area, often with only a rudimentary appreciation of possible linkages among them. On some occasions, they will fail to see important linkages where they exist (as did Lyndon Johnson in the relationship between the Vietnam War and global inflation). On other occasions, they may create linkages that previously did not exist in order to justify their behavior. Many factors are likely to contribute to shaping the perceptions of decisionmakers about the nature of linkages and the relative costs and benefits imposed by interdependence/dependence. Among these are subjective definitions, political obligations, ideology, memories (individual and organizational), and personality attributes. Objective indicators like transaction flows and the availability of alternatives may encourage the theorist to advise the decisionmaker that he ought to feel interdependent or dependent or run the risk of dire consequences for himself and those for whom he is a surrogate. In the end, however, the latter's perceptions will be formed on the basis of both objective and subjective factors.

And even if there is consensus as to probable costs associated with severing ties or the availability of substitute partners, actors will vary dramatically in terms of the price they are willing to pay for principle. Where Neville Chamberlain was willing to go to great lengths in 1938 to avoid the terrible price of war, Hungary (1956) and Czechoslovakia (1968) were prepared to risk terrible costs to assert their independence of the Soviet Union. Similarly, Cuba was objectively "dependent" on the United States in 1960 (and Washington was confident it could tighten the screws sufficiently to keep Havana in line), but Fidel Castro (unlike Fulgencio Batista) chose to seek political and economic substitutes at great "objective" cost (though perhaps great "subjective" gain).[110]

## CONCLUSION

Theoretical debate regarding the degree to which international politics is characterized by anarchy or solidarity is an enduring one. There is no greater consensus today regarding this key assumption than there was in classical antiquity.[111] Nor is there theoretical consensus as to the impact of these features on behavior in world politics. Like other debates in international politics, the theoretical controversy over anarchy is colored by hidden normative and policy preferences, an absence of conceptual clarity, and the repeated intrusion of policymakers' concerns and slogans into intellectual discourse.

# 9

# The Elusive Quest

In recent years the quest for theory in international relations has become, if anything, increasingly elusive. Those embarked on that quest stand today as in the midst of a maze, with the paths they have elected to pursue quite probably leading nowhere. There is no longer any widespread confidence that the maze even has an entry or an exit, certainly no consensus as to what the objective is, and growing doubt as to whether what might be found is likely to be worth the effort of continuing to look for it.

The sad truth, of which there appears to be growing recognition and acknowledgment, is that international relations practitioners in governments, some of whom (perhaps mistakenly) in the 1950s and 1960s looked to the academic world for guidance in matters like deterrence, find very little of either interest or relevance in contemporary theory and therefore make little attempt to read it.

There has even been a marked decline in academic interest in the subject of theory. Many graduate students and professionals seem to have concluded that it is hardly worth trying to penetrate the turgid prose and jargon of many, if not most, theoretical books and journal articles because these have nothing particularly significant or useful to say. More and more academics seem to be turning to policy questions or purely descriptive analyses of current events and issues, without attempting to explore the theoretical implications of their work. The resulting analyses, predictably, are all too often merely journalistic or at least are soon overtaken by events. Leading departments of political science are increasingly regarded as those with an ability to place students in Washington rather than as producers of doctorates.

Without a reasonably coherent body of theory, we have previously observed, one might argue that a "field" of international relations exists, but it is a long way from having a true discipline. Indeed, to term the field an "emerging" discipline implies a large measure of faith that does not seem to be justified by either past experience or current trends. An absence of theory has serious consequences across all our concerns, just as McGowan and Shapiro maintain that it profoundly affects the study of foreign policy:

> Without theory we cannot explain the relationships we "discover" and we can only make predictions of the crudest sorts based upon projections from empirical trends, not upon a profound understanding of foreign policy behavior. Without theory to guide our research we must depend upon luck and educated guesses to come up with worthwhile research hypotheses. Without theory research becomes ad hoc in the extreme, with no justification provided for the selection of cases, with no system to the definition and measurement of concepts, and with no consistency in the use of research techniques and data-processing routines. In brief, a field without theory is hardly an area of disciplined scientific inquiry. Since the comparative study of foreign policy lacks both middle-range and general theories of foreign policy behavior it fails to meet the basic objective of any science: a body of theoretically organized knowledge that is based on cumulative empirical research.[1]

How far we are from fulfilling the bold aspirations of a quarter of a century ago when the scientific revolution was in full steam and it appeared that there were answers to most important questions just down the track! How far we are, in fact, from meeting even the less ambitious vision advanced in 1960 by Morton A. Kaplan:

> [O]ur explanations or theories can never have the authority of theory in physics, or its explanatory or predictive power. The important problem is whether they can be stated in ways that permit additional analysis and investigation. Whether they are tautological dead ends or fruitful aids to historical and scientific imagination, whether the statements in them permit at least reasonable analysis and investigation or whether they are dogmatic fiats, the science of the discipline does not lie in absolute certainty but in reasonable belief, in definite canons of procedure and investigation, and in the attempt to permit confirmation or falsification even though of an imprecise order. The object is not to seek a certainty or precision that the subject matter does not allow, but to reject a dogmatism that the subject matter does not make necessary. The very difficulties of theory building and

confirmation in international politics demand sincere dedication
to scientific canons of procedure.[2]

Why has our work fallen so far short of our goals? Although the
explanations in this volume go beyond those that Kaplan advanced, we
must agree with his conclusion that "the factors inhibiting the development of a powerful, predictive, theoretical social science are fundamental and . . . it is not merely a matter of waiting for a Galilean
breakthrough."[3] First, to state the obvious but nonetheless basic and
significant, students of international relations deal with matters that are
exceedingly complex. The distinguised physicist, Sir Brian Pippard,
remarks:

> In olden days a prince of the church would employ a chaplain to
> remind him of his mortality. It would be no bad custom if at
> prize-giving ceremonies it was whispered in the ears of mathema-
> ticians and scientists, in their hour of triumph, that they had
> succeeded because they had chosen to tackle relatively straight-
> forward problems; and that if politicians and social reformers
> [surely we might add persons studying international relations] are
> not so obviously successful it is because they have challenged
> problems of enormously greater complexity.[4]

In Pippard's view, the latter problems, "when represented by physical
models, seem to belong to that class of problems that physicists find
most difficult to reduce to order—problems of instability and chaos."[5]
The physical scientist, by contrast, normally focuses on problems in
which only a relatively few number of major variables are operative.
Moreover, as Kaplan stressed over a quarter of a century ago, the
physical scientist "carries on his studies and experiments in a laboratory that is closed to outer-world or historical forces." On the other
hand, "each science gets less theoretical as we move from laboratory
generalizations to engineering applications and to the complexities and
uncertainties of the real world."[6]

Students of international relations not only have a staggering number
of potentially relevant variables with which to wrestle outside of a
closed laboratory setting but also, unlike the physical scientists, must
proceed with precious little agreement as to how variables should be
labeled and defined. One would be hard-pressed to find very many
physical science terms as vague as social science concepts like personality, power, capability, state, open political system, and so on almost
ad infinitum. When concepts such as these require separate definition
by virtually every theoretician, needless to say, this rather seriously

undercuts the persuasiveness of generalizations resulting from their application. And agreement regarding definitions would be illusory at best because, as we have seen, meanings shift in time and place in reaction to changing human commitments.

Another difficulty arises from the fact that, in our effort to comprehend the world around us, we believe there is no alternative but to build theories or models that are inevitably gross oversimplifications. Robert Jervis correctly observes: "Pure empiricism is impossible: facts do not speak for themselves."[7] Adopting a theory/model then has the effect of channeling perceptions so as to filter out contradictory evidence, which, in turn, leaves the theory/model open to the charge that it has neglected an important part of the picture. Jervis again:

> The world is not so cleanly constructed that all the evidence supports only one theory. There are so many variables, accidents, and errors in observations that [in Thomas Kuhn's words] "There is no such thing as research with counter-instances." No parsimonious explanation for any actor's behavior in a complex set of cases will be completely satisfying. Some aspects of the truth simply do not make sense. . . . Because it is rare that all the facts are consistent with the same conclusion, the closer one looks at the details of a case the greater the chance that some of them will contradict the accepted explanation.[8]

Kaplan, an advocate of system-level explanations, phrases it that "as we come closer to reality . . . we lose generality":

> If we want to apply our models to concrete cases, we must choose just those factors and just those factor values that we have some reason to believe operate in the particular instance we wish to understand and explain. In the endeavor, as our analysis gains in richness of relevant detail, we face a continuing loss of generality and a growing vagueness and lack of specification concerning the weight that each factor contributes to the total event or situation. This is the price we must pay when we deal with actual history.[9]

An optimist might note that fragmentation in theory-building is merely a reflection of fragmentation of world politics itself and that a proliferation of perspectives is a necessary prelude to later coherence. But, one must not hide behind complexity alone, in the sense of numbers of variables. Marion Levy is probably correct in asserting that "the level of complexity that faces one varies as an inverse function of the state of one's theory."[10] We have no way of knowing in advance just how many variables are relevant to our concerns. There is a more important sort of complexity that becomes apparent in efforts to isolate and study specific variables; such reductionism isolates selected factors from their milieu when it is the milieu itself in which we are interested. Thus, empirical elements are sifted and viewed apart from the normative yeast that animates them and lends them meaning.

Were we advancing along the path outlined by Thomas Kuhn, the general-vs-specific dilemma and other issues would be resolved through a gradual refinement of models in the progress of normal science. When a model proves inadequate, Pippard comments, the usual and proper reaction is not to abandon it entirely, but to "modify it if we can or, at least, recognize its limitations—'I don't really understand so-and-so,' we say."[11] On the other hand, the eventual replacement even of a dominant paradigm with another is putatively possible and, indeed, necessary if too many anomalies are observed and problems of major importance, therefore, remain unsolved.

Kuhn's analysis of the process of scientific progress, as we have seen, was a tremendous encouragement to a post-World War II generation of scholars who were determined to make the study of international relations more "scientific." Many still hold that the theoretical fragmentation and ferment which ensued offer substantial evidence of real progress in Kuhnian terms.

However, any such interpretation betrays a serious misreading of Kuhn and tends to obscure the reasons for our current plight. Kuhn insists, in the first instance, that scientific progress must start with a genuine dominant paradigm. Retrospectively, realism seemed the nearest thing to such a paradigm in international relations, but it was—and is—far from a genuine one. As we have seen, it is less a theory than a set of normative emphases which shape theory, a self-contained syllogism that closes off further analysis and sustains a particular ideology. Second, Kuhn stresses that an existing paradigm is only discarded when an alternative is available and that, meanwhile, progress is achieved through the process of normal science within the accepted framework. In contrast, the self-styled scientific revolution in international relations was mainly methodological, and there was no agreement of any kind from the outset on a common research agenda. Theorists started off in any number of different directions, with scant consensus as to the basic puzzles to be addressed or the concepts and methodologies to be employed. Hence, lines of research have been essentially idiosyncratic, without the kind of convergence that seems to make for cumulative knowledge in the Kuhnian sense. Klaus Knorr and

Sidney Verba recognized in 1960 that: "[I]n the long run, progress will be made in theories of the international system only if various approaches begin to converge and move in the same direction. Only in that way will our work, both theoretical and empirical, begin to be cumulative."[12] Unfortunately, after a fairly long run of over twenty-five years, theory in the field appears more divergent and consequently less cumulative than ever before. Perhaps, we seriously misunderstood the enterprise itself.

The central thesis of this book is that ideas emerge and compete in international relations scholarship in a decidedly un-Kuhnian pattern—that is, in response to what we have called the normative temper of the times. Schools of thought in international relations reflect the *Zeitgeist* of their age fully as much as do ideas in art and literature. Different normative commitments lie behind debates regarding which actors should be studied, which levels of analysis are most useful, which variables are critical, which issues are most important, and so forth. This should not be at all surprising, considering that the very problems which scholars choose to study and the data they amass derive initially from a set of value-based concerns. These concerns are always to some extent personal, yet they also typically reflect the current preoccupations of political leaders and society at large, as well as intellectual fashions in the halls of academe. And what is a value priority today may run a distant second or third tomorrow. Psychological and material rewards go to those individuals and institutions working on the problems that governments and fellow citizens are worried about today. Moreover, academics who want to get grants and to advance their career (who doesn't?) are only too aware that their analyses had better be wearing this year's theoretical hat. Scholarship is thus inevitably influenced not only by major historical trends but also by more ephemeral considerations.

Value hierarchies and the global agenda of issues change in response to contextual or situational factors that heighten perceptions of deprivation of some values and reduce anxieties about others. The focus is on arms control when technological advances in weapon systems appear likely to escalate the arms race, on the environment when there are severe famines or dying rivers and lakes, on the international monetary system when currency fluctuations grow intolerable, on capital flows when debtor countries are on the verge of bankruptcy, and so on. Sometimes the changes to which theorists respond have been slow and evolutionary in nature; perhaps more often, theoretical shifts have reflected the impact of cataclysmic or at least profoundly disillusioning events. Wars have often been the catalyst: the Peloponnesian War that influenced Thucydides, the fall of Rome, the French invasion of Italy in 1498, the religious wars of the sixteenth and seventeenth centuries, the French Revolution and its Napoleonic aftermath, the two world wars, and Vietnam. Each ushered in a period of introspection, a general questioning of existing norms and ideas, and eventually led to the emergence of "new" norms and theories.

The quotation marks around the word "new" in the previous sentence are required, of course, because our second main assertion has been that what is remarkable about debates among international relations theorists—and what distinguishes them from debates among natural scientists—is that essentially the same (often stale) arguments and emphases tend to recur over and over again through time despite superficial changes in concepts and language. There are enduring normative themes like realism and idealism or anarchy and order. Each draws its inspiration from partial views of a world that, despite genuine evolution and critical events, is not changing nearly as much as shifting theoretical fashions and the rhetoric of scholarly contests might appear to suggest. Moreover, theoretical shifts occur, often at the same time, along several fairly constant dimensions, including those we have identified as being the most important: mutability/immutability, optimism/pessimism, competitiveness/community, and elitism/nonelitism.

We began our in-depth historical survey with medieval Europe to the Renaissance, or the Middle Ages to Machiavelli, two periods—like all other periods—in which theories of international relations were products of a prevailing social and cultural milieu. The medieval era is a millenium that has usually been overlooked by scholars, no doubt because its pattern of complex overlapping jurisdictions seems to make it even harder to comprehend in "modern" terms than the earlier epochs of classical Greece and Rome. However, as we pointed out, the medieval era did have autonomous actors, violence and war, system solidarity and culture, and supranational organization. This period is also interesting and significant, in part, because the very lack of a clear "domestic" arena entailed a "purer" *inter*state arena than was the case either before or after. Medieval theory of a universal imperium, an overarching Roman Church, and the ultimate perfectability of humanity as a spiritual collectivity mirrored an economically and socially stratified real world. Political and military power were local and limited, and differentiation between individual and collective interests, as well as between domestic and international politics, was practically impossible.

In our own era, the erosion of the distinction between the domestic and international realms served to undermine traditional realist theories; the effect on theory was no less profound, but the result realism, when the Middle Ages waned and the domestic/international distinction was rediscovered. The hardening of boundaries, growth of state power, shifts in the bases of economic and military power, the breakdown of feudal society, increasing secularization, and progress in science paved the way for Marsilio and Machiavelli. Machiavelli's political realism was an eloquent statement of the belief in the immutability of the security dilemma, basic pessimism, intense competition, and elitism that characterized his Renaissance age. But it was *not* the statement of some basic and permanent truths.

For several centuries thereafter, until World War I, conditions proved repeatedly conducive to the advance of one or another version of realism. Religious strife in France gave birth to Bodin's articulation of the doctrine of state sovereignty; Louis XIV consolidated a model centralized state resting on a divine right monarchy; and the 1648 Peace of Westphalia ushered in what is usually termed the modern state system. The eighteenth century was a veritable "age of realism," featuring absolute monarchy, intense competition among states, shifting alliances, limited wars, and yet cosmopolitan diplomacy and relative political stability. The French Revolution and the rise of Napoleon presented serious domestic and international threats to the rest of Europe, but fusion of the ideas of state and nation appeared to give additional vitality to the state concept. After the midnineteenth century, however, glorification of state and nation began a march toward pathological extremes, especially in Germany, with disastrous results.

The disillusionment with realism after World War I set the stage for a period of what realists characterized as "idealism, which was itself supplanted after World War II by resurgent realism and an attendant emphasis on the scientific method. Idealists blamed the useless bloodletting primarily on selfish and unbridled nationalism, authoritarian governments, manipulative professional diplomats, and greedy arms merchants. In contrast to the old realism, the new idealist phase emphasized optimism, social and political mutability, cooperation through international law and organization, and broader political participation. The latter was to be accomplished both by giving greater weight to the views of an educated public opinion at home and by allowing national self-determination for previously subject peoples throughout the world.

The failure of the League of Nations and Western governments to curb German and Japanese expansionism, the calamity of World War

II, and the onset of the Cold War ushered in another period of realism. If the eighteenth century had been the age of realism among foreign-policy practitioners, the years following World War II saw a realist perspective capture the imagination of foreign office professionals and academics alike. First and foremost, Hans Morgenthau, but also E. H. Carr, Kenneth Thompson, Reinhold Niebuhr, and others gave realism a rich new literature and intellectual respectability. Realism's claim to offer a "science," its stress on the unitary state as actor, its amoralism (except, as we have noted, its own normative bias), and its rational model of foreign-policy decisionmaking also meshed nicely with the aims of a new generation of American theorists who were determined to engineer a scientific revolution in the study of international politics. The "behavioralists" promised a value-free approach, precise concepts, hard data, and relentless testing of propositions in accordance with the scientific method. The magic key that would unlock all important secrets, it appeared, might well soon be in hand.

By the 1970s, not only was the magic key still missing but also both realism and the scientific approach came under increasing attack—not because they were less promising than they had been the decade before. Again, the reason was a shift in normative emphases occasioned by widespread disillusionment, this time over Vietnam and such matters as the energy crisis, endemic stagflation, environmental concerns, and North-South tensions. Theorists gave greater attention to the nonrational roots of decisionmakers' actions, to bureaucratic politics and organizational behavior, to transnationalism and interdependence, to nonstate actors, and to the impact of issues. With considerable justification, advocates of the scientific approach were accused of ignoring the inevitable influence of values in all inquiry, of generating useless jargon, of confusing methodology with theory, of gathering data and "number crunching" without clear purpose, and (most damning of all) of simply having precious few hard results to show for decades of work and countless research dollars spent. Faced with the normative demands of the period, both realists and aspiring scientists thus looked increasingly irrelevant.

In the 1980s, international conditions have continued to evolve, and both the world and international theory—perhaps symbolized by the "compromise" of neorealism—now seem to be more complex and confused than at any time in recent memory. And, as we observe the world, on the one hand, and our theories about it, on the other, the relationship between them appears increasingly muddy. While change is a natural feature of the former, it may be quite different than the changes identified by the latter. *Often it is not even that the world has changed as much as it is that theorists have noticed something that had always been there or have rediscovered something that is not new at all.*

What, then, will be the future course of theory and international relations? A few projections can be made with some confidence. First, the search for theory will proceed, although with no grand synthesis or true paradigm and hence certainly nothing like a Kuhnian progression. The scientific revolution, which never really got under way despite the best efforts of its advocates, has now been all but abandoned as a goal. Method without theory is no solution; and, regrettably, theory that could provide an adequate base for the extensive application of genuine scientific canons of procedure is likely to remain well beyond our grasp. Statistical ingenuity will resolve little; data collection without a consensual theoretical framework to guide it is senseless.

We can and must continue to use concepts heuristically, as aids to thinking, research, and, most importantly, teaching. Unfortunately, since there is no consensus as to the meaning of the key concepts in our field, we will have to go on defining them each time we use them. Partly for this reason, whether we undertake case studies, investigate particular issue-areas, or look for properties of the general international system—whatever we attempt—research will inevitably remain essentially idiosyncratic and noncumulative. As it has always done, the study of international relations will also continue to reflect the normative temper of its time and place and will alternate back and forth between familiar themes along the dimensions we have described.

What will the international milieu that shapes norms be like in years to come? The record of the tumultuous past two decades—from détente to renewed superpower rivalry, SALT I to Star Wars, energy shortage to oil glut, international monetary system controls to floating exchange rates, petrodollar recycling to an international debt crisis, stagflation to partial economic recovery in the West, New International Economic Order demands to an indefinite suspension of North-South dialogue—holds ample warning for those bold or foolish enough to try to read the future. To be sure, the present authors' crystal ball is no less cloudy than everyone else's.

Nevertheless, we can be certain that a complex world will continue to be sufficiently ambiguous to offer theorists plenty of room to maneuver. There will continue to be grounds for both optimism and pessimism, opportunities for change and apparently immutable factors, competition (chaos) and cooperation (order), and a large measure of elitism as well as equality. Which emphases will move to the forefront of theoretical fashion, and when, will depend entirely upon the vicissitudes of the normative climate, itself influenced by the surfacing of long-term trends and especially by traumatic events.

In sum, the search for theory in the field of international relations will go on, despite the existence of grave doubts about its accomplishments to date and long-range prospects. As T. S. Eliot stated in another context, "we shall not cease from exploration," largely because there just is not any acceptable alternative. Our field is too important to abandon, and confining ourselves to policy prescription and descriptive analyses of current events—which persons closer to the policymaking process and journalists, respectively, are often better equipped to do— is not the answer. Nor can we solemnly announce our own irrelevance. We obviously must move ahead as systematically as possible, and this means that we cannot escape the task of theory-building. However, if we are to proceed without illusion and with greater tolerance for diversity than some prophets of the scientific revolution (and some traditionalists) managed in the past, we have to recognize that the quest for theory will likely continue to be as elusive as ever and to understand the reasons why.

Is there any alternative to the bleak forecast we have ventured? Perhaps, but it would of necessity entail a fundamental transformation in the way we must think about our subject. This means abandoning the explicit and implicit analogies to the natural sciences and, instead, trying to make sense of the way in which humanists approach their materials. (Ironically, the humanities, too, are trying to develop "scientific" methods and become "disciplines" and, in doing so, are embarking upon a fruitless path.) We must confront squarely the political and normative environments that shape our consciousness and infuse our theories about the world around us. Only when our concepts, like Freud's, are "vibrant with special humanistic resonances"[13] will integrated explanations of international behavior begin to emerge. Indeed, Bruno Bettelheim's description of the effects of translating Freud into English might also refer to what has happened to international relations scholarship—"abstract, depersonalized, highly theoretical, erudite, and mechanized—in short, 'scientific! . . .' "[14] Theorists must retreat from reductionism and correlative analysis. Causal theory that aims at understanding the shifting *Gestalten* of societies should be their object. Above all, students of international relations should recall what Aristotle recognized—that politics is an architectonic subject so that efforts to build disciplinary walls around it are not possible.

# Notes

## Introduction

1. Gerald Abrahams, *The Chess Mind* (Baltimore: Penguin Books, 1960), 15.

2. An observer may detect changing fashion in academics from professional conferences, doctoral dissertations, academic funding decisions, and editorial policies of leading journals.

3. Ronald Rogowski, "Rationalist Theories of Politics: A Midterm Report," *World Politics* 30:2 (January 1978), 306.

4. Gerald N. Grob, "The Origins of American Psychiatric Epidemiology," *American Journal of Public Health* 75:3 (March 1985), 229.

5. Ibid., 230.

6. Ibid., 231.

7. Ibid., 229.

## Chapter One

1. An earlier version of this chapter appeared in Margaret P. Karns (ed.), *Persistent Patterns and Emerging Structures in a Waxing Century* (New York: Praeger, 1986), 11–34.

2. Some of the same issues that are addressed here echo concerns expressed by Stanley Hoffmann almost three decades ago. Hoffmann, "International Relations: The Long Road to Theory," *World Politics* 11:3 (April 1959), 346–377.

3. James N. Rosenau, "Before cooperation: Hegemons, regimes, and habit-driven actors in world politics," *International Organization* 40:4 (Autumn 1986), 853.

4. Friedrich Kratochwil and John Gerard Ruggie, "International organization: a state of the art on an art of the state," *International Organization* 40:4 (Autumn 1986), 754.

5. Thomas S. Kuhn, *The Structure of Scientific Revolutions,* expanded ed. (Chicago: University of Chicago Press, 1970), 175.

6. Little attention has been paid to boundary problems in recent years even though they have never been adequately addressed.

7. This movement was part of the behavioral revolution that was taking place throughout political science. See, for example, Heinz Eulau, *The Behavioral Persuasion in Modern Political Analysis* (Englewood Cliffs, NJ: Prentice-Hall, 1963). Actually, the behavioral movement has roots in the 1920s. See Bernard Crick, *The American Science of Politics* (Berkeley and Los Angeles: University of California Press, 1960).

8. Herbert Butterfield, *The Origins of Modern Science* (New York: Free Press, 1957),

**223**

7, 28. See also Robert K. Merton, "Priorities in Scientific Discovery: A Chapter in the Sociology of Science," *American Sociological Review* 22:6 (1957), 635–659.

9. See, for example, David Bloor, "Two Paradigms for Scientific Knowledge?" *Science Studies* 1:1 (1971), 101–115. For his part, Popper argued that a theory required in advance specification of what evidence would be sufficient to *disprove* it. Induction, he believed, could never prove a theory although it could falsify one. Karl Popper, *Logik der Forschung: The Logic of Scientific Discovery* (London: Hutchinson, 1935).

10. M. D. King, "Reason, Tradition, and the Progressiveness of Science," in Gary Gutting (ed.), *Paradigms and Revolutions: Appraisals and Applications of Thomas Kuhn's Philosophy of Science* (Notre Dame, IN: University of Notre Dame Press, 1980), 104, 105.

11. Kuhn himself admitted that he had failed to stipulate consistently and clearly what a paradigm is. He therefore added a postscript to the second edition of *The Structure of Scientific Revolutions* in which he sought to identify the two central meanings of paradigm: "On the one hand, it stands for the entire constellation of beliefs, values, techniques, and so on shared by members of a given community. On the other, it denotes one sort of element in that constellation, the concrete puzzle-solutions which, employed as models or examples, can replace explicit rules as the basis for the solution of the remaining puzzles of normal science" (175). Perhaps the most useful and succinct definition of a paradigm is that of a set of fundamental assumptions that scholars make about the world they are studying. See John A. Vasquez, *The Power of Power Politics: A Critique* (New Brunswick, NJ: Rutgers University Press, 1983), 5.

12. Thomas S. Kuhn, *The Structure of Scientific Revolutions*, 10.

13. Alan Ryan, *The Philosophy of the Social Sciences* (New York: Pantheon Books, 1970), 72.

14. Thomas S. Kuhn, *The Structure of Scientific Revolutions*, 24.

15. Puzzles, according to Kuhn, are discrete, often esoteric, problems for which there are assured solutions that are sought according to rules "that limit both the nature of acceptable solutions and the steps by which they are to be obtained." Thomas S. Kuhn, *The Structure of Scientific Revolutions*, 38.

16. Thomas S. Kuhn, *The Structure of Scientific Revolutions*, 52.

17. Ibid., 52–53.

18. J. W. N. Watkins, "Against Normal Science," in Imre Lakatos and Alan Musgrave (eds.), *Criticism and the Growth of Knowledge* (Cambridge: Cambridge University Press, 1970), 26.

19. Thomas S. Kuhn, *The Structure of Scientific Revolutions*, 84.

20. Imre Lakatos, "Falsification and the Methodology of Scientific Research Programmes," in Imre Lakatos and Alan Musgrave (eds.), *Criticism and the Growth of Knowledge*, 91–196.

21. See M. D. King, "Reason, Tradition, and the Progressiveness of Science," 112.

22. Thomas S. Kuhn, *The Structure of Scientific Revolutions*, 165.

23. Ibid., 163.

24. Ibid., 150.

25. See, for example, John D. Heyl, "Paradigms in Social Science," *Society* 12:5 (July/August 1975), 61.

26. Thomas S. Kuhn, *The Structure of Scientific Revolutions*, 19.

27. Ibid.

28. L. Lavdan, *Progress and Its Problems* (London: Routledge and Kegan Paul, 1977), 81.

29. Harold Guetzkow, "Sizing Up a Study in Simulated International Processes," in James N. Rosenau (ed.), *In Search of Global Patterns* (New York: Free Press, 1976), 91. See also Guetzkow, "Long-range Research in International Relations," *American Perspective* 4:4 (Fall 1950), 421–440.

30. In contrast, subspecialities in the natural sciences do not exist to gainsay one another's achievements. Rather they tend to represent efforts to solve different puzzles that are posed by the paradigms within which they exist.

31. Douglas Lee Eckberg and Lester Hill, Jr., "The Paradigm Concept and Sociology: A Critical Review," in Gary Gutting (ed.), *Paradigms and Revolutions*, 122.

32. Ibid., 123. See their table 1 (132).

33. See, for example, Henrika Kuklick, "A 'Scientific Revolution': Sociological Theory in the United States," *Sociological Inquiry* 43:1 (1972), 2–22. The ascendance of structural-functionalism in sociology in the late 1950s was paralleled by its entry into political science, and the debate between structural-functionalists and operationalists in some respects resembled that between "scientists" and "traditionalists" in international relations.

34. George Ritzer, *Sociology: A Multiple Paradigm Science* (Boston: Allyn & Bacon, 1975).

35. See, for example, C. G. A. Bryant, "Kuhn, Paradigms and Sociology," *British Journal of Sociology* 26:3 (September 1975), 354–359.

36. See, for example, R. Serge Denisoff, Orel Callahan, and Mark H. Levine, *Theories and Paradigms in Contemporary Sociology* (Itasca, IL: F. E. Peacock, 1974), and Andrew Effrat, "Power to the Paradigms: An Editorial Introduction," *Sociological Inquiry,* 42:3–4 (1972), 3–34.

37. Douglas Lee Eckberg and Lester Hill, Jr., "The Paradigm Concept and Sociology: A Critical Review," 131.

38. Mark Blaug, "Kuhn versus Lakatos, or Paradigms versus Research Programmes in the History of Economics," in Gary Gutting (ed.), *Paradigms and Revolutions*, 137.

39. David A. Hollinger, "T. S. Kuhn's Theory of Science and Its Implications for History," in ibid., 195.

40. See, for example, Jorg Baumberger, "No Kuhnian Revolution in Economics," *Journal of Economic Issues* 11:1 (1977), 1–20; Martin Bronfenbrenner, "The 'Structure of Revolutions' in Economic Thought," *History of Political Economy* 3:1 (Spring 1971), 136–151; A. W. Coates, "Is There a 'Structure of Scientific Revolutions' in Economics?" *Kyklos* 22:2 (1969), 289–295; and L. Kunin and F. S. Weaver, "On the Structure of Scientific Revolutions in Economics," *History of Political Economy* 3:2 (Fall 1971), 391–397.

41. Mark Blaug, "Kuhn versus Lakatos," 137.

42. David A. Hollinger, "T. S. Kuhn's Theory of Science and Its Implications for History," 203.

43. Sheldon S. Wolin, "Paradigms and Political Theories," in Gary Gutting (ed.), *Paradigms and Revolutions*, 174.

44. Ibid., 182, 183, 184. See also David A. Hollinger, "T. S. Kuhn's Theory of Science and Its Implications for History," 198.

45. Gary Gutting, "Introduction," in Gutting (ed.), *Paradigms and Revolutions*, 13.

46. Thomas S. Kuhn, "Reflections on My Critics," in Imre Lakatos and Alan Musgrave (eds.), *Criticism and the Growth of Knowledge*, 245.

47. James N. Rosenau, *The Scientific Study of Foreign Policy* (New York: Free Press, 1971), vii.

48. P. Terrence Hopmann, J. David Singer, and Dina A. Zinnes, "Introduction," in Hopmann, Zinnes, and Singer (eds.), *Cumulation in International Relations Research* (Denver: Graduate School of International Studies, University of Denver Monograph Series in World Affairs, 1981), 4.

49. Little agreement exists regarding the degree of progress in the field. See, for example, Raymond E. Platig, *International Relations Research: Problems of Evaluation and Advancement* (Santa Barbara, CA: Clio Press, 1967); Robert Pfaltzgraff, Jr., "International Studies in the 1970s," *International Studies Quarterly* 15:1 (March 1971), 104–128; and K. J. Holsti, "Along the Road to International Theory," *International Journal* 39:2 (Spring 1984), 337–365. For a more general analysis of the state of political science, see Dag Anckar and Etkki Berndtson (eds.), *The Evolution of Political Science,* special edition of *International Political Science Review* 8:1 (January 1987).

50. Richard K. Ashley, "Noticing Pre-paradigmatic Progress," in James N. Rosenau (ed.), *In Search of Global Patterns* (New York: Free Press, 1977), 150–151.

51. As in other social sciences, taxonomies are regularly imposed upon international relations scholarship in efforts to identify paradigms (e.g., realism/idealism, state-centric/multi-centric/global centric, and so forth). See, for example, R. Maghroori and B. Ramberg (eds.), *Globalism Versus Realism: International Relations' Third Debate* (Boulder, CO: Westview Press, 1982), and R. Meyers, "International Paradigms, Concepts of Peace, and the Policy of Appeasement," *War and Society* 1:1 (May 1983), 43–65.

52. P. Terrence Hopmann, "Identifying, Formulating, and Solving Puzzles in International Relations Research," in James N. Rosenau (ed.), *In Search of Global Patterns,* 192. See also Richard K. Ashley, "Noticing Pre-paradigmatic Progress," 151.

53. Robert Jervis, "Cumulation, Correlations, and Woozles," in ibid., 183.

54. Thomas S. Kuhn, *The Structure of Scientific Revolutions,* 24.

55. Richard K. Ashley, "Noticing Pre-paradigmatic Progress," 151.

56. G. R. Boynton, "Cumulativeness in International Relations," in James N. Rosenau (ed.), *In Search of Global Patterns,* 145.

57. P. Terrence Hopmann, J. David Singer, and Dina A. Zinnes, "Introduction," in Hopmann, Zinnes, and Singer (eds.), *Cumulation in International Relations Research,* 5.

58. Michael P. Sullivan and Randolph M. Siverson, "Theories of War: Problems and Prospects," in P. Terrence Hopmann, Dina A. Zinnes, and J. David Singer (eds.), *Cumulation in International Relations Research,* 10.

59. Brian L. Job, "Grins Without Cats: In Pursuit of Knowledge of International Alliances," in P. Terrence Hopmann, Dina A. Zinnes, and J. David Singer (eds.), *Cumulation in International Relations Research,* 55.

60. P. Terrence Hopmann, J. David Singer, and Dina A. Zinnes, "Introduction," 7.

61. Richard Smith Beal, "A Contra-Kuhnian View of the Discipline's Growth," in James N. Rosenau (ed.), *In Search of Global Patterns,* 159.

62. Sheldon S. Wolin, "Paradigms and Political Theories," 166.

63. M. D. King, "Reason, Tradition, and the Progressiveness of Science," 104, 105.

64. Ibid., 172–173.

65. Thomas S. Kuhn, *The Structure of Scientific Revolutions,* 35.

66. G. R. Boynton, "Cumulativeness in International Relations," 146. Emphasis in original.

67. Richard K. Ashley, "Noticing Pre-paradigmatic Progress," 152.

68. Ibid. Emphasis in original.

69. Ibid., 153.

70. Dina A. Zinnes, "The Problem of Cumulation," in James N. Rosenau (ed.), *In Search of Global Patterns,* 162. Emphasis in original. Zinnes sees additive cumulation as an "ingredient" of integrative cumulation.

71. Kenneth N. Waltz, *Theory of International Politics* (Reading, MA: Addison-Wesley, 1979), 9.

72. Ibid.

73. Dina A. Zinnes, "The Problem of Cumulation," 163. Emphasis in original.

74. "Behavioralism" is actually a misleading term because political analysts have been observing human behavior since at least biblical times. What distinguished the so-called behavioralists was their determination to introduce the methods common to the natural science into the study of politics.

75. J. David Singer, "The Incompleat Theorist: Insight Without Evidence," in Klaus Knorr and James N. Rosenau (eds.), *Contending Approaches to International Politics* (Princeton: Princeton University Press, 1969), 83–84.

76. Sheldon S. Wolin, "Paradigms and Political Theories," 181.

77. Arend Lijphart, "The Structure of the Theoretical Revolution in International Relations," *International Studies Quarterly* 18:1 (March 1974), 41–74.

78. See, for example, G. D. Wagner and J. Berger, "Do Sociological Theories Grow?" *American Journal of Sociology* 90:4 (1985), 702–704.

79. P. Terrence Hopmann, "Identifying, Formulating, and Solving Puzzles in International Relations Research," 196. Emphasis in original.

80. Ibid., 20.

81. John A. Vasquez, *The Power of Power Politics: A Critique,* chap. 4. The present authors, however, disagree with Vasquez's contention that "realism" itself constituted an overarching paradigm. See infra chapter 4.

82. G. R. Boynton, "Cumulativeness in International Relations," 147. Vasquez in ingenious fashion reviewed and tested hypotheses that were guided by realist assumptions between 1956 and 1970 and concluded that there is a connection between "the dominance of the realist paradigm in the field and the failure of the field to produce much new knowledge." *The Power of Power Politics,* 202.

83. G. R. Boynton, "Cumulativeness in International Relations," 147.

84. Dina A. Zinnes, "The Problem of Cumulation," 164.

85. See, for example, Richard N. Rosecrance, "The Failures of Quantitative Analysis: Possible Causes and Cures," in James N. Rosenau (ed.), *In Search of Global Patterns,* 177.

86. Dina A. Zinnes, "The Problem of Cumulation," 164.

87. See, for example, Harold D. Lasswell and Abraham Kaplan, *Power and Society* (New Haven, CT: Yale University Press, 1950), xxiv.

88. Richard W. Mansbach, Yale H. Ferguson, and Donald E. Lampert, *The Web of World Politics: Nonstate Actors in the Global System* (Englewood Cliffs, NJ: Prentice-Hall, 1976), 30.

89. P. Terrence Hopmann, "Identifying, Formulating, and Solving Puzzles in International Relations Research," 193.

90. P. Braillard, "The Social Sciences and the Study of International Relations," *International Social Science Journal* 102:4 (1984), 634.

91. J. David Singer, "Tribal Sins on the QIP Reservation," in James N. Rosenau (ed.), *In Search of Global Patterns,* 171.

**Chapter Two**

1. See Klaus Knorr and James N. Rosenau (eds.), *Contending Approaches to Interna-

*tional Politics* (Princeton, NJ: Princeton University Press, 1969).

2. Thomas S. Kuhn, *The Structure of Scientific Revolutions,* expanded ed. (Chicago: University of Chicago Press, 1970), 164.

3. Ibid.

4. Patrick J. McGowan and Howard B. Shapiro, *The Comparative Study of Foreign Policy: A Survey of Scientific Findings* (Beverly Hills, CA: Sage Publications, 1973), 223.

5. Ibid., 224.

6. E. H. Carr, *The Twenty Years' Crisis 1919-1939* (New York: St. Martin's Press, 1962), 2.

7. By norms, we refer to considerations that are viewed as ethically compelling.

8. E. H. Carr, *The Twenty Years' Crisis,* 4.

9. R. J. Rummel, "The Roots of Faith," in James N. Rosenau (ed.), *In Search of Global Patterns* (New York: Free Press, 1976), 11. For an interesting "apologia" entailing value change, see Glenn D. Paige, "On Values and Science: *The Korean Decision* Reconsidered," *American Political Science Review* 71:4 (December 1977), 1603-1609.

10. Jacob Bronowski, *The Origins of Knowledge and Imagination* (New Haven, CT: Yale University Press, 1978), 127-129.

11. Ibid., 129. Natural scientists are no more consensual as regards normative commitment than are social scientists. Such commitments are often revealed when scientists are called upon to give advice about controversial public issues like the SALT II Treaty or the Strategic Defense Initiative. For analysis of scientists as advocates, see Robert Gilpin, *American Scientists and Nuclear Weapons Policy* (Princeton: Princeton University Press, 1962); Harold K. Jacobson and Eric Stein, *Diplomats, Scientists, and Politicians* (Ann Arbor, MI: University of Michigan Press, 1966); Eugene B. Skolnikoff, *Science, Technology, and American Foreign Policy* (Cambridge, MA: MIT Press, 1967); and C. P. Snow, *Science and Government* (Cambridge, MA: Harvard University Press, 1961).

12. For a similar approach, see F. Parkinson, *The Philosophy of International Relations: A Study in the History of Thought* (Beverly Hills, CA: Sage Publications, 1977). The varied normative cleavages in classical Greece are discussed in E. R. Dodds's *The Greeks and the Irrational* (Berkeley, CA: University of California Press, 1964).

13. See chapter 4, infra.

14. See Friedrich Meinecke, *Machiavellism: The Doctrine of Raison d'Etat and Its Place in Modern History,* trans. Douglas Scott (New Haven: CT: Yale University Press, 1957). Significant idealists in the European tradition might include Dante, Emeric Crucé, the Duc de Sully, William Penn, the Abbé de Saint Pierre, Rousseau, and Kant.

15. See José Ortega Y Gasset, *The Dehumanization of Art and Other Essays on Art, Culture and Literature* (Princeton: Princeton University Press, 1948), 4.

16. See Lionel Trilling, *Beyond Culture* (New York: Harcourt, Brace, Jovanovich, 1965), 81.

17. Pierre Bourdieu, *Distinction: A Social Critique of the Judgement of Taste,* trans. Richard Nice (Cambridge, MA: Harvard University Press, 1984), 6.

18. The following discussion is partly based on Richard W. Mansbach and John A. Vasquez, *In Search of Theory: A New Paradigm for Global Politics* (New York: Columbia University Press, 1981), 57-60.

19. Among the key values that have been identified as universal are wealth, security, order, freedom, peace, status, health, equality, justice, knowledge, beauty, honesty, and love. See Harold J. Lasswell and Abraham Kaplan, *Power and Society* (New Haven, CT:

Yale University Press, 1950), 55–56, and Ted Robert Gurr, *Why Men Rebel* (Princeton: Princeton University Press, 1970), 24–26. All are subjective constructs that express human aspirations for self-improvement.

20. Efforts to identify relatively permanent value hierarchies are at best elusive and, at worst, probably wrongheaded. See, for example, A. H. Maslow, "A Theory of Human Motivation," *Psychological Review* 50:4 (1943), 370–396, and Vernon Venable, *Human Nature: The Marxist View* (Cleveland, OH: Meridian, 1966), 74–97. Strict Freudians would in all likelihood disagree with this claim.

21. Barbara W. Tuchman, *A Distant Mirror: The Calamitous Fourteenth Century* (New York: Knopf, 1978), 104–105.

22. Hugh Thomas, *A History of the World* (New York: Harper & Row, 1979), 61.

23. James N. Rosenau, "Before cooperation: hegemons, regimes, and habit-driven actors in world politics," *International Organization* 40:4 (Autumn 1986), 861.

24. For a discussion of these variables and the manner in which they function, see Richard W. Mansbach and John A. Vasquez, *In Search of Theory*, 59–63 and 87–124.

25. "Actor" in this context should not be equated with "state" or "government." Rather the concept refers to any purposive group that behaves in a collective and autonomous fashion.

26. Cited in E. H. Carr, *The Twenty Years' Crisis*, 11. Carr argues that the realism-idealism dichotomy reflects the contrast between a belief in determinism and in free will (11–12), yet the Marxian tour de force was precisely turning Hegel on his head and enrolling determinism in the service of idealism. Carr also sees realism as the philosophy of the hard-headed practitioner in contrast to the utopian intellectual (12–19). This, too, seems superficial. There are practitioners and theorists of both stripes, and great leaders—Napoleon, Hitler, Lincoln, Franklin Roosevelt, et al.—tend to portray themselves as devotees of first one and then the other school. And a "realist" leader like Ronald Reagan has little difficulty in rejecting his predecessor's devotion to human rights as quixotic while embracing a technological fix like SDI as the solution to the fear of nuclear war.

27. Hans J. Morgenthau, *Politics Among Nations*, 5th ed., revised (New York: Knopf, 1978), 4.

28. Ibid.

29. Ibid., 3.

30. Kenneth N. Waltz, *Man, the State, and War* (New York: Columbia University Press, 1959), 18ff.

31. Among natural scientists, Freudian psychologists may be viewed as relative pessimists owing to the dark forces that they see as inherent in the human psyche and the putative intractability of these forces. Nevertheless, even this relative pessimism has been recently and eloquently challenged by Bruno Bettelheim. See Bruno Bettelheim, *Freud and Man's Soul* (New York: Knopf, 1983), esp. 103ff. See also Erich Fromm, *Beyond the Chains of Illusion* (New York: Simon & Shuster, 1962), 174ff.

32. See Kenneth N. Waltz, *Man, the State, and War.* Richard K. Ashley characterizes "neorealist" theory as lending "itself wonderfully well to becoming an apologia for the status quo, an excuse for domination." "The Poverty of Neorealism," *International Organization* 38:2 (Spring 1984), 257.

33. See E. H. Carr, *The Twenty Years' Crisis*, 22–27.

34. A similar logic had governed the views of Rousseau and Kant in the eighteenth century.

35. George Soule, *The Coming American Revolution* (New York: Macmillan, 1935),

20. See also Crane Brinton, *The Anatomy of Revolution* (New York: Norton, 1938).

36. By contrast, Edmund Burke in his *Reflections on the Revolution in France* (Garden City, NY: Doubleday, 1961) represented the views of a pessimist whose conservatism would not allow him to accept unbridled change.

37. See Kenneth N. Waltz, "The Stability of a Bipolar World," *Daedalus* 93 (Summer 1964), 881–909, and *Theory of International Politics* (Reading, MA: Addison-Wesley, 1979). The arguments of neorealism and its opponents are summarized in Robert O. Keohane (ed.), *Neorealism and Its Critics* (New York: Columbia University Press, 1986).

38. Robert Heilbroner, *An Inquiry into the Human Prospect* (New York: Norton, 1975), 136–137. Ronald Reagan's rejection of the pessimism of the Carter years was an important factor in his 1980 electoral victory.

39. Sheldon S. Wolin, *Politics and Vision: Continuity and Innovation in Western Political Thought* (Boston: Little, Brown, 1960), 218.

40. Hans J. Morgenthau, *Politics Among Nations,* 231.

41. George F. Kennan, *American Diplomacy 1900–1950* (Chicago: University of Chicago Press, 1951), 82.

42. James Burnham, *The Machiavellians: Defenders of Freedom* (Chicago: Henry Regnery, 1943), 34.

43. For an effort to find a middle path, see Hedley Bull, *The Anarchical Society: A Study of Order in World Politics* (New York: Columbia University Press, 1977). For his part, Robert O. Keohane seeks to provide a less stringent and abstract definition of self-interest based on "a less egotistical formulation of the concept." Robert O. Keohane, *After Hegemony: Cooperation and Discord in the World Political Economy* (Princeton: Princeton University Press, 1984), 110. See also 111–132.

44. Kenneth W. Thompson, "The Study of International Politics: A Survey of Trends and Developments," *Review of Politics* 11:4 (October 1952), 443.

45. Cited in Kenneth N. Waltz, *Man, the State and War,* 97.

46. The distinction between these two emphases reflects the problem of private versus collective benefits. See Mancur Olson, Jr., *The Logic of Collective Action* (Cambridge, MA: Harvard University Press, 1965).

47. Arnold Wolfers, "The Role of Power and the Pole of Indifference," in Wolfers, *Discord and Collaboration: Essays on International Politics* (Baltimore: Johns Hopkins Press, 1962), 86.

48. Kenneth N. Waltz, "International Structure, National Force, and the Balance of World Power." *Journal of International Affairs* 21:2 (1967), 215–231, and Waltz, "The Stability of a Bipolar World."

49. The relationship between status and conflict has become an important and unresolved issue in international relations research. The work of scholars such as Johan Galtung, R. J. Rummel, Manus Midlarsky, and Michael Wallace is especially relevant. Their conclusions largely deny the validity of the elitist assumptions of realists.

50. For an excellent critique of Morgenthau's version of balance of power that shows how its empirical and prescriptive elements become entangled, see Inis L. Claude, Jr., *Power and International Relations* (New York: Random House, 1962), 25–37.

51. Although realism as a whole is largely macroanalytic, individual realists have not been deterred by levels of analysis. Indeed, *The Prince* can, in part, be understood as a "lower level" version of some of the same ideas Machiavelli presents in *The Discourses.* For a discussion of the so-called level-of-analysis problem, see J. David Singer, "The Level-of-Analysis Problem in International Relations," in Klaus Knorr and Sidney Verba

(eds.), *The International System: Theoretical Essays* (Princeton: Princeton University Press, 1961), 77–92.

52. Walter Lippmann, *The Public Philosophy* (New York: Mentor, 1955), 29.

53. Alexis de Tocqueville, *Democracy in America* (New York: Knopf, 1945), vol. I, 234.

54. George F. Kennan, *American Diplomacy 1900–1950,* 81.

55. Hans J. Morgenthau, *Politics Among Nations,* 547.

56. Training in the discipline will, therefore, continue to be characterized by diversity, and this, in turn, will tend to perpetuate competition among theories.

**Chapter Three**

1. This chapter is, of course, focusing upon the evolution of ideas in a Western context. However, we believe our perspective is applicable outside that context and suspect, in fact, that it will rouse less controversy in non-Western contexts where the tradition of "science" described here is less deeply embedded. It is important to note that ethnocentrism remains a significant problem in international relations theory.

2. Philippe Contamine, *War in the Middle Ages,* trans. Michael Jones (Oxford: Basil Blackwell Ltd., 1984), 15. This description conforms to John H. Herz's idea of the "impenetrable" territorial nation-state successfully affording a protective "hard shell" for its inhabitants. *International Politics in the Atomic Age* (New York: Columbia University Press, 1959), 96–108.

3. Philippe Contamine, *War in the Middle Ages,* 15.

4. Ibid., 31.

5. Ibid., 43.

6. Clive Perry, "The Function of Law in the International Community," in Max Sorensen (ed.), *Manual of Public International Law* (New York: St. Martin's Press, 1968), 11.

7. Adda B. Bozeman, *Politics and Culture in International History* (Princeton: Princeton University Press, 1960), 264.

8. Feudalism achieved its highest form in the eleventh and twelfth centuries after the decline of the Frankish empire.

9. See Marc Bloch, *Feudal Society,* trans. L. A. Manyon, vol. 2 (Chicago: University of Chicago Press, 1961).

10. Ibid., vol. 1, 295.

11. Ibid., 296, 297.

12. Adda B. Bozeman, *Politics and Culture in International History,* 273.

13. Marc Bloch, I, *Feudal Society,* 296.

14. For additional information on the evolution of papal doctrine and the position of individual popes on this question, see Nicholas Cheetham, *Keepers of the Keys: A History of the Popes from St. Peter to John Paul II* (New York: Charles Scribner's Sons, 1983).

15. Adda B. Bozeman, *Politics and Culture in International History,* 243.

16. John of Salisbury, "The Statesman's Book" in William Ebenstein (ed.), *Great Political Thinkers,* 4th ed. (New York: Holt, Rinehart & Winston, 1969), 203.

17. Adda B. Bozeman, *Politics and Culture in International History,* 255.

18. Ibid., 256.

19. Ibid.

20. Dante Alighieri, "De Monarchia," in Williams Ebenstein (ed.), *Great Political Thinkers,* 4th ed., 250–260.

21. Ibid.

22. George H. Sabine, *A History of Political Theory,* 3rd ed. (New York: Holt, Rinehart & Winston, 1961), 261.

23. Pierre Dubois, *Recovery of the Holy Land,* cited in Adda B. Bozeman, *Politics and Culture in International History,* 247.

24. Marsilio of Padua, "The Defender of Peace," in William Ebenstein (ed.), *Great Political Thinkers,* 281.

25. Cited in James Burnham, *The Machiavellians: Defenders of Freedom* (Chicago: Henry Regnery Co., 1943), 84–85.

26. For example, Hans Morgenthau in *Politics Among Nations,* 5th ed., revised (New York: Knopf, 1978) cites Machiavelli on alliances, conceptions of politics, limited war, and revolutions in warfare. Raymond Aron in *Peace and War: A Theory of International Relations* (New York: Praeger, 1968) refers to him and/or his ideas on fourteen occasions; Arnold Wolfers in *Discord and Collaboration: Essays on International Politics* (Baltimore: Johns Hopkins Press, 1962) refers to Machiavelli on nine occasions; he is cited on seven occasions in Herbert Butterfield and Martin Wight (eds.), *Diplomatic Investigations: Essays in the Theory of International Politics* (Cambridge, MA: Harvard University Press, 1968); and E. H. Carr cites him even more often in *The Twenty Years' Crisis, 1919–1939* (New York: St. Martin's Press, 1962).

27. Kenneth N. Waltz, *Theory of International Politics* (Reading, MA: Addison-Wesley, 1979), 117.

28. E. H. Carr, *The Twenty Years' Crisis,* 63.

29. J. L. Brierly, *The Law of Nations: An Introduction to the International Law of Peace,* 5th ed. (New York: Oxford University Press, 1955), 6.

30. *The Prince,* chap. XV. We have used the Modern Library Edition of *The Prince and The Discourses,* introduction by Max Lerner (New York: Random House, 1950).

31. Winfried Franke, "The Italian City-State System as an International System," in Morton A. Kaplan (ed.), *New Approaches to International Relations* (New York: St. Martin's Press, 1968), 426. See also Adda B. Bozeman, *Politics and Culture in International History,* 485–489.

32. See, for example, Adda B. Bozeman, *Politics and Culture in International History,* 464–477.

33. Ibid., 477.

34. Ibid., 479.

35. Francesco Guicciardini, *The History of Italy,* trans. Sidney Alexander (London: Collier-Macmillan Ltd., 1969), 48–49.

36. *The Prince,* XXVI.

37. In *The Discourses* (Book 3, XXXI), Machiavelli reiterated this theme. Indeed, *The Art of War* was written by him explicitly to instruct his countrymen how to wage war successfully against countries such as France and Spain.

38. Felix Gilbert, "Machiavelli: The Renaissance of the Art of War," in Edward Mead Earle (ed.), *Makers of Modern Strategy: Military Thought from Machiavelli to Hitler* (New York: Atheneum, 1967), 5.

39. Francesco Guicciardini, *Storie Fiorentine,* cited in Felix Gilbert, "Machiavelli: The Renaissance of the Art of War," 8.

40. *The Prince,* XII. Emphasis added.

41. *The Discourses,* Book 3, XL.

42. See, for example, Sheldon S. Wolin, *Politics and Vision: Continuity and Innovation in Western Political Thought* (Boston: Little, Brown, 1960), 195–203.

43. Ibid., 201.

44. E. H. Carr, *The Twenty Years' Crisis*, 64.

45. See *The Prince*, XI.

46. *The Discourses*, Introduction to Book 2. As for the common man: "For it may be said of men in general that they are ungrateful, voluble, dissemblers, anxious to avoid danger, and covetous of gain. . . ." *The Prince*, XVII.

47. Sheldon S. Wolin, *Politics and Vision*, 209.

48. Friedrich Meinecke, *Machiavellism: The Doctrine of Raison D'Etat and Its Place in Modern History*, trans. Douglas Scott (New Haven: Yale University Press, 1957), 33.

49. See *The Prince*, XXV, and *The Discourses*, Book 2, XXIX. Machiavelli's "fortune" is not unlike what Clausewitz later called "friction" in his discussion of war. Carl Maria von Clausewitz, *On War*, edited and translated by Michael Howard and Peter Paret (Princeton: Princeton University Press, 1976), Book 1, VII.

50. Friedrich Meinecke, *Machiavellism*, 37.

51. *The Discourses*, Book 1, I.

52. *The Prince*, XV.

53. Ibid., XVIII, and *The Discourses*, Book 2, XIII.

54. Friedrich Meinecke, *Machiavellism*, 42.

55. *The Prince*, XXI.

56. *The Discourses*, Book 3, XLI.

**Chapter Four**

1. From time to time, realists themselves are prepared to see their ideas as part of more general worldviews that come to dominate particular periods of history. See Kenneth W. Thompson, *Political Realism and the Crisis of World Politics* (Princeton: Princeton University Press, 1960), 71.

2. See John A. Vasquez, *The Power of Power Politics: A Critique* (New Brunswick: Rutgers University Press, 1983). Ironically, behavioral research—even while retaining realist assumptions—contributed mightily to provoking doubts about the adequacy of its ideas by falsification of its propositions. Such research has been an important factor in producing theoretical fragmentation in the field even while encouraging new methodological orthodoxies.

3. John H. Herz, *The Nation-State and the Crisis of World Politics* (New York: David McKay Co., 1976), 74.

4. See, for example, Robert E. Osgood, *Ideals and Self-Interest in America's Foreign Relations* (Chicago: University of Chicago Press, 1953); George F. Kennan, *American Diplomacy 1900–1950* (Chicago: University of Chicago Press, 1951); and Norman A. Graebner, *Ideas and Diplomacy: Readings in the Intellectual Tradition of American Foreign Policy* (New York: Oxford University Press, 1964).

5. As Inis Claude observed: "I have noted . . . a series of charges that Woodrow Wilson, being a critic of the balance of power and an advocate of collective security, thereby stamped himself as a man unable to stomach the reality of power. This conclusion can be sustained only by indulging in the following process of deduction: Everybody who is realistic about power in international relations believes in the the balance of power; anybody who attacks the idea of the balance of power is *ipso facto*, unrealistic about power; Wilson attacked the balance of power, thereby showing himself as one possessed by the illusion that the power problem is unreal and that power is unimportant in international relations. It is *not* a conclusion which can withstand careful consideration

of the evidence about Wilson." *Power and International Relations* (New York: Random House, 1962), 95. Emphasis in original.

6. Alfred Zimmern, *The Greek Commonwealth: Politics and Economics in Fifth-Century Athens* (New York: Oxford University Press, 1961), 199.

7. Friedrich Meinecke, *Machiavellism* (New Haven: Yale University Press, 1957), 208.

8. Arnold Wolfers and Laurence W. Martin (eds.), *The Anglo-American Tradition in Foreign Affairs* (New Haven: Yale University Press, 1956), xxv.

9. Ibid., xviii. It is probably not coincidental that a number of leading postwar American realists, like Morgenthau and Reinhold Neibuhr, reached maturity in Europe.

10. See Kenneth N. Waltz, *Theory of International Politics* (Reading, MA: Addison-Wesley, 1979).

11. Luther's expedient endorsement of state power as necessary to achieve heavenly paradise resembles Lenin's later compromise with state power as necessary for the achievement of an earthly paradise and the "withering" of the state itself.

12. See, for example, the Huguenot tract *Vindiciae contra tyrannos* published in 1579 under the pseudonym of Stephen Junius Brutus.

13. For an excellent analysis of Bodin's ideas and their context, see Julian H. Franklin, *Jean Bodin and the Rise of Absolutist Theory* (Cambridge: Cambridge University Press, 1973).

14. Richard N. Rosecrance, *Action and Reaction in World Politics: International Systems in Perspective* (Boston: Little, Brown, 1963), 25.

15. Edward Vose Gulick, *Europe's Classical Balance of Power: A Case History of the Theory and Practice of One of the Great Concepts of European Statecraft* (New York: Norton, 1955), 4. Emphasis in original.

16. See J. D. B. Miller, "Sovereignty as a source of vitality for the state," *Review of International Studies* 12:2 (1986), 79–89. In contemporary international politics, recognition of the sovereign independence of a political entity is less a source of "vitality" than it is a *post hoc* acknowledgment by the international community (or some group within it) that the entity is already playing a significant international role. Or, in the case of many new states, recognition of sovereignty is merely an honorific appellation that only marginally alters their impotence and dependence.

17. Harold Nicolson, *Diplomacy,* 3rd ed. (New York: Oxford University Press, 1963), 24.

18. Cited in Kenneth N. Waltz, *Man, the State and War* (New York: Columbia University Press, 1959), 101.

19. Cited in Paul H. Beik and Laurence Lafore, *Modern Europe: A History Since 1500* (New York: Henry Holt, 1959), 335.

20. The hypothesis that revolution is an expression of frustrated optimism is articulated by James C. Davies, "Toward a Theory of Revolution," *American Sociological Review* 27:1 (February 1962), 6.

21. René Albrecht-Carrié, *The Concert of Europe* (New York: Harper & Row, 1968), 4.

22. Richard N. Rosecrance, *Action and Reaction in World Politics: International Systems in Perspective,* 55–56.

23. John Bowle, *Politics and Opinion in the Nineteenth Century* (New York: Oxford University Press, 1964), 27.

24. Hegel, for one, enthusiastically greeted the invading French armies as harbingers of cultural advance. See Shlomo Avinieri, "Hegel and Nationalism" in Walter Kaufmann (ed.), *Hegel's Political Philosophy* (New York: Atherton Press, 1970), 110.

25. John Bowle, *Politics and Opinion in the Nineteenth Century,* 30.

26. Ibid., 37. For a persuasive argument that Hegel was actually antinationalist but was misunderstood by his followers, see Shlomo Avinieri, "Hegel and Nationalism," 109–136.

27. Ibid., 42.

28. Cf. the ebullient and optimistic nationalism of *Fidelio* with the racist mythology of *Siegfried.*

29. The French attitude is perhaps best summarized in Léon Gambetta's advice regarding the lost provinces—"Think of it always, speak of it never." Cited in René Albrecht-Carrié, *A Diplomatic History of Europe Since the Congress of Vienna* (New York: Harper & Row, 1958), 167. In Russia, the individual who perhaps best reflected prevailing currents of Panslav nationalism was Mikhail Nikoforovich Katkov, editor of *Moskovskie Vyedomosti.* See George F. Kennan, *The Decline of Bismarck's European Order: Franco-Russian Relations, 1875–1890* (Princeton: Princeton University Press, 1979), 33, 94–95.

30. Heinrich von Treitschke, "The State Idea," in M. G. Forsyth, H. M. A. Keens-Soper, P. Savigear (eds.), *The Theory of International Relations; Selected Texts from Gentili to Treitschke* (New York: Atherton Press, 1970), 326.

31. Heinrich von Treitschke, "International Law and International Intercourse," in ibid., 338.

32. Ibid., 339.

33. Heinrich von Treitschke, "The State Idea," in M. G. Forsyth, et al., (eds.), *The Theory of International Relations,* 327.

34. John Bowle, *Politics and Opinion in the Nineteenth Century,* 299.

35. Alfred Zimmern, *The League of Nations and the Rule of Law, 1935–1938* (London: Macmillan, 1939), 2.

36. See E. H. Carr, *The Twenty Years' Crisis 1919–1939* (New York: St. Martin's Press, 1962), 2.

37. See Kenneth W. Thompson, "The Study of International Politics: A Survey of Trends and Developments," *Review of Politics* 14:4 (October 1952), 437–439.

38. David Wilkinson, *Deadly Quarrels: Lewis F. Richardson and the Statistical Study of War* (Berkeley, CA: University of California Press, 1980), 7.

39. John A. Vasquez, *The Power of Power Politics,* 14.

40. Kenneth W. Thompson, "The Study of International Politics," 434.

41. Ibid., 438.

42. Ibid., 437.

43. Cited in William T. R. Fox, "Interwar International Relations Research: The American Experience," *World Politics* 2:1 (October 1949), 68.

44. Hedley Bull, "The Theory of International Politics 1919–1969," in B. Porter (ed.), *The Aberystwyth Papers: International Politics 1919–1969* (London: Oxford University Press, 1972), 34.

45. Kenneth N. Waltz, *Man, the State and War,* 111.

46. Woodrow Wilson, "The World Must Be Made Safe for Democracy," from an address to Congress, April 2, 1917 in John A. Vasquez (ed.), *Classics of International Relations* (Englewood Cliffs, NJ: Prentice-Hall, 1986), 16.

47. Woodrow Wilson, "The Fourteen Points," from an address to Congress, January 8, 1918 in ibid., 18. This passage well reflects the influence that Immanual Kant had on Wilson.

48. Such analogies were sharply denounced by realists as false and misleading. In Hans Morgenthau's words: "All history shows that nations active in international politics

are continuously preparing for, actively involved in, or recovering from organized violence in the form of war. In the domestic politics of Western democracies, on the other hand, organized violence as an instrument of political action on an extensive scale has become a rare exception." *Politics Among Nations: The Struggle for Power and Peace,* 5th ed., revised (New York: Knopf, 1978), 42.

49. Woodrow Wilson, cited in Kenneth N. Waltz, *Man, the State and War,* 118.

50. Ibid. See also Arnold Wolfers, "The Pole of Power and the Pole of Indifference," in Wolfers, *Discord and Collaboration: Essays on International Politics* (Baltimore: Johns Hopkins Press, 1962), 101.

51. John A. Vasquez, *The Power of Power Politics,* 15.

52. *The Prince,* xv.

53. See, for example, Hans J. Morgenthau, "Another Great Debate: The National Interest of the United States," *American Political Science Review* 46:4 (December 1952), 961–988. See also Morgenthau, *In Defense of the National Interest* (New York: Knopf, 1951).

54. See James E. Dougherty and Robert L. Pfaltzgraff, Jr., *Contending Theories of International Relations: A Comprehensive Survey,* 2nd ed. (New York: Harper & Row, 1981), 10 and 45, footnote 38. International relations courses in the 1950s consisted largely of realist texts and analyses of U.S.-Soviet relations.

55. John A. Vasquez, *The Power of Power Politics,* 17.

56. In recent years, heated disputes arising from shifting normative emphases have been clearly reflected in analyses of the causes of the Cold War, but they were equally characteristic of analyses of earlier wars as well. Revisionist history is an almost inevitable companion of changing social norms.

57. Hans J. Morgenthau, *Politics Among Nations,* 5th ed., revised, 134–155.

58. Ibid., 158.

59. Relatively little has been written regarding the utility of Kuhn's framework to international relations. For contrasting views, see Richard Smith Beal, "A Contra-Kuhnian View of the Discipline's Growth," in James N. Rosenau (ed.), *In Search of Global Patterns* (New York: Free Press, 1976), 158–161, and Arend Lijphart, "The Structure of the Theoretical Revolution in International Relations," *International Studies Quarterly* 18:1 (March 1974), 41–74. The "paradigm" concept is finding increasing acceptance in the discipline, though often in a largely metaphorical sense. Of special interest in this regard is the recent work of Hayward R. Alker, Jr. See Alker and Thomas J. Biersteker, "The Dialectics of World Order: Notes for a Future Archeologist of International Savoir Faire," *International Studies Quarterly* 28:2 (June 1984), 121–142.

60. Thomas S. Kuhn, *The Structure of Scientific Revolutions,* expanded ed. (Chicago: University of Chicago Press, 1970), 52–53.

61. See, for example, Hans J. Morgenthau, *Politics Among Nations,* 5th ed., revised, 193. Realists were especially enamored of European balance-of-power practice, frequently alleging that Americans had been able to ignore this practice—at their peril—because of the fortunate circumstances of geography. See Robert E. Osgood, *Ideals and Self-Interest in America's Foreign Relations.*

62. Hans J. Morgenthau, *Politics Among Nations,* 5th ed., revised, 3.

63. Ibid., 16.

64. Realists have astutely pointed out that a nation-state's self-image is not always compatible with the "realities" of power. This insight has provided a basis for theories of status equilibrium and disequilibrium.

65. Hans J. Morgenthau, *Politics Among Nations,* 5th ed., revised, 12.

66. See Robert A. Packenham, *Liberal America and the Third World: Political Development Ideas in Foreign Aid and Social Science* (Princeton: Princeton University Press, 1973), 245.

67. Bernard Brodie, *War and Politics* (New York: Macmillan, 1973), 368, 365.

68. Richard J. Barnet, *The Roots of War* (Baltimore: Penguin, 1973), 65.

69. David Halberstam, *The Best and the Brightest* (New York: Random House, 1972), 69.

70. Arnold Wolfers, "National Security as an Ambiguous Symbol," in Wolfers, *Discord and Collaboration*, 147.

71. Richard J. Barnet, *Roots of War*, 109ff.

72. Hans J. Morgenthau, *Politics Among Nations*, 5th ed., revised, 7.

73. Thomas S. Kuhn, *The Structure of Scientific Revolutions*, 34. Perhaps the best analysis of the work of behavioral and quantitative scholars in this context is John A. Vasquez, *The Power of Power Politics*.

74. See, for example, Robert Jervis, *Perception and Misperception in International Politics* (Princeton, NJ: Princeton University Press, 1976).

75. See, for example, Charles F. Hermann, *Crises in Foreign Policy* (Indianapolis: Bobbs-Merrill, 1969).

76. See, for example, Graham T. Allison, *Essence of Decision: Explaining the Cuban Missile Crisis* (Boston: Little, Brown, 1971), and Morton H. Halperin, *Bureaucratic Politics and Foreign Policy* (Washington, DC: Brookings, 1974).

77. See, for example, Robert O. Keohane and Joseph Nye, Jr. (eds.), *Transnational Relations and World Politics* (Cambridge, MA: Harvard University Press, 1972), and Keohane and Nye, *Power and Interdependence: World Politics in Transition* (Boston: Little, Brown, 1977).

78. See, for example, Richard W. Mansbach, Yale H. Ferguson and Donald E. Lampert, *The Web of World Politics: Nonstate Actors in the Global System* (Englewood Cliffs, NJ: Prentice-Hall, 1976).

79. See, for example, Edward L. Morse, *Modernization and the Transformation of International Relations* (New York: Free Press, 1976), and Richard W. Mansbach and John A. Vasquez, *In Search of Theory: A New Paradigm for Global Politics* (New York: Columbia University Press, 1981).

80. Thomas S. Kuhn, *The Structure of Scientific Revolutions*, 182. See also Kuhn, "Second Thoughts on Paradigms," in F. Suppe (ed.), *The Structure of Scientific Theories* (Urbana, IL: University of Illinois Press, 1971), 462–463 and Kuhn, *The Essential Tension* (Chicago: University of Chicago Press, 1977), xvi–xxiii.

81. See, for example, Harold D. Lasswell, *World Politics and Personal Insecurity* (New York: McGraw-Hill, 1935), and Alexander and Juliette George, *Woodrow Wilson and Colonel House* (New York: Day, 1956).

82. See, for example, Samuel P. Huntington, *The Common Defense* (New York: Columbia University Press, 1961), and Warner R. Schilling, Paul Hammond, and Glenn Snyder (eds.), *Strategy, Politics, and Defense Budgets* (New York: Columbia University Press, 1962).

83. See, for example, Ernst B. Haas, *The Uniting of Europe: Political, Social and Economic Forces* (Stanford: Stanford University Press, 1958).

84. See, for example, Bruce M. Russett, *Trends in World Politics* (New York: Macmillan, 1965), and Raymond Vernon, *Sovereignty at Bay: The Multinational Spread of U.S. Enterprises* (New York: Basic Books, 1971).

85. The postwar explosion of scholarly publications in international relations theory

was dominantly American. Consequently, perceived changes in American status have had a fundamental impact on theory. See K. J. Holsti, *The Dividing Discipline: Hegemony and Diversity in International Theory* (Boston: Allen & Unwin, 1985), 102–128.

86. See, for example, Michael Howard, "Reassurance and Deterrence: Western Defense in the 1980s," *Foreign Affairs* 61:2 (Winter 1982–83), 309–324.

87. See Richard W. Mansbach and John A. Vasquez, *In Search of Theory*, 110–113. The concept of "critical issue" has been analyzed largely in the context of American politics and has to date received little attention in international relations. At present, the process in which a single all-encompassing issue arrives at the apex of the global agenda is only poorly understood.

88. See, for example, Dennis Pirages, *A New Context for International Relations: Global Ecopolitics* (North Scituate, MA: Duxbury Press, 1978).

89. See Richard K. Ashley, "The Poverty of Neorealism," *International Organization* 38:2 (Spring 1984), 232.

90. See, for example, Robert O. Keohane and Joseph S. Nye, Jr. (eds.), *Transnational Relations and World Politics;* Ole R. Holsti, Randolph M. Siverson and Alexander George (eds.), *Change in the International System* (Boulder, CO: Westview/Praeger, 1980); Stephen D. Krasner (ed.), *International Regimes* (Ithaca, NY: Cornell University Press, 1983); and John Gerard Ruggie (ed.), *The Antinomies of Interdependence: National Welfare and the Division of Labor* (New York: Columbia University Press, 1983).

91. See Robert O. Keohane, *After Hegemony: Cooperation and Discord in the World Political Economy* (Princeton, NJ: Princeton University Press, 1984), esp. 5–17. See also Keohane, "Theory of World Politics: Structural Realism and Beyond," in Keohane (ed.), *Neorealism and Its Critics* (New York: Columbia University Press, 1986), 158–203.

92. Kenneth N. Waltz, *Theory of World Politics.* In "The Poverty of Neorealism," Richard Ashley argues that a new synthesis—"neorealism"—has already emerged to replace classical realism, and he declares that: "In the United States of the 1980s, neorealism and its structural theory of hegemony frames the measured discourse and ritual of a generation of graduate students in international politics" (227). In addition, Ashley provides something of a *Weltgeist* interpretation for this development by viewing it as paralleling "structuralist triumphs in such fields as linguistics, sociology, anthropology, and philosophy" (234). While some of his criticisms of neorealism are telling (e.g., reliance on economic logic and revival of state-centricity), his argument is diluted by a self-conscious polemicism. See Robert G. Gilpin's response, "The Richness of the Tradition of Political Realism," *International Organization* 38:2 (Spring 1984), esp. 289. Nevertheless, Ashley correctly sees a renewed emphasis upon immutability (structural dominance), pessimism, competitiveness, and elitism (hegemony). These and several other arresting critiques of neorealism are reproduced in Robert O. Keohane (ed.), *Neorealism and Its Critics.*

93. Robert O. Keohane, *After Hegemony*, 105.

94. At the time this is being written it remains unclear whether or not the "Iranagua" scandal will prove sufficiently serious to trigger a new normative crisis in the United States.

95. Charles E. Lindblom and David Cohen, *Usable Knowledge: Social Science and Social Problem Solving* (New Haven: Yale University Press, 1979), 79. See also Oran R. Young, "The Perils of Odysseus: On Constructing Theories of International Relations," *World Politics* 24: Supplement (Spring 1972), 179–203.

96. See, for example, Michael Useem, "Government Influence on the Social Science Paradigm," *Sociological Quarterly* 17:2 (Spring 1976), 159–160.

97. Bernard Barber, *Science and the Social Order* (London: Allen & Unwin, 1953), 4. See also Duncan J. Macrae, *The Social Function of Social Science* (New Haven: Yale University Press, 1976), passim.

## Chapter 5

1. Martin Wight, "Why Is There No International Theory?" in Herbert Butterfield and Martin Wight (eds.), *Diplomatic Investigations: Essays in the Theory of International Politics* (Cambridge: MA: Harvard University Press, 1968), 17. For a more positive evaluation of the state of international relations theory, see Warren R. Phillips, "Where Have All the Theories Gone?" *World Politics* 26:2 (January 1974), 155–188.

2. Wight, "Why Is There No International Theory?" 18.

3. Ibid., 21.

4. Hans J. Morgenthau, *Politics among Nations: The Struggle for Power and Peace,* 5th ed. rev. (New York: Knopf, 1978), esp. chap. 1 and part III.

5. Inis L. Claude, Jr., "Myths about the State," *Review of International Studies,* 12:1 (1986), 1.

6. Claude discusses seven "myths" that he sees as having grown up in specialized contexts and eras. Ibid., 1–10.

7. Benjamin N. Cardozo, *The Nature of the Judicial Process* (New Haven: Yale University Press, 1921), 13.

8. William J. Brennan, Jr., "The Constitution of the United States: Contemporary Ratification," Text and Teaching Symposium, Georgetown University, Washington, DC, October 12, 1985, 9.

9. Oliver Wendell Holmes, *The Common Law* (1881), cited in Jack Greenberg, "Litigation for Social Change: Methods, Limits and Role in Democracy," *Record of the Association of the Bar of the City of New York* 29 (1974), 347.

10. Benjamin N. Cardozo, *The Nature of the Judicial Process,* 76–77, 81–82, 82–83.

11. It was this concern that prompted the present authors to examine the concept of "international actor" over a decade ago. See Richard W. Mansbach, Yale H. Ferguson, and Donald E. Lampert, *The Web of World Politics: Nonstate Actors in the Global System* (Englewood Cliffs, NJ: Prentice-Hall, 1976). At that time, the authors argued that among the factors that accounted for the longevity of the concept were the relatively easy availability of aggregate data regarding states, the desire of scholars to work with readily comparable data, and their preference for units of analysis that did not overlap (30). We have no reason to revise that assessment but have concluded that the problem has significantly deeper sources than we then suspected.

12. F. H. Hinsley, *Sovereignty,* 2nd ed. (Cambridge: Cambridge University Press, 1986), 120.

13. Immanuel Wallerstein, *The Modern World-System: Capitalist Agriculture and the Origins of the European World-Economy in the Sixteenth Century* (New York: Academic Press, 1974), 357.

14. Nicos Poulantzas, *State, Power, Socialism,* trans. Patrick Camiller (London: NLB, 1978), 7.

15. J. P. Nettl, "The State as a Conceptual Variable," *World Politics* 20:4 (July 1968), 559.

16. Stephen D. Krasner, "Approaches to the State: Alternative Conceptions and Historical Dynamics," *Comparative Politics* 16:2 (January 1984), 223.

17. Stephen D. Krasner, "State Power and the Structure of International Trade," *World Politics* 28:3 (April 1976), 317.

18. Stephen D. Krasner, "Approaches to the State," 244.

19. Sabino Cassese, "The Rise and Decline of the Notion of State," *International Political Science Review* 7:2 (April 1986), 121.

20. J. W. Burton, *Systems, States, Diplomacy and Rules* (New York: Cambridge University Press, 1968), 9.

21. Donald J. Puchala, *International Politics Today* (New York: Harper & Row, 1971), 28.

22. Bertrand Badie and Pierre Birnbaum, *The Sociology of the State,* trans. Arthur Goldhammer (Chicago: University of Chicago Press, 1983), 139–140.

23. Ronald Cohen, "Introduction" in Ronald Cohen and Elman R. Service (eds.), *Origins of the State: The Anthropology of Political Evolution* (Philadelphia: ISHI, 1978), 8. For intriguing support from the perspective of natural selection theory that "the state" emerged from processes of both cooperation and conflict, see Roger D. Masters, "The Biological Nature of the State," *World Politics* 35:2 (January 1983), 161–193.

24. Ronald Cohen, "Introduction" in Ronald Cohen and Elman R. Service (eds.), *Origins of the State,* 8.

25. Ibid., 2. As we suggest elsewhere in this book, Cohen's personal definition is essentially Weberian. See also Ronald Cohen, "State Origins: A Reappraisal" in Henri J. M. Claessen and Peter Skalnik (eds.), *The Early State* (The Hague, The Netherlands: Mouton Publishers, 1978), 31–75. Two additional essays in Part One of this collection are particularly useful: the editors' "The Early State: Theories and Hypotheses," 3–29; and Anatoli M. Khazanov, "Some Theoretical Problems of the Study of the Early State," 77–92.

26. Jonathan Haas, *The Evolution of the Prehistoric State* (New York: Columbia University Press, 1982), 2–3. Emphasis added.

27. Ernest Gellner, *Nations and Nationalism* (Ithaca, NY: Cornell University Press, 1983), 5. Emphasis in original. See also: George Modelski, "Agraria and Industria: Two Models of the International System" in Klaus Knorr and Sidney Verba (eds.), *The International System* (Princeton: Princeton University Press, 1961), 125ff.; and Roger D. Masters, "World Politics as a Primitive Political System," *World Politics* 16:4 (July 1964), 595–619.

28. Bertrand Badie and Pierre Birnbaum, *The Sociology of the State,* 65.

29. Ibid., 103.

30. Ibid., 60.

31. Ibid., 105.

32. Ibid., 105–115.

33. Ibid., 103–104.

34. Morton H. Fried, "The State, the Chicken, and the Egg: or What Came First?" in Ronald Cohen and Elman R. Service (eds.), *Origins of the State,* 37.

35. Oran R. Young, "The Actors in World Politics," in James N. Rosenau, Vincent Davis, and Maurice A. East (eds.), *The Analysis of International Politics* (New York: Free Press, 1972), 127.

36. For example, see Adda B. Bozeman, *Politics and Culture in International History* (Princeton: Princeton University Press, 1960); Robert G. Wesson, *State Systems: International Pluralism, Politics, and Culture* (New York: Free Press, 1978); Allen W. John-

son and Timothy Earle, *The Evolution of Human Societies: From Foraging Group to Agrarian State* (Stanford, CA: Stanford University Press, 1987; S. N. Eisenstadt, *The Political Systems of Empires* (New York: Free Press, 1963); John H. Kautsky, *The Politics of Aristocratic Empires* (Chapel Hill, NC: University of North Carolina Press, 1982); M. I. Finley, *Politics in the Ancient World* (Cambridge: Cambridge University Press, 1983); John A. Armstrong, *Nations before Nationalism* (Chapel Hill, NC: University of North Carolina Press, 1982); Anthony D. Smith, *The Ethnic Origins of Nations* (Oxford: Blackwell, 1986); and John H. Hall (ed.), *States in History* (Oxford: Oxford University Press, 1986).

37. Charles W. Kegley, Jr., and Eugene R. Wittkopf, *World Politics: Trends and Transformation*, 2nd ed. (New York: St. Martin's Press, 1985), fn. 78–79.

38. David Vital, "Back to Machiavelli," in Klaus Knorr and James N. Rosenau (eds.), *Contending Approaches to International Politics* (Princeton: Princeton University Press, 1969), 155–156. Emphasis in original.

39. Oran R. Young, "The Actors in World Politics," 131. See also Richard W. Mansbach, Yale H. Ferguson, and Donald E. Lampert, *The Web of World Politics*, 22–25.

40. William W. Bishop, Jr., *International Law: Cases and Materials*, 3rd ed. (Boston: Little, Brown, 1971), 306–307.

41. Bruce M. Russett and Harvey Starr, *World Politics: The Menu for Choice* (San Francisco: W. H. Freeman, 1981), 68. Emphasis in original.

42. See Johan Galtung, "The Social Sciences: An Essay on Polarization and Integration," in Klaus Knorr and James N. Rosenau (eds.), *Contending Approaches to International Politics*, 243–285.

43. See, for example, J. David Singer, *The Wages of War, 1816–1965: A Statistical Handbook* (New York: Wiley, 1972). Efforts by COW (Correlates of War) scholars to test hypotheses about the onset of war using status ordering, alliance aggregation, and so forth as intervening variables are complicated by uncertainty as to the comparability of the units that constitute the global system during different historical eras.

44. This is the thrust of the model advanced in F. H. Hinsley, *Sovereignty.*

45. John A. Hall, *States in History*, 16–17.

46. John H. Herz, *International Politics in the Atomic Age* (New York: Columbia University Press, 1959), chaps. 2–4. See also John H. Herz, *The Nation-State and the Crisis of World Politics* (New York: David McKay, 1976), chaps. 3 and 8. In addition, see especially on this period: Charles Tilly (ed.), *The Formation of National States in Western Europe* (Princeton: Princeton University Press, 1975).

47. J. P. Nettl observes: "It is significant that the word *l'État* in French should be the only one normally beginning with a capital letter." ("The State as a Conceptual Variable," 567).

48. Bertrand Badie and Pierre Birnbaum, *The Sociology of the State*, 114.

49. Ibid., 105.

50. Peter Worsley, *The Three Worlds: Culture and World Development* (Chicago: University of Chicago Press, 1984), 273.

51. Wesson describes the process of decay in the latter stages of Louis XIV's long reign: "The model monarchy of Louis XIV decayed in its last decades, and some began calling for security of property and an end to religious persecution and arbitrary government. . . . Personal monarchy decayed into bureaucratic as government became professionalized. Roads, communications, and postal services that governments fostered for ease of administration and improvement of national economies, made for greater political awareness. New middle classes deriving wealth from nonofficial sources acquired more

importance . . . and there was a revolutionary increase of foreign trade, . . . Growing knowledge of far off lands broadened horizons and assisted criticisms of domestic foibles. The idea that the wealth of the people made the greatness of the sovereign . . . grew into the thesis of 'benevolent despotism,' by which it became fashionable to think of princes ruling not by divine mandate, which lost intellectual respectability, but because enlightened, therefore benevolent despots were responsible for the progress and happiness of their people—a doctrine dangerous for monarchy. Although the philosophers saw no alternative to monarchy, recollection of medieval natural law gave a basis for new ideas of rights; and several thinkers derived sovereignty directly from the people. Power became a trust rather than a God-given privilege, a mandate to be exercised by reason. Contract theories of the state, a reflection of the importance of commercial relations, gained in importance" (*State Systems*, 142).

52. Among the extensive literature on nationalism, see, Ernest Gellner, *Nations and Nationalism;* Hugh Seton-Watson, *Nations and States* (Boulder, CO: Westview Press, 1977); Hans Kohn, *The Idea of Nationalism* (New York: Macmillan, 1944); and Frederick Hertz, *Nationality in History and Politics* (New York: Humanities Press, 1944).

53. Ernest Gellner, *Nations and Nationalism*, 56.

54. Ibid., 34.

55. Peter Worsley, *The Three Worlds*, 292.

56. See John A. Armstrong, *Nations before Nationalism* and Anthony D. Smith, *The Ethnic Origin of Nations*. Armstrong and Smith both emphasize the importance of ethnicity in the world's political evolution. Ethnic identities are real and widespread; many have a long history, in some cases actually extending into prehistory; and the existence of an ethnic core was critical to establishment of some modern states. Nevertheless, continued ethnic fragmentation remains a major challenge to many present "nation-builders" (and maintainers).

57. Ernest Gellner, *Nations and Nationalism*, 55–56.

58. Peter Worsley, *The Three Worlds*, 252.

59. This postwar development is not unprecedented. The breakup of the Austro-Hungarian and Russian empires as a consequence of World War I and the spreading of the "national principle" by Western liberals produced a host of weak and economically dependent states in Central Europe that proved ready prey for Nazi influence in the 1930s. Arguably, the erosion of the Roman Empire had the same consequences.

60. Peter Worsley, *The Three Worlds*, 290.

61. Ibid.

62. Ibid., 289.

63. W. Raymond Duncan, *Latin American Politics; A Developmental Approach* (New York: Praeger, 1976), 121.

64. Alessandro Passerin D'Entreves, *The Notion of the State: An Introduction to Political Theory* (London: Oxford University Press, 1967), 96.

65. Clifford Geertz, *Negara: The Theatre State in Nineteenth Century Bali* (Princeton: Princeton University Press, 1981).

66. J. P. Nettl, "The State as a Conceptual Variable," 560.

67. F. H. Hinsley, *Sovereignty*, 1. Hinsley's is a brilliant study, by far the best to date, of the historical evolution of the concept.

68. Alan James, *Sovereign Statehood: The Basis of International Society* (London: Allen & Unwin, 1986), 25.

69. Ibid., especially 180ff.

70. Ibid., 276–277.

71. See especially Robert H. Jackson and Carl G. Rosberg, "Why Africa's Weak States Persist: The Empirical and the Juridical in Statehood," *World Politics* 35:1 (October 1982), 1–24; Robert H. Jackson, "Negative Sovereignty in Sub-Saharan Africa," *Review of International Studies* 12:4 (October 1986), 246–264; and Robert H. Jackson, "African States and International Theory," paper delivered at the British International Studies Association annual meeting, University of Reading, Reading, England, 16 December 1986.

72. Robert H. Jackson, "African States and International Theory," 29.

73. Ibid., 4–7. See also James Mayall, "The Variety of States," paper delivered at the British International Studies Association annual meeting, University of Reading, Reading, England, 16 December 1986.

74. Robert H. Jackson, "African States and International Theory," 33.

75. Ibid., 36–38. The reference is to J. D. B. Miller, "Sovereignty as a Source of Vitality for the State," *Review of International Studies* 12:2 (April 1986), 79–91.

76. Robert H. Jackson and Carl G. Rosberg, "Why Africa's Weak States Persist," 13–14.

77. John Gerard Ruggie, "Continuity and Transformation in the World Polity: Toward a Neorealist Synthesis," *World Politics* 35:2 (January 1983), 275–276.

78. Ibid., footnote 39, 276. The present authors see no reason to alter those views.

79. Kenneth N. Waltz, *Theory of International Politics* (Reading, MA: Addison-Wesley, 1979), 96.

80. John Gerard Ruggie, "Continuity and Transformation in the World Polity," footnote 39, 276.

81. Ibid., 276. Emphasis in original.

82. Ibid., 280. Emphasis in original.

83. For a careful analysis of Weber's writings on the state and citations to his major works, see Bertrand Badie and Pierre Birnbaum, *The Sociology of the State,* 17–24. We have drawn heavily on Badie and Birnbaum in our discussions of Weber, as well as of Durkheim and Parsons infra.

84. Eric A. Nordlinger, *On the Autonomy of the Democratic State* (Cambridge, MA: Harvard University Press, 1981).

85. Bertrand Badie and Pierre Birnbaum, *The Sociology of the State,* 23–24.

86. Quoted in ibid., 12.

87. Ibid., 28.

88. Ibid., 27.

89. Ibid., 56.

90. Ibid., 49.

91. Ibid., 60.

92. Ibid., 62.

93. Ibid., 100–101. See also Howard J. Wiarda, *Ethnocentrism in Foreign Policy: Can We Understand the Third World?* (Washington, DC: American Enterprise Institute for Public Policy Research, 1985). On participation, see especially Samuel P. Huntington and Joan M. Nelson, *No Easy Choice: Political Participation in Developing Countries* (Cambridge, MA: Harvard University Press, 1976).

94. Stephen D. Krasner, *Defending the National Interest: Raw Materials Investments and U.S. Foreign Policy* (Princeton: Princeton University Press, 1978), 21. For a succinct description of the Marxist model of international relations, see Wojciech Kostecki, "A Marxist Paradigm of International Relations," *International Studies Notes* 12:1 (Fall 1985), 19–21.

95. Stephen D. Krasner, *Defending the National Interest*, 27.

96. Associated especially with the work of Graham Allison and Morton Halperin. We will examine this approach in chapter 7.

97. Stephen D. Krasner, "Approaches to the State," 224–225.

98. Eric A. Nordlinger, *On the Autonomy of the Democratic State*, 11. Emphasis added.

99. Ibid., 9–10.

100. Ibid., 8.

101. Ibid., 7.

102. Ibid., 186–187. Emphasis in original.

103. In Great Britain, devices such as cabinet responsibility serve to perpetuate the same myth.

104. Manfred Wilhelmy, "Politics, Bureaucracy, and Foreign Policy in Chile" in Heraldo Muñoz and Joseph S. Tulchin (eds.), *Latin American Nations in World Politics* (Boulder, CO: Westview Press, 1984), 50.

105. Dina A. Zinnes, "Prerequisites for the Study of System Transformation" in Ole R. Holsti, Randolph M. Silverson, and Alexander L. George (eds.), *Change in the International System* (Boulder, CO: Westview Press, 1980), 5.


## Chapter Six

1. Efforts to study national attributes in order to predict and explain behavior avoid the need to assume rationality. The results of this research have, however, been disappointing to date. Even more importantly, such research is difficult to relate to policy because the variables upon which it focuses tend to be nonmanipulable.

2. John A. Vasquez, *The Power of Power Politics: A Critique* (New Brunswick, NJ; Rutgers University Press, 1983), 205. Emphasis added. As noted earlier, the present authors do not consider realism to be a genuine paradigm.

3. Hans J. Morgenthau, *Politics among Nations*, 5th ed., revised (New York: Knopf, 1978), 5. Emphasis added.

4. Steve Smith, "Theories of Foreign Policy: An Historical View," *Review of International Studies* 12:1 (January 1986), 14–15.

5. Hans J. Morgenthau, *Politics among Nations*, 5th ed., revised, 4.

6. Ibid., 5. Emphasis added.

7. Ibid., 7.

8. Ibid., 8.

9. John A. Vasquez, *The Power of Power Politics*, 216.

10. Ibid.

11. Ibid., 17.

12. Sidney Verba, "Assumptions of Rationality and Non-Rationality in Models of the International System" in Klaus Knorr and Sidney Verba (eds.), *The International System: Theoretical Essays* (Princeton: Princeton University Press, 1961), 95. This model was always regarded as an "ideal type." Neither sufficient information nor information-processing capability was believed to be available to individuals for its attainment.

13. Richard W. Cottam, *Foreign Policy Motivation* (Pittsburgh: University of Pittsburgh Press, 1977), 3.

14. Thomas C. Schelling, *The Strategy of Conflict* (New York: Oxford University Press, 1963), and Schelling, *Arms and Influence* (New Haven: Yale University Press, 1966).

15. Herman Kahn, *Thinking about the Unthinkable* (New York: Horizon Press, 1962).

16. Herman Kahn, *On Escalation: Metaphors and Scenarios* (New York: Praeger, 1965).

17. John D. Steinbruner, *The Cybernetic Theory of Decision: New Dimensions of Political Analysis* (Princeton, NJ: Princeton University Press, 1974), 9.

18. Richard J. Barnet, *Roots of War: The Men and Institutions behind U.S. Foreign Policy* (Baltimore: Penguin, 1973), 44.

19. Richard W. Cottam, *Foreign Policy Motivation*, 6. For a penetrating analysis of the effect of Vietnam on American views, see Ole R. Holsti and James N. Rosenau, *American Leadership and World Affairs: Vietnam and the Breakdown of Consensus* (Boston: Allen & Unwin, 1984).

20. See, for example, Richard J. Barnet, *Roots of War*, chap. 2.

21. John D. Steinbruner, *The Cybernetic Theory of Decision*, 27.

22. Ibid.

23. "Decision-Making as an Approach to the Study of International Politics" in Richard C. Snyder, H. W. Bruck, and Burton Sapin (eds.), *Foreign Policy Decision-Making* (New York: Free Press, 1962), 14–185.

24. Harold and Margaret Sprout, *Man-Milieu Relationship Hypotheses in the Context of International Politics* (Princeton: Center of International Studies, 1956); *The Ecological Perspective on Human Affairs* (Princeton: Princeton University Press, 1965); and *An Ecological Paradigm for the Study of International Politics*, Research Monograph No. 30 (Princeton: Center of International Studies, 1968).

25. Joseph H. de Rivera, *The Psychological Dimension of Foreign Policy* (Columbus, OH: Charles E. Merrill, 1968), 21. Emphasis in original.

26. Paul Dickson, *The Official Explanations* (New York: Delacorte Press, 1980), 28.

27. Joseph H. de Rivera, *The Psychological Dimension of Foreign Policy*, 43. Emphasis in original.

28. Sidney Verba, "Assumptions of Rationality and Non-Rationality."

29. Ibid., 109.

30. Ibid.

31. Ibid., 110.

32. Ibid., 112.

33. Ibid., 113.

34. See especially James G. March and Herbert Simon, *Organizations* (New York: Wiley, 1957); and by Herbert Simon, *Models of Man* (New York: Wiley, 1957), and *Administrative Behavior: A Discussion of Decision-making Process in Administrative Organization*, 2d ed. (New York: Macmillan, 1961).

35. See especially Charles E. Lindblom, *The Policy-making Process* (Englewood Cliffs, NJ: Prentice-Hall, 1968), and "The Science of Muddling Through," *Public Administration Review* 19:2 (Spring 1959), 79–88. For a careful comparison of the assumptions of the rational model with those advanced by Simon and Lindblom, see also William I. Bacchus, *Foreign Policy and the Bureaucratic Process: The State Department's Country Director System* (Princeton: Princeton University Press, 1974), 19–23.

36. There is a growing body of research by political psychologists on the psychological and perceptual dimensions of foreign policy. See, for example, Margaret G. Hermann, *How Leaders Shape Foreign Policy* (Columbia, SC: University of South Carolina Press, forthcoming).

37. Arnold A. Rogow, *James Forrestal: A Study in Personality, Politics, and Policy* (New York: Macmillan, 1963).

38. Alexander L. George and Juliette L. George, *Woodrow Wilson and Colonel House: A Personality Study* (New York: Day, 1956).

39. See, for example, Alexander L. George, "The 'Operational Code': A Neglected Approach to the Study of Political Leaders and Decision-Making," *International Studies Quarterly* 13:2 (June 1969), 190–222.

40. See, for example, Ole R. Holsti, *Toward a Typology of "Operational Code" Belief Systems.* Final Report to the National Science Foundation (Chapel Hill, NC: Duke University, 1977), and Holsti, "The Operational Code Approach: Problems and Some Solutions" in Christer Jonsson (ed.), *Cognitive Dynamics and International Politics* (New York: St. Martin's Press, 1982), 75–90.

41. See, for example, Ole R. Holsti, "The Belief System and National Images: A Case Study" in James N. Rosenau (ed.), *International Politics and Foreign Policy,* rev. ed. (New York: Free Press, 1969), 542–550.

42. Robert A. Isaak, *Individuals and World Politics,* 2d ed. (North Scituate, MA: Duxbury Press, 1981).

43. Joseph H. de Rivera, *The Psychological Dimension of Foreign Policy,* especially chap. 5.

44. Margaret G. Hermann and Thomas W. Milburn (eds.), *A Psychological Examination of Political Leaders* (New York: Free Press, 1977).

45. Lloyd S. Etheridge, *A World of Men: The Private Sources of American Foreign Policy* (Cambridge, MA: MIT Press, 1978).

46. See, for example, Margaret G. Hermann, "When Leader Personality Will Affect Foreign Policy: Some Propositions" in James N. Rosenau (ed.), *In Search of Global Patterns* (New York: Free Press, 1976), 326–333. For a useful summary of the propositions advanced in the literature, see also Charles W. Kegley, Jr., and Eugene R. Wittkopf, *American Foreign Policy: Pattern and Process,* 2nd ed. (New York: St. Martin's Press, 1982), 512–516.

47. Joseph H. de Rivera, *The Psychological Dimension of Foreign Policy,* 168. The barriers to adequate conceptualization of psychological constructs are epitomized in James David Barber, *The Presidential Character: Predicting Performance in the White House* (Englewood Cliffs, NJ: Prentice-Hall, 1972).

48. Ibid.

49. Ibid., 167.

50. On this point, see especially Gunnar Sjoblom, "Some Problems of the Operational Code Approach" in Christer Jonsson (ed.), *Cognitive Dynamics and International Politics,* 37–74.

51. Ibid., 45.

52. Ole Holsti takes strong exception to Sjoblom's argument along this line, but his counter is little more than an assertion than an emphasis on organizations and/or bureaucracies entails even more severe theoretical problems. It is significant, as Sjoblom and several of the other authors in the Jonsson collection note, that the term "operational code" was actually coined back in the early 1950s by Nathan Leites to describe aspects of Bolshevik doctrine, rather than individual behavior. See Nathan Leites, *The Operational Code of the Politburo* (New York: McGraw-Hill, 1951).

53. Richard C. Snyder et al. (eds.), *Foreign Policy Decision-making,* 5–6. Emphasis in original.

54. Robert Jervis, *Perception and Misperception in International Politics* (Princeton: Princeton University Press, 1976), 29. See also Jervis's seminal article: "Hypotheses on Misperception," *World Politics* 20:3 (April 1968), 454–479.

55. Joseph H. de Rivera, *The Psychological Dimension of Foreign Policy.*

56. Alexander L. George, *Presidential Decision-making: The Effective Use of Information and Advice* (Boulder, CO: Westview Press, 1980), especially 25–55.

57. John D. Steinbruner, *The Cybernetic Theory of Decision*, chap. 4.

58. On this subject see also especially, Ernest R. May, *"Lessons" from the Past: The Use and Misuse of History in American Foreign Policy* (New York: Oxford University Press, 1973); and Yaacov Y. I. Vertzberger, "Foreign Policy Decisionmakers as Practical-intuitive Historians: Applied History and Its Shortcomings," *International Studies Quarterly* 30:2 (June 1986), 223–247.

59. Robert Jervis, *Perception and Misperception in International Politics*, 29.

60. Ibid., 20.

61. Raymond Cohen, *Threat Perception in International Crisis* (Madison, WI: University of Wisconsin Press, 1979), 189.

62. Ibid., 181.

63. Robert Jervis, *Perception and Misperception in International Politics*, 62.

64. Charles F. Hermann, "International Crisis as a Situational Variable" in James N. Rosenau (ed.), *International Politics and Foreign Policy*, rev. ed., 409–421.

65. Richard Ned Lebow, *Between Peace and War: The Nature of International Crisis* (Baltimore: Johns Hopkins Press, 1981), 7–12.

66. Richard W. Cottam, *Foreign Policy Motivation*, 7. See also William A. Gamson and Andre Modigliani, *Untangling the Cold War* (Boston: Little, Brown, 1971).

67. Richard W. Cottam, *Foreign Policy Motivation*, 87.

68. Ibid., 89.

69. Ibid.

70. See, for example, Robert Jervis, *Perception and Misperception in International Politics*, 102–202 and chap. 12; Alexander L. George, "The Case for Multiple Advocacy in Making Foreign Policy," *American Political Science Review* 66:3 (September 1972), 751–785; Richard W. Cottam, *Foreign Policy Motivation* 11 and 332–333; and Yaacov Y. I. Vertzberger, "Foreign Policy Decisionmakers as Practical-intuitive Historians," 243–244.

71. John D. Steinbruner, *The Cybernetic Theory of Decision*, 338.

72. Richard C. Snyder, et al., *Foreign Policy Decision-making*, 5.

73. Christer Jonsson, "Introduction: Cognitive Approaches to International Politics," in Jonsson, *Cognitive Dynamics and International Politics*, 7.

74. Ibid. Jonsson observes: "No 'hard' data on the cognitive beliefs or processes of decisionmakers exist. Nor is there agreement as to what constitutes the best available 'soft' data, or the appropriate categories into which whatever data are available can be coded" (Ibid., 9).

75. John D. Steinbruner, *The Cybernetic Theory of Decision*, 136. Emphasis in original.

76. Ibid., 150.

77. Robert Jervis, *Perception and Misperception in International Politics*, 31.

78. Hedley Bull, "International Theory: The Case for a Classical Approach," in Klaus Knorr and James N. Rosenau (eds.), *Contending Approaches to International Politics* (Princeton: Princeton University Press, 1969), 20.

79. Robert Jervis, *Perception and Misperception in International Politics*, 342.

**Chapter Seven**

1. Sigmund Freud, "Why War?" in Melvin Small and J. David Singer (eds.), *International War: An Anthology and Study Guide* (Homewood, IL: Dorsey Press, 1985), 161.

2. Paul Dickson, *The Official Explanations* (New York: Delacorte Press, 1980).

3. For example, the issue of what is "policy" arises in discussions about the validity of events data.

4. Steve Smith, "Theories of Foreign Policy: An Historical View," *Review of International Studies* 12:1 (January 1986), 15.

5. This was as true of early Machiavellians as it is of twentieth-century realists.

6. "Assumptions of Rationality and Non-Rationality in Models of the International System" in Klaus Knorr and Sidney Verba (eds.), *The International System: Theoretical Essays* (Princeton: Princeton University Press, 1961), 111.

7. For an analysis of "unitariness" as a variable, see Richard W. Mansbach and John A. Vasquez, *In Search of Theory: A New Paradigm for Global Politics* (New York: Columbia University Press, 1981), 165–185.

8. John A. Vasquez summarizes these neatly in *The Power of Power Politics: A Critique* (New Brunswick, NJ: Rutgers University Press, 1983), 215.

9. Steve Smith, "Theories of Foreign Policy: An Historical View," 15. Emphasis in original.

10. Kenneth N. Waltz, *Theory of International Politics* (Reading, MA: Addison-Wesley, 1979), and Waltz, "Reflections on *Theory of International Politics:* A Response to My Critics," in Robert O. Keohane (ed.), *Neorealism and Its Critics* (New York: Columbia University Press, 1986), 322–345.

11. Robert O. Keohane, *After Hegemony: Cooperation and Discord in the World Political Economy* (Princeton: Princeton University Press, 1984).

12. See especially Immanuel Wallerstein, *The Capitalist World-Economy* (New York: Cambridge University Press, 1979), and *The Politics of the World-Economy: The States, the Movements, and the Civilizations* (New York: Cambridge University Press, 1984).

13. Kenneth N. Waltz, *Theory of International Politics*, 113.

14. John Gerard Ruggie, "Continuity and Transformation in the World Polity: Toward a Neorealist Synthesis," *World Politics*, 35:2 (January 1983), 270.

15. Robert O. Keohane, *After Hegemony*, 64.

16. Immanuel Wallerstein, *The Politics of the World-Economy*, 182.

17. Charles W. Kegley and Eugene R. Wittkopf, *American Foreign Policy: Pattern and Process*, 2nd ed. (New York: St. Martin's, 1982), 516–517.

18. Richard J. Barnet, *Roots of War: The Men and Institutions Behind U.S. Foreign Policy* (Baltimore: Penguin, 1973), 5.

19. Ibid.

20. Ibid., 6.

21. Ibid., 7.

22. Ibid., 8–9.

23. Robert Jervis, *Perception and Misperception in International Politics* (Princeton: Princeton University Press, 1976), 26.

24. Morton H. Halperin, *Bureaucratic Politics and Foreign Policy* (Washington, DC: The Brookings Institution, 1974), 11–12.

25. Ibid., 14.

26. Robert A. Packenham, *Liberal America and the Third World* (Princeton: Princeton University Press, 1973).

27. Thomas R. Dye, *Who's Running America? The Conservative Years*, 4th ed. (Englewood Cliffs, NJ: Prentice-Hall, 1986), 273–274.

28. Ibid., 267.

29. Ibid., 268. Emphasis in original.

30. Ibid., 271.

31. Ibid., 272–273. Emphasis in original.

32. Comparing 1976 and 1980 samples designed to illuminate the foreign-policy beliefs of U.S. leaders, it is interesting that Ole R. Holsti and James N. Rosenau found remarkable stability *but* "deep cleavages on many fundamental issues." See Holsti and Rosenau, "A Leadership Divided: The Foreign Policy Beliefs of American Leaders, 1976–1980" in Charles W. Kegley, Jr., and Eugene R. Wittkopf (eds.), *Perspectives on American Foreign Policy: Selected Readings* (New York: St. Martin's Press, 1983), 196–212.

33. Morton H. Halperin, *Bureaucratic Politics and Foreign Policy,* 14–15.

34. Richard W. Cottam, *Foreign Policy Motivation* (Pittsburgh: University of Pittsburgh Press, 1977), 9–11.

35. Morton H. Halperin, *Bureaucratic Politics and Foreign Policy,* 15.

36. Ibid.

37. See especially Irving L. Janis, *Victims of Groupthink: A Psychological Study of Foreign-Policy Decisions and Fiascoes* (Boston: Houghton Mifflin, 1972). See also Irving L. Janis and Leon Mann, *Decision Making: A Psychological Analysis of Conflict, Choice, and Commitment* (New York: Free Press, 1977).

38. John D. Steinbruner, *The Cybernetic Theory of Decision: New Dimensions of Political Analysis* (Princeton: Princeton University Press, 1974), especially chap. 3. For a rather frightening analysis of the implications of this approach for strategic deterrence, see Steinbruner, "Beyond Rational Deterrence: The Struggle for New Conceptions," *World Politics* 28:2 (January 1976), 223–245.

39. Ibid., 13.

40. Ibid., 50–51.

41. Joseph H. de Rivera, *The Psychological Dimension of Foreign Policy* (Columbus, Ohio: Charles E. Merrill, 1968), 59–60. See also Charles F. Hermann, "Bureaucratic Constraints on Innovation in American Foreign Policy" in Charles W. Kegley, Jr., and Eugene R. Wittkopf (eds.), *Perspectives on American Foreign Policy: Selected Readings,* 390–409.

42. John D. Steinbruner, *The Cybernetic Theory of Decision,* 13–14.

43. Ibid., 14.

44. Joseph H. de Rivera, *The Psychological Dimension of Foreign Policy,* 46.

45. Ibid.

46. Graham T. Allison, *Essence of Decision: Explaining the Cuban Missile Crisis* (Boston: Little, Brown, 1971), 164. On the governmental (bureaucratic) politics approach, see also especially: Graham T. Allison and Morton H. Halperin, "Bureaucratic Politics: A Paradigm and Some Policy Implications" in Raymond Tanter and Richard N. Ullman (eds.), *Theory and Policy in International Relations* (Princeton: Princeton University Press, 1972), 40–79; Morton H. Halperin, *Bureaucratic Politics and Foreign Policy;* and Morton H. Halperin and Arnold Kanter (eds.), *Reading in Foreign Policy: A Bureaucratic Perspective* (Boston: Little, Brown, 1973).

47. Graham T. Allison, *Essence of Decision,* 178.

48. Stephen D. Krasner, "Are Bureaucracies Important? (Or Allison Wonderland)," *Foreign Policy,* No. 7 (Summer 1972), 179. Krasner thus defends both approaches to reform—get better leaders and pursue the "right" values—that, as we have noted, cognitive theory suggests are unlikely to be productive.

49. Kim Richard Nossal, "Bureaucratic Politics and the Westminster Model" in Robert O. Matthews, Arthur G. Rubinoff, and Janice Gross Stein (eds.), *International Con-*

*flict and Conflict Management* (Englewood Cliffs, NJ: Prentice-Hall, 1984), 125.

50. John D. Steinbruner, *The Cybernetic Theory of Decision*, 147.

51. Robert J. Art, "Bureaucratic Politics and American Foreign Policy: A Critique" in Robert J. Art and Robert Jervis (eds.), *International Politics: Anarchy, Force, Political Economy, and Decision-Making*, 2nd ed. (Boston: Little, Brown, 1985), 470.

52. Morton H. Halperin, *Bureaucratic Politics and Foreign Policy*, 16.

53. Graham T. Allison, *Essence of Decision*, 166. Emphasis in original.

54. Stephen D. Krasner, *Defending the National Interest: Raw Materials Investments and U.S. Foreign Policy* (Princeton: Princeton University Press, 1978), 88–89. It should be mentioned that Krasner also argues: "[E]ven in a weak political system the state is not merely an epiphenomenon: central decision-makers can still resist pressures from private groups; they can still formulate preferences related to general societal goals." What is critical, according to Krasner, is which decisionmaking "arena" is used to decide an issue, and this is "partly a function of [the] inherent nature [of the issue] and partly a function of the way it is defined." In his view, leaders may be able to change "the way societal groups perceive a particular problem" and "thereby the arena in which it is decided and the final policy outcome" (89–90).

55. Stephen D. Cohen, *The Making of United States International Economic Policy*, 2nd ed. (New York: Praeger, 1981), 89.

56. Graham T. Allison, *Essence of Decision*, 168.

57. Stephen D. Krasner, "Are Bureaucracies Important?"

58. James N. Rosenau, "Capabilities and Control in an Interdependent World," *International Security* 1:2 (Fall 1976), 40–42.

59. Ibid., 42. There is little consensus in the literature even with respect to the classification of issues. John Spanier and Eric M. Uslaner, for example, offer a threefold typology: crisis, security, and intermestic issues. As they see it, crisis issues involve only a few top officials in the executive; security issues involve those actors mentioned by Rosenau, plus Congress, because of budgetary considerations; and intermestic issues (energy is the example) "mobilize all the actors that domestic politics do: the executive agencies whose jurisdiction is basically domestic, Congress, interest groups, and public opinion." (*American Foreign Policy and the Democratic Dilemmas*, 4th ed. [New York: Holt, Rinehart and Winston, 1985], 17–18.)

Despite taxonomic problems, issue analysis has become very popular. See, for example, Theodore J. Lowi, "American Business, Public Policy, Case Studies and Political Theory," *World Politics* 16:4 (July 1964), 677–715; William Zimmerman, "Issue Area and Foreign-Policy Process: A Research Note in Search of a General Theory," *American Political Science Review* 67:4 (December 1973), 1204–1212; Thomas L. Brewer, "Issue and Context Variation in Foreign Policy," *Journal of Conflict Resolution* 17:1 (March 1973), 89–115; Michael K. O'Leary, "The Role of Issues," in James N. Rosenau (ed.), *In Search of Global Patterns* (New York: Free Press, 1976), 318–326; and Richard W. Mansbach and John A. Vasquez, *In Search of Theory*, 28–67.

60. Glenn H. Snyder and Paul Diesing would add an eighth, their charge that the approach gives too little attention to the constraints on policy emanating from the external environment. (*Conflict Among Nations: Bargaining, Decision Making, and System Structure in International Crisis* [Princeton: Princeton University Press, 1977], 511–523.) This appears to be a variant of Arnold Wolfers's fire-in-the-house argument.

61. James N. Rosenau, "Comparative Foreign Policy: Fad, Fantasy, or Field?" in Rosenau, *The Scientific Study of Foreign Policy* (New York: Free Press, 1971), 67.

62. James N. Rosenau, "Pre-Theories and Theories of Foreign Policy" in R. Barry Farrell (ed.), *Approaches to Comparative and International Politics* (Evanston, IL: Northwestern University Press, 1966), 27–93. A good deal of subsequent research in the field entailed investigation and elaboration of the Rosenau pre-theory and its taxonomy. While many of its findings were of interest, they did little to advance the field theoretically beyond the pre-theory. Recently, Rosenau described the pre-theory as "a static product of a static era" and concluded "that to aspire to theoretical breakthroughs we need to return to fundamentals. . . ." Rosenau, "A Pre-Theory Revisited: World Politics in an Era of Cascading Interdependence," *International Studies Quarterly* 28:3 (September 1984), 246, 247.

63. Christer Jonsson, "Introduction: Cognitive Approaches to International Politics," in Jonsson (ed.), *Cognitive Dynamics and International Politics* (New York: St. Martin's, 1982), 1.

64. Patrick J. McGowan and Howard B. Shapiro, *The Comparative Study of Foreign Policy: A Survey of Scientific Findings*, vol. 4, Sage Library of Social Research (Beverly Hills, CA: Sage, 1973), 215. See also James N. Rosenau (ed.), *Comparing Foreign Policies: Theories, Findings and Methods* (New York: Wiley, 1974).

65. Linda P. Brady, "A Proposal" in Patrick C. Callahan, Linda P. Brady, and Margaret G. Hermann (eds.), *Describing Foreign Policy Behavior* (Beverly Hills, CA: Sage, 1982), 29. Emphasis in original. The entire volume unintentionally reveals how little the field of comparative foreign policy had advanced to that time.

66. Patrick J. McGowan and Howard B. Shapiro, *The Comparative Study of Foreign Policy*, 218.

67. Ibid., 214–224. It is remarkable that fully thirteen years after McGowan and Shapiro had argued that "the evaluation of past policy from a normative point of view . . . and the *prescription* of future policy" were an "essential aspect of the comparative study of foreign policy" (223), John Vasquez was again calling for foreign-policy evaluation. "The Need for Foreign Policy Evaluation," in John A. Vasquez (ed.), *Evaluating U.S. Foreign Policy* (New York: Praeger, 1986), 3–16.

68. Bahgot Korany, "Foreign Policy in the Third World: An Introduction" in Korany (ed.), *Foreign Policy Decisions in the Third World*, topical issue of *International Political Science Review*, 5:1 (1984), 7–8. For an excellent review of the strengths and weaknesses of the research record compiled in the comparative study of foreign policy, see Charles W. Kegley, Jr., *The Comparative Study of Foreign Policy: Paradigm Lost?*, Essay Series No. 10, Institute of International Studies, The University of South Carolina (1980).

69. K. J. Holsti, "National Role Conceptions in the Study of Foreign Policy," *International Studies Quarterly* 14:3 (September 1970), 233–309. See also Christer Jonsson and Ulf Westerlund, "Role Theory in Foreign Policy Analysis" in Jonsson (ed.), *Cognitive Dynamics and International Politics*, 122–157.

70. Christer Jonsson and Ulf Westerlund observe: "As with most prevalent concepts, there exists no one agreed definition of the concept of role." ("Role Theory in Cognitive Analysis," 124.)

71. Henry A. Kissinger, *American Foreign Policy: Three Essays* (New York: Norton, 1969), chap. 3.

72. Kim Richard Nossal discusses these three reasons at some length in his essay, "Bureaucratic Politics and the Westminster Model," 120–121.

73. See especially Jerel A. Rosati, "A Neglected Actor in American Foreign Policy: The Role of the Judiciary," *International Studies Notes*, 12:1 (Fall 1985), 10–15.

74. See Wayne Selcher, "Brazil's Foreign Policy: More Actors and Expanding Agendas" in Jennie K. Lincoln and Elizabeth G. Ferris (eds.), *The Dynamics of Latin American Foreign Policies: Challenges for the 1980s* (Boulder, CO: Westview Press, 1984), 103–107. On the relevance of general theories of foreign-policy decisionmaking to Latin America, see especially: Yale H. Ferguson, "Analyzing Latin American Foreign Policies," *Latin American Research Review* (forthcoming). Howard J. Wiarda explores some of the policy implications for the United States of Latin American "differentness" in his *Ethnocentrism in Foreign Policy: Can We Understand the Third World?* (Washington, DC: American Enterprise Institute, 1985).

75. Kim Richard Nossal, "Bureaucratic Politics and the Westminster Model," 146.

76. Stephen D. Cohen, *The Making of United States International Economic Policy*, chap. 8.

77. See, for example, David Collier (ed.), *The New Authoritarianism in Latin America* (Princeton: Princeton University Press, 1979).

78. See, for example, Gerhard Lehmbruch and Philippe C. Schmitter (eds.), *Patterns of Corporate Policy Making* (Beverly Hills, CA: Sage, 1982), and Philippe C. Schmitter, "Democratic Theory and Neocorporatist Practice," *Social Research* 50:4 (Winter 1983), 885–928.

79. Bernard C. Cohen, *The Public's Impact on Foreign Policy* (Boston: Little, Brown, 1973), 188–189. Emphasis in original. See also especially Gabriel A. Almond, *The American People and Foreign Policy* (New York: Praeger, 1960), and James N. Rosenau, *Public Opinion and Foreign Policy* (New York: Random House, 1961).

80. Bernard C. Cohen, *The Public's Impact on Foreign Policy*, 178. Emphasis in original.

81. Richard L. Merritt, "Public Opinion and Foreign Policy in West Germany" in Patrick J. McGowan (ed.), *Sage International Yearbook of Foreign Policy Studies: Volume One* (Beverly Hills, CA: Sage, 1973), 271.

82. See Ivo D. Duchacek, "The International Dimension of Subnational Self-Government," *Publius* 14:4 (Fall 1984), 5–31.

83. See, for example, Louis L. Synder, *Global Mini-Nationalisms: Autonomy or Independence?* (Westport, CT: Greenwood Press, 1982), and *Ethnicity and Regionalism*, topical issue of *International Political Science Review* 6:2 (1985).

84. See especially James N. Rosenau, *Linkage Politics* (New York: Free Press, 1969).

## Chapter Eight

1. See Hedley Bull, *The Anarchical Society* (New York: Columbia University Press, 1977) and his earlier article, "Society and Anarchy in International Relations," in Herbert Butterfield and Martin Wight (eds.), *Diplomatic Investigations* (London: Allen & Unwin, 1966), 40–48. Bull argues that there is a high degree of order within the apparent anarchy of world politics. See also Oran R. Young, "Anarchy and Social Choice: Reflections on the International Polity," *World Politics* 30:2 (January 1978), 241–263.

2. See K. J. Holsti, *The Dividing Discipline: Hegemony and Diversity in International Theory* (Boston: Allen & Unwin, 1985), 23–27.

3. See, for example, Fred W. Riggs, "International Relations as a Prismatic System," in Klaus Knorr and Sidney Verba (eds.), *The International System: Theoretical Essays* (Princeton: Princeton University Press, 1961), 141–181.

4. Kenneth N. Waltz, *Man, the State and War* (New York: Columbia University Press, 1959), 232.

5. See, for example, Peter J. Katzenstein, "International interdependence: Some long-term trends and recent changes," *International Organization* 29:4 (Autumn 1975), 1021–1034.

6. R. Rosecrance, A. Alexandroff, W. Koehler, J. Kroll, S. Laqueur, and J. Stocker, "Whither Interdependence?" *International Organization* 31:3 (Summer 1977), 426.

7. Ibid., 426–427. Emphasis in original.

8. Robert O. Keohane and Joseph S. Nye, Jr., *Power and Interdependence: World Politics in Transition* (Boston: Little, Brown, 1977), 9–10.

9. Ibid., 11–19.

10. Kenneth N. Waltz, "Will the Future Be Like the Past?" in Nissan Oren (ed.), *When Patterns Change: Turning Points in International Politics* (New York: St. Martin's Press, 1984), 26. Waltz's definition of interdependence is very similar to that of Keohane and Nye.

11. R. Rosecrance et al., "Whither Interdependence?" 441–444. Differing conceptualizations of interdependence naturally lead to measurement disputes. See, for example, Mary Ann Tetreault, "Measuring interdependence," *International Organization* 34:3 (Summer 1980), 429–443; Richard N. Rosecrance and William Gutowitz, "Measuring interdependence: a rejoinder," *International Organization* 35:3 (Summer 1981), 553–556; and Mary Ann Tetreault, "Measuring interdependence: a response," *International Organization* 35:3 (Summer 1981), 557–560.

12. Stephen D. Cohen, *The Making of United States International Economic Policy,* 2nd ed. (New York: Praeger, 1981), 85, 89.

13. Robert O. Keohane, *After Hegemony: Cooperation and Discord in the World Political Economy* (Princeton: Princeton University Press, 1984), 5.

14. Kenneth N. Waltz, "Will the Future Be Like the Past?" 27.

15. See James A. Caporaso (ed.), *Dependence and dependency in the global system,* special issue, *International Organization* 32:1 (Winter 1978).

16. This is perhaps not surprising in view of the potent ideological commitments evident in earlier discussions of this issue. See Osvaldo Sunkel, "The Crisis of the Nation-State in Latin America: Challenge and Response," in Yale H. Ferguson and Walter F. Weiker (eds.), *Continuing Issues in International Politics* (Pacific Palisades, CA: Goodyear, 1973), 352–368; Sunkel, "Big Business and 'Dependencia': A Latin American View," *Foreign Affairs* 50:3 (April 1972), 517–531; Fernando Enrique Cardoso, *Dependencia y desarrollo en America Latina* (Mexico: Siglo Veintiuno Editores, 1969); and Theontonio dos Santos, *El Nuevo caracter de la dependencia* (Santiago, Chile: Cuadernos de CESO, 1968).

17. Alberto van Klaveren, "The Analysis of Latin American Foreign Policies: Theoretical Perspectives," in Heraldo Muñoz and Joseph S. Tulchin (eds.), *Latin American Nations in World Politics* (Boulder, CO: Westview Press, 1984), 8.

18. William E. Brock, "Trade and Debt: The Vital Linkage," *Foreign Affairs* 62:5 (Summer 1984), 1045.

19. Dennis K. Gordon, "Argentina's Foreign Policies in the Post-Malvinas Era," in Jennie K. Lincoln and Elizabeth G. Ferris (eds.), *The Dynamics of Latin American Foreign Politics: Challenges for the 1980s* (Boulder, CO: Westview Press, 1984), 98.

20. David Leyton-Brown, "The Nation-State and Multinational Enterprise: Erosion or Assertion," in Robert O. Matthews, Arthur G. Rubinoff, and Janice Gross Stein (eds.), *International Conflict and Conflict Management: Reading in World Politics* (Scarborough, Ontario: Prentice-Hall, 1984), 339. See also Joseph M. Grieco, "Between depen-

dency and autonomy: India's experience with the international computer industry," *International Organization* 36:3 (Summer 1982), 609–632.

21. Norman Angell, *The Great Illusion* (London: Heinemann, 1914).

22. See Karl W. Deutsch, et al., *Political Community and the North Atlantic Area* (Princeton: Princeton University Press, 1957), and Ernst B. Haas, *Beyond the Nation-State: Functionalism and International Organization* (Stanford: Stanford University Press, 1964).

23. Cited in Kenneth N. Waltz, *Man, the State and War*, 183.

24. Jean-Jacques Rousseau, "Abstract of the Abbé de Saint-Pierre's Project for Perpetual Peace," in M. G. Forsyth, H. M. A. Keens-Soper and P. Savigear (eds.), *The Theory of International Relations: Selected Texts from Gentili to Treitschke* (New York: Atherton Press, 1970), 148.

25. See Kenneth N. Waltz, *Man, the State and War*, 163 ff. for a discussion of the stag-hare exemplar.

26. Cited in Herbert Butterfield, "The Balance of Power," in Herbert Butterfield and Martin Wight (eds.), *Diplomatic Investigations: Essays in the Theory of International Politics* (London: Allen & Unwin, 1966), 144. In a more recent incarnation, Burke's argument is reflected in Richard N. Rosecrance's discussion of bipolarity. "Bipolarity, Multipolarity, and the Future," *Journal of Conflict Resolution* 10:3 (September 1966), 318.

27. A common observation about World War I was that the existence of continental alliance systems in 1914 transformed a local conflict between Serbia and Austria-Hungary into a global one.

28. See F. Parkinson, *The Philosophy of International Relations: A study in the history of thought* (Beverly Hills, CA: Sage Publications, 1977), 45–48.

29. Emmerich de Vattel, "The Just Causes of War," in M. G. Forsyth, H. M. A. Keens-Soper, and P. Savigear (eds.), *The Theory of International Relations*, 118.

30. See Karl W. Deutsch and J. David Singer, "Multipolar Power Systems and International Stability," *World Politics* 16:3 (April 1964), 390–406; Richard N. Rosecrance, "Bipolarity, Multipolarity and the Future"; and Kenneth N. Waltz, "The Stability of a Bipolar World," *Daedalus* 93 (Summer 1964), 881–909. A useful recent anthology of such research is Allen Ned Sabrosky (ed.), *Bipolarity and War* (Boulder, CO: Westview Press, 1985).

31. See, for example, J. David Singer, S. Bremer, and J. Stuckey, "Capability Distribution, Uncertainty, and Major Power War, 1820–1965," in Bruce M. Russett (ed.), *Peace, War, and Numbers* (Beverly Hills, CA: Sage, 1972), 19–48; Michael Wallace, "Status, Formal Organization, and Arms Levels as Factors Leading to the Onset of War, 1820–1964," in ibid., 49–71; and Wallace, "Alliance Polarization, Cross-cutting, and International War, 1815–1964," *Journal of Conflict Resolution* 17:4 (December 1973), 575–604. Such research was responsible for generating important insights into the role of status inconsistency and the onset of war.

32. J. David Singer, *A General Systems Taxonomy for Political Science* (New York: General Learning Press, 1971), 9.

33. See, for example, Morton A. Kaplan, *System and Process in International Politics* (New York: Wiley, 1957), 22–36, and A. F. K. Organski, *World Politics* (New York: Knopf, 1958), chaps. 11, 12, 14.

34. See, for example, Ernst B. Haas, "The Balance of Power: Prescription, Concept or Propaganda?" *World Politics* 5:4 (July 1953), 442–477.

35. See, for example, Inis L. Claude, Jr., *Power and International Relations* (New York: Random House, 1962), chaps. 2–3.

36. See Donald Reinken, "Computer Explorations of the 'Balance of Power': A Project Report" (459–481); Hsi-Sheng Chi, "The Chinese Warlord System as an International System" (405–425); and Winfried Franke, "The Italian City-State System as an International System" (426–458), all in Morton A. Kaplan, *New Approaches to International Politics* (New York: St. Martin's Press, 1968).

37. Robert J. Lieber, *Theory and World Politics* (Cambridge, MA: Winthrop, 1972), 123. The only exception to this was "general systems theory," a highly abstract mode of analysis that posited isomorphisms among variables in very different types of systems. See, for example, Anatol Rapoport, "Foreword," in Walter Buckley (ed.), *Modern Systems Research for the Behavioral Sciences* (Chicago: Aldine, 1968), and Ludwig von Bertalanffy, "General System Theory," in J. David Singer (ed.), *Human Behavior and International Politics: Contributions from the Social-Psychological Sciences* (Chicago: Rand McNally, 1965), 20–31.

38. Morton A. Kaplan, *Macropolitics* (Chicago: Aldine, 1969), 66. The use of jargon to describe the commonplace did nothing to improve the prose of scholars.

39. Harold and Margaret Sprout, *The Ecological Perspective on Human Affairs with Special Reference to International Politics* (Princeton: Princeton University Press, 1965), 208.

40. The work of Karl W. Deutsch, perhaps more than that of any other political scientist, reflects a debt to cybernetic theory. See Deutsch, *The Nerves of Government* (New York: Free Press, 1964).

41. A. Hall and R. Fagen, "Definition of a System," *General Systems*, I (1956), 18. Emphasis in original.

42. See, for example, K. J. Holsti, *International Politics: A Framework for Analysis*, 4th ed. (Englewood Cliffs, NJ: Prentice-Hall, 1983), 27–64.

43. See, for example, Michael Banks, "Systems Analysis and the Study of Regions," *International Studies Quarterly* 13:4 (December 1969), 335–360; Louis J. Cantori and Steven L. Spiegel, *The International Politics of Regions: A Comparative Approach* (Englewood Cliffs, NJ: Prentice-Hall, 1970); and William R. Thompson, "The Regional Subsystem: A Conceptual Explication and a Propositional Inventory," *International Studies Quarterly* 17:1 (March 1973), 89–117.

44. See Oran R. Young, "Political Discontinuties in the International System," *World Politics* 20:3 (April 1968), 369–392, and Donald E. Lampert, Lawrence L. Falkowski and Richard W. Mansbach, "Is There an International System?" *International Studies Quarterly* 22:1 (March 1978), 143–166.

45. Jerome Stephens, "An Appraisal of Some Systems Approaches in the Study of International Systems," *International Studies Quarterly* 16:3 (September 1972), 328.

46. John Spanier, *Games Nations Play: Analyzing International Politics*, 4th ed. (New York: Holt, Rinehart & Winston, 1981), 10.

47. See Immanual Wallerstein, *The Capitalist World-Economy* (New York: Cambridge University Press, 1979) and *The Politics of the World-Economy: The States, the Movements, and the Civilizations* (New York: Cambridge University Press, 1984). Useful critiques of Wallerstein include: Aristide R. Zolberg, "Origins of the Modern World System: A Missing Link," *World Politics* 23:2 (January 1981), 253–281; Robert Brenner, "The Origins of Capitalist Development: A Critique of Neo-Smithian Marxism," *New Left Review* 104 (July/August 1976), 25–92; Theda Skocpol, "Wallerstein's World Capi-

talist System: A Theoretical Critique," *American Journal of Sociology* 82:5 (March 1977), 1075–1090; and Peter Worsley, *The Three Worlds: Culture and World Development* (Chicago: University of Chicago Press, 1984), 312–313.

48. Kenneth N. Waltz, *Theory of International Politics* (Reading, MA: Addison-Wesley, 1979), 98–99.

49. John Gerard Ruggie, "Continuity and Transformation in the World Polity: Toward a Neorealist Synthesis," *World Politics* 35:2 (January 1983), 281. See also Richard N. Rosecrance, "International Theory Revisited," *International Organization* 35:4 (Autumn 1981), 691–713; Kenneth N. Waltz, "Letter to the editor," *International Organization* 36:3 (Summer 1982), 679–681; and Richard N. Rosecrance, "Reply to Waltz," *International Organization* 36:3 (Summer 1982), 682–685.

50. Interestingly, it is generally accepted that research in most of the natural sciences is inductive, reducing a problem into components and observing relations among these. This was not the case with the systems approach.

51. Edward Vose Gulick, *Europe's Classical Balance of Power* (Ithaca: Cornell University Press, 1955), 35.

52. Cited in Lynn Montross, *War Through the Ages*, 3rd ed. (New York: Harper & Row, 1960), 315.

53. René Albrecht-Carrié, *The Concert of Europe* (New York: Harper & Row, 1968), 4.

54. See Richard B. Elrod, "The Concert of Europe: A Fresh Look at an International System," *World Politics* 28:2 (January 1976), 159–174.

55. See Kenneth N. Waltz, *Theory of International Politics*, passim.

56. Although the preference of such scholars for stability is rarely expressed openly, it is implicit in their tendency to evaluate alternative systems in terms of the stability they afford. See, for example, Kenneth N. Waltz, *Theory of International Politics*, 161 ff.

57. Edward Shils, *Political Development in the New States* (The Hague, the Netherlands: Mouton, 1962), 10.

58. Reinhard Bendix, cited in Paul T. McClure, "The Organizational Approach versus the Society Approach to Development in Emerging Nations," P-3927 (Santa Monica, CA: Rand Corporation, February 1969), 26.

59. Leonard Binder, cited in Fred W. Riggs, "The Theory of Developing Politics," *World Politics* 16:1 (October 1963), 156. For a classic statement that economic development does not assure political stability, infused with a strong bias toward stability and order, see Samuel P. Huntington, *Political Order in Changing Societies* (New Haven: Yale University Press, 1968).

60. David Mitrany, *A Working Peace System* (London: Royal Institute of International Affairs, 1943). See also Inis L. Claude, Jr., *Swords into Plowshares*, 3rd ed. (New York: Random House, 1964), chap. 17, and James P. Sewell, *Functionalism and World Politics* (Princeton: Princeton University Press, 1966).

61. See Richard A. Falk, *This Endangered Planet* (New York: Random house, 1971); Richard A. Falk, "Contending Approaches to World Order," *Journal of International Affairs* 31 (Fall/Winter 1977), 171–198; and Saul H. Mendlowitz, "The program of the Institute of World Order," *Journal of International Affairs* 31 (Fall/Winter 1977), 259–266.

62. James P. Sewell, *Functionalism and World Politics*, 3.

63. In effect, functionalists shared the deterministic fallacy with classical Marxists and suffered a similar disappointment.

64. Karl W. Deutsch, "Nation and World," in Ithiel de Sola Pool (ed.), *Contemporary*

*Political Science: Toward Political Theory* (New York: McGraw-Hill, 1967), 218. Interestingly, John H. Herz, a leading realist, came to a similar conclusion about the indefensability of the nation-state, which led him to believe, like the functionalists, that the state would disappear. He later came to revise this claim significantly. See his *International Politics in the Atomic Age* (New York: Columbia University Press, 1959), and "The Territorial State Revisited: Reflections on the Future of the Nation-State," in James N. Rosenau (ed.), *International Politics and Foreign Policy,* rev. ed. (New York: Free Press, 1969), 76–89.

65. Both Robert Keohane and Joseph Nye in *Power and Interdependence* and Rosecrance et al. in "Whither Interdependence?" view transaction flows as "horizontal interdependence" which "implies only interconnectedness" ("Whither Interdependence?," 427). Genuine interdependence, according to Rosecrance et al., is "vertical" (ibid., 429).

66. This includes mass media exchange such as radio, television, newspapers, and films; and interpersonal communications such as mail and telephone calls.

67. Sophisticated methods were developed to measure economic and sociocultural transactions with an eye to discerning the development of transnational society. See, for example, Leon N. Lindberg and Stuart A. Scheingold (eds.), *Regional Integration: Theory and Research* (Cambridge, MA: Harvard University Press, 1970).

68. See Karl W. Deutsch et al., *Political Community and the North Atlantic Area: International Organization in the Light of Historical Experience* (Princeton: Princeton University Press, 1957); Bruce M. Russett, *Community and Contention: Britain and America in the Twentieth Century* (Cambridge, MA: MIT Press, 1963); and Richard E. Neustadt, *Alliance Politics* (New York: Columbia University Press, 1970).

69. Richard Meier, "Information, Resources and Economic Growth," in J. J. Spengler (ed.), *National Resources and Economic Growth* (Washington, DC: Resources for the Future, n.d.), 113.

70. Robert O. Keohane, *After Hegemony: Cooperation and Discord in the World Political Economy,* 100, 101.

71. See, for example, Ernst B. Haas, *The Uniting of Europe: Political, Social and Economic Forces, 1950–1957* (Stanford: Stanford University Press, 1958), and Leon Lindberg, *The Political Dynamics of European Economic Integration* (Stanford: Stanford University Press, 1963).

72. See Joseph S. Nye, Jr. (ed.), *International Regionalism: Readings* (Boston: Little, Brown, 1968).

73. Similarly, American scholarly interest in deterrence and strategic theory waxed during the period in which American leaders were seeking to find a coherent NATO defense policy and trying to persuade France that its efforts to establish a national nuclear force were in error.

74. Modernization theory served as a justification for U.S. foreign aid during much of the 1950s and 1960s.

75. The issue reappeared as Robert O. Keohane and Joseph S. Nye, Jr. (eds.), *Transnational Relations and World Politics* (Cambridge, MA: Harvard University Press, 1972).

76. Joseph S. Nye, Jr. and Robert O. Keohane, "Transnational Relations and World Politics: An Introduction," in ibid., xii.

77. Ibid., xvii.

78. Joseph S. Nye, Jr., and Robert O. Keohane, "Transnational Relations and World Politics: A Conclusion," in ibid., 374–376. See also James A. Field, Jr., "Transnational-

ism and the New Tribe," in ibid., 3–32.

79. For example, ITT involvement in the overthrow of Chile's Salvador Allende, the OPEC oil embargo, the end of the Vietnam War, the intensification of international monetary and debt instabilities, persistent problems of global "stagflation," and several ecological disasters.

80. Robert O. Keohane and Joseph S. Nye, Jr., *Power and Interdependence*, 24–37.

81. Ibid., 25. For the evolution of the Keohane's and Nye's ideas on this subject, see their "Introduction: The Complex Politics of Canadian-American Interdependence," and Joseph S. Nye, Jr., "Transnational Relations and Interstate Conflicts: An Empirical Analysis," both in *International Organization* 23:4 (Autumn 1974), 495–607, 961–996; Keohane and Nye, "Transgovernmental Relations and International Organizations," *World Politics* 27:1 (October 1974), 39–62; and C. Fred Bergsten, Robert O. Keohane, and Joseph S. Nye, Jr., "International Economics and International Politics: A Framework for Analysis," *International Organization* 29:1 (Winter 1975), 3–36.

82. Robert O. Keohane and Joseph S. Nye, Jr., *Power and Interdependence*, 227.

83. Ibid., 229. Keohane and Nye strongly insist that regimes must be based on mutual interests. See Robert O. Keohane and Joseph S. Nye, Jr., "Two Cheers for Multilateralism," *Foreign Policy*, no. 60 (Fall 1985), 148–167.

84. Robert O. Keohane and Joseph S. Nye, Jr., *Power and Interdependence*, 19. See also Oran R. Young, "International Regimes: Problems of Concept Formation," *World Politics* 32:3 (April 1980), 331–356; Ernst B. Haas, "Why Collaborate? Issue-Linkage and International Regimes," *World Politics* 32:3 (April 1980), 357–405; Ernst B. Haas, "On Systems and International Regimes," *World Politics* 27:2 (January 1975), 147–174; and Stephen D. Krasner (ed.), "International Regimes," special issue of *International Organization* 36:2 (Spring 1982). The contributors to that volume apparently reached a consensus on defining international regimes as "sets of implicit or explicit principles, norms, rules, and decision-making procedures around which actors' expectations converge in a given area of international relations." Stephen D. Krasner, "Structural causes and regime consequences: regimes as intervening variables," in ibid., 186.

85. Robert O. Keohane, "The Theory of Hegemonic Stability and Changes in International Economic Regimes, 1967–1977," in Ole R. Holsti, Randolph M. Siverson and Alexander L. George (eds.), *Change in the International System* (Boulder, CO: Westview Press, 1980), 133.

86. Stephen D. Krasner, "Structural causes and regime consequences: regimes as intervening variables," 185–186.

87. Arthur A. Stein, "Coordination and collaboration: regimes in an anarchic world," *International Organization* 36:2 (Spring 1982), 299, 316.

88. Donald J. Puchala and Raymond F. Hopkins, "International regimes: lessons from inductive analysis," *International Organization* 36:2 (Spring 1982), 247. Emphasis added. See also Oran R. Young, "Regime dynamics: the rise and fall of international regimes," *International Organization* 36:2 (Spring 1982), 277–297.

89. Stephen D. Krasner, "Structural causes and regime consequences: regimes as intervening variables," 193.

90. Hedley Bull, "The Groatian Conception of International Society," in Herbert Butterfield and Martin Wight (eds.), *Diplomatic Investigations: Essays in the Theory of International Politics*, 52.

91. Stephen D. Krasner, "Structural causes and regime consequences: regimes as intervening variables," 187.

92. Robert O. Keohane, *After Hegemony*, 64.

93. Hedley Bull, *The Anarchical Society*, 161.

94. Stephen D. Krasner, "Structural causes and regime consequences: regimes as intervening variables," 189. Emphasis added.

95. Ibid., 202.

96. Arthur A. Stein, "Coordination and collaboration: regimes in an anarchic world," 299, 300. See also Susan Strange, *"Cave! hic dragones:* a critique of regime analysis," *International Organization* 36:2 (Spring 1982), 480–486.

97. Susan Strange, *"Cave! hic dragones:* a critique of regime analysis," 487.

98. Ibid., 481.

99. Ibid., 488, 491.

100. Richard W. Mansbach and John A. Vasquez, *In Search of Theory: A New Paradigm for Global Politics* (New York: Columbia University Press, 1981), 281–328.

101. For a counterargument to the "decline in hegemony" thesis, see Bruce M. Russett, "The mysterious case of vanishing hegemony: or, Is Mark Twain really dead?" *International Organization* 39:2 (Spring 1985), 207–231.

102. Recent years have witnessed some ingenious efforts to study this issue empirically. See, for example, Mark J. Gasiorowski, "Economic Interdependence and International Conflict: Some Cross-national Evidence," *International Studies Quarterly* 30:1 (March 1986), 23–38.

103. Roy Licklider, "Political Power and the Arab Oil Weapon: The Netherlands, Great Britain, Canada, Japan, and the United States," MS. (April 1986), 416–417, 419.

104. Ibid., 419.

105. On the other side, Arab leaders have for many years been constrained from taking steps toward reconciliation with Israel by fears of assassination, coup, or massive unrest. The fate of leaders such as King Abdullah of Jordan and Anwar Sadat of Egypt is sobering indeed to those who might wish to reach an agreement.

106. A. W. DePorte, *Europe Between the Superpowers* (New Haven: Yale University Press, 1979), vii.

107. Stephen Szabo et al., *The Successor Generation: International Perspectives* (London: Butterworth, 1983).

108. Regime theorists correctly point out that national bureaucracies occasionally form transnational alliances in support of particular arrangements of mutual benefit. To this extent, they may represent the other side of the coin. See, for example, Raymond F. Hopkins, "The international role of 'domestic' bureaucracy," *International Organization* 30:3 (Summer 1976), 405–432.

109. Roy Licklider, "Political Power and the Arab Oil Weapon: The Netherlands, Great Britain, Canada, Japan, and the United States," 429.

110. Currently, analysts argue over the extent to which Cuba's support for Soviet objectives in areas like Africa and Central America is compelled by dependency on the USSR or stems from Castro's own perception of Cuban interests. Contrast, for example, Juan del Aguila, "Cuba's Foreign Policy in Central America and the Caribbean," in Jennie K. Lincoln and Elizabeth G. Ferris (eds.), *The Dynamics of Latin American Foreign Policies,* 251–266, with Cole Blasier, *The Giant's Rival: The USSR and Latin America* (Pittsburgh: University of Pittsburgh Press, 1983), chap. 5.

111. See F. Parkinson, *The Philosophy of International Relations,* 9–25.

## Chapter Nine

1. Patrick J. McGowan and Howard B. Shapiro, *The Comparative Study of Foreign Policy: A Survey of Scientific Findings,* vol. 4, Sage Library of Social Research (Beverly Hills, CA: Sage, 1973), 214.

2. Morton A. Kaplan, "Problems of Theory Building and Theory Confirmation in International Politics" in Klaus Knorr and Sidney Verba (eds.), *The International System: Theoretical Essays* (Princeton: Princeton University Press, 1961), 23–24.

3. Ibid., 10.

4. Sir Brian Pippard, "Instability and Chaos: Physical Models of Everyday Life," *Interdisciplinary Science Review* 7:2 (1982), 93.

5. Ibid., 101.

6. Morton A. Kaplan, "Problems of Theory Building and Theory Confirmation in International Politics," 7–8.

7. Robert Jervis, *Perception and Misperception in International Politics* (Princeton: Princeton University Press, 1976), 158.

8. Ibid.

9. Morton A. Kaplan, "Problems of Theory Building and Theory Confirmation in International Politics," 8–9.

10. Marion J. Levy, Jr., "Does It Matter If He's Naked? Bawled the Child," in Klaus Knorr and James N. Rosenau (eds.), *Contending Approaches to International Politics* (Princeton: Princeton University Press, 1969), 89.

11. Sir Brian Pippard, "Instability and Chaos: Physical Models of Everyday Life," 92.

12. Klaus Knorr and Sidney Verba, "Introduction" in Knorr and Verba (eds.), *The International System*, 1–2.

13. Bruno Bettelheim, *Freud and Man's Soul* (New York: Knopf, 1983), 8.

14. Ibid., 5.

# Bibliography

Albrecht-Carrié, René (1958). *A Diplomatic History of Europe Since the Congress of Vienna* (New York: Harper & Row).

Albrecht-Carrié, René (1968). *The Concert of Europe* (New York: Harper & Row).

Alker, Hayward R., Jr. and Thomas J. Biersteker (1984). "The dialectics of world order: notes for a future archeologist of international savoir faire." *International Studies Quarterly,* vol. 28, no. 2 (June), pp. 121–142.

Allison, Graham T. (1971). *Essence of Decision: Explaining the Cuban Missile Crisis* (Boston: Little, Brown).

Allison, Graham T. and Morton H. Halperin (1972). "Bureaucratic politics: a paradigm and some policy implications." In Raymond Tanter and Richard H. Ullman (eds.), *Theory and Policy in International Relations* (Princeton: Princeton University Press), pp. 40–79.

Almond, Gabriel A. (1960). *The American People and Foreign Policy* (New York: Praeger).

Anckar, Dag and Erkki Berndtson (eds.) (1987). *The Evolution of Political Science: Selected Case Studies.* Special edition of *International Political Science Review,* vol. 8, no. 1 (January).

Angell, Norman (1914). *The Great Illusion* (London: Heinemann).

Armstrong, John A. (1982). *Nations Before Nationalism* (Chapel Hill, NC: University of North Carolina Press).

Aron, Raymond (1968). *Peace and War: A Theory of International Relations* (New York: Praeger).

Art, Robert J. (1985). "Bureaucratic politics and American foreign policy: a critique." In Art and Robert Jervis (eds.), *International Politics: Anarchy, Force, Political Economy, and Decision-Making,* 2nd ed. (Boston: Little, Brown), pp. 467–490.

Art Robert J. and Robert Jervis (eds.) (1985). *International Politics: Anarchy, Force, Political Economy, and Decision-Making,* 2nd ed. (Boston: Little, Brown).

Ashley, Richard K. (1976). "Noticing pre-paradigmatic progress." In James N.

**261**

Rosenau (ed.), *In Search of Global Patterns* (New York: Free Press), pp. 161–166.

Ashley, Richard K. (1984). "The poverty of neorealism." *International Organization*, vol. 38, no. 2 (Spring), pp. 225–286.

Avinieri, Shlomo (1970). "Hegel and nationalism." In Walter Kaufmann (ed.), *Hegel's Political Philosophy* (New York: Atherton Press), pp. 109–136.

Bacchus, William I. (1974). *Foreign Policy and the Bureaucratic Process: The State Department's Country Director System* (Princeton: Princeton University Press).

Badie, Bertrand and Pierre Birnbaum (1983). *The Sociology of the State*, trans. Arthur Goldhammer (Chicago: University of Chicago Press).

Banks, Michael (1969). "Systems analysis and the study of regions." *International Studies Quarterly*, vol. 13, no. 4 (December), pp. 335–360.

Barber, Bernard (1953). *Science and the Social Order* (London: Allen & Unwin).

Barber, James David (1972). *The Presidential Character: Predicting Performance in the White House* (Englewood Cliffs, NJ: Prentice-Hall).

Barnet, Richard J. (1973). *The Roots of War: The Men and Institutions Behind U.S. Foreign Policy* (Baltimore: Penguin).

Baumberger, Jorg (1977). "No Kuhnian revolution in economics." *Journal of Economic Issues*, vol. 11, no. 1, pp. 1–20.

Beik, Paul H. and Laurence Lafore (1959). *Modern Europe: A History Since 1500* (New York: Henry Holt).

Bergsten, C. Fred, Robert O. Keohane, and Joseph S. Nye, Jr. (1975). "International economics and international politics: a framework for analysis." *International Organization*, vol. 29, no. 1 (Winter), pp. 3–36.

Bertalanffy, Ludwig von (1965). "General system theory." In J. David Singer (ed.), *Human Behavior and International Politics: Contributions from the Social-Psychological Sciences* (Chicago: Rand McNally), pp. 20–31.

Bettelheim, Bruno (1983). *Freud and Man's Soul* (New York: Knopf).

Bishop, William W., Jr. (1971). *International Law: Cases and Materials*, 3rd ed. (Boston: Little, Brown).

Blasier, Cole (1983). *The Giant's Rival: The USSR and Latin America* (Pittsburgh: University of Pittsburgh Press).

Blaug, Mark (1980). "Kuhn versus Lakatos, or paradigms versus research programmes in the history of economics." In Gary Gutting (ed.), *Paradigms and Revolutions: Appraisals and Applications of Thomas Kuhn's Philosophy of Science* (Notre Dame, IN: University of Notre Dame Press), pp. 137–160.

Bloch, Marc (1961). *Feudal Society*, 2 vols., trans. L. A. Manyon (Chicago: University of Chicago Press).

Bloor, David (1971). "Two paradigms for scientific knowledge?" *Science Studies*, vol. 1, no. 1, pp. 101–115.

Bourdieu, Pierre (1984). *Distinction: A Social Critique of the Judgement of Taste*, trans. Richard Nice (Cambridge, MA: Harvard University Press).

Bowle, John (1964). *Politics and Opinion in the Nineteenth Century* (New York: Oxford University Press).

Boynton, G. R. (1976). "Cumulativeness in international relations." In James N. Rosenau (ed.), *In Search of Global Patterns* (New York: Free Press), pp. 145–150.

Bozeman, Adda B. (1960). *Politics and Culture in International History* (Princeton: Princeton University Press).

Brady, Linda P. (1982). "A proposal." In Patrick C. Callahan, Linda P. Brady, and Margaret G. Hermann (eds.), *Describing Foreign Policy Behavior* (Beverly Hills, CA: Sage), pp. 17–30.

Braillard, P. (1984). "The social sciences and the study of international relations." *International Social Science Journal*, vol. 102, no. 4, pp. 627–642.

Bremer, Stuart A. (1976). "Obstacles to the accumulation of knowledge." In James N. Rosenau (ed.), *In Search of Global Patterns* (New York: Free Press), pp. 204–212.

Brennan, William J., Jr. (1985). "The Constitution of the United States: Contemporary Ratification." Text and Teaching Symposium, Washington, DC.

Brenner, Robert (1976). "The origins of capitalist development: a critique of neo-Smithian Marxism." *New Left Review*, no. 104 (July/August), pp. 25–92.

Brewer, Thomas L. (1973). "Issue and context variation in foreign policy." *Journal of Conflict Resolution*, vol. 17, no. 1 (March), pp. 89–115.

Brierly, J. L. (1955). *The Law of Nations: An Introduction to the International Law of Peace*, 5th ed. (New York: Oxford University Press).

Brinton, Crane (1938). *The Anatomy of Revolution* (New York: Norton).

Brock, William E. (1984). "Trade and debt: the vital linkage." *Foreign Affairs*, vol. 62, no. 5, pp. 1037–1057.

Brodie, Bernard (1973). *War and Politics* (New York: Macmillan).

Bronfenbrenner, Martin (1971). "The 'structure of revolutions' in economic thought." *History of Political Economy*, vol. 3, no. 1 (Spring), pp. 136–151.

Bronowski, Jacob (1978). *The Origins of Knowledge and Imagination* (New Haven, CT: Yale University Press).

Bryant, C. G. A. (1975). "Kuhn, paradigms and sociology." *British Journal of Sociology*, vol. 26, no. 3 (September), pp. 354–359.

Buckley, Walter (ed.) (1968). *Modern Systems Research for the Behavioral Sciences* (Chicago: Aldine).

Bull, Hedley (1966). "Society and anarchy in international relations." In Herbert Butterfield and Martin Wight (eds.), *Diplomatic Investigations: Essays in the Theory of International Politics* (London: Allen & Unwin), pp. 40–48.

Bull, Hedley (1966). "The Groatian conception of international society." In Herbert Butterfield and Martin Wight (eds.), *Diplomatic Investigations: Essays in the Theory of International Politics* (London: Allen & Unwin), pp. 51–73.

Bull, Hedley (1969). "International theory: the case for a classical approach." In Klaus Knorr and James N. Rosenau (eds.), *Contending Approaches to*

*International Politics* (Princeton: Princeton University Press), pp. 20–38.

Bull, Hedley (1972). "The theory of international politics 1919–1969." In B. Porter (ed.), *The Aberystwyth Papers: International Politics 1919–1969* (London: Oxford University Press), pp. 30–56.

Bull, Hedley (1977). *The Anarchical Society: A Study of Order in World Politics* (New York: Columbia University Press).

Burke, Edmund (1961). *Reflections on the Revolution in France* (Garden City, NY: Doubleday).

Burnham, James (1943). *The Machiavellians* (Chicago: Henry Regnery).

Burton, J. W. (1968). *Systems, States, Diplomacy and Rules* (New York: Cambridge University Press).

Butterfield, Herbert (1957). *The Origins of Modern Science* (New York: Free Press).

Butterfield, Herbert (1966). "The balance of power." In Butterfield and Martin Wight (eds.), *Diplomatic Investigations: Essays in the Theory of International Politics* (London: Allen & Unwin), pp. 149–175.

Butterfield, Herbert and Martin Wight (eds.) (1966). *Diplomatic Investigations: Essays in the Theory of International Politics* (London: Allen & Unwin).

Callahan, Patrick C., Linda P. Brady, and Margaret G. Hermann (eds.) (1982). *Describing Foreign Policy Behavior* (Beverly Hills, CA: Sage).

Cantori, Louis J. and Steven L. Spiegel (1970). *The International Politics of Regions: A Comparative Approach* (Englewood Cliffs, NJ: Prentice-Hall).

Caporaso, James A. (ed.) (1978). *Dependence and dependency in the global system.* Special issue of *International Organization,* vol. 32, no. 1 (Winter).

Cardoso, Fernando Enrique. *Dependencia y desarrollo en America Latina* (Mexico: Siglo Veintiuno Editores).

Cardozo, Benjamin N. (1921). *The Nature of the Judicial Process* (New Haven: Yale University Press).

Carr, E. H. (1962). *The Twenty Years' Crisis 1919–1939* (New York: St. Martin's Press).

Cassese, Sabino (1986). "The rise and decline of the notion of state." *International Political Science Review,* vol. 7, no. 2 (April), pp. 120–130.

Cheetham, Nicholas (1983). *Keepers of the Keys: A History of the Popes from St. Peter to John Paul II* (New York: Charles Scribner's Sons).

Chi, Hsi-Sheng (1968). "The Chinese warlord system as an international system." In Morton A. Kaplan (ed.), *New Approaches to International Politics* (New York: St. Martin's Press), pp. 405–425.

Claessen, Henri J. M. and Peter Skalnik (eds.) (1978). *The Early State* (The Hague, The Netherlands: Mouton Publishers).

Claessen, Henri J. M. and Peter Skalnik (1978). "The early state: theories and hypotheses." In Claessen and Skalnik (eds.), *The Early State* (The Hague, The Netherlands: Mouton Publishers), pp. 77–92.

Claude, Inis L., Jr. (1962). *Power and International Relations* (New York: Random House).

Claude, Inis L., Jr. (1964). *Swords into Plowshares,* 3rd ed. (New York: Random House).

Claude, Inis L., Jr. (1986). "Myths about the state." *Review of International Studies,* vol. 12, no. 1, pp. 1–11.

Coates, A. W. (1969). "Is there a 'structure of revolutions' in economics?" *Kyklos,* vol. 22, no. 2, pp. 289–295.

Cohen, Benjamin J. (1982). "Balance-of-payments financing: evolution of a regime." *International Organization,* vol. 36, no. 2 (Spring), pp. 457–478.

Cohen, Bernard C. (1973). *The Public's Impact on Foreign Policy* (Boston: Little, Brown).

Cohen, Raymond (1979). *Threat Perception in International Crisis* (Madison, WI: University of Wisconsin Press).

Cohen, Ronald (1978). "Introduction." In Cohen and Elman R. Service (eds.), *Origins of the State: The Anthropology of Political Evolution* (Philadelphia: ISHI), pp. 141–160.

Cohen, Ronald (1978). "State origins: a reappraisal." In Henri J. M. Claessen and Peter Skalnik (eds.), *The Early State* (The Hague, The Netherlands: Mouton Publishers), pp. 31–75.

Cohen, Ronald and Elman R. Service (eds.) (1978). *Origins of the State: The Anthropology of Political Evolution* (Philadelphia: ISHI).

Cohen, Stephen D. (1981). *The Making of United States International Economic Policy,* 2nd ed. (New York: Praeger).

Collier, David (ed.) (1979). *The New Authoritarianism in Latin America* (Princeton: Princeton University Press).

Contamine, Philippe (1984). *War in the Middle Ages,* trans. Michael Jones (Oxford: Basil Blackwell, Ltd.).

Cottam, Richard W. (1977). *Foreign Policy Motivation* (Pittsburgh: Pittsburgh University Press).

Crick, Bernard (1960). *The American Science of Politics* (Berkeley and Los Angeles: University of California Press).

Dahl, Robert (1963). *Modern Political Analysis* (Englewood Cliffs, NJ: Prentice-Hall).

Davies, James C. (1962). "Toward a theory of revolution." *American Sociological Review,* vol. 27, no. 1 (February), pp. 5–19.

De Rivera, Joseph H. (1968). *The Psychological Dimension of Foreign Policy* (Columbus, OH: Charles E. Merrill).

De Tocqueville, Alexis (1945). *Democracy in America,* vol. 1 (New York: Knopf).

Del Aguila, Juan (1984). "Cuba's foreign policy in Central America and the Caribbean." In Jennie K. Lincoln and Elizabeth G. Ferris (eds.), *The Dynamics of Latin American Foreign Policies: Challenges for the 1980s* (Boulder, CO: Westview Press), pp. 251–266.

Denisoff, R. Serge, Orel Callahan, and Mark H. Levine (1974). *Theories and Paradigms in Contemporary Sociology* (Itasca, IL: F. E. Peacock).

DePorte, A. W. (1979). *Europe Between the Superpowers* (New Haven: Yale

University Press).

Deutsch, Karl W. (1964). *The Nerves of Government* (New York: Free Press).

Deutsch, Karl W. (1967). "Nation and world." In Ithiel de Sola Pool (ed.), *Contemporary Political Science: Toward Political Theory* (New York: McGraw-Hill), pp. 204–227.

Deutsch, Karl W., S. Burrell, R. Kann, M. Lee, M. Lichterman, R. Lindgren, F. Lowenheim, and R. Van Wagenen (1957). *Political Community and the North Atlantic Area: International Organization in the Light of Historical Experience* (Princeton: Princeton University Press).

Deutsch, Karl W. and J. David Singer (1964). "Multipolar power systems and international stability." *World Politics,* vol. 16, no. 3 (April), pp. 390–406.

Dickson, Paul (1980). *The Official Explanations* (New York: Delacorte Press).

Dodds, E. R. (1964). *The Greeks and the Irrational* (Berkeley, CA: University of California Press).

Dos Santos, Theontonio (1968). *El Nuevo carácter de la dependencia* (Santiago, Chile: Cuadernos de CESO).

Dougherty, James E. and Robert L. Pfaltzgraff, Jr. (1981). *Contending Theories of International Relations: A Comprehensive Survey,* 2nd ed. (New York: Harper & Row).

Duchacek, Ivo D. (1984). "The international dimension of subnational self-government." *Publius,* vol. 14, no. 4 (Fall), pp. 5–31.

Duncan, W. Raymond (1976). *Latin American Politics: A Developmental Approach* (New York: Praeger).

Dye, Thomas R. (1986). *Who's Running America? The Conservative Years,* 4th ed. (Englewood Cliffs, NJ: Prentice-Hall).

Earle, Edward Mead (ed.) (1967). *Makers of Modern Strategy: Military Thought from Machiavelli To Hitler* (New York: Atheneum).

Ebenstein, William (ed.) (1969). *Great Political Thinkers,* 4th ed. (New York: Holt, Rinehart & Winston).

Eckberg, Douglas Lee and Lester Hill, Jr. (1980). "The paradigm concept and sociology: a critical review." In Gary Gutting (ed.), *Paradigms and Revolutions; Appraisals and Applications of Thomas Kuhn's Philosophy of Science* (Notre Dame, IN: University of Notre Dame Press), pp. 117–137.

Effrat, Andrew (1972). "Power to the paradigms: an editorial introduction." *Sociological Inquiry,* vol. 42, no. 3–4, pp. 3–34.

Eisenstadt, S. N. (1963). *The Political Systems of Empires* (New York: Free Press).

Elrod, Richard B. (1976). "The concert of Europe: a fresh look at an international system." *World Politics,* vol. 28, no. 2 (January), pp. 159–174.

Etheridge, Lloyd S. (1978). *A World of Men: The Private Sources of American Foreign Policy* (Cambridge, MA: MIT Press).

Eulau, Heinz (1963). *The Behavioral Persuasion in Politics* (New York: Random House).

Falk, Richard A. (1971). *This Endangered Planet* (New York: Random House).

Falk, Richard A. (1977). "Contending approaches to world order." *Journal of International Affairs,* vol. 31 (Fall/Winter), pp. 171–198.

Farrell, R. Barry (ed.) (1966). *Approaches to Comparative and International Politics* (Evanston, IL: Northwestern University Press).

Ferguson, Yale H. and Walter F. Weiker (eds.) (1973). *Continuing Issues in International Politics* (Pacific Palisades, CA: Goodyear).

Field, James A., Jr. (1972). "Transnationalism and the new tribe." In Robert O. Keohane and Joseph S. Nye, Jr. (eds.). *Transnational Relations and World Politics* (Cambridge, MA: Harvard University Press), pp. 3–32.

Finifter, Ada W. (ed.) (1983). *Political Science: The State of the Discipline* (Washington, DC: American Political Science Association).

Finley, M. I. (1983). *Politics in the Ancient World* (Cambridge: Cambridge University Press).

Fleisher, Martin (ed.) (1972). *Machiavelli and the Nature of Political Thought* (New York: Atheneum).

Forsyth, M. G., H. M. A. Keens-Soper, P. Savigear (eds.) (1970). *The Theory of International Relations: Selected Texts from Gentili to Treitschke* (New York: Atherton Press).

Fox, William T. R. (1949). "Interwar international relations research: the American experience." *World Politics,* vol. 2, no. 1 (October), pp. 67–80.

Franke, Winfried (1968). "The Italian city-state system as an international system." In Morton A. Kaplan (ed.), *New Approaches to International Relations* (New York: St. Martin's Press), pp. 426–458.

Franklin, Julian H. (1973). *Jean Bodin and the Rise of Absolutist Theory* (Cambridge: Cambridge University Press).

Fried, Morton H. (1978). "The state, the chicken, and the egg: or what came first?" In Ronald Cohen and Elman R. Service (eds.), *Origins of the State: The Anthropology of Political Evolution* (Philadelphia: ISHI), pp. 35–47.

Fromm, Erich (1962). *Beyond the Chains of Illusion* (New York: Simon & Schuster).

Galtung, Johan (1969). "The social sciences: an essay on polarization and integration." In Klaus Knorr and James N. Rosenau (eds.), *Contending Approaches to International Politics* (Princeton: Princeton University Press), pp. 243–286.

Gamson, William A. and Andre Modigliani (1971). *Untangling the Cold War* (Boston: Little, Brown).

Gasiorowski, Mark J. (1986). "Economic interdependence and international conflict: some cross-national evidence." *International Studies Quarterly,* vol. 30, no. 1 (March), pp. 23–28.

Geertz, Clifford (1981). *Negara: The Theatre State in Nineteenth Century Bali* (Princeton: Princeton University Press).

Gellner, Ernest (1983). *Nations and Nationalism* (Ithaca, NY: Cornell University Press).

George, Alexander L. (1969). "The 'operational code': a neglected approach to the study of political leaders and decision-making." *International Studies*

*Quarterly,* vol. 13, no. 2 (June), pp. 190–222.

George, Alexander L. (1972). "The case for multiple advocacy in making foreign policy." *American Political Science Review,* vol. 66, no. 3 (September), pp. 751–785.

George, Alexander L. (1980). *Presidential Decision-Making: The Effective Use of Information and Advice* (Boulder, CO: Westview Press).

George, Alexander L. and Juliette George (1956). *Woodrow Wilson and Colonel House* (New York: Day).

Gilbert, Felix (1967). "Machiavelli: the renaissance of the art of war." In Edward Mead Earle (ed.), *Makers of Modern Strategy: Military Thought from Machiavelli to Hitler* (New York: Atheneum), pp. 3–25.

Gilpin, Robert (1962). *American Scientists and Nuclear Weapons Policy* (Princeton: Princeton University Press).

Gilpin, Robert G. (1984). "The richness of the tradition of political realism." *International Organization,* vol. 38, no. 2 (Spring), pp. 287–304.

Gordon, Dennis K. (1984). "Argentina's foreign policies in the post-Malvinas era." In Jennie K. Lincoln and Elizabeth G. Ferris (eds.), *The Dynamics of Latin American Foreign Policies: Challenges for the 1980s* (Boulder, CO: Westview Press), pp. 85–100.

Graebner, Norman A. (1964). *Ideas and Diplomacy: Readings in the Intellectual Tradition of American Foreign Policy* (New York: Oxford University Press).

Greenberg, Jack (1974). "Litigation for social change: methods, limits and role in democracy." *Record of the Association of the Bar of the City of New York,* vol. 29.

Grieco, Joseph M. (1982). "Between dependency and autonomy: India's experience with the international computer industry." *International Organization,* vol. 36, no. 3 (Summer), pp. 609–632.

Guetzkow, Harold (1950). "Long-range research in international relations." *American Perspective,* vol. 4, no. 4 (Fall), pp. 421–440.

Guetzkow, Harold (1976). "Sizing up a study in simulated international processes." In James N. Rosenau (ed.), *In Search of Global Patterns* (New York: Free Press), pp. 91–105.

Guicciardini, Francesco (1969). *The History of Italy,* trans. Sidney Alexander (London: Collier-Macmillan Ltd.).

Gulick, Edward Vose (1955). *Europe's Classical Balance of Power: A Case History of the Theory and Practice of One of the Great Concepts of European Statecraft* (New York: Norton).

Gurr, Ted Robert (1970). *Why Men Rebel* (Princeton: Princeton University Press).

Gutting, Gary (1980). "Introduction." In Gutting (ed.), *Paradigms and Revolutions: Appraisals and Applications of Thomas Kuhn's Philosophy of Science* (Notre Dame, IN: University of Notre Dame Press), pp. 1–23.

Gutting, Gary (ed.) (1980). *Paradigms and Revolutions: Appraisais and Applications of Thomas Kuhn's Philosophy of Science* (Notre Dame, IN: University of Notre Dame Press).

Haas, Ernst B. (1953). "The balance of power: prescription, concept or propaganda?" *World Politics,* vol. 5, no. 4 (July), pp. 442–477.

Haas, Ernst B. (1958). *The Uniting of Europe: Political, Social and Economic Forces* (Stanford: Stanford University Press).

Haas, Ernst B. (1964). *Beyond the Nation-State: Functionalism and International Organization* (Stanford: Stanford University Press).

Haas, Ernst B. (1975). "On systems and international regimes." *World Politics,* vol. 27, no. 2 (January), pp. 147–174.

Haas, Ernst B. (1980). "Why collaborate? Issue-linkage and international regimes." *World Politics,* vol. 32, no. 3 (April), pp. 357–405.

Haas, Ernst B. (1982). "Words can hurt you; or, who said what to whom about regimes." *International Organization,* vol. 36, no. 2 (Spring), pp. 207–243.

Haas, Jonathan (1982). *The Evolution of the Prehistoric State* (New York: Columbia University Press).

Halberstam, David (1972). *The Best and the Brightest* (New York: Random House).

Hall, John H. (ed.) (1986). *States in History* (Oxford: Oxford University Press).

Halperin, Morton H. (1974). *Bureaucratic Politics and Foreign Policy* (Washington, DC: Brookings).

Halperin, Morton H. and Arnold Kanter (eds.) (1973). *Readings in Foreign Policy: A Bureaucratic Perspective* (Boston: Little, Brown).

Heilbroner, Robert (1975). *An Inquiry into the Human Prospect* (New York: Norton).

Hermann, Charles F. (1969). *Crises in Foreign Policy* (Indianapolis: Bobbs-Merrill).

Hermann, Charles F. (1969). "International crisis as a situational variable." In James N. Rosenau (ed.), *International Politics and Foreign Policy,* rev. ed. (New York: Free Press), pp. 409–421.

Hermann, Charles F. (1983). "Bureaucratic constraints on innovation in American foreign policy." In Charles W. Kegley, Jr. and Eugene R. Wittkopf (eds.), *Perspectives on American Foreign Policy: Selected Readings* (New York: St. Martin's Press), pp. 390–409.

Hermann, Margaret G. (1976). "When leader personality will affect foreign policy; some propositions." In James N. Rosenau (ed.), *In Search of Global Patterns* (New York: Free Press), pp. 326–333.

Hermann, Margaret G. (forthcoming). *How Leaders Shape Foreign Policy* (Columbia, SC: University of South Carolina Press).

Hermann, Margaret G. and Thomas W. Milburn (eds.) (1977). *A Psychological Examination of Political Leaders* (New York: Free Press).

Hertz, Frederick (1944). *Nationality in History and Politics* (New York: The Humanities Press).

Herz, John H. (1959). *International Politics in the Atomic Age* (New York: Columbia University Press).

Herz, John H. (1969). "The territorial state revisited: reflections on the future of the nation-state." In James N. Rosenau (ed.), *International Politics and*

*Foreign Policy,* rev. ed. (New York: Free Press), pp. 76–89.

Herz, John H. (1976). *The Nation-State and the Crisis of World Politics* (New York: David McKay).

Heyl, John D. (1975). "Paradigms in social science." *Society,* vol. 12, no. 5 (July/August), pp. 61–67.

Hinsley, F. H. (1986). *Sovereignty,* 2nd ed. (Cambridge: Cambridge University Press).

Hoffmann, Stanley (1959). "International relations: the long road to theory." *World Politics,* vol. 11, no. 3 (April), pp. 346–377.

Hollinger, David A. (1980). "T. S. Kuhn's theory of science and its implications for history." In Gary Gutting (ed.), *Paradigms and Revolutions: Appraisals and Applications of Thomas Kuhn's Philosophy of Science* (Notre Dame, IN: University of Notre Dame Press), pp. 195–223.

Holsti, K. J. (1970). "National role conceptions in the study of foreign policy." *International Studies Quarterly,* vol. 14, no. 3 (September), pp. 233–309.

Holsti, K. J. (1983). *International Politics: A Framework for Analysis,* 4th ed. (Englewood Cliffs, NJ: Prentice-Hall).

Holsti, K. J. (1984). "Along the road to international theory." *International Journal,* vol. 39, no. 2 (Spring), pp. 337–365.

Holsti, K. J. (1985). *The Dividing Discipline: Hegemony and Diversity in International Theory* (Boston: Allen & Unwin).

Holsti, Ole R. (1969). "The belief system and national images: a case study." In James N. Rosenau (ed.), *International Politics and Foreign Policy,* rev. ed. (New York: Free Press), pp. 542–550.

Holsti, Ole R. (1977). *Toward a Typology of "Operational Code" Belief Systems,* Final Report to the National Science Foundation (Chapel Hill, NC: Duke University).

Holsti, Ole R. (1982). "The operational code approach; problems and some solutions." In Christer Jonsson (ed.), *Cognitive Dynamics and International Politics* (New York: St. Martin's Press).

Holsti, Ole R. and James N. Rosenau (1983). "A leadership divided: the foreign policy beliefs of American leaders, 1976–1980." In Charles W. Kegley, Jr., and Eugene R. Wittkopf (eds.), *Perspectives on American Foreign Policy: Selected Readings* (New York: St. Martin's Press), pp. 196–212.

Holsti, Ole R. and James N. Rosenau (1984). *American Leadership and World Affairs: Vietnam and the Breakdown of Consensus* (Boston: Allen & Unwin).

Holsti, Ole R., Randolph M. Siverson, and Alexander L. George (eds.) (1980). *Change in the International System* (Boulder, CO: Westview Press).

Hopkins, Raymond F. (1976). "The international role of 'domestic' bureaucracy." *International Organization,* vol. 30, no. 3 (Summer), pp. 405–432.

Hopkins, Raymond F. and Richard W. Mansbach (1973). *Structure and Process in International Politics* (New York: Harper & Row).

Hopmann, P. Terrence (1976). "Identifying, formulating, and solving puzzles in international relations research." In James N. Rosenau (ed.), *In Search of Global Patterns* (New York: Free Press), pp. 192–197.

Hopmann, P. Terrence, Dina A. Zinnes and J. David Singer (eds.) (1981). *Cumulation in International Relations Research* (Denver: Graduate School of International Studies, University of Denver Monograph Series in World Affairs).

Hopmann, P. Terrence, J. David Singer, Dina A. Zinnes (1981). "Introduction." In Hopmann, Zinnes and Singer (eds.), *Cumulation in International Relations Research* (Denver: Graduate School of International Studies, University of Denver Monograph Series in World Affairs), pp. 3-8.

Hopple, Gerald W. and Paul J. Rossa (1981). "International crisis analysis: recent developments and future directions." In P. Terrence Hopmann, Dina A. Zinnes and J. David Singer (eds.). *Cumulation in International Relations Research* (Denver: Graduate School of International Studies, University of Denver Monograph Series in World Affairs), pp. 65-97.

Howard, Michael (1982-83). "Reassurance and deterrence: western defense in the 1980s." *Foreign Affairs,* vol. 61, no. 2 (Winter), pp. 309-324.

Huntington, Samuel P. (1961). *The Common Defense* (New York: Columbia University Press).

Huntington, Samuel P. (1968). *Political Order in Changing Societies* (New Haven: Yale University Press).

Huntington, Samuel P. and Joan M. Nelson (1976). *No Easy Choice: Political Participation in Developing Countries* (Cambridge, MA: Harvard University Press).

IPSR Editorial Committee (1985). *Ethnicity and Regionalism,* topical issue of *International Political Science Review,* vol. 6, no. 2.

Isaak, Robert A. (1981). *Individuals and World Politics,* 2nd ed. (North Scituate, MA: Duxbury Press).

Jackson, Robert H. (1986). "African states and international theory." Paper delivered at the British International Studies Association annual meeting, University of Reading, Reading England.

Jackson, Robert H. (1986). "Negative sovereignty in sub-Saharan Africa." *Review of International Studies,* vol. 12, no. 4 (October), pp. 246-264.

Jackson, Robert H. and Carl G. Rosberg (1982). "Why Africa's weak states persist: the empirical and the juridical in statehood." *World Politics,* vol. 35, no. 1 (October), pp. 1-24.

Jacobson, Harold K. and Eric Stein (1966). *Diplomats, Scientists, and Politicians* (Ann Arbor, MI: University of Michigan Press).

James, Alan (1986). *Sovereign Statehood: The Basis of International Society* (London: Allen & Unwin).

Janis, Irving L. (1972). *Victims of Groupthink: A Psychological Study of Foreign-Policy Decisions and Fiascoes* (Boston: Houghton Mifflin).

Janis, Irving L. and Leon Mann (1977). *Decision Making: A Psychological Analysis of Conflict, Choice, and Commitment* (New York: Free Press).

Jervis, Robert (1968). "Hypotheses on misperception." *World Politics,* vol. 20, no. 3 (April), pp. 454-479.

Jervis, Robert (1976). "Cumulation, correlations, and woozles." In James N.

Rosenau (ed.), *In Search of Global Patterns* (New York: Free Press), pp. 181–185.

Jervis, Robert (1976). *Perception and Misperception in International Politics* (Princeton: Princeton University Press).

Jervis, Robert (1982). "Security regimes." *International Organization,* vol. 36, no. 2 (Spring), pp. 357–378.

Job, Brian L. (1981). "Grins without cats: In pursuit of knowledge of international alliances." In P. Terrence Hopmann, Dina A. Zinnes and J. David Singer (eds.), *Cumulation in International Relations Research* (Denver: Graduate School of International Studies, University of Denver Monograph Series in World Affairs), pp. 39–63.

Johnson, Allen W. and Timothy Earle (1987). *The Evolution of Human Societies: From Foraging Group to Agrarian State* (Stanford, CA: Stanford University Press).

Jonsson, Christer (ed.) (1982). *Cognitive Dynamics and International Politics* (New York: St. Martin's Press).

Jonsson, Christer (1982). "Introduction: cognitive approaches to international politics." In Jonsson (ed.), *Cognitive Dynamics and International Politics* (New York: St. Martin's Press), pp. 1–18.

Jonsson, Christer and Ulf Westerlund (1982). "Role theory in foreign policy analysis." In Jonsson (ed.), *Cognitive Dynamics and International Politics* (New York: St. Martin's Press), pp. 122–157.

Kahn, Herman (1962). *Thinking About the Unthinkable* (New York: Horizon Press).

Kahn, Herman (1965). *On Escalation: Metaphors and Scenarios* (New York: Praeger).

Kaplan, Morton A. (1957). *System and Process in International Politics* (New York: Wiley).

Kaplan, Morton A. (1961). "Problems of theory building and theory confirmation in international politics." In Klaus Knorr and Sidney Verba (eds.), *The International System: Theoretical Essays* (Princeton: Princeton University Press), pp. 6–24.

Kaplan, Morton A. (ed.) (1968). *New Approaches to International Relations* (New York: St. Martin's Press).

Kaplan, Morton A. (1969). *Macropolitics* (Chicago: Aldine).

Kaplan, Morton A. (1969). "The new great debate: traditionalism vs. science in international relations." In Klaus Knorr and James N. Rosenau (eds.), *Contending Approaches to International Politics* (Princeton: Princeton University Press), pp. 39–61.

Karns, Margaret P. (ed.) (1986). *Persistent Patterns and Emerging Structures in a Waxing Century* (New York: Praeger).

Katzenstein, Peter (1975). "International interdependence: some long-term trends and recent changes." *International Organization,* vol. 29, no. 4 (Autumn), pp. 1021–1034.

Kaufmann, Walter (ed.) (1970). *Hegel's Political Philosophy* (New York: Atherton Press).

Kautsky, John H. (1982). *The Politics of Aristocratic Empires* (Chapel Hill, NC: University of North Carolina Press).

Kegley, Charles W., Jr., and Eugene R. Wittkopf (1982). *American Foreign Policy: Pattern and Process*, 2nd ed. (New York: St. Martin's Press).

Kegley, Charles W., Jr., and Eugene R. Wittkopf (eds.) (1983). *Perspectives on American Foreign Policy: Selected Readings* (New York: St. Martin's Press).

Kegley, Charles W., Jr., and Eugene R. Wittkopf (1985). *World Politics: Trends and Transformation*, 2nd ed. (New York: St. Martin's Press).

Kelman, Herbert C. (ed.) (1965). *International Behavior: A Social-Psychological Analysis* (New York: Holt, Rinehart & Winston).

Kennan, George F. (1951). *American Diplomacy 1900–1950* (Chicago: University of Chicago Press).

Kennan, George F. (1979). *The Decline of Bismarck's European Order: Franco-Russian Relations, 1875–1890* (Princeton: Princeton University Press).

Keohane, Robert O. (1980). "The theory of hegemonic stability and changes in international economic regimes, 1967–1977." In Ole R. Holsti, Randolph M. Siverson and Alexander L. George (eds.), *Change in the International System* (Boulder, CO: Westview Press), pp. 131–162.

Keohane, Robert O. (1982). "The demand for international regimes." *International Organization*, vol. 36, no. 2 (Spring), pp. 325–355.

Keohane, Robert O. (1984). *After Hegemony: Cooperation and Discord in the World Political Economy* (Princeton: Princeton University Press).

Keohane, Robert O. (ed.) (1986). *Neorealism and Its Critics* (New York: Columbia University Press).

Keohane, Robert O. (1986). "Theory of world politics: structural realism and beyond." In Keohane (ed.), *Neorealism and Its Critics* (New York: Columbia University Press), pp. 158–203.

Keohane, Robert O. and Joseph S. Nye, Jr. (eds.) (1972). *Transitional Relations and World Politics* (Cambridge, MA: Harvard University Press).

Keohane, Robert O. and Joseph S. Nye, Jr. (1974). "Introduction: the complex politics of Canadian-American interdependence." *International Organization*, vol. 23, no. 4 (Autumn), pp. 495–607.

Keohane, Robert O. and Joseph S. Nye, Jr. (1974). "Transgovernmental relations and international organizations." *World Politics*, vol. 27, no. 1 (October), pp. 39–62.

Keohane, Robert O. and Joseph S. Nye, Jr. (1974). "Transnational relations and interstate conflicts: an empirical analysis." *International Organization*, vol. 22, no. 4 (Autumn), pp. 961–996.

Keohane, Robert O. and Joseph S. Nye, Jr. (1977). *Power and Interdependence: World Politics in Transition* (Boston: Little, Brown).

Keohane, Robert O. and Joseph S. Nye, Jr. (1985). "Two cheers for multilateralism." *Foreign Policy,* no. 60 (Fall), pp. 148–167.

Khazanov, Anatoli M. (1978). "Some theoretical problems of the study of the early state." In Henri J. M. Claessen and Peter Skalnik (eds.), *The Early State* (The Hague, The Netherlands: Mouton Publishers), pp. 77–92.

King, M. D. (1980). "Reason, tradition, and the progressiveness of science." In Gary Gutting (ed.), *Paradigms and Revolutions: Appraisals and Applications of Thomas Kuhn's Philosophy of Science* (Notre Dame, IN: University of Notre Dame Press), pp. 97–117.

Kissinger, Henry A. (1969). *American Foreign Policy: Three Essays* (New York: Norton).

Knorr, Klaus and James N. Rosenau (eds.) (1969). *Contending Approaches to International Politics* (Princeton: Princeton University Press).

Knorr, Klaus and James N. Rosenau (1969). "Tradition and science in the study of international politics." In Knorr and Rosenau (eds.), *Contending Approaches to International Politics* (Princeton: Princeton University Press), pp. 3–19.

Knorr, Klaus and Sidney Verba (eds.) (1961). *The International System: Theoretical Essays* (Princeton: Princeton University Press).

Kohn, Hans (1944). *The Idea of Nationalism* (New York: Macmillan).

Korany, Bahgot (1984). "Foreign Policy Decisions in the Third World: and introduction." In Korany (ed.), *Foreign Policy Decisions in the Third World,* topical issue of *International Political Science Review,* vol. 5, no. 1, pp. 7–20.

Krasner, Stephen D. (1972). "Are bureaucracies important? (Or Allison wonderland)." *Foreign Policy,* no. 7 (Summer), pp. 159–179.

Krasner, Stephen D. (1976). "State power and the structure of international trade." *World Politics,* vol. 28, no. 3 (April), pp. 317–347.

Krasner, Stephen D. (1978). *Defending the National Interest: Raw Materials Investments and U.S. Foreign Policy* (Princeton: Princeton University Press).

Krasner, Stephen D. (ed.) (1982). "International Regimes." Special issue of *International Organization,* vol. 36, no. 2 (Spring).

Krasner, Stephen D. (1982). "Regimes and the limits of realism: regimes as autonomous variables." *International Organization,* vol. 36, no. 2 (Spring), pp. 497–510.

Krasner, Stephen D. (1982). "Structural causes and regime consequences: regimes as intervening variables." *International Organization,* vol. 36, no. 2 (Spring), pp. 185–205.

Krasner, Stephen D. (1984). "Approaches to the state: alternative conceptions and historical dynamics." *Comparative Politics,* vol. 16, no. 2 (January), pp. 223–246.

Kratochwil, Friedrich and John Gerard Ruggie (1986). "International organization: a state of the art on an art of the state." *International Organization,* vol. 40, no. 4 (Autumn), pp. 753–775.

Kuhn, Thomas S. (1970). *The Structure of Scientific Revolutions,* expanded ed. (Chicago: University of Chicago Press).

Kuhn, Thomas S. (1971). "Second thoughts on paradigms." In F. Suppe (ed.), *The Structure of Scientific Theories* (Urbana, IL: University of Illinois Press), pp. 459–517.

Kuhn, Thomas S. (1977). *The Essential Tension* (Chicago: University of Chicago Press).

Kuklick, Henrika (1972). "A 'scientific revolution': sociological theory in the United States." *Sociological Inquiry,* vol. 43, no. 1, pp. 2–22.

Kunin, L. and F. S. Weaver (1971). "On the structure of scientific revolutions in economics." *History of Political Economy,* vol. 3, no. 2 (Fall), pp. 391–397.

Lakatos, Imre (1970). "Falsification and the methodology of scientific research programmes." In Imre Lakatos and Alan Musgrave (eds.), *Criticism and the Growth of Knowledge* (Cambridge: Cambridge University Press), pp. 91–196.

Lakatos, Imre and Alan Musgrave (eds.) (1970). *Criticism and the Growth of Knowledge* (Cambridge: Cambridge University Press).

Lampert, Donald E., Lawrence L. Falkowski, and Richard W. Mansbach (1978). "Is there an international system?" *International Studies Quarterly,* vol. 22, no. 1 (March), pp. 143–166.

Lasswell, Harold D. (1935). *World Politics and Personal Insecurity* (New York: McGraw-Hill).

Lasswell, Harold D. and Abraham Kaplan (1950). *Power and Society* (New Haven, CT: Yale University Press).

Lavdan, L. (1977). *Progress and Its Problems* (London: Routledge & Kegan Paul).

Lebow, Richard Ned (1981). *Between Peace and War: The Nature of International Crisis* (Baltimore: Johns Hopkins Press).

Lehmbruch, Gerhard and Philippe C. Schmitter (eds.) (1982). *Patterns of Corporate Policy Making* (Beverly Hills, CA: Sage).

Leites, Nathan (1951). *The Operational Code of the Politburo* (New York: McGraw-Hill).

Levy, Marion J., Jr. (1969). " 'Does it matter if he's naked?' bawled the child." In Klaus Knorr and James N. Rosenau (eds.), *Contending Approaches to International Politics* (Princeton: Princeton University Press), pp. 87–109.

Leyton-Brown, David (1984). "The nation-state and multinational enterprise: erosion or assertion." In Robert O. Matthews, Arthur G. Rubinoff, and Janice Gross Stein (eds.), *International Conflict and Conflict Management: Readings in World Politics* (Scarborough, Ontario: Prentice-Hall), pp. 330–340.

Licklider, Roy (1986). "Political Power and the Arab Oil Weapon: The Netherlands, Great Britain, Canada, Japan, and the United States." Manuscript.

Lieber, Robert J. (1972). *Theory and World Politics* (Cambridge, MA: Winthrop).

Lijphart, Arend (1974). "The structure of the theoretical revolution in international relations." *International Studies Quarterly,* vol. 18, no. 1 (March), pp. 41–74.

Lincoln, Jennie K. and Elizabeth G. Ferris (eds.) (1984). *The Dynamics of Latin American Foreign Policies: Challenges for the 1980s* (Boulder, CO: Westview Press).

Lindberg, Leon N. (1963). *The Political Dynamics of European Economic Integration* (Stanford: Stanford University Press).

Lindberg, Leon N. and Stuart A. Scheingold (eds.) (1970). *Regional Integration: Theory and Research* (Cambridge, MA: Harvard University Press).

Lindblom, Charles E. (1959). "The science of muddling through." *Public Administration Review,* vol. 19, no. 2 (Spring), pp. 79–88.

Lindblom, Charles E. (1968). *The Policy-Making Process* (Englewood Cliffs, NJ: Prentice-Hall).

Lindblom, Charles E. and David Cohen (1979). *Usable Knowledge: Social Science and Social Problem Solving* (New Haven: Yale University Press).

Lippmann, Walter (1955). *The Public Philosophy* (New York: Mentor).

Lipson, Charles (1982). "The transformation of trade: the sources and effects of regime change." *International Organization,* vol. 36, no. 2 (Spring), pp. 417–455.

Lowi, Theodore J. (1964). "American business, public policy, case studies and political theory." *World Politics,* vol. 16, no. 4 (July), pp. 677–715.

Machiavelli, Niccolo (1950). *The Prince and The Discourses,* introduction by Max Lerner (New York: Random House).

Macrae, Duncan J. (1976). *The Social Function of Social Science* (New Haven: Yale University Press).

Maghroori, R. and B. Ramberg (eds.) (1982). *Globalism Versus Realism: International Relations' Third Debate* (Boulder, CO: Westview Press).

Mansbach, Richard W., Yale H. Ferguson, and Donald E. Lampert (1976). *The Web of World Politics: Nonstate Actors in the Global System* (Englewood Cliffs, NJ: Prentice-Hall).

Mansbach, Richard W. and John A. Vasquez (1981). *In Search of Theory: A New Paradigm for Global Politics* (New York: Columbia University Press).

March, James G. and Herbert Simon (1957). *Organizations* (New York: Wiley).

Martin, Wayne Richard (1976). "Cumulation, cooperation, and commitment." In James N. Rosenau (ed.), *In Search of Global Patterns* (New York: Free Press), pp. 212–215.

Maslow, A. H. (1943). "A theory of human motivation." *Psychological Review,* vol. 50, no. 4, pp. 370–396.

Masters, Roger D. (1964). "World politics as a primitive political system." *World Politics,* vol. 16, no. 4 (July), pp. 595–619.

Masters, Roger D. (1983). "The biological nature of the state." *World Politics,* vol. 35, no. 2 (January), pp. 161–193.

Matthews, Robert O., Arthur G. Rubinoff, and Janice Gross Stein (eds.) (1984). *International Conflict and Conflict Management* (Scarborough, Ontario: Prentice-Hall).

May, Ernest R. (1973). *"Lessons" from the Past: The Use and Misuse of History in American Foreign Policy* (New York: Oxford University Press).

Mayall, James (1986). "The variety of states." Paper delivered at the British International Studies Association annual meeting, University of Reading, Reading, England.

McClure, Paul T. (1969). "The Organizational Approach versus the Society Approach to Development in Emerging Nations," P-3927 (Santa Monica, CA: RAND Corporation).

McGowan, Patrick J. (ed.) (1973), *Sage International Yearbook of Foreign Policy: Volume One* (Beverly Hills, CA: Sage).

McGowan, Patrick J. (1976). "The future of comparative studies: an evangelical appeal." In James N. Rosenau (ed.), *In Search of Global Patterns* (New York: Free Press), pp. 217–235.

McGowan, Patrick J. and Howard B. Shapiro (1973). *The Comparative Study of Foreign Policy: A Survey of Scientific Findings*, vol. 4, Sage Library of Social Research (Beverly Hills, CA: Sage Publications).

Meinecke, Friedrich (1956). *Machiavellism: The Doctrine of Raison D'Etat and Its Place in Modern History*, trans. Douglas Scott (New Haven, CT: Yale University Press).

Mendlowitz, Saul H. (1977). "The program of the Institute of World Order." *Journal of International Affairs*, vol. 31 (Fall/Winter), pp. 259–266.

Merritt, Richard L. (1973). "Public opinion and foreign policy in West Germany." In Patrick J. McGowan (ed.), *Sage International Yearbook of Foreign Policy Studies: Volume One* (Beverly Hills, CA: Sage), pp. 255–274.

Merton, Robert K. (1957). "Priorities in scientific discovery: a chapter in the sociology of science." *American Sociological Review*, vol. 22, no. 6, pp. 635–659.

Meyers, R. (1983). "International paradigms, concepts of peace, and the policy of appeasement." *War and Society*, vol. 1, no. 1 (May), pp. 43–65.

Miller, J. D. B. (1986). "Sovereignty as a source of vitality for the state." *Review of International Studies*, vol. 12, no. 2 (April), pp. 79–91.

Mitrany, David (1943). *A Working Peace System* (London: Royal Institute of International Affairs).

Modelski, George (1961). "Agraria and industria: two models of the international system." In Klaus Knorr and Sidney Verba (eds.), *The International System* (Princeton: Princeton University Press), pp. 118–143.

Montross, Lynn (1960). *War Through the Ages*, 3rd ed. (New York: Harper & Row).

Morgenthau, Hans J. (1951). *In Defense of the National Interest* (New York: Knopf).

Morgenthau, Hans J. (1952). "Another great debate: the national interest of the United States." *American Political Science Review*, vol. 46, no. 4 (December 1952), pp. 961–988.

Morgenthau, Hans J. (1978). *Politics Among Nations: The Struggle for Power and Peace*, 5th ed., revised (New York: Knopf).

Morse, Edward L. (1976). *Modernization and the Transformation of Interna-*

*tional Relations* (New York: Free Press).

Muñoz, Heraldo and Joseph S. Tulchin (eds.) (1984). *Latin American Nations in World Politics* (Boulder, CO: Westview Press).

Nettl, J. P. (1968). "The state as a conceptual variable." *World Politics,* vol. 20, no. 4 (July), pp. 559–592.

Neustadt, Richard (1970). *Alliance Politics* (New York: Columbia University Press).

Nicolson, Harold (1963). *Diplomacy,* 3rd ed. (New York: Oxford University Press).

Nordlinger, Eric A. (1981). *On the Autonomy of the Democratic State* (Cambridge, MA: Harvard University Press).

Nossal, Kim Richard (1984). "Bureaucratic politics and the Westminster model." In Robert O. Matthews, Arthur G. Rubinoff, and Janice Gross Stein (eds.), *International Conflict and Conflict Management* (Scarborough, Ontario: Prentice-Hall), pp. 120–127.

Nye, Joseph S., Jr. (ed.) (1968). *International Regionalism: Readings* (Boston: Little, Brown).

Nye, Joseph S., Jr. and Robert O. Keohane (1972). "Transnational relations and world politics: a conclusion." In Robert O. Keohane and Joseph S. Nye, Jr. (eds.), *Transnational Relations and World Politics* (Cambridge, MA: Harvard University Press), pp. 371–398.

Nye, Joseph S., Jr. and Robert O. Keohane (1972). "Transnational relations and world politics: an introduction." In Robert O Keohane and Joseph S. Nye, Jr. (eds.), *Transnational Relations and World Politics* (Cambridge, MA: Harvard University Press), pp. ix–xxix.

O'Leary, Michael K. (1976). "The role of issues." In James N. Rosenau (ed.), *In Search of Global Patterns* (New York: Free Press), pp. 318–326.

Olson, Mancur, Jr. (1965). *The Logic of Collective Action* (Cambridge, MA: Harvard University Press).

Oren, Nissan (ed.) (1984). *When Patterns Change: Turning Points in International Organization* (New York: St. Martin's Press).

Organski, A. F. K. (1958). *World Politics* (New York: Knopf).

Ortega y Gasset, José (1948). *The Dehumanization of Art and Other Essays on Art, Culture and Literature* (Princeton: Princeton University Press).

Osgood, Robert E. (1953). *Ideals and Self-Interest in America's Foreign Relations* (Chicago: University of Chicago Press).

Packenham, Robert A. (1973). *Liberal America and the Third World: Political Development Ideas in Foreign Aid and Social Science* (Princeton: Princeton University Press).

Paige, Glenn D. (1977). "On values and science: *The Korean Decision* reconsidered." *American Political Science Review,* vol. 71, no. 4 (December), pp. 1603–1609.

Parkinson, F. (1977). *The Philosophy of International Relations: A Study in the History of Thought* (Beverly Hills, CA: Sage Publications).

Passerin D'Entreves, Alessandro (1967). *The Notion of the State: An Introduc-*

*tion to Political Theory* (London: Oxford University Press).

Perry, Clive (1968). "The function of law in the international community." In Max Sorensen (ed.), *Manual of Public International Law* (New York: St. Martin's Press), pp. 1–54.

Pfaltzgraff, Robert, Jr. (1971). "International Studies in the 1970s." *International Studies Quarterly*, vol. 15, no. 1 (March), pp. 104–128.

Phillips, Warren R. (1974). "Where have all the theories gone?" *World Politics*, vol. 26, no. 2 (January), pp. 155–188.

Pippard, Sir Brian (1982). "Instability and chaos: physical models of everyday life." *Interdisciplinary Science Reviews*, vol. 7, no. 2, pp. 92–101.

Pirages, Dennis (1978). *A New Context for International Relations: Global Ecopolitics* (North Scituate, MA: Duxbury Press).

Platig, Raymond E. (1967). *International Relations Research: Problems of Evaluation and Advancement* (Santa Barbara, CA: Clio Press).

Pool, Ithiel de Sola (ed.) (1967). *Contemporary Political Science: Toward Political Theory* (New York: McGraw-Hill).

Popper, Karl (1935). *Logik der Forschung: The Logic of Scientific Discovery* (London: Hutchinson).

Porter, B. (ed.) (1972). *The Aberystwyth Papers: International Politics 1919–1969* (London: Oxford University Press).

Poulantzas, Nicos (1978). *State, Power, Socialism* (London: NLB).

Puchala, Donald J. (1971). *International Politics Today* (New York: Harper & Row).

Puchala, Donald J. and Raymond F. Hopkins (1982). "International regimes: lessons from inductive analysis." *International Organization*, vol. 36, no. 2 (Spring), pp. 245–275.

Reinken, Donald (1968). "Computer explorations of the 'balance of power': a project report." In Morton A. Kaplan (ed.), *New Approaches to International Politics* (New York: St. Martin's Press), pp. 459–481.

Riggs, Fred W. (1961). "International relations as a prismatic system." In Klaus Knorr and Sidney Verba (eds.), *The International System: Theoretical Essays* (Princeton: Princeton University Press).

Riggs, Fred W. (1963). "The theory of developing politics." *World Politics*, vol. 16, no. 1 (October), pp. 147–171.

Ritzer, George (1975). *Sociology: A Multiple Paradigm Science* (Boston: Allyn & Bacon).

Rogow, Arnold A. (1963). *James Forrestal: A Study in Personality, Politics, and Policy* (New York: Macmillan).

Rosati, Jerel A. (1985). "A neglected actor in American foreign policy: the role of judiciary." *International Studies Notes*, vol. 12, no. 1 (Fall), pp. 10–15.

Rosecrance, Richard N. (1963). *Action and Reaction in World Politics: International Systems in Perspective* (Boston: Little, Brown).

Rosecrance, Richard N. (1966). "Bipolarity, multipolarity, and the future." *Journal of Conflict Resolution*, vol. 10, no. 3 (September), pp. 314–327.

Rosecrance, Richard N. (1976). "The failures of quantitative analysis: possible causes and cures." In James N. Rosenau (ed.), *In Search of Global Patterns* (New York: Free Press), pp. 174–180.

Rosecrance, Richard N. (1981). "International theory revisited." *International Organization*, vol. 35, no. 4 (Autumn), pp. 691–713.

Rosecrance, Richard N. (1982). "Reply to Waltz." *International Organization*, vol. 36, no. 3 (Summer), pp. 682–685.

Rosecrance, Richard N., A. Alexandroff, W. Koehler, J. Kroll, S. Laqueur, and J. Stocker (1977). "Whither interdependence?" *International Organization*, vol. 31, no. 3 (Summer), pp. 425–444.

Rosecrance, Richard N. and William Gutowitz (1981). "Measuring interdependence: a rejoinder." *International Organization*, vol. 35, no. 3 (Summer), pp. 553–556.

Rosenau, James N. (1961). *Public Opinion and Foreign Policy* (New York: Random House).

Rosenau, James N. (1966). "Pre-theories and theories of foreign policy." In R. Barry Farrell (ed.), *Approaches to Comparative and International Politics* (Evanston, IL: Northwestern University Press), pp. 27–93.

Rosenau, James N. (ed.) (1969). *International Politics and Foreign Policy*, rev. ed. (New York: Free Press).

Rosenau, James N. (1971). "Comparative foreign policy: fad, fantasy, or field?" In Rosenau, *The Scientific Study of Foreign Policy* (New York: Free Press), pp. 67–94.

Rosenau, James N. (1971). *The Scientific Study of Foreign Policy* (New York: Free Press).

Rosenau, James N. (ed.) (1974). *Comparing Foreign Policies: Theories, Findings and Methods* (New York: Wiley).

Rosenau, James N. (1976). "Capabilities and control in an interdependent world." *International Security*, vol. 1, no. 2 (Fall), pp. 32–49.

Rosenau, James N. (ed.) (1976). *In Search of Global Patterns* (New York: Free Press).

Rosenau, James N. (1984). "A pre-theory revisited: world politics in an era of cascading interdependence." *International Studies Quarterly*, vol. 28, no. 3 (September), pp. 245–305.

Rosenau, James N. (1986). "Before cooperation: Hegemons, regimes, and habit-driven actors in world politics." *International Organization*, vol. 40, no. 4 (Autumn), pp. 849–894.

Rosenau, James N., Vincent Davis, and Maurice A. East (eds.) (1972). *The Analysis of International Politics* (New York: Free Press).

Ruggie, John Gerard (1982). "International regimes, transactions, and change: embedded liberalism in the postwar economic order." *International Organization*, vol. 36, no. 2 (Spring), pp. 379–415.

Ruggie, John Gerard (1983). "Continuity and transformation in the world polity: toward a neorealist synthesis." *World Politics*, vol. 35, no. 2 (January), pp. 261–285.

Ruggie, John Gerard (ed.) (1983). *The Antimonies of Interdependence: National Welfare and the Division of Labor* (New York: Columbia University Press).

Rummel, R. J. (1976). "The roots of faith." In James N. Rosenau (ed.), *In Search of Global Patterns* (New York: Free Press), pp. 10–30.

Russett, Bruce M. (1963). *Community and Contention: Britain and America in the Twentieth Century* (Cambridge, MA: MIT Press).

Russett, Bruce M. (1965). *Trends in World Politics* (New York: Macmillan).

Russett, Bruce M. (ed.) (1972). *Peace, War, and Numbers* (Beverly Hills, CA: Sage).

Russett, Bruce M. (1976). "Apologia pro vita sua." In James N. Rosenau (ed.), *In Search of Global Patterns* (New York: Free Press), pp. 31–37.

Russett, Bruce M. (1985). "The mysterious case of vanishing hegemony; or, Is Mark Twain really dead?" *International Organization,* vol. 39, no. 2 (Spring), pp. 207–231.

Russett, Bruce M. and Harvey Starr (1981). *World Politics: The Menu for Choice* (San Francisco: W. H. Freeman).

Ryan, Alan (1970). *The Philosophy of the Social Sciences* (New York: Pantheon Books).

Sabine, George H. (1961). *A History of Political Theory* (New York: Holt, Rinehart & Winston).

Sabrosky, Allen Ned (ed.) (1985). *Polarity and War* (Boulder, CO: Westview Press).

Schelling, Thomas C. (1963). *The Strategy of Conflict* (New York: Oxford University Press).

Schelling, Thomas C. (1966). *Arms and Influence* (New Haven: Yale University Press).

Schilling, Warner R., Paul Hammond, and Glenn Snyder (eds.) (1962). *Strategy, Politics, and Defense Budgets* (New York: Columbia University Press).

Schmitter, Philippe C. (1983). "Democratic theory and neocorporatist practice." *Social Research,* vol. 50, no. 4 (Winter), pp. 885–928.

Selcher, Wayne (1984). "Brazil's foreign policy: more actors and expanding agendas." In Jennie K. Lincoln and Elizabeth G. Ferris (eds.), *The Dynamics of Latin American Foreign Policies: Challenges for the 1980s* (Boulder, CO: Westview Press), pp. 101–123.

Seton-Watson, Hugh (1977). *Nations and States* (Boulder, CO: Westview Press).

Sewell, James P. (1966). *Functionalism and World Politics* (Princeton: Princeton University Press).

Shils, Edward (1962). *Political Development in the New States* (The Hague, The Netherlands: Mouton).

Simon, Herbert (1957). *Models of Man* (New York: Wiley).

Simon, Herbert (1961). *Administrative Behavior: A Discussion of Decision-Making Process in Administration Organization,* 2nd ed. (New York: Macmillan).

Singer, J. David (1961). "The level-of-analysis problem in international relations." In Klaus Knorr and Sidney Verba (eds.), *The International System: Theoretical Essays* (Princeton: Princeton University Press), pp. 77–92.

Singer, J. David (ed.) (1968). *Quantitative International Politics: Insights and Evidence* (New York: Free Press).

Singer, J. David (1969). "The incompleat theorist: insight without evidence." In Klaus Knorr and James N. Rosenau (eds.), *Contending Approaches to International Politics* (Princeton: Princeton University Press), pp. 62–86.

Singer, J. David (1972). *The Wages of War, 1816–1965: A Statistical Handbook* (New York: Wiley).

Singer, J. David (1976). "Tribal sins on the QIP reservation." In James N. Rosenau (ed.), *In Search of Global Patterns* (New York: Free Press), 167–173.

Singer, J. David (1981). *A General Systems Taxonomy for Political Science* (New York: General Learning Press).

Singer, J. David, S. Bremer, and J. Stuckey (1972). "Capability distribution, uncertainty, and major power war, 1820–1965." In Bruce M. Russett (ed.), *Peace, War, and Numbers* (Beverly Hills, CA: Sage), pp. 19–48.

Siverson, Randolph M. (1976). "Some suggestions for improving cumulation." In James N. Rosenau (ed.), *In Search of Global Patterns* (New York: Free Press), pp. 198–204.

Sjoblom, Gunnar (1982). "Some problems of the operational code approach." In Christer Jonsson (ed.), *Cognitive Dynamics and International Politics* (New York: St. Martin's Press), pp. 37–74.

Skocpol, Theda (1977). "Wallerstein's world capitalist system: a theoretical critique." *American Journal of Sociology,* vol. 82, no. 5 (March), pp. 1075–1090.

Skolnikoff, Eugene B. (1967). *Science, Technology, and American Foreign Policy* (Cambridge, MA: MIT Press).

Small, Melvin and J. David Singer (eds.) (1985). *International War: An Anthology and Study Guide* (Homewood, IL: Dorsey Press).

Smith, Anthony D. (1986). *The Ethnic Origins of Nations* (Oxford: Blackwell).

Smith, Steve (1986). "Theories of foreign policy: an historical view." *Review of International Studies,* vol. 12, no. 1 (January), pp. 13–29.

Smoke, Richard (1976). "Theory for and about policy." In James N. Rosenau (ed.), *In Search of Global Patterns* (New York: Free Press), pp. 185–191.

Snow, C. P. (1961). *Science and Government* (Cambridge, MA: Harvard University Press).

Snyder, Glenn H. and Paul Diesing (1977). *Conflict Among Nations: Bargaining, Decision Making, and System Structure in International Crisis* (Princeton: Princeton University Press).

Snyder, Louis L. (1982). *Global Mini-Nationalisms: Autonomy or Independence?* (Westport, CT: Greenwood Press).

Snyder, Richard C., H. W. Bruck, and Burton Sapin (eds.) (1962). *Foreign Policy Decision-Making* (New York: Free Press).

Soule, George (1935). *The Coming American Revolution* (New York: Macmillan).

Spanier, John (1981). *Games Nations Play: Analyzing International Politics*, 4th ed. (New York: Holt, Rinehart & Winston).

Spanier, John and Eric M. Uslaner (1985). *American Foreign Policy and the Democratic Dilemmas*, 4th ed. (New York: Holt, Rinehart & Winston).

Spengler, J. J. (ed.) (n.d.). *National Resources and Economic Growth* (Washington, DC: Resources for the Future).

Sprout, Harold and Margaret Sprout (1956). *Man-Milieu Relationship Hypotheses in the Context of International Politics* (Princeton: Center of International Studies).

Sprout, Harold and Margaret Sprout (1965). *The Ecological Perspective on Human Affairs with Special Reference to International Politics* (Princeton: Princeton University Press).

Sprout, Harold and Margaret Sprout (1968). *An Ecological Paradigm for the Study of International Politics*, Research Monograph No. 30 (Princeton: Center of International Studies).

Stein, Arthur A. (1982). "Coordination and collaboration: regimes in an anarchic world." *International Organization*, vol. 36, no. 2 (Spring), pp. 299–324.

Steinbruner, John D. (1974). *The Cybernetic Theory of Decision: New Dimensions of Political Analysis* (Princeton: Princeton University Press).

Steinbruner, John D. (1976). "Beyond rational deterrence: the struggle for new conceptions." *World Politics*, vol. 28, no. 2 (January), pp. 223–245.

Stephens, Jerome (1972). "An appraisal of some systems approaches in the study of international systems." *International Studies Quarterly*, vol. 16, no. 3 (September), pp. 321–350.

Strange, Susan (1982). "*Cave! hic dragones:* a critique of regime analysis." *International Organization*, vol. 36, no. 2 (Spring), pp. 479–496.

Sullivan, Michael P. and Randolph M. Siverson (1981). "Theories of war: problems and prospects." In P. Terrence Hopmann, Dina A. Zinnes and J. David Singer (eds.), *Cumulation in International Relations Research* (Denver: Graduate School of International Studies, University of Denver Monograph Series in World Affairs), 9–37.

Sunkel, Osvaldo (1972). "Big business and 'dependencia': a Latin American view." *Foreign Affairs*, vol. 50, no. 3 (April), 517–531.

Sunkel, Osvaldo (1973). "The crisis of the nation-state in Latin America: Challenge and Response." In Yale H. Ferguson and Walter F. Weiker (eds.), *Continuing Issues in International Politics* (Pacific Palisades, CA: Goodyear), pp. 352–368.

Szabo, Stephen, et al. (1983). *The Successor Generation: International Perspectives* (London: Butterworth).

Tanter, Raymond and Richard H. Ullman (eds.) (1972). *Theory and Policy in International Relations* (Princeton: Princeton University Press).

Tetreault, Mary Ann (1980). "Measuring interdependence." *International Organization,* vol. 34, no. 3 (Summer), pp. 429–443.

Tetreault, Mary Ann (1981). "Measuring interdependence: a response." *International Organization,* vol. 35, no. 3 (Summer), pp. 557–560.

Thomas, Hugh (1979). *A History of the World* (New York: Harper & Row).

Thompson, Kenneth W. (1952). "The study of international politics: a survey of trends and developments." *Review of Politics,* vol. 11, no. 4, pp. 433–443.

Thompson, Kenneth W. (1960). *Political Realism and the Crisis of World Politics* (Princeton: Princeton University Press).

Thompson, William R. (1973). "The regional subsystem: a conceptual explication and a propositional inventory." *International Studies Quarterly,* vol. 17, no. 1 (March), pp. 89–117.

Thucydides (1954). *The Peloponnesian War,* trans. Rex Warner (Baltimore: Penguin Books).

Tilly, Charles (ed.) (1975). *The Formation of National States in Western Europe* (Princeton: Princeton University Press).

Trilling, Lionel (1965). *Beyond Culture* (New York: Harcourt, Brace, Jovanovich).

Tuchman, Barbara W. (1978). *A Distant Mirror: The Calamitous 14th Century* (New York: Knopf).

Useem, Michael (1976). "Government influence on the social science paradigm." *Sociological Quarterly,* vol. 17, no. 2 (Spring), pp. 146–161.

Van Klaveren, Alberto (1984). "The analysis of Latin American foreign policies: theoretical perspectives." In Heraldo Muñoz and Joseph S. Tulchin (eds.), *Latin American Nations in World Politics* (Boulder, CO: Westview Press), pp. 1–21.

Vasquez, John A. (1983). *The Power of Power Politics: A Critique* (New Brunswick, NJ: Rutgers University Press).

Vasquez, John A. (ed.) (1986). *Classics of International Relations* (Englewood Cliffs, NJ: Prentice-Hall).

Vasquez, John A. (ed.) (1986). *Evaluating U.S. Foreign Policy* (New York: Praeger).

Vasquez, John A. (1986). "The need for foreign policy evaluation." In Vasquez (ed.), *Evaluating U.S. Foreign Policy* (New York: Praeger), pp. 3–16.

Venable, Vernon (1966). *Human Nature: The Marxist View* (Cleveland, OH: Meridian).

Verba, Sidney (1961). "Assumptions of rationality and non-rationality in models of the international system." In Klaus Knorr and Verba (eds.), *The International System: Theoretical Essays* (Princeton: Princeton University Press), pp. 93–117.

Vernon, Raymond (1971). *Sovereignty at Bay: The Multinational Spread of U.S. Enterprises* (New York: Basic Books).

Vertzberger, Yaacov, Y. I. (1986). "Foreign policy decisionmakers as practical-intuitive historians: applied history and its shortcomings." *International Studies Quarterly,* vol. 30, no. 2 (June), pp. 223–247.

Vital, David (1969). "Back to Machiavelli." In Klaus Knorr and James N. Rosenau (eds.), *Contending Approaches to International Politics* (Princeton: Princeton University Press), pp. 144–157.

Wagner, G. D. and J. Berger (1985). "Do sociological theories grow?" *American Journal of Sociology,* vol. 90, no. 4 (January), pp. 697–728.

Walker, R. B. J. (1987). "Realism, change, and international political theory." *International Studies Quarterly,* vol. 31, no. 1 (March), pp. 65–86.

Wallace, Michael (1972). "Status, formal organization and arms levels as factors leading to the onset of war, 1820–1964." In Bruce M. Russett (ed.), *Peace, War, and Numbers* (Beverly Hills, CA: Sage), pp. 49–71.

Wallace, Michael (1973). "Alliance polarization, cross-cutting, and international war, 1815–1964." *Journal of Conflict Resolution,* vol. 17, no. 4 (December), pp. 575–604.

Wallerstein, Immanuel (1974). *The Modern World-System: Capitalist Agriculture and the Origins of the European World-Economy in the Sixteenth Century* (New York: Academic Press).

Wallerstein, Immanuel (1979). *The Capitalist World-Economy* (New York: Cambridge University Press).

Wallerstein, Immanuel (1984). *The Politics of the World-Economy: The States, the Movements, and the Civilizations* (New York: Cambridge University Press).

Waltz, Kenneth N. (1959). *Man, the State, and War* (New York: Columbia University Press).

Waltz, Kenneth N. (1964). "The stability of a bipolar world." *Daedalus,* vol. 93 (Summer), pp. 881–909.

Waltz, Kenneth N. (1967). "International structure, national force, and the balance of world power." *Journal of International Affairs,* vol. 21, no. 2, pp. 215–231.

Waltz, Kenneth N. (1979). *Theory of International Politics* (Reading, MA: Addison-Wesley).

Waltz, Kenneth N. (1982). "Letter to the editor." *International Organization,* vol. 36, no. 3 (Summer), pp. 679–681.

Waltz, Kenneth N. (1984). "Will the future be like the past?" In Nissan Oren (ed.), *When Patterns Change: Turning Points in International Politics* (New York: St. Martin's Press), pp. 16–36.

Waltz, Kenneth N. (1986). "Reflections on *Theory of International Politics:* a response to my critics." In Robert O. Keohane (ed.), *Neorealism and Its critics* (New York: Columbia University Press), pp. 322–345.

Watkins, J. W. N. (1970). "Against normal science." In Imre Lakatos and Alan Musgrave (eds.), *Criticism and the Growth of Knowledge* (Cambridge: Cambridge University Press), pp. 25–37.

Wesson, Robert G. (1978). *States Systems: International Pluralism, Politics, and Culture* (New York: Free Press).

Wiarda, Howard J. (1985). *Ethnocentrism in Foreign Policy: Can We Understand the Third World?* (Washington, DC: American Enterprise Institute for Public Research).

Wight, Martin (1966). "Why is there no international theory?" In Herbert Butterfield and Martin Wight (eds.), *Diplomatic Investigations: Essays in the Theory of International Politics* (London: Allen & Unwin Press), pp. 17–34.

Wilhelmy, Manfred (1984). "Politics, bureaucracy, and foreign policy in Chile." In Heraldo Muñoz and Joseph S. Tulchin (eds.), *Latin American Nations in World Politics* (Boulder, CO: Westview Press), pp. 45–62.

Wilkinson, David (1980). *Deadly Quarrels: Lewis F. Richardson and the Statistical Study of War* (Berkeley, CA: University of California Press).

Wolfers, Arnold (1962). *Discord and Collaboration: Essays on International Politics* (Baltimore: Johns Hopkins Press).

Wolfers, Arnold and Laurence W. Martin (eds.) (1956). *The Anglo-American Tradition in Foreign Affairs* (New Haven: Yale University Press).

Wolin, Sheldon S. (1960). *Politics and Vision: Continuity and Innovation in Western Political Thought* (Boston: Little, Brown).

Wolin, Sheldon S. (1980). "Paradigms and political theories." In Gary Gutting (ed.), *Paradigms and Revolutions: Appraisals and Applications of Thomas Kuhn's Philosophy of Science* (Notre Dame: IN: University of Notre Dame Press), pp. 160–195.

Worsley, Peter (1984). *The Three Worlds: Culture and World Development* (CHicago: University of Chicago Press).

Young, Oran R. (1968). "Political discontinuities in the international system." *World Politics*, vol. 20, no. 3 (April), pp. 369–392.

Young, Oran R. (1972). "The actors in world politics." In James N. Rosenau, Vincent Davis and Maurice A. East (eds.), *The Analysis of International Politics* (New York: Free Press), pp. 125–144.

Young, Oran R. (1972). "The perils of Odysseus: on constructing theories of international relations." *World Politics*, vol. 24: Supplement (Spring), pp. 179–203.

Young, Oran R. (1978). "Anarchy and social choice: reflections on the international polity." *World Politics*, vol. 30, no. 2 (January), pp. 241–263.

Young, Oran R. (1980). "International regimes: problems of concept formation." *World Politics*, vol. 32, no. 3 (April), pp. 331–356.

Young, Oran R. (1982). "Regime dynamics: the rise and fall of international regimes." *International Organization*, vol. 36, no. 2 (Spring), pp. 277–297.

Zimmerman, William (1973). "Issue area and foreign-policy process: a research note in search of general theory." *American Political Science Review*, vol. 67, no. 4 (December), pp. 1204–1212.

Zimmern, Alfred (1939). *The League of Nations and the Rule of Law 1935–1938* (London: Macmillan).

Zimmern, Alfred (1961). *The Greek Commonwealth: Politics and Economics in Fifth-Century Athens* (New York: Oxford University Press).

Zinnes, Dina A. (1976). "The problem of cumulation." In James N. Rosenau (ed.), *In Search of Global Patterns* (New York: Free Press), pp. 161–166.

Zinnes, Dina A. (1980). "Prerequisites for the study of system transformation." In Ole R. Holsti, Randolph M. Siverson, and Alexander L. George (eds.), *Change in the International System* (Boulder, CO: Westview Press), pp. 1–21.

Zolberg, Aristide R. (1981). "Origins of the modern world system: a missing link." *World Politics,* vol. 23, no. 2 (January), pp. 253–281.

# Name Index

# Subject Index

Africa: "negative sovereignty" (Jackson) of states, 132–133
American Revolution, 127
anarchy: as characteristic of international relations, 8, 40, 111, 156, 160, 186ff.; as a characteristic of international relations theories, 160
Anglo-Saxon distinctive intellectual tradition, 83, 99–102, 169, 195–196
"anomalies" as condition for scientific advance, 16, 25, 38, 99, 216
anthropology: relevance to international relations theory, 23
architectonic conception of politics, 23, 222
Aristotle: influence on early Christian doctrine, 62–64; as progenitor of contemporary scientific theory, 14–15, 23; as model for future theory, 222
art and literature: parallel to theory, 36, 38

balance of power theory, 192–194, 197–198
"behavioralism" in social science, 27–32, 108, 186, 210, 220
Belgium government's concern for minorities, 184
biology: relevance to international relations theory, 23
bureaucratic approach to foreign policy. See governmental (bureaucratic) approach
"bureaucratic machismo" as concept, 102
Byzantine Empire, 50–51, 57

canon law, 53–54
Carter administration in United States: contrast with Reagan administration on human rights, 171, 180
cataclysmic events as influence on theory, 37ff., 71–73, 107, 217–218, 222
change on "domestic" and "international" levels: impact on theory, 36ff., 49ff., 67ff., 83ff., 186ff., 207ff., 218ff.
"chaos" concept relevance to international relations theory, 214
Christian commonwealth myth (St. Augustine and Dante), 52ff.
Christian thought of early church, 50ff., 76–78, 218–219
Cluny reform movement in early Christian church, 59, 61
cognitive approach to foreign policy, 154–160, 173, 175, 180, 220
Cold War, 97, 99, 104, 116, 156, 195, 220–221
comparative study of foreign policy, 8, 178–185
competitiveness/community as key normative dimension, 43–45, 76–78, 81, 83, 86, 88, 92–94, 104, 186ff., 218–219, 221
conceptual anarchy in the study of international relations, 7–9, 13, 111ff.
Concert of Europe, 87, 198
Congress of Vienna, 87
Congress role in U. S. foreign policy, 176–177, 180, 183
conservatism and its relation to theory, 81, 87

**296**